TEACHING GENERAL MUSIC IN GRADES 4–8

A Musicianship Approach

THOMAS A. REGELSKI

State University of New York at Fredonia

New York   Oxford
Oxford University Press
2004

Oxford University Press

Oxford   New York
Auckland   Bangkok   Buenos Aires   Cape Town   Chennai
Dar es Salaam   Delhi   Hong Kong   Istanbul   Karachi   Kolkata
Kuala Lumpur   Madrid   Melbourne   Mexico City   Mumbai
Nairobi   São Paulo   Shanghai   Taipei   Tokyo Toronto

Copyright © 2004 by Oxford University Press, Inc.

Published by Oxford University Press, Inc.
198 Madison Avenue, New York, New York, 10016
www.oup.com

Oxford is a registered trademark of Oxford University Press

Library of Congress Cataloging-in-Publication Data
Regelski, Thomas A., 1941–
     Teaching general music in grades 4–8 : a musicianship approach / by Thomas A. Regelski.
     p. cm.
     Includes index.
     ISBN 0-19-513778-7 (alk. paper)
     1. School music—Instruction and study—United States. I. Title.

MT3.U5R44 2004
372.87′044—dc22   2003053652

Printing number: 9 8 7 6 5 4 3 2 1

Printed in the United States of America
on acid-free paper

This book is dedicated to the general music teachers everywhere whose commitment is to making a difference in students' musical lives through general music instruction.

Contents

APPENDIX C

APPENDIX D

Preface

AGE RELEVANCE

Teaching General Music in Grades 4–8 focuses on the special instructional needs of students in *general music classes* in grades 4–8, that is, from preadolescence (ages 9–11) through the end of early adolescence (11–14). Focusing on this grade range provides more than just a co-ordination of curriculum between elementary and middle school. Given the important developmental changes increasingly indicated by developmental and educational psychologists and educators, *Teaching General Music in Grades 4–8* is innovatively predicated on making fundamental instructional and curricular modifications for grades 4–6 in formal anticipation of middle school, rather than to continue K–3 teaching methods with pre- and early adolescents in the intermediate grades.

The recommended change to a different style of teaching beginning in fourth grade is in direct consideration of the important *developmental and behavioral changes* that begin to appear then and thereafter in grades five and six. *Teaching General Music in Grades 4–8* thus overlaps and bridges the traditional division between elementary and middle school. It is designed, then, for use in conjunction with other age-relevant materials in the wide variety of elementary, secondary, or K–12 general/vocal methods course formats or teaching assignments that exist today. Elementary general music teachers can beneficially apply this text to the changing needs of their older students, middle school teachers to all their students, and teachers whose assignment spans elementary and middle school will be assisted by it in making the difficult but important transition from elementary to middle school general music.

ACTION LEARNING FOR TANGIBLE MUSICIANSHIP

This text is predicated on the new praxial theory of music and music education and focuses on real-life uses of music in everyday life. Thus, after the traditional early childhood approaches to general music used in the primary grades (K–3), an Action Learning approach is advanced for the intermediate grades that progressively bases instruction on likely real-life models of lifelong musical interest and use. This results in fostering tangible and observable musicianship skills in grades 4–6 that provide a secure foundation for middle school classes. The sense of relevance that Action Learning fosters is well suited to the musical attitudes and interests of both pre- and early adolescents. In a situation where a teacher is responsible only for middle school, the approach taken here can begin in middle school. Though not as much skill can ultimately be developed as if Action Learning had begun in grade 4 or 5, beginning it in middle school will still produce major gains in musicianship, attitudes and values, especially if grade 6 is included in the middle school.

Middle school general music itself is the "capstone," the *value-added* fulfillment of the entire K–8 general music program. Therefore general music classes for grades 4–8 are approached here as an apprenticeship for lifelong musical involvement. Where high school electives are not offered, the middle school will typically be the last formal general music instruction for the majority of students. Accordingly, instruction needs to promote the musical independence students need to make meaningful musical choices that enable them to be more effectively involved with music throughout life than just as listeners of the latest "pop" music.

GENERAL APPLICABILITY

General music classes vary incredibly in terms of scheduling, resources, curriculum, teacher preparation and an unending list of other unavoidable influences and limitations. This text, then, specifically avoids "how to" recipes or "idealized" lessons plans. Such inflexible or supposedly "teacher proof" lessons would inevitably be doomed by the necessary, unavoidable, and usually decisive differences between teachers and situations—differences that, among other factors, promote teacher and teaching uniqueness. Appropriately, a range of *general* formats for different kinds of lessons is offered in terms of background foundations that allow the teacher to customize plans to local conditions and changing circumstances over time. Throughout, the teacher is encouraged to be a *professional* who diagnoses, hypothesizes, acts, and reflects on results in terms of expectations and professional accountability. In fact, the main rewards of teaching are seen as being a direct result of the professionalism that successfully accounts for differences between teachers and their teaching situations.

Specifics of assessment, grading, and the like also vary greatly, of course, according to school, state, and region and between individual teachers in the same school district. Nonetheless, guidelines are addressed throughout as they apply to specific lessons and common issues. Enormous diversity also exists in the availability of computers and music software for general music instruction from school to school, even within the same district. Therefore this text is predicated on no more "technology" than a sound system and an overhead projector. However, relevant general suggestions are made so that teachers who have and can use computers and other advanced technology can enhance instruction as local resources allow. Curriculum is approached in this text as the professional responsibility of the teacher (or faculty group). However, specific issues of curricular implementation are addressed throughout and guidelines for curriculum development are provided.

Teaching General Music in Grades 4–8 is divided into three parts. Part One presents theoretical background and other general foundations that review and apply developmental psychology, educational psychology, philosophy, and sociology to the special needs of teaching general music in grades 4–8 covered later in the text. Part Two applies the basics of Part One to general teaching protocols for performing, listening, and compositional lessons. Part Three considers the important variables between teaching situations, including curriculum and classroom management needs. A technical glossary and three practical appendices are also included in this part.

PART I: USEFUL FOUNDATIONS AND GENERAL PLANNING BASICS

The **Introduction** establishes the nature of general music instruction as music learning that is basic to the *general education of all students* and explains why the text focuses on the special needs of grades 4–8 (ages 9–14). A rationale of teachers as professionals is offered. It is predicated on the need for a teacher, as a professional, to use various theoretical foundations of teaching and learning to diagnose students' needs and local instructional variables. Hence, the effective general music teacher is seen as engaged in a *professional praxis* that puts theory into action in insuring effective results *for* students, not as a *technician* who regards teaching as a "technology" of methods and materials imposed *on* students.

Chapter 1 introduces and explains the Action Learning model upon which this text is based. Rather than just learning "about" music academically in class, the importance of personal *musical* goals on the part of students for "doing" music in life is stressed for general music classes grades 4–8. A pragmatic account of "what music is good for in life" is developed in connection with general music instruction as a practicum for real-life musical actions, and is contrasted with teaching music as a discipline for its own sake.

Chapter 2 provides important and practical foundations for understanding and working with pre- and early-teens. Physical development and characteristics of " 'tween-agers" are outlined, and the cognition, perception, attention and memory, and social and personality traits of the age group are explained. Attention deficit disorder is also discussed. Relevant developmental characteristics are analyzed in terms of their use for general music teaching and their implications for effective teachers of this age group. Differences between elementary, middle school, and junior high school are also analyzed in terms of the consequences for general music instruction.

Chapter 3 presents general planning guidelines to be applied to the different lesson formats presented in Part Two. A seven-part process for planning is outlined and ten "generative themes" are offered by which teachers can organize and unify instruction across the different kinds of lessons modeled in each of the chapters that follow in Part Two.

PART II: TEACHING FORMATS AND PROTOCOLS*

Chapter 4 provides the detailed bases for teaching musicianship skills and rudiments of music theory through *composing diatonic melodies in small part forms*. Lesson protocols are provided for various types of content focus. Practical "Nuts 'n' bolts 'n' cautions" are provided to assist the mechanics of planning and delivering lessons.

Chapter 5 covers lessons for teaching musicianship skills through *"sound compositions."* These mini-"symphonies," and so forth, are usually done in cooperative groups. They enable students to understand larger forms (i.e., problems of unity and variety) and to explore musical techniques and effects relevant to contemporary and even non-Western musics. Once again, plenty of practical "Nuts 'n' bolts 'n' cautions" are provided.

Chapter 6 presents formats and strategies for improving aural acuity through various types of listening lessons. The nature and instructional challenges of promoting *audience listening* as its own musical praxis are stressed, and listening is addressed as an active process where listeners construct their own responses. An analysis of the listening process and the need for "directed listening" precede nineteen general types of listening lessons. Specific practical suggestions are given for minimizing problems and maximizing results for the special challenges of teaching listening lessons.

Chapter 7 deals with teaching *music reading* and *singing*. Singing is addressed in terms of its value as recreation outside the classroom and throughout life. The nature of the changing voice—especially in boys—is analyzed in relation to strategies for encouraging enthusiastic and satisfying singing. Practical advice and cautions are provided in connection with using singing activities with this age group.

---

*No recommended sequence or priority is implied by the order of the chapters.

Chapter 8 addresses teaching *recreational instruments* in the general music class. The emphasis is on developing beginning competence that can initiate a lifelong amateur interest in performing for personal and social pleasures.

PART III: APPENDICES

Chapter 9 addresses the many and highly variable conditions different teachers must consider in implementing instruction, including differences of physical plant, scheduling, resources, curriculum, and the like. A detailed discussion of classroom management is also provided.

The **Critical Glossary of Key Ideas and Terms** explains or critically analyzes important technical terms and key ideas used in the text. *Technical terms*, especially those from disciplines outside of music that are central to educational discourse and praxis, are defined and discussed in terms of their functional implications for general music teaching. *Key ideas*, especially those commonly taken for granted or misunderstood, are analyzed and clarified for teaching purposes. Throughout each chapter, ideas and terms central to a clear-cut understanding of the discussion at hand are highlighted in boldface font for easy reference.

Appendix A presents guidelines for curriculum development in connection with an actual sample of an Action Learning curriculum for grade 6 general music that can be used as a model.

Appendix B describes the use of "rubrics" and other considerations for evaluating learning and teaching success.

Appendix C includes teaching materials and resources. Given the abundance of commercial resources found in the many catalogues and teaching journals and on the Internet, and the exceedingly rapid changes in technology and related materials, general resources are suggested so they will not be out of date by the time the text is read.

Appendix D is a description of information and software for MIDI Classroom Work Stations.

ACKNOWLEDGMENTS

Several people need to be thanked for their specific contributions: Sylvia Sharp, for formatting the musical examples, Todd Cruikshank for the graphics and diagrams, and Eric Wills for recommendations concerning MIDI workstations and computer software. Special thanks go to Rick Bunting, whose approach to teaching social instruments greatly influenced Chapter 8, and to T. J. Smith for permission to use his curriculum as a model. Thanks are also due to the many teachers over the years who allowed me into their classrooms and otherwise shared their expertise, in particular Kent Knappenberger of the Westfield (NY) Academy and Central School, where Action Learning in general music class is an everyday reality.

TEACHING GENERAL MUSIC
IN GRADES 4–8

INTRODUCTION

GENERAL MUSIC AS BASIC TO "GENERAL EDUCATION"

General music is the "core curriculum" for all musical studies. However, such classes are not simply the feeder program for the minority of students in ensembles. "General music" is the curricular means by which music contributes to students' "general education." The adjective "general" does *not* refer, then, to "music *in general*"—to a superficial music appreciation survey course or a sampling of musical skills and **musics**.* It refers instead to the musical learning *all students* are believed to need to be "generally well educated."

What it means to be "generally well educated" is widely contested. Traditionalists view general education as the mastery of learning and skill developed and transmitted by previous generations and that perpetuates existing social structures and practices. In this *transmission* view, schools exist to help individuals adjust to *existing* social patterns, to contribute to *social stability* and to profit from the *social status quo*. However, a newer and competing view of general education seeks to study the past, but in terms of its implications—positive or negative—for the present and, especially, as a basis for improving society and the individuals who constitute society.

This *transformation* view is the position taken by this text. In this model, traditions and legacies are not accepted without question as inert or given "facts." Given the changing present and unknowable future, the past is evoked 'critically'[†] and selectively and new practices that will become the traditions of the future are initiated. In this view, **curriculum** is an ever-evolving conversation between the past and present that brings the past "to life," but in terms of the present and with flexibility toward the unpredictable needs and conditions of the future, as well.

At one time being a generally well-educated person meant being musically educated enough to partake of one or more forms of **musicking**. Such "classy" people were expected to be able to sing and play instruments, and to listen with intelligence and refined discrimination. Many tried their hand at amateur composing, and wrote or otherwise remained informed about music theorizing and criticism. However, all this was before the days of universal **schooling**. Now that the ideal of a comprehensive education is sought not for just the aristocratic or higher classes but for all, the ideal of being generally well educated has not focused on the type of learning necessary to be inducted into a high social station. Rather, being generally well educated promotes being able to live the "good life." While earlier ideals of being generally well educated focused on "classy" musics, the democratization of school-

---

*Throughout, words appearing in **boldface** will be defined, explained, or otherwise 'critically' clarified in the Glossary in terms of specific use in music education and in this text. A term will appear (or reappear) in boldface when it is central to the discussion at hand, which might be more than once throughout the text but not every time it is used.

[†]References in this text to 'critical' thinking and critical theory should be understood in terms of the kind of 'critique' that takes place in a music lesson. Such critiques serve positive and constructive ends rather than simply finding fault or complaining.

ing and cultural pluralism have led to a similar democratization and pluralism of musical choices as a result of formal schooling in music.

The current inclusion of **multicultural** and **world musics** in schools is only one step in this process. Now skills needed for musicking in life are made available to all children as part of their general education so they can be musically active in ways they find to be personally satisfying and rewarding. In an egalitarian and pluralistic society, music education naturally reflects many views of musical value, not just the "good tastes" of previous generations, present authorities or dominant social classes—whether of the "art music" or any other established genre.

However, if general music teaching is to go beyond the transmission model that only passes on the traditions and practices of "good music" dictated by socially, economically, or politically dominant classes and authorities, then it is necessary for general music teachers to function as *cultural mediators*. This means that general music programs rooted in personal and social transformation models of curriculum seek to develop a *capacity for successful cultural analysis on the part of students regarding music*—what it "is" and is "good for"—in culture and, most importantly, in their personal lives. Such instruction helps them to be more aware of the sometimes limiting and narrow (or contradictory) influences of cultural institutions and ethnocentric assumptions, including their own. At the same time, however, their musical choices are increased, enhanced, and enriched by formal instruction in school, and this, in turn, opens new musical horizons. For some, general music class will also formally extend and refine musical skills and tastes they learned informally in the home, church, and community.

The specific two-part ideal envisaged by this text for general music students, then, is (a) to promote thoughtfulness concerning their present musical tastes and choices and (b) to increase the usually narrow range of musical choices provided by their informal music education. A broader ideal is to renew, revitalize, and even transform those kinds of musics and the kinds of personal musical involvement that warrant inclusion in schools because they advance the well-being of individuals and society. Viewed from this perspective, general music seeks to *transform* the musical lives of individuals and therefore of society! Because the type of music people make and consume has a strong bearing on sociocultural attitudes and values that go well beyond music, general music teachers can and must seek to transform people individually and collectively though the kinds of musical values that influence and mediate social and cultural values.

This text is predicated on just such a concern and, in particular, with modeling and otherwise advancing musical choices of the kind that lead to a life well lived; the kinds of choices in particular that are otherwise unlikely in students' informal music education outside of school. *Teaching General Music in Grades 4–8*, then, seeks to motivate students "into action" musically in ways and to a degree that can be directly attributed to general music class. The general criterion for such teaching is the tangible "value added" by instruction to students' musical lives outside of and after graduation from school.

UNIQUE NEEDS OF PRE- AND EARLY ADOLESCENTS

Research has documented significant *developmental changes* in students as early as fourth grade and typically by fifth grade. These changes signal the beginnings of what used to be called "middle childhood" (approximately ages 9–11, grades 4–5) and now is more typically called **preadolescence**. Preadolescence is an important transition to the "late childhood" that the modern world calls **adolescence**. *Early* adolescence encompasses the modern middle school (i.e., "junior high school" in the old lingo) while *late* adolescence refers to high school and even the late teen years. Although the timing of such changes is variable for individuals and according to local and regional patterns and even gender and ethnic background, the physical, cognitive, and emotional developmental changes of preadolescents have important implications for teaching and curriculum. However, elementary general music is typically conceived as kindergarten through grade 6 (K–6), both as a teaching assignment and in university methods courses. Once a pattern of instruction is established in and for "early childhood" (i.e., "primary school," K–3), then, general music teachers often tend to teach the preadolescents of the intermediate grades (4–6) in a very similar manner to the way they teach primary grade children, despite the older students' new needs and characteristics.

Contrary to this tendency, developmental and educational psychology both point to *the need for clearly distinct approaches to early and middle childhood*—that is, between instruction for K–3 (primary grades) and for grades 4–6 (intermediate grades). Indeed, separate programs and teaching certification for "early childhood education" have been promoted in recent years predicated on precisely the different needs of primary and intermediate grades. Also, with the ever-earlier signs of **pubescence** (and earlier symptoms and traits of preadolescence), children in grades 4–6 progressively resist instructional methods and content they view as "childish" and as lacking in the tangible and 'grown-up' progress they experience in their other studies!

The usefulness or value of reading, writing, and arithmetic becomes apparent to them at this age, but the continuation of instruction in general music based only on exploring music or "experiencing concepts" fails to promote clear visions of the *value or usefulness of music in their future lives*. While musical activities may be fun, on the other hand they are less often interested in gaining the kind of useful know-how in music *class* that results from their other studies. Some begin to "act out" in a manner that anticipates the discipline problems of middle school. Most, however, passively go along with the fun, but with little specific **intentionality** for improving their *musical* skills and understandings. As a result, *pleasure does not arise from new competence* and tangible musical skill gained from the last few years of elementary general music class. Musical learning is often insignificant when compared to progress made in other subjects.

Educational leaders (and critics) are increasingly aware of the special needs and problems of these age groups. The fact that states are instituting progress checks in certain subjects at the end of fourth and eighth grades illustrates how important the five years of pre- and early adolescence are for future success in education and life. If music education is to be taken as seriously as it should, general music teachers must also adjust their curriculum and teaching accordingly. Instrumental teachers—at least in North America—already focus their attention on this age level as the time for beginning instrumental lessons that will serve students musically for the future. The preadolescent years are also the last years during which impressive cognitive gains and attitudinal foundations for music learning can be set in place *before* the full and often disrupting onset of early adolescence and middle school.

Two issues are clear. First, preadolescents often regard K–3 teaching formats as "childish" because they now see themselves as more "grown up." Instruction in grades 4–6, then, benefits from being revised in the more "grown-up" terms of impending middle school. Secondly, this shift anticipates and prepares the way for the behavior and learning styles as well as the new types of content of instruction that will characterize middle school general music class. Intermediate level students are fully capable of succeeding to learn and benefiting from many types of learning. For example, they can notate and perform their own compositions, learn to play electronic keyboards and other "real" **social and traditional instruments**, and use **MIDI technology** or other means to organize sound compositions of various kinds. At this age, in comparison to middle school students, they thrive on such challenges with *open and receptive minds*. While their accomplishments are necessarily less refined than what middle school students (ages 10/11–14) can achieve, they provide an important **readiness stage** in the transition from early childhood to early adolescence and middle school.

For similar reasons, the organized sports—for example, softball, soccer, and baseball leagues—that are important in middle school begin during the preadolescent years. At this age, **fine** and **gross motor control** are also ready for specialized development and refinement as *musical skills*. Likewise, preadolescents now possess the mental and intellectual capacities needed for both understanding the importance of practice to progress, and for guiding the practice needed to develop skills that, in turn, promote musical satisfaction. These developments highlight this age group as a prime target for initiating a commitment to lifelong *musical* involvement! Therefore, students with such a rich and functional background in grades 4–5 come into middle school general music classes (typically grades 6–8) attitudinally "turned on" to the relevance of music learning and appropriately to general music class.

A "MUSICIANSHIP LABORATORY" FOR THE NEEDS OF 'TWEENS

Social psychology points out that commercial media, adult role models, and peers stimulate the musical interests and aspirations of pre- and early adolescents more than any influence of music classes. Their transitory status be*tween* childhood and adolescence—thus making them *'tweens* not *teens*—makes them increasingly vulnerable to the models of teens. During the fifth grade, most students begin to acquire "tastes" for *teen music* and manifest other signs of *teen culture* (e.g., clothing, slang, dancing) that demonstrate their self-awareness and anticipation of approaching adolescence. As a result, rather than spending time on the playground simply releasing excess energy, more and more of the free "playtime" (in and outside of school) is spent on hobbies, sports, computers, and similar activities that *'practice' and develop knowledge skills and interests* that often continue into later life. This, too, makes the preadolescent stage crucial in identifying or initiating, then developing and sustaining, musical choices to which students can begin to commit their free time for life.

With this foundation in the intermediate grades, the middle school curriculum can challenge early (middle school) adolescents musically, socially, and educationally in ways that channel their energies and interests into significant musical competence. Rather than having to "con" middle school general music students in order to avoid a "**performance strike**" (for example by bribing them with "their" pop music in order to get them to study other music), the patterns, content, and perceived value of musical instruction will already have been established in the open-minded receptiveness of the intermediate grades. Rather than rejection or resistance, students who bring skills developed in the intermediate grades to middle school general music classes instead develop **pragmatic** skills of **musicianship** that can and will be used outside of school—in the present and, more likely, throughout life.

The model for general music classes adopted in this text is that of a *musicianship laboratory*. Classes experiment with and investigate **real-life musical actions** of the kind that are clearly most relevant to students because their lifelong potential is obvious. Thus, for example, learning to play a guitar or electronic keyboards, developing an interest in MIDI software, or enjoying musical theater or drum circles—all examples of what Chapter 1 describes as Action Learning—are specific starting points on a **spiral curriculum** that continues to unfold and develop to a degree limited only by the student's desire and native ability. Physical education teachers inspired by the "new phys ed" have just this in mind, too, when they introduce tennis, golf, archery, gymnastics, aerobics, wall-climbing and the like in their classes as real-life pursuits that have long-term health and recreational value. Physical education teachers who do not follow this model, and who, like some general music teachers, just involve kids in "fun activities" and "games" of one kind or another, fail to help students develop functional skills. Both kinds of teachers run the risk of denying students important opportunities for personal and **lifelong learning** and **recreation**. A person who is "turned on" to a sport will continue to "play" (i.e., **practice-in-action**) as often as time and resources allow. Similarly, this text is predicated on starting students on their way to such lifelong musical "play" by addressing real-life models of musicking beginning in the intermediate grades.

Such **holistic** real-life musical pursuits in general music classes also address the **need to achieve**—the productive relationship between accomplishment and self-concept that is so crucial to pre- and early adolescents. Pursuits of this kind promote the concrete achievement that helps define self-identity and develops a positive self-worth, both of which are important **growth tasks** for pre-, early, and late adolescents alike.

Just as intermediate level general music classes prepare the way for and lead directly to middle school, so the middle school music curriculum is the basis for high school electives. School programs that successfully engage intermediate students' interests in general music ultimately generate demand for high school general music electives. Such courses should exist not just for students who anticipate musical careers but also for students who simply want to advance their opportunities and skills for lifelong musicking.

MUSIC AND ITS VALUE FOR LIFE

Whoever wrote, "Nothing is so practical as a good theory" was right on target. Theory and practice are inseparable, and just as much so for education as elsewhere. Of course, music teachers study music theory, but other theory-based questions are involved daily in teaching and curriculum:

1. What music *is*, and when and where music exists?
2. What musical meaning is, and how it comes about?
3. What music is "good for"—or the value of music for life?
4. And, what constitutes "good music"?

The first question above is addressed, for example, when children are taught to sing rather than shout. But some music teachers often unwittingly convey to students that "music is the notation" when, in fact, notation is not necessary to create music, and learning to decode notation is not the same as making music. In many cases, the assumption (usually inherited from university training) is accepted that music—at least the "good music" to be studied in school—exists to be contemplated for its own sake; that it involves *aesthetic meanings* that are either objectively "in" musical works or are subjectively "triggered" by them.

Conventional **aesthetic theories of music** and musical value do not, however, account for—or, for some aestheticians, approve of—the many everyday uses of music in contemporary society and the democratization and pluralism of musics mentioned earlier. While such musics may be seen by orthodox aesthetic theories as having *use* value (e.g., music for worship, film music, caroling), they are not accorded *aesthetic* value as such because aesthetic values of music are said to be pure, cerebral, and contemplated for their own sake. However, in our multicultural and pluralistic world, intellectualized contemplation is clearly not regarded as what music *is* or is "good for" by most people. To the contrary, outside of concerts of Western "classics," music is valued everywhere in the world precisely *for* its use-functions.

A new **praxial theory of music** has emerged that defines music in part according to how, when, where, and by whom it is used and especially in terms of why it is used—that is, what important personal and social uses it serves. Seen this way, music's most prevalent value throughout the world is its **pragmatic** use for a variety of personal and social values and pleasures. Even concerts of "classics" are seen as a particular use-function; the use, depending on the audience member's musical values, can range from lofty intellectual interest to emotional delight. "Good music," in such a praxial theory, then, is determined by the "goods" served by music, whether those involve amateur and recreational performance, dancing, worship, going to concerts, and the like. Among the otherwise infinite uses of music, then, only one use is to serve the lofty contemplative interests of expert connoisseurs. The minority status and intellectual demands of that *kind* of "music appreciation" typically make it a "difficult sell" in the general music classroom.

This text therefore applies a praxial approach to musical value and to teaching music. Since music as **praxis** by definition accounts for *all* musical praxis, praxial theory also includes **"just listening"** to the "classics" of any genre at concerts and to recordings at home. Given the realities of general music classes in today's schools—the incredible diversity of students, the extreme variability of resources, and so forth—such a pragmatic approach can reach all students; it can add some significant musical benefits and skills for the life well lived, regardless of whether these values fit the orthodox aesthetic **paradigm**. Connoisseurship models of general music based on "aesthetic appreciation" and watered down history surveys typically run afoul of pre- and early adolescent's resistance to learning abstract concepts and background information as a basis for their listening to music of any type. But since "just listening" is a major and readily available source of real-life musical pleasure available to all, the Action Learning paradigm of this text promotes *active listening* and *enhanced aural acuity* that can serve many types and styles of listening and musical praxis—from "refined" or rarefied to ubiquitous and everyday.

CRITICAL AND REFLECTIVE PRAXIS FOR PROFESSIONALIZING TEACHING

Music teachers cannot avoid the many social, economic, and political theories concerning the *purpose and value of schooling* and, thus, of the role of music in schooling. These conflicting theories all regularly influence the day-to-day facts of teaching. In fact, the jeopardized status of music in the schools is due in part to music teachers taking for granted the value of music and music education in ways and to a degree that are not taken for granted by taxpayers and politicians, parents, and students! Financial and other resources certainly do not support the noble and lofty sounding "artistic" values of music education exalted by many teachers and parents.

This is one reason why this text applies **critical theory** to issues commonly taken for granted by many general music teachers. Critical theory involves the kind of concerned and constructive 'criticism' that is best compared to the 'critique' every music student comes to expect in a music lesson. Without such a critique of last week's practice, students make little or no progress. Similarly, without a critique of past practices, music teaching can make little progress coping with changing times. Five "themes" of critical theory can be sketched in relation to schooling, and are shown in Figure I.1.

FIGURE I.1 Five Themes of Critical Theory in Education

1. Critical theorists challenge any taken-for-granted "methods" of teaching, especially those where claims of "it works" are said to be "proven" by science or experience and those advanced as "technologies" of prescriptive or recipe teaching. The uncritical devotion to, or worship of, such *technicist* approaches to teaching I call **methodolatry**. Critical theorists see such approaches as denying the freedom and variety that is inherent in human nature and as not in the best interests of teachers or their students.

2. Critical theory reminds us that students, teachers, and schools cannot be reduced to "laws," one-mold-fits-all teaching techniques, or "methods" that assume "training" a student is comparable to "shaping" a clay pot and that teaching is merely a hand-me-down *craft* that takes place in schools run like factories. In fact, in the **professions**, it is precisely the *differences* between people and situations characteristic of a particular profession that make these fields interesting and rewarding. In education, this means that both students and teachers are different according to their **life-worlds**, skills, interests, personalities, values, and the like. All teaching is also **situated** within a context of restraints and resources that varies within a school, between schools and between communities and regions.

3. Because of this situatedness, variation between teachers is expected. But teachers in the "trenches" often become *too situated* and therefore can barely see beyond their own foxholes! College and university theorists, on the other hand, have a fine view of big trends, issues, and problems from their "Ivory Towers" but often lack the down-to-earth details and hands-on skills. The view of each group, then, becomes **ideological** in its autonomy and is narrow and limiting. Teachers as a result, criticize as "merely theoretical" the recommendations of educational theorists and theorists blame teachers for being "merely expedient"; they point out that what is "merely **practicable**" is not always *pragmatic* in the results brought about by the teaching praxis. Whatever the reason, it is recognized that "teachers teach they way they were taught" and that progress in teaching has therefore been glacial compared to other professions. Criticism of teachers and schools is widespread, not the least because parents (even grandparents) do not see much change for the better since they were students.

4. Key to a critical theory of teaching, then, is the need and ability for each teacher and theorist to engage in *ideology critique*. This involves taking nothing for granted and hence the need to challenge all pat and pet, personal and professional assumptions. The intention is to challenge one's current ways of thinking and to teach beyond what was perhaps only blindly accepted during the individual's own **socialization** into teaching. A teacher who works at remaining critically self-aware of major assumptions, influences, and past practices is not beguiled into accepting that one way "works" for all students or times, and never accepts that his teaching is "good enough." Teaching, in this view, is a self-reflective *praxis* in just the same way that, say, a doctor reflects on her practice

in terms of tangible benefits for the people served. Teaching is similarly *professionalized* when the teacher functions as a *reflective practitioner* and reflects on actual benefits of instruction for students.

5. Ongoing ideology critique profits from going beyond the individual teacher and taking into consideration other music instruction, at least within the same school. Educational sociologists long ago pointed out that teachers in the same school typically operate their classrooms as one-room schools under the same roof. This problem is compounded when there are multiple schools in a district. A need for communication and community between teachers is certainly one condition that has a bearing on the overall effectiveness of and public opinion concerning schooling.

Critical theory aims at **empowering** teachers to develop and acknowledge as a matter of community and professionalism certain **action ideals** for "good practice" that will guide and govern their collective teaching praxis. This process is similar to the way such ideals in medicine guide doctors and surgeons while nonetheless allowing and empowering them to develop personalized habits of praxis. Instead of expecting a set "method" or standard "technique" to be followed rigorously, teachers (like doctors or lawyers) are empowered to and must therefore be responsible for developing their own "theory of practice" according to certain action ideals they hold consciously and explicitly in common. These ideals, as we shall see, constitute the basis for curriculum.

Critically reflective teachers are not captivated by a methodolatry or technicism of "how to" teach, or "what works" in teaching that falsely—from both the scientific and philosophical points of view—claims universal application. Instead, they first diagnose the particulars of their teaching situations. With such situated "realities" in mind, they hypothesize both the tangible **ends** and "goods" they will seek for students (curriculum) *and* (only) then the **means** they will use (instruction) to bring about such results. Reflective practice comes into play, then, as they judge the effectiveness of both curriculum and instruction in terms of tangible results *for students*. "Good methods" are not something declared or "proven" *in advance* by so-called experts and authorities. Rather, "good methods" are those that bring about "good" (i.e., intended) *curricular consequences* of a tangible nature in a particular situation.

Accordingly *this text does not propose or aspire to be a "method," or a "how-to," or a "what works" technology*. It presents a theoretical *model* called Action Learning (explained in Chapter 1) by which general music teachers can organize their thinking about curriculum, formulate their plans, gather their resources, guide their teaching, and evaluate the results of both their teaching and of their curriculum—all along similar lines. This model can be compared to a "jazz chart" that presents a "theme" and its chord progressions. Lessons conceived according to the Action Learning model therefore guide the teacher through what, given the variability of any class or school day, is essentially a controlled "improvisation" according to the Action Learning model, not the "delivery" of recipe-like lessons.

The results will be individual according to the musical background and personal profile of each teacher as realized within the particular set of circumstances provided by the curriculum and school. Descriptions of lesson formats, then, are presented only as general **protocols**; they outline general procedures, guidelines, and rules of thumb. They are not formulas or recipes. Rather, in practice, they should guide individual teachers along similar lines

---

FIGURE I.2 Summary

Reflective Praxis of Critical Theory

1. Critiques one-mold-fits all, "it works" kinds of *methodolatry*.

2. Acknowledges that the *situatedness* of students, teachers, and schools needs to be taken into consideration.

3. Points out, however, that subjective differences between teachers too often become *ideological* and limiting. An "it works" (or even "it works for me") becomes a cop-out that refuses professional responsibility and the need for ever-more effective teaching.

4. Recommends, then, that ongoing *ideology critique* and *reflective teaching* are needed to overcome complacency and to promote ever-improved teaching praxis.

5. Concludes that such a critique will overcome the subjectivity of 3. and 4. and meet the varied needs of students and teachers best by *communication* and engagement within a professional community that starts at least at the local level.

---

of *theoretical control of teaching*, according to related action ideals of a curricular nature, and by means of common procedural steps for planning, teaching, and evaluating lessons. However, because different teachers will follow the guiding model and curriculum in individual and unique ways, they escape the factory model of **technicist** teaching.

With the protocols from Part Two in mind as guidelines, general music teachers in the same schools and districts can communicate in similar terms—for example, the elementary and middle school general music teachers can actually achieve a **vertical alignment of curriculum** in practice, not just on paper. Teachers accustomed to types of lessons that arise from such approaches as Orff or Kodaly (just to mention two well-known traditions) will be pleased to find that many of their teaching "tools" fit very comfortably within the Action Learning model and lesson protocols, once the general theoretical framework of Chapter 1 is understood. Appropriately, selected approaches from K–3 instruction can continue to serve for grades 4–8 (e.g., use of Orff instruments and improvisations) once adjusted to the Action Learning framework. There still is, however, a need for a major "shift" of planning and teaching around grade 4 and no later than grade 5 which has students increasingly working toward acquiring functional musicianship skills that lead to productive real-life musicking,

TEACHING AS "ACTION RESEARCH"

A profession as understood in sociology, is not simply a highly skilled way of making a living, for example, as a 'professional' athlete, barber, or plumber. A profession—particularly any of the "helping professions" such as teaching, health care, and so forth—is a *practice based on theory and research* rather than just taken for granted skills, hand-me-down, how-to, recipe knowledge, formulas, or methodolatry and it has an *ethic* to serve its "clients" well. Artisanship is involved, of course: It arises naturally from hands-on experience. But professional praxis is not the "practice" of a beginning piano student, nor does it proceed from simple trial and error. It builds from the start on theory and research. New experience arising from ongoing praxis is interpreted in terms of the theory behind the praxis.

FIGURE I.3 Problems with Teaching's Empirical Research Base

1. Philosophers, humanists and social theorists criticize the assumption that matters of teaching and learning can be adequately "quantified" and rendered in terms of laws. At best, such research can describe what *is* the statistical (normal) case, but not what *ought* or *might* be the case in particular circumstances rather than in experimental conditions.

2. The ideal of objective, value-free, and universally valid results requires such research to be conducted in experimental conditions where variables are highly controlled. The "real world" of teachers, however, is incredibly variable and therefore such research cannot be directly put into practice.

3. Such educational research is floated down from some anonymous "elsewhere," often in forbidding statistical and technical terms; as a result, teachers often do not understand it well enough to try, or know how, to adapt it to their unique circumstances.

4. The "law like" claims or implications of such research present a "how-to," technicist model of teaching that is akin to a factory production line: Do certain teaching operations *on* students according to these laws of learning or "findings" and you will obtain certain results within statistical norms.

5. As seen by sociologists of education, the previous situation has led to de-professionalizing, "de-skilling" and disempowering of teachers, making them, instead, mere technical functionaries in the institutional machinery of schooling.

A problem in all teaching fields is that much empirical research is being conducted by university-based researchers, not by practitioners *in* and *for* their own teaching situations and needs. The claims of such experimental and quantitative educational research to "universality" is challenged by critical theorists on the grounds explained in points 1 and 2 of Figures I.1 and I.2 mentioned earlier. Further problems are summarized in Figure I.3.

The problem, then, is the usefulness of research for improving a teacher's *own* practice. Findings from developmental psychology, for example those presented in Chapter 2 of this text, *can* be very useful in guiding teachers' diagnoses of teaching needs and choice of pedagogy. But such findings *cannot* be translated directly into action as some kind of "universal method," nor do they automatically adjust to any particular "method." So, to be a reflective professional, professional judgment is needed by the teacher concerning which research might be relevant and how it is to be adapted for the teacher's particular circumstances.

However, teachers, particularly early in their careers often become captivated by the first "new" (to them) theory they encounter—whether it is introduced in college courses, student teaching, or in-service education. Unfortunately, familiarity gained under such circumstances rarely is broad based. Undaunted by the existence of competing or alternative theories, and unaware of shortcomings, many teachers then settle in with their new but now comfortable theory. They take it for granted and the idea of other "research" applications for their own teaching does not occur to them because they assume that "good methods" that "work" (or "work for me") have already been found. On the other hand, those who seek "new ideas" are typically committed to a technicist mind-set focused on new "strategies" that "work." Such strategies are widely available in certain books, texts, education journals, and on the Internet. Various in-service conferences consist mainly of such "how-to" teaching strategies.

In countering the problems of such unreflective, craft-like teaching, critical theory approaches teaching as a *professional practice* (i.e., as a **praxis**) rather than as a *technology* or craft. As mentioned in Figure I.3, traditional transmission views of schooling treat teachers as merely technical functionaries in a kind of assembly line process. They are expected to accept the 'product' being produced, and so are left only to master and execute the technologies (i.e., the methods) of 'production' that are currently in vogue. In this traditional model, teachers are viewed—and, subconsciously come to view themselves—as part of the "machinery" of an educational "factory"; or merely as artisans who execute a repeatable and therefore predictable sequence of techniques and activities applied to certain 'raw materials' (the students). The value of results is simply taken for granted as "good" or "good enough" because they mistakenly assume the use of "good methods" guarantees "good results."

The professionalized view of teaching—teaching as reflective praxis—that is the basis of this text, requires the same kind of *informed judgment* that uses theory and research as guidelines for diagnosis, action, and evaluation as, for example, in the medical or legal professions. And, as in other professions, such reflective action continually generates new **praxial knowledge** that improves future teaching. It is precisely *praxis* that is at stake when we say that a doctor, dentist, or lawyer sets up "practice." This is not the "practice" of students mastering a score; it is the praxis that results in the improved savvy of individual judgment informed by personal experience that, in turn, is given shape for the future by theoretical understanding. Accordingly, no status quo is ever good enough, no ethical standard of care is 'care-full' enough, no final or absolute, true or best solution is ever attained. No 'canned' or teacher-proof lessons can *ethically* or *pragmatically* meet the varied changing needs of real students in a rapidly changing world. So reflective teachers, as true professionals, constantly push the status quo—at least their own—to ever new and more improved levels or dimensions.

This is accomplished in teaching by, in effect, considering the *everyday act of teaching as being research.* This means that the teacher is at least *informally* engaged in **action research**—research undertaken by a practitioner for the purposes of improving his or her *own* praxis. Such action research does not typically seek results that can be generalized to other teachers. When the findings of such teaching-as-research are understood in terms of the theoretical premises involved (rather than presented as "how-to" recipes), they sometimes can be exchanged profitably between teachers. But in general, conclusions are not drawn for all teachers in all places. Instead, action research is typically hypothesized as applying only to the foreseeable future for this teacher (or cooperating faculty), in this situation.

The enabling condition for action research, then, is the ongoing *ethical* realization and acceptance that results can always be improved as long as some students do not succeed. Teachers who think they have found "the" best way to teach simply do not meet this ethical condition to serve students' needs. A reflective teacher, instead, reflects on the inadequacies of present results and correspondingly is always self-critical in a constructive sense of creative improvement *for the benefit of students.* The Action Learning teacher, as we shall see in more detail, appropriately considers teaching as an activity where *theory guides praxis.*

CURRICULAR AND INSTRUCTIONAL HYPOTHESES AND TEACHING AS REFLECTIVE PRAXIS

There are two main levels of theorizing that are centrally involved in general music teaching as a theory-guided praxis. At the first or *curricular level of theorizing*, what the teacher (or

FIGURE I.4 Two Levels of Action Research and Reflective Praxis

1. **Curriculum**: *Formal curriculum writing is a process of hypothesizing certain ends as being of more value than others.* Such *curricular hypotheses* need ongoing "testing in action" to verify their actual goodness for students now and in the future.

The abstract concepts and isolated skills of technicist teaching leave untested and unverified whether or what such learning is "good for." An Action Learning approach to general music class, in contrast, hypothesizes real-life, holistic musicking as valuable because people already choose these real-life pursuits. The focus, then, is on types of musicking that have the likelihood of beginning a lifetime of musical involvement. The "test results" of such curricular hypotheses are seen in the "actions" of typical students in real-life simulations in school and in real life outside of school.

2. **Instruction**: *Planning instruction begins by hypothesizing certain teaching strategies and materials as the most effective and efficient means for implementing the formal curriculum.*

Rather than methodolatry where "good methods" are assumed to always produce good results, Action Learning evaluates instructional means in terms of how *well* (or *whether*) the intended curricular ends are actually realized. Such reflective teaching amounts to action research: it is predicated on putting (curriculum) theory into (instructional) practice in the local teaching situation. The "test results" of instructional hypotheses can be seen in the functional value added to students' functional musicianship, choices for musicking and, so, their lives.

group) chooses to include and teach is *hypothesized as valuable* in terms of the educational and musical contribution it is predicted to bring for typical students. The "test results" of such hypotheses must be observed "in action"—which is to say, whether the "good results" predicted are actually good "in action" as demonstrated by students. If, for example, music reading is included in the *formal curriculum* in the belief that students will be more competent or more often involved in high school ensembles, church choirs, or personal musicking, then this hypothesized "good result" needs to be observed in order to confirm the curricular hypothesis!

A second and subsequent *instructional level of theorizing* is based on the aforestated curricular theorizing. Each teacher, following the formal curriculum, further hypothesizes as valuable certain instructional tools, techniques, materials, and conditions as the *instruction* by which learning on the part of typical students is most likely to occur. Given the hypothetical value of the *ends* predicted by the curriculum (which, remember, is never taken for granted), the second level of hypothesizing concerns the selection of instructional *means*.

Most technicist "methods" choose their "tools" first and regard their preferred instructional techniques and materials *as* the curriculum—that is, whatever the "tools" can build *is* the curriculum—rather than choosing the tools in light of the tangible ends hypothesized by the formal curriculum as desirable. The assumption is that results are good (or good enough) if the "good method" is employed properly. However the critical and reflective teacher is a *theorist-researcher*, and unlike the teacher as *method-technician*, is concerned first with the hypotheses of value associated with the content of the formal curriculum; that is, with the musical "goods" predicted for students. These provide the criteria by which the success of the hypothesized methods, materials, and other conditions of instruction can be judged. In other words, the success of instructional *means* is judged only to the degree that *ends* are realized that represent a musically unambiguous "value added" for students.

When *curricular* "goods" turn out not as hypothesized, remedial diagnosis centers on whether the hypothesized value needs revision or replacement. However, it may be that the *instructional* means and materials chosen are poorly hypothesized for the curricular ends in question, or that the means simply need improvement in order to succeed. Either way, new hypothesizing and new "action tests" are required.

This text, then, is not intended to promote "going through the motions" of teaching set strategies or canned lessons that result in no (or a negative) impact. Also avoided will be any learning that either *can't* (or won't) be used outside the classroom. It does no good and much harm when valuable learning is taught in ways that students fail to want to use in life. Poetry, for example, is often taught in a way that turns kids off to reading or writing poetry for life. This must be avoided at all costs in general music classes.

Teaching is approached in this text as a type of *informal action research by which teachers constantly improve their own teaching through reflective praxis*. More precisely, it is the process by which teachers "teach themselves"—that is, create their own praxial knowledge—through various kind of organized theorizing and reflective practice in order to facilitate predictable and valuable results for their "clients," the students. This usually requires ongoing attention to changing philosophical, social, psychological, and pedagogical issues, the selecting of ever-new hypotheses for "testing" in action, the "observing" of actual results in terms of predicted hypotheses, a professional restlessness or curiosity, and an ethical commitment to students.

With these various considerations in mind, we are ready to turn to a more specific consideration of action theory, Action Learning, and the details of music and teaching as praxis.

CHAPTER ONE

ACTION LEARNING AND "BREAKING 100 IN MUSIC"

In the sixteenth century legend of the "Pied Piper of Hamelin," the flutist entranced the children: They followed him unquestioningly but ultimately were led astray. Something similar can happen in elementary general music classes. Children like their teacher and unquestioningly follow their teacher's lead because the activities are fun. However, by preadolescence, if general music classes do not begin to model and inspire visions of a life of *active* musicking, too many graduates remain only passive consumers of music, which seems to be the present case.

Action Learning is a teaching paradigm rooted in **action theory**. It uses that theory to get students "into action" musically by increasing or enhancing the typically limited musical choices with which they enter school, and by promoting the musical independence needed for musicking throughout life. Music classes are still fun and challenging, but have the specific purpose of modeling and nurturing choices for lifelong involvement in music.

THEORY AND ACTION THEORY

Praxis based on **theory** is, as was discussed in the Introduction, a primary characteristic of a profession. For any professional, theory is not "merely theoretical" or "for its own sake"; it takes *applied* form—for instance, the physics and other theory needed to guide a spaceship to the moon. Theory in this sense, then, is incredibly practical and is used even for everyday actions. When we enter a dark room we reach for the light switch on the theory that it will enable us to turn on the lights. If it does not, we theorize that the bulb is faulty or we check to see if the lamp is plugged in—and so on.

Theorizing at any level—everyday, professional, scientific—is not uninformed speculation; it results from the data of experience or experiment. Furthermore, theories are not "proven," then used; they predict certain results (e.g., that the light will go on). When theories predict well, they are very useful and are likely to be used again. When failures or inconsistencies arise, theories either get adjusted or replaced with more adequate ones.

Theories also generate new information; in scientific experiments, for instance, they produce new data. In life, too, various folk and other theories guide our everyday actions and determine what we "learn from experience." Likewise, the theory guiding professional praxis determines the new knowledge newly learned from hands-on experience. The "facts" of experience or experiment, then, are data interpreted in light of a particular theory. Different theories, however, can interpret the same data as different "facts."

This variability explains major differences within a profession. For example, the important distinction between a Medical Doctor (M.D.) and an Osteopathic Doctor (D.O.) is a result of the differences between the theories of allopathy and osteopathy and their respective (but contrasting) paradigms for defining and promoting "good health." While both kinds of doctor have studied supporting theories from biology, chemistry, and physics, they have different approaches to medical practice; in fact, hospitals predicated on one theory used to exclude doctors subscribing to the other theory.

Action Learning is similarly distinguished from other "active" approaches to learning music by its reliance on *action theory* from sociology, psychology, and philosophy. Understanding action theory is thus as vitally important to Action Learning as allopathy and osteopathy are to the medical practices of doctors who subscribe to those theories. Action Learning is a model of defining and promoting musical "good health."

This chapter, then, is practical, not "merely theoretical." Understanding action theory is essential to understanding and achieving the all-important distinctions between teaching as a *professional praxis* and the *technicist teaching* discussed in the Introduction. Action theory, then, is not simply "background"; it must be in the "foreground" of the readers' thinking throughout the remaining chapters of this text that put this theory into practice.

TRADITIONS AND PRECEDENTS FOR ACTION LEARNING IN GENERAL EDUCATION

- The term "Action Learning" was first used in the 1960s to refer to *learning experiences that closely duplicate real life outside of school*. Programs and instruction were designed to get students involved with productive *adult and adult-like activities* in a direct attempt to connect school to out-of-school life. Typically such Action Learning involved students in actual **apprenticeships**, **practicums**, internships and externships, and with frequent field trips to the workplace. Vocational education is also predicated on Action Learning,

- Action Learning also encompasses *in-school simulation of out-of-school activities and roles*. In such classes, teachers formally structure learning to model the conditions under which it will be applied in real life. Language immersion is a good example: When students walk into a Spanish or German class of this kind, no English is spoken and the content of the class models being in the target country. Simulations where, for example, elementary students "role-play" making change in a store are also models of Action Learning.

- Action Learning is also used with learning disabled students. Their schooling consists largely of *learning by doing* typical tasks needed to succeed in life.

- Another variety of Action Learning is the use of "games"—that is, "game theory." In educational "games," realistic problems are posed that require *action strategies* (i.e., choices and decisions) that, in turn, must be acted upon. Thus students "live" and actually experience the inner workings of the undertaking in question as realistically as can be approximated in formal school settings. The social studies teacher who has students "play" the stock market for several months is involved in Action Learning.

Action Learning precedents all attempt to (a) *import and validate real life* as a central part of the school curriculum and learning process; and (b) *export learning to life outside of and after graduation from school*. Both conditions are highly motivating, especially beginning with preadolescents.

FUNDAMENTALS AND CHARACTERISTICS OF ACTION LEARNING

Action Learning is rooted in research from a wide variety of supporting disciplines.

1. Action Theory

At the root of action theory is the idea of a purposive **agent**—that is, a person who *acts mindfully* to bring about a desired result. Thus an **action** is not just any 'behavior' or 'activity.' By definition, an action is guided by **intentionality**: the *meanings, values, and purposes* that an agent 'tries to' achieve.

Action Learning within music education is therefore concerned with modeling and developing meanings, values, and purposes of a specifically *musical* kind. Teaching in ways that evoke and nurture such *musical* intentionality is distinguished from the "Pied Piper" kind of teaching where students "go along" with the fun of musical "activities" without any clear sense, image, or model of their long-term purpose or value.

> Action Learning teachers try to get students to have *musical intentions* in mind; students do not just go along simply for fun, for fear of not doing so, or for grades. For example, in composing a song (Chapter 4) their intentions are focused specifically on the *musical* results and on gaining new mastery of *musical* materials, not just in the "activity" for its own sake—though composing is fun and rewarding at this age. Musical intentionality is fostered when real-life models of musicking are at stake and where part of the intention is to be musically more "grown up."

2. Brain Research and Cognitive Psychology

The "mindfulness" of intentionality is reinforced by psychological theory that points to the importance of the *mental actions* that direct overt musical doings. **Behavior**, as defined by behaviorists, is not intentional or mindful. Rather, behavior is mere 'activity' that involves *conditioned* responses, thoughtless reactions and even instincts that are not consciously directed.

> Lessons taught only as "activities" often elicit this kind of indifferent "going along" and unthinking, reactive *behavior*, rather than the conscious "trying to" of a specifically musical kind that Action Learning seeks.

Constructivism: Findings of modern brain and cognitive theory also point out that *knowledge is a personal construction*. Any knowledge base from the past—from a discipline or from a student's past—necessarily gets "in-formed" (inwardly shaped or constructed) and personalized in terms of the learner's present experience, needs, intentions, uses. As long as "information" is only "passed on" as *preformed* in someone else's terms (e.g., the teacher or text author), learning qualifies only as *short-term memory*, not as knowledge as such.

Action Learning for general music class stresses that, (a) **concepts** are constructed by learners in terms of the context of certain situated musicianship demands or needs, and that (b) concepts are unique between people and also between musical practices. A student's "concept of," say "form" at any moment is uniquely "constructed" by each student over time as based on all composing lessons (Chapters 4, 5) where unity and variety are at stake; in singing and playing lessons (Chapters 7, 8) where recognizing repetition and contrast aids the performance; and particularly in listening lessons (Chapter 6) where students "in-form" or give their own inward organization or structure to perceptions.

3. Philosophy Contributes Three Theories of Special Importance to Action Learning

Pragmatism teaches that the truth or value of a proposition or method is seen in the tangible consequences that result from its application "in action." If the consequences of general music instruction are not *tangible*, and if they do not *make a difference* in the musical values (choices) and capabilities of most students, they are *not pragmatic*. Importantly, then, not everything that is practicable to teach, promotes pragmatic results.

Action Learning for general music seeks to make such a pragmatic musical difference for students beyond what might reasonably be expected without general music class. It is concerned with what students can *do*—at all, better or to new ends—as a result of instruction! This is the "value added" mentioned in the Introduction.

Utilitarianism advises that a 'right act' is one that actually or most probably produces, directly or indirectly, "goods" for the greatest number of people involved. By this criterion, an Action Learning teacher attempts to model those kinds of musical choices and benefits that have *the greatest likelihood of benefiting the largest number of students*, not just an elite few.

In Action Learning, a full range of musics and musicking are offered, not just the European "classics." The emphasis is on modeling the *everyday benefits and uses of music* and of developing musicianship skills that enable and enthuse students to be active musickers.

Humanistic and **existential** philosophies tell us that *meaning is made*, not found or passed on ready-made from the past or others. These philosophies show that *meaning—*including, importantly, self-meaning; one's sense of personal value—*is constructed by and revealed through personal choices and actions.*

Action Learning classes *facilitate meaning-making* rather than assuming in advance that meaning and value are absolutes to be imposed on or discovered by students. Just as a tennis ball 'affords' many uses beyond playing tennis, the **affordances of music** make available many kinds or types of meaning and value. Only learning that is personally meaningful to students will last outside the classroom and after the school years. Thus increasing and enhancing personal *musical choice making*— whether that be in relation to a listening response (Chapter 6) or new options for performing (Chapters 7, 8)—is an important goal.

4. Educational Theories

Transfer of learning refers, first of all, to the ability to use learning in new situations. For Action Learning this means using school-based learning in out-of-school applications, rather than simply accumulating information or concepts or learning "basic skills" that end up being not used and thus basic to nothing. Two major principles of transfer involve (a) similarity of the *task* and (b) the *timing* between learning and its transfer.

For Action Learning, then, (a) lessons and practice tasks need to resemble as closely as possible (given the age and classroom conditions) the anticipated out-of-school applications. And, (b) any study, practice, drill or memorization is applied to anticipated uses during the same or next lesson or class period, not as a final project. The increased musical rewards of learning are thus seen by students to justify the practice or study.

Secondly, *teaching for transfer* also means that learning is not just accumulated from one class to another, but that instruction in subsequent classes builds on, applies, and otherwise develops previous learning.

In Action Learning, this means a **spiral curriculum** where musicianship becomes stronger, richer, and more productive as it approaches *evermore realistic models* of musicking. Thus, for example, a new chord learned in playing the guitar or ukulele (Chapter 8) or in composing songs and melodies (Chapter 4) functions as a stepping stone to a new, more realistic and thus more personally meaningful and satisfying stage of musicianship.

Holistic learning: Instead of learning *atomistic* bits and pieces of information or skills, or addressing isolated concepts in the abstract, the focus of a lesson always occurs in a holistic musical context where, for example, many concepts interact in producing the overall result. The more it is holistic, the more musicking is "realistic" in its fullness and satisfactions.

A focus on say, melody, takes place in the context of rhythm and harmony (Chapter 4), not in isolation. Similarly, a sound composition (Chapter 5) employs formal and expressive dimensions holistically rather than simply improvising on, say, a single musical focal point or variable. Holism of instruction is more satisfying because of its greater realism and its greater realism contributes to the synthesis of effective musicianship, which is always holistic in praxis.

Knowing-in-action is stressed rather than knowing-out-of-context. When learning is relative to and evaluated only in terms of decontextualized, neutral classroom conditions, then only "merely academic" school learning is at stake, not the student's ability and intention to use the learning in personally meaningful ways. "School music" thus fails to lead to lifelong musicking.

Knowing-in-action is best facilitated by *learning*-in-action and **practicing-in-action** where outside-of-school models of musicking become the vehicles for in-class learning and pracice, thus increasing the student's ability and desire to place the learning in personal context. Sound composition "advertisements" for products or as "sound tracks" for videos (Chapter 5), or musical "valentines" (Chapter 4) demonstrate the importance of the 'fit' between use and music.

Authentic learning and assessment: Musical learning is best seen and assessed "authentically"—which is to say, in action through **real-life** models of singing, performing, composing or listening; not on unmusical, written, abstract, or arbitrary classroom evaluations that bear no relation to holistic and *authentic musicking* in real life. The term "authentic learning" in education today is virtually synonymous with Action Learning!

If recreational playing of instruments is a curricular ideal (Chapter 8; Appendix A), authentic assessment involves determining how well and enjoyably the student actually plays relative to the age group. By the end of middle school, considerable **musical independence** ought to be the criterion for all musicking.

Essentialism and **perennialism**: The former claims that certain "basics" are "essential" to general education. However, because such teaching is taught as a "discipline" and rarely demonstrates *what* such learning *is basic to* in terms of real life musical actions, learning is usually "merely academic." Perennialism holds that the "classics" have "perennial value" for everyone, forever. Advocates make rather absolute—and often arbitrary-sounding—claims for "good music" and for what students *should* learn, whether interested or not.

Action Learning, instead, is *student centered* and *action focused,* two principles of **progressivism**, and important to philosophies of **humanism** and **reconstructionism**. With student-centered learning, students actively construct and negotiate their own meanings (i.e., constructivism), in contrast to *teacher-dominated* instruction of essentialism and perennialism where the teacher is active and students are passive. Action-focused learning can and is put "into action," compared to the learning-for-its-own-sake that characterizes the *subject matter-centered* teaching of essentialism and perennialism. Thus Action Learning also shares the forward-looking trait of **futurism**.

The focus of Action Learning is to inspire students *to want to* and *to be able to* live life more fully through musicking of some kind. The real-life models on which curriculum focuses inspire student intentionality. General music, thus, becomes not a "survey" of music in general, or a "discipline" studied for its own sake; it is taught and learned for personal use. Meaning and value, then, are seen in use.

"BREAKING 100 IN MUSIC": A SPORTS ANALOGY

That *meaning is seen in use* is illustrated and summarized by comparing music to golf and bowling. A leading manufacturer of sporting goods noted that when individuals can score less than 100 in golf and more than 100 in bowling they begin to think of themselves, respectively, as "golfers" and "bowlers" and thus spend more time and money on the sport. Even though music has no numerical score as an indicator of accomplishment, important parallels exist between this attitude of "breaking 100" and musicking.

1. *Music can be enjoyed alone or in groups.* Each has different value.

2. *Music is an extremely important recreational pastime for large numbers of musically minded individuals.* The key for Action Learning is to get students to become musically minded. This is done by curriculum that models the kinds of musicking that are the most likely avenues of musical enjoyment throughout life.

3. *Music, like sports, derives at least some of its pleasures from maintaining or increasing mastery* (i.e., practice). Recreational activities that involve no challenge, skill development, or effort offer little interest. *Achievement increases rewards*; thus time and effort spent practicing are thus seen as **"good time"**—time well spent.

4. *As in sports, various professional or expert models define the upper limits of music skill.* Realistically, however, most amateurs engage "seriously" in their choice of musicking with no intentionality for reaching such heights of artistry. Personal musicking is satisfying to them despite falling short of professional standards. Thus, just as with amateur golfers and bowlers, "good time" in music is relative to the interests and abilities of the individual and is afforded by different kinds and levels of expertise.

5. *Nonetheless expert models serve as ideals for potential improvement and its rewards.* In sports, individual skill development is usually limited by native ability and available practice time. Whatever the expertise, the individual continues to be involved for the pleasures made possible by the quality of play afforded by that expertise—for example, in friendly competition with others of similar ability. In music, similarly, native ability, practice time, and competing interests influence an individual's skill development. The pleasures and rewards, then, are commensurate with the *type* of competence. Thus, for example, guitar skills for folk music and sing-alongs provide types of musical pleasure that are simply different than (not of lesser value than) the kinds of skills involved in other types of guitar playing.

6. *Students who are not enabled to develop a level of musical competence and independence sufficient to musicking at personal levels of satisfaction while in the general music program are not likely to ever "break 100 in music."* The Action Learning teacher is thus not satisfied to have "taught" things to students if such learning

does not result in "good time" from present and future musicking. Moreover, Action Learning avoids teaching "good things" in "bad ways" that turn students off to musicking for the future.

> The analogy with golf and bowling is perhaps best understood in relation to musicking as a recreational performance. However, Action Learning for general music also addresses other potential types of "breaking 100 in music," such as listening, music criticism and journalism, many forms of composing and arranging (such as MIDI) and a whole host of music-based amateur involvements from building personal record collections to pursuing certain music interests on the Internet.

MUSIC IN ACTION

As mentioned in the opening, music teachers generally tend to take the value of music, and thus the reasons for its inclusion in general education, for granted. However, starting with preadolescence, a typical student's concept of what music *is* and is "good for" increasingly becomes influenced by older adolescents and the commercial media.

Action Learning teachers, then, need to think more about what music *is* and "is good for" in the lives of ordinary people. Virtually everything they teach, and how they teach and evaluate learning and teaching, is predicated on a philosophy of music and musical value. Exclusive emphasis on decoding notation, for example, fails to account for most of the music in the world that has no score. Focusing solely on European "art music" conveys the false notion that listening involves "receiving" aesthetic meanings, messages, or pleasures the piece is said to "express," "contain," or "make us feel." However, most listeners in the world would greet the Western idea of *listening-as-contemplation* with great surprise. Most listening in the world involves active musical participation, such as moving, dancing, clapping, and so on. It fulfills an entirely different and altogether more personally interactive and social role than is expected of a Western audience member.

- Action Learning, thus, focuses on a **praxial theory of music** that fully accounts for *all* musicking the world has to offer. For praxial theory, music is sound used to make human occasions and cultural events of all kinds *special*. A wedding without its chosen music, for example, is less exceptional, less meaningful in key ways, and music is chosen for parties, worship, and aerobics with special care.

> *Implications for general music:*
> Music is not just a "fun" thing to do, and not simply the "icing on the cake of life." It provides very basic and pragmatic "goods," among which are the various occasions of its use to enhance human life in various ways.
>
> 1. Showing *that* and *how* music is useful or pragmatic—*how* and *what* it *adds* to important occasions and life—is particularly appealing to pre- and early adolescents (not to mention most adults) for whom tangible and down-to-earth values are more attractive than claims that "proper" musical meaning and value are abstract, timeless, and cerebrally highbrow.

2. Music is "good" when it serves valued human needs and does so success-fully enough to be appreciated as "good time"—as time well spent. General music classes should always address, model, or exemplify these "goods" (uses) and teachers need to promote "good time" (but not just "fun") as the major consequence of learning.

- For praxial theory, *that* sounds are "music" and the specific *nature* of those sounds, are both determined in part by the **situated context** that occasions its use! Thus, the specific conditions of the use-occasion are part of its meaning or value. A Bach chorale *as worship* is considerably different "music"—that is, has different requirements and meanings—than the same score performed by a trained chorus for a secular concert audience. What "good music" is and what a "good performance" is will vary, then, according to situated variables.

Implications for general music:

1. Meaning is not strictly "in" music's sounds. It is "in" the relationship between the sounds, the social praxis those sounds are "making special," and the in-dividual or individuals who are to benefit. Meaning is a *process*, an inter-action, conversation or negotiation between those three aspects. Rather than a single or singular *product*, musical **affordances** vary according to that process. The verb form "musicking" conveys this 'doing' or praxial aspect in comparison to the noun form "music" which problematically conveys the idea of musical "works" as "things" or fixed products.

2. General music teachers need to constantly emphasize that "good music" is sound employed to bring about "right results" for the intentionality of an in-dividual or group in a particular situation. Stressing the different situations in life to which music is central and analyzing the criteria of "good music" in terms of the "goods" served for such situations should begin in general music classes of pre- and early adolescents.

- A praxial theory of music does not treat music as a transcendent "rising above" time and place, an ethereal or intangible, mystical, spiritual, or obscure meaning of some kind that is absolute and unchanging. Instead, music's "meanings" or "goods" arise in the present in terms of this or that praxis. Music is not, then, some historical artifact—a "work"—that is rooted in and thus tied to the meanings and values of the past. It is an ongoing, always contemporary praxis that derives its "goods" from the particulars of its use in the present. A Bach harpsichord piece is given new "life"—is new music—in the present when played on piano or marimba. Similarly, compositions created for one pur-pose can find new "life" in the present, for example in movies, advertising, and the like.

Implications for general music:

1. Music is a "living" art form meant for people whose lives are made more "lively" or full of life as a result. It is important to model, therefore, that mu-

sical meaning is not unchanging; rather, its value is seen in the wide range of human needs it continues to serve. Emphasizing these contemporary needs or uses is of key importance beginning with preadolescence.

2. Musical "expression" is not tied to fixed "aesthetic emotions"—intellectual purifications of "real emotions" into abstract "ideas of feelings"—that are idealized and thus the same for all people. Music affords meanings that vary according to this person, in this time and place; thus meaning is always "contemporary" in the sensibilities that it is **expressive of**. Not "anything goes," however; music's *expressive* affordances are necessarily derived from its actual features, which are objective.

- For Action Learning, musics that have promise of continual renewal hold the most potential "good" for instruction. These, regardless of style, ethnic origin, genre, or the like, properly constitute the "classics."

Implications for music education:

1. A useful long-term strategy for this age group is to make a distinction between "classics" of any praxis and the "merely popular" music of passing fashion. General music classes should model a diverse range of such "classics" with the intention of discerning the musical features responsible for that status, and for the purposes of attracting students' interests to such musics.

2. Since a main use of "merely popular" music is to make money by manipulating popular consumption habits, pre- and early adolescents are susceptible to economic and social exploitation and need to be **empowered** to be critical consumers and producers of music.

3. "Teen music," while of passing interest, does fulfill a valuable and defining role for "teen culture." However, students are already well versed in it and its short shelf life makes it a poor candidate for lifelong learning. To the degree it functions as a form of rebellion, however, adolescents may resent its inclusion in the school curriculum or react to its inclusion in ways the teacher does not expect.

- The praxial view of Action Learning puts a particular emphasis on developing *a lifelong* **amateur** *interest and involvement* in some personally valued form of musicking. Action Learning takes the pragmatic position that musical values and meanings—however elevated or everyday—are seen only in action. Thus it aims to get students into action musically in personally rewarding ways that are directly modeled in general music classes.

Implications for general music:

1. Claims for musical values that cannot be observed or evaluated give way with Action Learning to teaching a broad variety of **musicianship skills** that

are rooted in the "classics" of musical traditions most likely to be available to students outside of schooling now and in the future.

2. Despite music's down-to-earth nature and everyday value, it profits from formal learning in order to fully use and savor its benefits. Such "schooling" in music necessarily should help students incorporate themselves in musical traditions beyond those already immediately at hand. If general education is to prepare students "in general" for a changing world, so must general music education prepare students for similarly changing musical choices.

THEORY INTO PRACTICE: ACTION LEARNING VERSUS ACTIVITIES APPROACHES TO GENERAL MUSIC

The "active" agency of Action Learning is often misunderstood to mean mere "hands on" learning or "learning by doing." Such "active learning" *is* part of it. But the "actions" of Action Learning are different in important ways from the "activities" of other approaches to teaching. On the other hand, some of those "activities" can be easily and suitably re-adapted according to Action Learning theory. The following outline summarizes the most important theoretical distinctions.

1. Activities Versus Actions

- Recall, first of all, that **actions** are guided by intentions (goals, desires, values) for reaching certain musical results. *Musical* actions involve mindfully "trying-to" bring about certain desired *musical* results. When students are clear as to the nature and value of musical results, their intentions inevitably advance music learning in line with the competencies demanded by such results.

- "Activities" involve *mere* **behavior** that is somewhat mindless, or it is directed by *non*-musical or *un*musical intentions, such as pleasing the teacher or just having fun. Thus while students may appear to be enjoying or otherwise going along with the lesson, musical learning may be nonexistent, slight, or haphazard.

2. Musical Experience

- "*An* experience" is the result of an intentional action. It is necessarily holistic because it weds: (a) "intending" a musical result, (b) diagnosing and hypothesizing means of reaching it, (c) "initiating" and "undergoing" the action, and (d) the "done" (or the result) in a unified whole. If results are not as intended, **adaptive action** is employed: then (b) is reanalyzed and leads to a new action (c), and new reflection on results.

- "*To* experience" something is when it "happens" *to* us without our intending. It does not conclude with any intended learning or result. Much experience where students are "active" in the presence of music "happens" reactively by them without any musical intentions on their parts. Therefore the experience is not necessarily "musical" or even "educational" and without intentions there is no adaptive action—no "mindful" learning.

3. Teaching musicianship Skills as Cognitive Actions Versus "Teaching Concepts"

- **Concepts** are *mental action patterns*; they are in effect the cognitive 'software' behind experiences of 'things' and 'doings.' Often we have abstract words (terms, labels) and definitions to refer to such 'things' (e.g., "melody," "harmony," "rhythm") and 'doings' (e.g., "singing," "dancing"). However, these *words* are not the concepts. Rather, *the experience* (of, for example, "melody," "harmony," "rhythm" as such) *itself is the concept at work*. Verbal labels have the negative effect of separating and isolating concepts into abstractions that in actual use actually overlap and interact holistically. Thus, for example, "melody," "harmony," "rhythm," "form," "meter," "timbre," and "pitch" are not separable in experience; even when **focal attention** is on one, all the others (and many more) are unavoidably involved. Thus, *having* "an experience" already involves **concepts-in-action**; and any conceptual focus always holistically involves other interactive and collaborative concepts.

- Action Learning, addresses musical concepts then, as *holistic cognitive actions*—as **musicianship skills**—not as abstract labels or definitions. They develop over time (often throughout life) *through realistic musical uses* where, for example, "melody," "harmony" and "rhythm" (etc.) function in natural **synergy**. Thus, instead of planning separate "activities" in order to "experience" or "understand" this or that abstract concept *preliminary to use*, Action Learning instead promotes concepts *through use*—that is, as functional 'doings' of various kinds in relation to a curriculum of real-life models. Thus a student's concept of, say, "melody" is constructed over time by means of what Piaget described as **assimilation** and **accommodation**. Such concepts evolve; they grow progressively richer, more "realistic" and thus ever more functional as they are developed in connection with a spiral curriculum of real-life (authentic, holistic, synergic) musical uses. The holism of such praxial learning insures that lessons are *useful* (and thus perceived by pre- and early adolescents as relevant) and that the learning—the conceptual skill—is *actually used*, rather than abstract, isolated, or disconnected from real and future uses.

4. Practice-in-Action Versus "Skill Drill" and Isolated Memorization

- Mere "skill drill" is typically mindless repetition or **rote** learning. **Practice**, instead, is mindful of desired results and thus engages **adaptive action** to correct mistakes. Furthermore, a drill (such as clapping a set pattern) is only a self-contained "activity"; as such, it does not necessarily transfer to holistic use in the future. Memorization is sometimes necessary, of course (e.g., key signatures). But such information is best learned and "tested" by regular aplication to real-life uses where it becomes functional rather than forgotten.

- Action Learning thus provides an apprenticeship of *general* musicianship that is **practiced-in-action** through application to ever new and more realistic musical needs. Learning progresses by basing lessons *progressively* on evermore realistic musical actions drawn from musical traditions and practices that are hypothesized to be of present interest and future value to students. Upon such a general base, the *specialized* musicianship skills of particular musics can be extended; for example, jazz chords are built on triads; "oomp-chunk-chunk" strums are expanded to rhythmically more interesting strums. Such specialized musicianship most likely awaits high school electives or out-of-school pursuit based on individual interest.

5. *Using* Instructional Plans as "Tools" Versus *Teaching* "Activities" as Ends-in-Themselves

- With Action Learning, individual lessons are not taught as self-contained "activities." Instead, lessons are "tools" for progressively building concepts-in-action; that is, functional musicianship skills in connection with authentic musical learning. Thus lessons taught in accordance with the protocols of Part II of this text (i.e., song writing, sound compositions, listening lessons, and recreational singing and playing) should be approached as a *practicum* of lessons that *build on each other*, not as freestanding "activities." A lesson should always (a) be predicated on a realistic musical use, (b) and serve as a "tool" for building new learning to evermore authentic applications. This promotes fruitful **transfer** of learning between lessons and to life.

- A song is sung, then, (a) to model the pleasures of recreational singing and (b) to advance students' singing or music-reading ability, and so on. The song is thus *used* to practice-in-action (i.e., get better at) the learning at stake in addition to its musical pleasures (which, in any case, are enhanced as skills improve). In addition, the materials promoting such growth need (c) to be chosen for the other important contributions they can make to the students' general musicianship. Thus, for example, songs to be sung should be related to composing and listening skills.

6. "Problem Solving" and Decision Making Versus "Teaching Creativity" for Its Own Sake

- Action Learning teachers use **problem-based learning**. Musical problems are projects that involve *experiments* and *challenges* predicated on attractive and real-life musical "goods." Learning arises from analyzing, deciding on, and experimenting with solutions, observing results and, if needed, acting adaptively. Students' different solutions to the same problems demonstrate the inherent variability and creativity of musicking. Problems are chosen to elicit decision making among certain musical possibilities and according to specified musicianship *criteria*: For example, the challenge of fostering "unity" in a sound composition (Chapter 5) when restricted to the use of heterogeneous timbres; explorations of creating "variety" when restricted to homogenous timbres; experiments for adding "rhythmic interest" to the basic prosody of a song's words (Chapter 4). Because such problems are musically holistic, learning is similarly holistic in its potential relevance and satisfactions.

- Such problem solving involves creativity. But because problems are *predicated on musicianship criteria* (e.g., "unity," "variety," "rhythmic interest," in the previous examples) such creativity is not just a matter of spontaneity or improvisation. Even where students' solutions may not seem "creative" to the teacher in the 'imaginative' or 'inspired' sense (though such judgments are arguably subjective), they will be more or less successful in meeting the stated criteria and students typically derive satisfaction from their creative efforts.

7. Action-Centered Pragmatism Versus Child-Centered Progressivism

- By itself, the earlier mentioned child-centered approach based on students' interests does not necessarily result in learning that is applicable, tangible, long lasting, or satisfying. Choosing activities *solely* on the basis of present interest and fun—for example, singing seasonal songs—is unproductive, therefore, if such lessons do not *also* advance students' musical abilities in consequential, long-term ways. Furthermore, if the child's *present* interests are the sole or main criterion, much of potential value to their musical *future* gets left out.

- Action Learning is therefore *action*-centered, not simply *child*-centered. What the student is able to do—at all, or better, or to new ends—as a result of instruction is primary. If learning can be advanced beyond mere "fun motivation," then it is useful to draw upon students' existing interests. But Action Learning teachers also feel free to *stimulate interest* in musical practices students may not even know exist. Then the "fun" comes from accomplishing something they would not have thought was interesting, or from mastering something that was initially difficult to do. So, Action Learning teachers regularly *tempt* students in new directions in a way that involves them involved in learning they would not have at first been interested in but can soon find satisfying as skill improves.

SUMMARY
PUTTING ACTION LEARNING THEORY INTO PRACTICE IN THE GENERAL MUSIC CLASSROOM

1. Action Learning Advances "General Musicianship" Knowledge and Skills

- It advances the skills predictably useful to typical adults throughout life: for example, recreational singing, music reading sufficient to church and community choirs, "making sense" of music and enjoyment through listening, and the like.

- It is not a survey of disconnected musical generalities, a superficial sampling of music "in general"; boiled-down theory, history, appreciation; or introduction to the "discipline" of music as a "subject" of study for its own sake.

- *Instead,* it promotes the broad musicianship skills and positive attitudes for "breaking 100" that *enable* students to be musically independent and active outside of class and after graduation, and to *want to* be musically active as part of the life well lived.

2. Action Learning Addresses Music from a Praxial Philosophy and Rationale

- It studies music, first, in terms of what music is "good for" in life. Secondly, "good music" is music that serves a human "good" very well. Thirdly, music is studied in school as a potential "good" in the life of each student. Thus, and finally, it is studied in terms of its tangible contribution to society and culture.

- "Just listening" is treated as only one among a multitude of human activities that music is "good for." Audience listening of all kinds is best addressed by improving aural acuity (Chapter 6) not specifically to promote "good taste" or the "appreciation" of a particular kind of music.

- Music from other cultures is studied: (a) to learn what music is "good for" in human cultures and societies; and, (b) for the contribution such study makes to understanding other cultures and societies; but mainly, (c) for the rewards such musical knowledge and skill can contribute specifically to the individual and his or her *personal* musical life.

- Music is **embodied**: Its "feelingfulness" is a construction by the individual's mind-body. Such feelings are "felt" rather than "understood" or "received" as intellectual or aesthetic abstractions and therefore they are personally meaningful. Because human bodies are similar, such "felt" bases of musicking are also shared between humans; however, such feelingfulness varies according how music is organized by and contributes to the sociality of different groups and their traditions. Thus viewed, music unifies mind and body, and individual and community.

3. Action Learning Expands or Extends the Musical Choices and Options Available to Students "In Life" Beyond Those Already Easily Accessible without Instruction

- *It respects the present musical values of students.* It may even advance skills learning in connection with music of the home (ethnic group, church, etc.) and everyday music in terms of the "goods" thus made available by such musics for life.

- A hallmark of Action Learning is the *"value added" to students' musical choices and options* as a result of instruction. The lack of value added fails to "turn on" students to "breaking 100 in music," often leads to "burn out" by teachers, and is a source of the problems music teachers have with budgets, class size, scheduling, and so forth.

- Successful teaching in general music class results in the *progressive demonstration of learning and skill that can be directly attributed to instruction* and that can be put "into action" musically and independently outside of class or after graduation from school. Instead of mere fun, students "intend" to advance their musical learning through study and practice because it leads to new or newly increased *musical* pleasures.

- Important to Action Learning are *changes of attitude and valuing* that can be seen when students choose to be musically active in and out of school in ways that formal schooling made possible (e.g., enrolling in—or calling for—high school general music electives; joining a church choir). *Musical independence* and *competence* are prerequisites for lifelong musical involvement but cannot be forced on students by teaching means that turn them off from using such learning outside of class and school.

4. Action Learning has an Ethical Criterion to "Do No Harm" to the Natural Interest and Love Children Exhibit for Music

- Children in grades K–3 naturally get into the natural "flow" of musicking simply for its joys. In the intermediate grades, however, this natural appeal needs to be focused on new, more adult-like models. If music class does not thereafter promote skill and learning in ways that advance musical rewards and pleasures, then students become more and more resistant to musicking outside of school beyond teen music.

- Action Learning seeks to directly nurture the *attitudes, values, and rewards* that are the value of any musicking. It seeks to cultivate positive visions of the active role of music in the life well lived.

- The learner's *need to achieve* is addressed musically by tangibly advancing musicianship skills and by demonstrating that improved competency increases musical satisfaction.

CHAPTER TWO

'TWEEN-AGERS—THEIR SCHOOLS AND THEIR TEACHERS

Pre- and early adolescents (grades 4–8) are 'tween-agers; that is, somewhere be*tween* being little children and being young adults. Before the 'tween-age years, children are seldom very far from adult control and supervision, and with **adolescence** they become progressively autonomous. Grades 4–8 provide the transition from early childhood (K–3) to adolescence (high school).

Developmental psychologists see this transition as an independent **stage of development** that is *as critical as the first two years of life*. It has been called **transescence** and encompasses the years just prior to **pubescence** (ages 9–10) through early adolescence (ages 13–14). This is the age this text addresses. Transescence presents special developmental **growth-tasks** and school should help them meet these needs.

Key Traits of Transescence:

1. Highly variable physical change has important consequences for emotional and social development.
2. A spurt in brain growth between ages 10–12 has important implications for teaching and learning.
3. Peers exert a new influence that previously had been solely the province of adults.
4. They need, nonetheless, to develop functional relations with adults, and to understand the adult world they are about to enter.
5. A major developmental task is cultivating a sense of values, especially a positive sense of *self-worth*.
6. Many traits (and problems) of early adolescence are seen in budding form; for example, styles of dress and music.

'Tween-agers have an ambivalent relation with adults. Formerly they were dependent on and naturally looked up to adults. With transescence, however, they increasingly seek more physical separation and independence and, especially, psychological and social independence from adults. They are keenly aware of adult models, but typically 'put up with' adults, but look forward to being grown up and free to make their own choices.

Although their energies sometimes spin out of control, children K–3 are generally responsive to adult direction. After the 'antsyness' of the primary grades, fourth graders are more focused. But this is only a short-lived "calm before the storm." By fifth grade students begin to be more socially aware of and interested in peers and the adolescent subculture, and give increasing evidence that they no longer take the adult world or authority for granted.

They are more likely to question adult authority—at least in indirect, attitudinal ways, but increasingly in the form of direct challenges. By middle or junior high school direct challenges and misbehavior are predictable.

This developmental drift from cute to contentious is well underway by fourth and fifth grade and has implications general music teachers need to consider. The basic instructional protocols recommended in Part Two of this text *must be modified to suit the changing needs of each grade level.*

For clarity, developmental traits of 'tween-agers are broken down in this text into two groups: *intermediate* (grades 4–6) and *middle school* (grades 6–8). However, it is important to stress that individual students will vary, sometimes greatly. And because a given fifth grade may have more early maturers than another fifth grade, it is usually necessary to make adjustments for differences between individual classes. Furthermore, in one geographic area or school, fifth graders may tend to act more maturely or respectfully than in another. Developmental differences also vary according to ethnic group and gender. Important gender differences will be noted here, but teachers need to become informed about differences related to the ethnic diversity of their communities.

In some schools sixth grade is part of the elementary school and others place it in (or at least treat it as) middle school. Thus the distinction in this text between "intermediate" and "middle" school applies to grades 4 and 5, and 7 and 8, respectively, because grade 6 is handled differently in different communities. It is important to note, however, that as the oldest in elementary school, sixth graders act somewhat differently than they do when they are the youngest in middle school!

DEVELOPMENTAL CHARACTERISTICS OF INTERMEDIATE AND MIDDLE SCHOOL STUDENTS

Descriptions of developmental differences between genders are statistical findings based on research, not stereotypes. The degree to which differences are due to nature or nurture is an open question.

PHYSICAL

Intermediate Grades

- Height and weight gains are continuous and steady.
- Girls generally develop earlier than boys and, by the end of this period, are often taller and more physically mature than boys.
- A significant growth spurt of the brain occurs between ages 10–12, and the process of **myelinization** continues into early adolescence. Connections within the brain progress from the *motor areas* (physical control) in the back of the brain to the *abstract thinking* areas in the frontal lobes. Thus physical abilities develop well before abstract thinking, and "thinking" at this stage still requires many of the tangible actions **Jean Piaget** called *concrete operations.*
- Girls' brains typically develop more quickly than boys; thus they gain earlier control of verbal skills and abstract thinking. Boys generally need more overt, physical involvement. This has important implications for the relatively different learning styles of boys and girls at this age and on their behavioral tendencies. Generally, school fa-

vors the developing girls' brain at this age and thus some boys can struggle until about ninth grade.

- Motor development profits from general growth and strength, and preadolescents have more fine muscle coordination. Their reaction times also improve, making this a prime time for development of both musical and athletic skill. However, keeping with their earlier development, girls tend to develop refined coordination earlier or easier than boys.

Middle School

- Girls generally reach puberty between the ages of 10 and 14 (i.e., as early as fifth grade, and as late as eighth) with the average being roughly age 12. For boys it is generally reached between age 12 and 14.
- The hormonal changes of puberty result in the appearance of secondary sex characteristics, and in a new interest in the opposite sex.
- Adult-like proportions and bodily features develop. Legs grow first, followed by growth of the trunk and arms. Both contribute to the long-legged look and to clumsiness since the individual has to learn how to coordinate these new physical dimensions.
- The boy's changing voice occurs during this time and causes a similar but temporary lack of vocal 'coordination.'
- The *rate* of physical growth peaks for girls on the average at age 12-plus, and for boys at age 14-plus, although some further growth continues in high school.
- Early or late maturation has its special problems. *Early maturing boys* enjoy certain social advantages among peers, and elicit favorable responses for their more "mature" ways from teachers. *Early maturing girls* can find their physical changes, and the reaction of others to these changes, stressful. *Late maturing girls* are often more at ease and eventually tend to enjoy certain social dividends.
- In general, *body image* has considerable bearing on the developing self-concept; whether the resulting self-esteem is positive or negative depends on many variables.

COGNITION, PERCEPTION, ATTENTION, AND MEMORY

Intermediate Grades

- This period is centered on Piaget's *concrete operational stage* where "logical thinking" is largely limited to events and "things" that are present here and now. Such thinking is developed through hands-on actions.
- Concrete operations serve as the basis for the abstract or *formal operational* thinking of high school. However, the first steps toward thinking abstractly begin in middle school. Thus "cause and effect" relationships progressively begin develop a web of abstract mental patterns (i.e., **concepts**) that function as hypotheses that need "testing" in action.
- Intermediate children no longer see things only from their own perspectives. They begin to realize that others perceive the world differently and they can increasingly see issues, events, or objects from multiple perspectives.
- Preadolescents are less distracted by irrelevant details than they were in grades K–3 and thus can focus attention on variables central to solving a problem. They can also

shift attention when needed to new or more relevant aspects, are less dominated by the most striking features, and can attend to detail.

- Learning proceeds by grouping and classifying 'things' according to similarities and this process becomes less context-dependent and more analytic (abstract) with age and experience.

- As a result, the hypotheses needed to solve problems focus on relevant information (or asking questions to obtain it) and narrowing down options, rather than the trial and error or spontaneous approaches of early childhood.

- Because the brain growth spurt takes place earlier for girls, and because it progresses from motor to verbal and other abstract learning, girls are typically more advanced in *verbal skills* and *abstract thinking* at this age. In contrast, boys are more *concrete* in their thinking and thus more at home with *hands-on* "doing."

- Since the capacity for abstract thought develops last, and since this capacity is needed for forethought and planning, the slower maturation of boys' brains results in *more impulsive behavior;* they are less able to anticipate the consequences of their behavior in advance. This often results in more "acting out" on the part of boys that is **growth typical**, not instances of intentional misbehavior, or hyperactivity. This energy is constructively channeled by action-focused lessons. Misbehavior and hyperactivity are predictable, however, when learning is abstract or passive.

Middle School

- *Formal operational (abstract) thinking* slowly evolves. However, plenty of concrete operations are still warranted to meets the needs of boys, and it also helps most girls because their cognitive growth still falls far short of fully abstract thinking.

- More (but not all) early adolescents can create concepts that function as *hypotheses for action*. These need to be "tested." Successful results strengthen the concept (Piaget's *assimilation*) and unsuccessful results require opportunities for altering the original concept and acting anew (Piaget's *accommodation*).

- Abstract thinking allows students to understand present problems in terms of future possibilities that are only, at the moment, intangible ideas.

- When clear about the nature of a future possibility and interested in its achievement, they are capable of *problem setting* as well as *problem solving*—although both still benefit from considerable teacher guidance and structure.

- Problem solving is now more step-by-step, even methodical, instead of the haphazard trial and error more typical in K–3. Students are increasingly able to pay attention to and coordinate multiple and variable aspects of a situation.

- Perception, attention, and memory are highly influenced by the context—including, importantly, the governing interest (value; **intentionality**). Thus conception develops most fruitfully in holistic, concrete, and situated action frameworks rather than in abstract, detached conditions.

- As logical and abstract thinking evolve, middle school students become increasingly capable of considering what "might" or even "should" be the case. This often results in "adolescent idealism" that questions or challenges what the early adolescent often sees as the illogical, inconsistent, or unfair realities of the adult world.

- This age is, for the same reason, often interested in philosophical, social, and moral questions—as long as they are posed in terms of *present relevance*, rather than abstractly. Despite the capacity for future planning and idealist thought, the early adolescent is firmly rooted in the present.

THE SOCIAL SELF AND PERSONALITY

Intermediate Ages

- According to **Eric Erikson**, children should begin the process of relating achievement to social acceptance and feelings of self-worth at this age. Failure to develop this sense of *industry* and responsibility (in general, or in particular areas of study or domains of development) results in a sense of inferiority, or of learned helplessness, and thus of giving up and no longer even trying to achieve.

- Groups—tightly knit *cliques* and larger *crowds* of friendly cliques—become important as the child moves progressively away from sole involvement within the family orbit. Social groups form as much on the basis of convenience (e.g., neighborhood friends) as on mutual interests. Shared interests and mutual support, however, lead to friendships that extend beyond the group.

- Groups are informal rather than having formal rules for membership; membership is therefore flexible rather than cohesive or exclusive.

- Boys and girls start to separate into their own groups, often according to different interests and activities.

- Boys' groups tend to be larger, louder, and more rough-and-tumble, and thus require the outdoors or large spaces. Girls' groups tend to be smaller and their interactions tend to reinforce "feminine" stereotypes*—although girls' sports at this age promote alternative **roles**.

- Boys are prone to sex stereotyping (even male chauvinism) and often resist activities which girls typically pursue (e.g., playing the flute). On the other hand, more and more girls participate in competitive sports.

- Students in the intermediate grades are more and more influenced by the opinions and actions of others than they were in primary school. This includes, of course, peers and the various outlets of mass media that shape their impressions of adult life and the world.

- Ethical judgment (and hence behavior) changes with cognitive and social development. As new possibilities for "might" and "should"' interact with present values and intentions, more options are considered. Ethical thinking is thus more complex than early childhood because preadolescents no longer see "rules" as absolute.

- With increasing self-consciousness, *popularity* becomes an issue. Social acceptance is defined according to criteria that vary widely. A social hierarchy evolves, separately and differently, for boys' and girls' groups. However, within groups of boys, athletic ability (or physical stature or prowess in general), leadership, and an outgoing personality are typical virtues. There is a certain noticeable contentiousness within any group of boys that sometimes erupts in overt but usually short-lived conflict. Groups of girls on the other hand tend to favor quietness, friendliness, politeness, and physi-

---

*Whether this *should* be the case is of interest to feminists.

cal appearance.* Girls are less overtly quarrelsome; their "fights" may be more subtle than boys' but are no less disturbing of the learning atmosphere.

- Unpopularity results from uncooperative, aggressive, and selfish behavior. Such youngsters tend to become excluded from activities, or are rejected as members of study groups, committees, and the like. Whether shyness is a cause or result of unpopularity is not clear.

Middle School

- A major growth task facing adolescents is *identity*—a stable and valued sense of Self. This need is a result of the changes in appearance, cognitive processes, and social interactions of this age group.

- Self-identity requires increasing *differentiation*, especially from family, but it paradoxically entails growing *closer* with peers; then the peer group in general differentiates itself from adults. The peer group provides stability (or consistency) and provides the opportunity to practice social relationships and roles.

- Acceptance by peers is of prime concern, especially to early adolescents, and is of particular concern to girls.

- Popularity is associated with humor, enthusiasm, tolerance, and sympathetic helpfulness. Popular adolescents are accepting of others and have ideas that are enjoyed by others as well.

- Students who possess a strong sense of identity are most confident and autonomous, conform less within the peer group and are most likely to be leaders.

- Lack of an effective *sense of identity* (e.g., insecurity, shyness) is associated with being socially isolated. Unpopularity and rejection often result in aggressive, demanding, and conceited behavior, or in compensatory attention seeking behavior.

- *Role confusion* results from a weak or dysfunctional sense of identity. It takes several forms: (a) a permanently *negative* (socially undesirable) role; (b) prolonged *identity confusion* (lack of a stable identity); (c) *role diffusion* (experimenting with several); or (d) *prematurely settling on an identity* (one that is thus eventually threatened with "loss of Self" when inadequate for later life).

- *Risk taking* is a predictable result of *experimentation* with roles and identity. Because some degree of identity confusion is growth-typical, some degree of psychological instability (or at least unpredictability) is not uncommon.

- Early adolescents generally display greater conformity than they will in the later years of high school but "peer pressure" is often more subtle and indirect than the stereotype assumes.

- *Adolescent egocentrism* takes the form of (a) an *imaginary audience* for which they perform as though always "on stage," and (b) a *personal fable* about the complete uniqueness of their own lives.

- Same-sex cliques eventually give way to interaction between the sexes. This, in turn, results in dual-sex cliques. Eventually, in high school, dating reduces the influence of the clique.

---

*Whether this *should* be the case is of interest to feminists.

- Premarital sex, pregnancy, delinquency, drugs, depression, and suicide are at the top of the list of *at risk behaviors* that often begin in the middle school. (The last two are increasingly problematic in grades 5 and 6, as well.)

- Ethical thinking is still conventional in trying to please others. However, social, political, philosophical, economic, and religious issues are also of concern, and these provide a basis for discussing and evaluating behavior.

- "Storm and stress" is not a universal experience of early adolescence. Some individuals are (or seem to be) well adjusted. However, students who fail to cope with their growth needs at this time continue to suffer them as "unfinished business" later in (or throughout) life!

Attention Deficit Disorder and Hyperactivity

These conditions are diagnosed more frequently than in the past and have repercussions for music classes. As mentioned, the "antsy" behavior of pre- and early adolescent boys is growth-typical. But Attention Deficit Disorder (ADD) and ADD with hyperactivity (ADDH)[†]—and learning disabilities in general—are, in fact, far *more common in boys* than in girls.

Authorities disagree on what degree of such restless, impatient, inattentive behavior amounts to pathology and what (if anything) to do about it in terms of medical treatment or therapy. Because the line between normal and pathological behavior is vague, it is all too easy for teachers to assume that impulsive students are hyperactive or suffer from attention disorders.

When lessons involve long periods of concentrating on abstract and verbal learning, wandering attention easily becomes physical restlessness. The unsuspecting teacher can easily diagnose this restlessness as hyperactivity. But, a certain degree of restive or unsettled behavior is typical at this age and *more than a few "discipline problems" are normal reactions to abstract, boring, and irrelevant lessons.* On the other hand, when an individual regularly exhibits many of the following symptoms in comparison to others students and for other teachers, then a referral to school health officials is warranted.

ADD with Hyperactivity (ADDH)

1. Little self-control: impulsive and emotional outbursts
   - "Acts out" without thinking
   - Interrupts with remarks, and with undesirable musical "improvisations"
   - Blurts out answers, or shouts comments unrelated to the lesson
   - Cannot resist socializing or interacting inappropriately with neighbors
   - Engages in rough or even dangerous behavior, such as pushing and shoving

---

[†]Also called Attention Deficit Hyperactive Disorder (ADHD) by some experts.

- Cannot wait for his or her turn
- Easily gets off-task; mind follows bodily impulses

2. Constantly active
    - Squirms in seat; bolts to stand when others are sitting; cannot stay put
    - Easily distracted; fools around with objects within reach; cannot hold a musical instrument quietly until it is time to play
    - Fidgets with hands; legs and feet are restless, even when seated

3. Overreacts
    - Is easily overstimulated during movement activities
    - Reacts aggressively to classmates

4. Easily frustrated
    - Low self-esteem
    - Little "stick-to-it-iveness"; gives up easily
    - Throws "tantrums"; gets upset when problems arise
    - Turns attention to other divertissements (usually misbehavior)

5. Adapts slowly and with difficulty to change
    - Has difficulty getting settled at the beginning of music class
    - Needs variety, yet transitions between activities are challenging
    - "Gets into" a new lesson more slowly and with less focus than others

6. Social immaturity
    - Does not relate easily or well with classmates.
    - Argumentative, bossy, "bullheaded"

ADD without Hyperactivity (ADD)

Many ADDH symptoms also apply to ADD. Because the "hyper" part of ADDH is so easily noticed and is much more common in boys, ADD *without the hyperactive behavior often goes unnoticed, particularly among girls.* ADD without hyperactivity is also much *more likely for girls.*

1. Poor concentration
    - Difficulty staying "on-task"

2. Attention wanders
    - Easily distracted by competing interests, and by extraneous stimuli or other activity in the room

3. Daydreaming; "spacing out"

4. Problem handling directions
    - Does not listen carefully (i.e., cannot focus on directions in terms of expectations)
    - Does not follow directions carefully or at all

5. Working, studying or practicing alone is difficult

6. Study or practicing skills are poor and work is inconsistent
   • Disorganized and unsystematic

TRANSESCENCE: ESSENTIAL GENERAL IMPLICATIONS AND APPLICATIONS FOR GENERAL MUSIC

PHYSICAL FACTORS

1. The physical growth and improved coordination of fourth and fifth graders is well suited to beginning musical skills. General music classes that only "expose" students to various abstract concepts or provide fragmented musical "experiences" fail to focus specifically on practicing skills and acquiring tangible knowledge in a way and to a degree that students of this age consider worthwhile. Music class thus risks becoming a music-based *recreation* period that, by age 10 or so, seems less and less "fun" or credible since little learning of any value seems to occur there. More "acting out" is the predictable result. Practicing skills students find relevant motivates students and helps ADDH students focus their attention.

2. The faster growth of girls' bodies and brains gives them a head start with both verbal and abstract learning and psychomotor skills. Girls, however, still benefit greatly from hands-on learning. Because girls with ADD do not act 'hyper' when struggling to learn, their learning problems go undiagnosed more often than boys'.

3. The slower neurological maturation of boys at this age leads many to be "antsy" and they need physical and concrete involvement to stay "on-task" and learn.

4. Individuals progress at different rates and thus need some individual attention. Without concentrating on individual skills—that is, if, instead, the whole class always responds (especially with singing and playing)—*the averaging effect of large numbers gives the false appearance of progress* when in fact many are not learning at all or are not developing **musical independence**. Students need and can accept more individual diagnosis and evaluation beginning at the preadolescent age.

5. Skills accomplished in fourth and fifth grade—especially boys' singing skills—may regress (or reach a *plateau* in the **learning curve** for a certain skill) for a while in the middle school as students regain control over new growth. New resistance to skills taught for their own sake compounds their resulting frustration and the growth of musicianship skills comes to a screeching halt.

6. Students who developed no or few musical skills in grades 4 and 5 also must contend with the new growth. However, their difficulties are often complicated by problems of self-esteem, self-concept, and psychosocial results of repeated failure.

7. The teacher needs to be very alert to the consequences of continued failure. "Failure" at this age is a subjective perception that has no necessary relation to objective judgments of others and is a leading factor in adolescent suicide.

COGNITIVE FACTORS

1. Cognitive development requires a steady diet of *concrete* musical actions, reflection on results (**reflective abstraction**) and opportunities for **acting adaptively**. These are the bases for constructing *functional* concepts for future use.

2. Despite advances in abstract thinking, neither the intermediate nor the middle school student responds with much enthusiasm when abstractions (e.g., labels, terms, facts, dates, and information) are the content of instruction. Such information is best learned when its *present value* for *personal use* is clear, and it will be learned functionally through repeated opportunities for such use at progressively more complex levels.

3. Since both memory for specific details and musical interest are **context** dependent, learning proceeds best in real-life contexts. The more real-life the learning, the more holistic, progressively complex, and personally rewarding it is for the student.

4. Now students can increasingly see music from varied perspectives and can pay attention to relevant details. Thus *selective attention* needs to be developed by *directing it* to ever more refined details and features. Without such direction they continue to relate in childlike ways to only the most striking musical features and are distracted by the very details that would otherwise advance their musicianship and pleasure. This is especially the case with the **directed listening** covered in Chapter 6.

5. Students need to be engaged in **problem-based learning**. Lessons need to present *choices*—options for action testing—where there are different routes to meeting the lesson's criteria and curricular intentions. Students also progressively need to *set their own problems* within guidelines and models of *systematic* problem solving (e.g., Chapter 4, concerned with writing melodies). Once these are mastered, however, they should be encouraged to develop and pursue their own approaches.

6. 'Tweens profit from imaginative "what if . . . ?" kinds of musical challenges and experiments, and from "listening through the ears" of others. Such techniques promote multiple perspectives beyond the "personal fable," advance cognitive possibilities, and are motivating.

7. Increasing idealism and interest in philosophical, social, and moral questions can be turned to musical ends by predicating lessons on such interests (e.g., a text about ecology accompanied by a sound composition). Investigating music for its social and ethical implications also motivates them—for example, analyzing the musical qualities (i.e., apart from words) that make some songs "good for" protest and others "good for" for patriotism or worship.

THE SOCIAL SELF

1. The **need for achievement** is especially decisive at this age in relationship to self-concept, self-esteem, and self-worth! *Musical skills* provide the opportunity for meeting this need to be good at something, and can be a prime source of overt pride and personal pleasure.

2. "Music" is first associated with Self during pre- and early adolescence. When musicking is one of the things "*I do* (well and enjoy)" it becomes central to "who *I am*" and the stage has been set for "breaking 100 in music" for life. After middle school, it is progressively unlikely that this identification of Self with music will ever develop.

3. The process of identify formation makes this age a good time to explore multicultural musics and to develop critical perspectives on "merely popular" music. Stressing the diversity of musical interests and tastes within and across age groups and exploring the influence of region, geography, and socioeconomic factors on musical tastes is also beneficial.

4. Beginning in fourth grade, teachers should be alert to, and should attempt to avoid student stereotyping of certain music or types of musicking—especially singing—as for "girls" versus "boys." At the same time, lessons of the kind featured in the earlier elementary grades can now feel "childish" and should give way to lessons preadolescents see as more "grown-up." These should involve the kinds of problem posing, problem solving, and nurturing of adult-like skills associated with real-life models of musicking students can now begin to see as relevant for their present and future lives.

5. **Cooperative learning** particularly benefits this age—especially projects based on small groups! Small group work draws upon the social needs of the age group by getting boys and girls, shy and outgoing, early and late maturers, high and low achievers working together. Group projects also lead to improved or unique results that no single individual could otherwise produce.

6. Socially isolated students can be socially integrated in healthy ways with students in such music classes. **Special education** students and students with other special needs (e.g., students for whom English is a new language) can experience social and musical success, as well, via small group work.

7. With group work, since no "one" is the focus of attention, students take risks and experiment in ways they might not if working alone. Similarly, the perception of *personal* "failure" is minimized, yet everyone in a group generally takes some feeling of credit for success.

8. When the unique products of different groups are compared—groups that already cut across cliques, crowds and friendship boundaries—rich multiplicity replaces the uniformity usually associated with the age group. This is not only a social benefit but, in strictly musical terms, it models the inherent sociability, social variability, and social benefits of music as praxis.

POSSIBLE ADD AND ADDH (AND OVERLY RESTLESS STUDENTS IN GENERAL)

1. Action Learning helps focus students' mental and physical energies on concrete and holistic results that interest them, focus and hold their attention and therefore help guide and control their behavior.

2. The social and tangible nature of musicking and group work both address the needs of students who are more 'hyper' than the teacher might wish. Just as they can participate in ensembles (as long as they are busy performing rather than bored by too much teacher-talk), so they can also participate successfully in group work and classroom musicking that involves tangible results they value.

3. The physically active nature of performing and composing is well suited to these students—when musicianship skills and musical criteria are stressed rather than just "fooling around" with music. However, listening must also be approached actively (i.e., mentally and/or physically) and, even then, it remains a challenge.

4. In comparison to abstract and "academic" lessons, real-life musicking attracts and sustains the attention of these students, just as when you stop swimming or biking the immediate benefits cease.

THE SCHOOL SETTING

The school setting influences all the preceding physical, mental and social variables of transescence. Different arrangements for organizing schools, teachers, and curriculum have different implications for general music teachers and instruction.

ELEMENTARY SCHOOL

Schools are organized in factory-like ways that are basically "unnatural" to the impulses of children. Defenders argue that this regimentation is needed for the **socialization** of students into the adult world. Unfortunately, much of *what* is taught by such means does not naturally carry over to life outside of school.

> General music class, however, is one "subject" that can have a very natural **transfer of learning** to real life outside of school—IF the teacher regularly makes that connection evident via Action Learning's real-life curricular focus.

Students are "drafted" and *institutionalized* in the pursuit of purposes about which they are unclear and thus unsure. The prevailing metaphor for school is "jail," and attitudes and behavior often reflect this understanding, beginning especially with preadolescence.

> Students in primary grade general music classes at first have no idea why they are there, but quickly catch on that they are supposed to sing, move, and "play" music. When the teacher does not inspire clear *musical* purposes and goals, **intentionality** quickly turns to merely 'playing around' with music. Thus, despite having fun *with* music, the growth of musical skill and musicianship rarely parallels students' growth in other school subjects. By at the end of elementary school, then, little of musical value has interested very many in the direction of "breaking 100 in music."

The elementary years are the foundation for general education. The "basics" learned in those years are refined and specialized in middle school, high school, and college.

> If no "basic musicianship" is developed in elementary school, it is altogether unlikely that any musicking will be attempted in later schooling or adult life, let alone further developed or refined. All elementary grade children—not just those in ensembles!—need basic musicianship, if only for singing hymns in church or to aid their listening abilities and thus to inform their tastes and enrich their choices.

Grades and competition are downplayed in most elementary settings, as is 'tracking' students according to perceived ability or accomplishment (special education students are obvious exceptions). The **sorting function** of schooling is minimized at this age in order to help each student develop basic skills to the fullest degree possible.

Without care, various economic and social forces can hinder children with disadvantaged backgrounds from the musical achievements that come perhaps more readily to children whose families are more directly supportive of musical interests and abilities. General music classes should be the mainstay of equal opportunity.

So-called "musical intelligence" is different from "general intelligence" (i.e., what IQ tests claim to measure) and students *can* succeed in music even if they struggle elsewhere in school.

When arriving at the elementary school, children encounter far more *heterogeneity* than they have experienced at home. Even neighborhood schools offer more diversity than in the past. While the status and role of children is unique at home, their grouping and treatment in school is based on *similarity* (i.e., age), and *conformity* to norms.

General music classes (along with art) can help rescue the individual from this anonymity by serving as an "oasis" in a school day where children are otherwise allowed little individuality or uniqueness. More importantly, however, individual achievement is the whole point of musical instruction! Therefore, treating the class as though it is a chorus, instrumental, or dance *ensemble* loses track of the individual and stresses only an anonymous contribution to the overall product. While this is sometimes useful (for example, modeling the pleasures of large-group performance), when overused it operates against the likelihood of developing the musical independence needed to be fruitfully involved in music in later life—even in large groups.

Along with the increased heterogeneity of people, students in elementary school first encounter a variety of *new values and roles*—even in religious schools!

Among these should be musical values and roles. Multicultural and world musics, for example, enhance students' awareness and choices. Rather than promoting one, or a few musics, to the exclusion of all others, Action Learning in general music class seeks instead to enhance the number and kinds of realistic choices for music action in real life. The general music teacher mediates musical values acquired at home and from the media and offers new options. Important, too, is the need for general music classes to model musical **roles**. Aside from potential career roles, adult forms of *musical amateurism* need to be modeled as roles to which students can aspire when they are "grown-up." Thus, it is *important to have adult role models in the school* as often as possible and to otherwise highlight adult amateurs (e.g., using videos).

Elementary schools teach students that "work" is what they are *told* to do (or otherwise *supposed* to do) for reasons not usually made clear to them by teachers; and "play" is what they want to or *enjoy* doing when given *free* choice. This socialization into "workers"—

especially by teachers who constantly refer to the class as "my good workers"—has the unfortunate result of making much learning and practice seem **other-directed**: it turns students off to the joys of learning for its own sake.

> Music, like sports, is an endeavor where "work" (effort) and "play" (fun) naturally intersect. Students can understand that "practice" leads to "greater enjoyment" as a result of new skills learned. However, if general music teachers ignore the need to inspire students to practice, or make practice into meaningless, uninspiring drill for its own sake, the "work" not only does *not* contribute to "playing" or "doing" music; it risks turning kids off to the intrinsic rewards of musical achievement.

Achievement is its own reward in the elementary school. Lack of achievement, then, is frustrating to the developing Self and students soon lose interest. Furthermore, the relationship between personal *evaluation* and *gratification* becomes important. Preschoolers evaluate their activities according to its gratification. But in school the teacher evaluates and rewards (or 'punishes') via grades, and so on. Gratification thus becomes other-directed and **extrinsic**. Receiving good grades or praise replaces the *natural* gratification of **intrinsic** rewards and pleasures. By its very nature, then, school tends to make much music learning progressively more extrinsic and ungratifying. As a result, *discipline* comes to mean "enforced control" rather than inner-directed *self*-discipline.

> Students need tangible achievement (and thus need to develop some diligence in practice and learning) if they are to reap the natural musical rewards of enhanced musical functioning. Without progress they lose interest and, at most, are other-directed toward extrinsic rewards. *Inner-direction* toward intrinsic rewards must be the focus. Action Learning helps them "intend" or "try to" acquire and improve musical skills because they "want" and "need" to use and benefit personally in terms of increased *musical* gratification (as opposed to grades, gold stars, and other extrinsic rewards).

Elementary schools teach students all kinds of categories and distinctions, especially the roles people "play" and the difference between "good" and "bad." The distinction between the role of "teacher" and "student" is taught in ways that translate as "boss" and "worker." The implication is learned that a "teacher" is an adult 'in the know' and "students" are kids who are 'ignorant.' Thus a "teacher" also comes to be seen not as an **authoritative** person of any age *from whom one learns*, but rather as an adult **authoritarian**. "Teaching" also comes to be seen as something that teachers do "to" or "for" you. "Good" and "bad" are seen, too, as judgments made according to usually abstract criteria by "authorities" (teachers or textbook authors), as are "right" and "wrong" ways of doing things. Thus the development of *personal or functional criteria of success* is replaced by abstract pronouncements that students resist, ignore, or never act upon.

> The role of "peer teachers" of any age and other authoritative adults should not be overlooked. Some students can usually "teach" or help others if the teacher sets up

the conditions. Similarly, many "teachers" (adult amateurs) from the community can be involved, at least as role models. Musical learning should be approached as *self-teaching*—a fact that every musician should appreciate since practicing between music lessons is exactly that. Thus a "teacher"—adult or not, certified or not—is an "authority" when she or helps students attain musical rewards that still require self-teaching (i.e., practice and study). Similarly, something is "good" relative to what it is "good for" (as seen by the learner), not as an abstract or force-fed decree. And "right" and "wrong" ways of attaining musical results become "better" versus "less successful," or "easier" versus "less efficient" ways. The music "teacher," like the good "coach," is thus a person whose personal authority is seen in action diagnosing new needs and recommending practice or study that "works" in getting results students find more rewarding.

Portfolios, anecdotal reports, and the like at the very least supplement traditional grades as the means of *recording* and *reporting* student evaluation and progress. "Grades," either as rewards, punishments, or goals, are less and less the focus of attention for elementary teachers, students, or parents than just a generation ago and also much less than in middle and high schools.

General music teachers need to be aware of these trends. The minority of students in ensembles does not demonstrate the value of an elementary music program. Failure to evaluate and report the progress of real musical learning to parents gives the impression that general music class is not "basic" but a frill. A sense of "standards" or "expectations"—for example, in the form of **rubrics** and *benchmarks*—counters this attitude on the part of both students and parents (and taxpayers, school officials, etc.).

ELEMENTARY SCHOOL ORGANIZATION

Elementary schools have a bewildering variety of organizational formats, often dictated by existing buildings and other considerations that are not primarily educational. Thus all of the following patterns can be found.

1. K–6, perhaps the most traditional grouping, is giving way to other formats. Even when grade 6 is in the elementary school *building*, some districts treat it distinctively as pre-middle school!

2. Some districts group K–2 or K–3 in a "primary school" building with 4–5 (or 4–6) in another building as "intermediate" school, or some similar label.

3. Sixth grade can variously be found grouped with fourth and fifth, just with fifth, sometimes by itself in a separate building or administrative unit, or, more and more commonly, within a middle school setting.

4. Individual "grade levels" in some schools give way to various other groupings.

   - "Half grades," particularly "pre–K and "pre–first" grade classes accommodate important differences at these crucial first stages of schooling.

- "Family groups" of self-contained classes include two or three grade levels of students and their teachers in one big "family." The family stays together as a *group* for two or three years, each year getting a group of new students at the youngest age. Teachers and students thus have extended contact over several years. However, teachers instruct their special subjects to all the students in the family. Importantly, students can be instructed together according to achievement rather than age. Thus a "third grader" who reads at the "fifth grade" level can actually study at that advanced level.

- "Multiage" groups will often encompass two or three age-grade levels and teachers teach across grade levels as well. Each teacher has children from all two or three age-grade groups in one "homeroom" or "home base," but teaches students from all homerooms on a daily or weekly basis.

- With "looping" classes, a teacher "travels" with the same class for one or more consecutive years. This allows the teacher to "fine tune" instruction over time, but otherwise instruction is often quite traditional because the class involves students of the same age.

- Team-teaching and departmental teaching are also finding their way into the elementary school. In the former, several teachers cooperate and cover all subjects collectively, while in the latter, teachers specialize in subjects.

Implications for General Music Classes and Teachers

- In fourth through sixth grades, musical learning does not necessarily or naturally follow age-grouped self-contained classes. Yet few provisions are made for different rates of learning or accomplishment. Individual attention is most needed for transfer students whose learning is greatly different than what is typical in their new school.

- The narrower the range of grades taught, the more specialized the music teacher's skills can become. However, a narrow range can, without care, lead to lazy teaching where "generic" lessons are planned that are basically repeated from one grade to the next, changing only the repertory from year to year.

- The wider the range of levels taught, the more variety teachers enjoy. Development of students' skills and attitudes over time is more easily noticed and appreciated. However, teaching across many grade or age levels means that teaching approaches need to vary in order to meet changing students needs and to avoid student boredom. When a general music teacher covers grades K–5 or K–6, learning will be less likely and misbehavior more likely if teaching has failed to accommodate the new traits, needs, and interests of the students when they were in grades 4 and 5.

- General music teaching also needs accommodate the underlying purpose or philosophy of multiage, family groups and the like. It is advantageous for the students and thus for their musical growth if general music teachers adapt and capitalize on these differences rather than "teach to the average student."

These formats and considerations are influenced, in particular, by whether the general music teacher has a "real" classroom. Having to teach in auditoriums, cafetoriums, or gymnasiums, or needing to move from one location to another, all have important implications that must be taken into consideration. In particular, the *itinerant teacher*, one without a permanent building assignment, needs to make changes in instruction over what would be realistic or possible under other circumstances. These variables are considered in Chapter 9.

SECONDARY SCHOOLS

The change from "elementary school" to middle or junior high school provides dramatic differences and new challenges for students and teachers alike because the assumptions, goals, and purposes of secondary schools are different than for elementary school. The already mentioned variables of socialization, involuntary attendance, basic skill instruction, heterogeneity of people, values and roles, problems of work versus play and good versus bad, and the need for achievement continue, but in new forms. These "new" changes in "old" patterns can be especially unsettling when taken in combination with the physical, emotional, social, and cognitive changes of pre- and early adolescence. They are combined, however, with altogether new ideals and new problems:

- Secondary school refines general education and develops advanced skills. "Subjects" are studied more or less "academically" rather than with a view to their relevance or interest to students or life—all the more so in the "high-stakes testing" climate of national and state "standards."
- Traditionally secondary school was a stepping-stone to the world of work for most graduates and prepared students in new ways to "appreciate" or understand the meaning of the word "work" and the conditions that apply to it. Vocational programs still fulfill this function.
- Secondary school increasingly provides preparation for specialized vocational and university education.
- Competition, or at least increasing comparisons among and between students, becomes even more pronounced than in the late stages of middle childhood. Competition is the main means by which the *sorting function* of schools is accomplished.
- Cocurricular and extracurricular activities develop and extend specialized skills, and promote personal and social traits, such as cooperation, teamwork, and the like.
- In addition to the "core" curriculum, advanced electives are offered.
- All studies, including vocational studies, are seen as preparing students for graduation. Ironically, a diploma is necessary to "get ahead" in the world even though a good deal of what is taught in schools is quickly forgotten by students.
- Finally, secondary school is supposed to accommodate the changes that arise with pubescence and adolescence. In particular, social activities are now an important part of school life.

JUNIOR HIGH SCHOOL

Around the beginning of the twentieth century, psychologists "discovered" (or, more correctly, "created") the concept of adolescence. As a result, the "junior high school" was invented as a step between "elementary" and "senior high school." By the 1920s, it was an accepted part of schooling and brought with it some important changes:

1. Junior high students moved from teacher to teacher. Students were no longer "taken" to and from class but had the freedom and responsibility to arrive at the right classes on time.

2. Teachers became more specialized both for core subjects and for the various "special" subjects.

3. The curriculum for core subjects prepared students for advanced or specialized study of the same subjects in high school. However, at the very least, reading, 'riting, 'rithmatic, and regurgitation of history had to serve the practical needs of those who dropped out of school after the mandatory years.

4. Special subjects were to offer greater depth than in elementary school with a view to experimentation and exploration for future career choices, or for certain predictable life functions. Thus, "music," "art," "homemaking," and "shop" classes were added in the 1950s. The last two were originally sexually stereotyped but the newly named "industrial" and "home arts" began to enroll both boys and girls, as did new technology courses of various kinds. Health and physical education focused on taming the coordination problems of adolescents and modeling good health practices by introducing physical activities that could be enjoyed throughout life.

5. After-school clubs and cocurricular activities developed to accommodate students' new interests and recreational commitments. Many of these, with the original exception of sports, brought boys and girls together socially and cooperatively in new ways. Dances and other extracurricular social events especially catered to the interaction of boys and girls.

There were (and still are, in cases where junior high exists in name or practice) certain problems with these arrangements.

- The plan varied between communities. When schools were small, junior high and senior high students were in the same building. Junior high students learned from the models of the older students in the halls. In larger schools, only grades 7 and 8 were typically segregated in their own buildings or programs and ninth grade was located "in" the high school. In other schools, a 7–9 pattern was used for junior high. Where ninth graders were the oldest students in junior high school, their somewhat more 'mature' behavior served as a good model for seventh and eighth graders. Otherwise, the often erratic behavior of eighth graders became the model for seventh graders.

- Grouping and instruction of students was still by chronological age even though boys and girls in early adolescence are still on different growth trajectories and often differ in cognitive (mental age) and physical development.

- Special subjects existed in a "never-never land" of contradictions. On one hand they were supposed to engage interest, exploration, and experimentation, but on the other they were graded and thus in theory could be "failed." This threat was of little solace to general music teachers since grades are not generally accepted as inducements or punishment by most students of this age. In any case, only rarely might a student be forced to repeat music class. And failing a student risked getting that student back again—something that, unfortunately, too many teachers fondly wished to avoid.

- Extracurricular interests—especially sports and selective musical ensembles—sometimes became the tail wagging the dog. Instead of simply meeting adolescents interests and social needs, these activities—particularly interscholastic sports—could tend to become virtually the sole focus of interest for some students.

Special Problems for the General Music Teacher

- Longer, often multiple weeks of instruction (daily or alternate days) gave more and more continuous time for music class instruction, but not for the entire year. This had obvious disadvantages for skill-based instruction, which is gradual and incremental and requires consistent practice.

- In particular, the voice change of boys could not be adequately monitored and handled since it might occur when a boy was not scheduled in a music class.

- Longer music classes were often predicated on a more "academic study" of music that paralleled studies in other subjects. This approach, however, was unsuited to the musical needs and interests of early adolescents, and frequent "discipline problems" were the proof.

- Over the years, this age group has increasingly identified with increasingly rebellious and even obscene rock music. Adolescent identification with music that is out-of-favor with adults (precisely *because* adults disapprove) presented new difficulties for teachers concerned mainly with the "good music," "good taste," and aesthetic appreciation of Eurocentric "classics," or with other types of musical studies students rejected out-of-hand, including instruction in the "history of rock."

- Singing continued to be the major focus of general music class. But this ran afoul of the many difficulties with the changing boy's voice, their stereotyping of singing as "sissy" or "female" (despite their rock and pop music heroes), and their reluctance to risk singing in front of (and looking "bad" for) peers.

- Curriculum for junior high music classes rarely had **vertical alignment** with elementary school. Particularly where several elementary schools "fed" into a single junior high, general music teachers were (and still are) faced with a bewildering diversity of musical abilities, attitudes, and values. Junior high teachers could count often on only a few predictable conditions: (a) that all students had studied the lines and spaces but could not read music unless they had studied an instrument; (b) that all students had studied the names of the instruments of the orchestra, but no longer wanted to play "guess that instrument"; (c) that most students in sixth grade did *not* look forward to general music class in junior high; and that, (d) each new junior high class essentially started from 'scratch' with students who, at this age, were now resistant to singing, playing "toy" instruments, studying "about" composers, and the like.

- Junior high general music classes rarely led to high school study or culminated in anything even reasonably approaching musical "competence" or "literacy." The last year of general music was, with the exception of the small percentage of students in ensembles, the last year of any musical instruction! "Demand" for high school electives was small—except, perhaps, for the few students considering careers in music. Only the wealthier schools could afford to offer these electives to such small numbers of students.

MIDDLE SCHOOL

This arrangement can be traced to the 1960s and 70s and to new research into child development. For the new middle school movement, neither the child-centered focus of the elementary school nor the subject-centered curriculum of junior or senior high school meet the special learning and developmental needs of this transitional age group. An altogether unique school program is needed.

Some school districts study and formally adopt a middle school *philosophy*, and then implement a program designed around it. In other districts, however, the "middle school" is only a convenient *name* for labeling certain grade-level groupings or buildings. For all practical purposes, these programs remain wed to the older assumptions, practices, and problems of the junior high school! There are, however, some schools that are still called junior high school but are close in practice to the middle school philosophy. Whether a school building is labeled junior high or middle school, then, is of little or no importance.

The following are important premises of middle school:

1. Extensive effort is provided to meet the *special learning and other developmental problems* of early adolescents.

   - In particular, school guidance systems and programs are created to give direction to students on personal, social, and school matters.

2. Focus is on active *problem solving, decision making, and creative thinking* that this group is not only now capable of, but responds well to in terms of interest and behavior.

   - Active learning capitalizes on the rapid brain growth that takes place at this age.

3. A special *transitional curriculum* is planned that not only bridges the time between elementary and high school, but that carefully articulates and coordinates instruction around the transescence growth profile and prepares students for future study.

   - Instruction focuses more on subject matter than was the case in elementary school, but specifically in terms of the needs and traits of the developmental stage—especially in comparison to the more "formal" and "academic" study that characterizes high school.

4. Courses and extracurricular activities are specifically designed to allow students to *explore and develop new interests*, commitments, and a sense of personal responsibility.

   - Emphasis is on participation by *all* students, but not on a competitive basis for selecting some and excluding others.

   - The opportunity to explore a variety of interests and abilities is seen as central to promoting flexibility, variety, and balance in instruction and curricular results.

5. Instruction is *flexible* and teaching strategies are selected and varied in order to address the learning style that is most typical for this group. Central are:

   - **Constructivism**
   - **Cooperative learning**
   - **Team-teaching**
   - Technology

6. *Scheduling and staffing* are specifically designed to facilitate the special needs of the middle school program and students.

   - While junior high schools tend to follow the high school type of schedule, middle school scheduling practices are often unique to the program.

- Faculty are not only subject-matter specialists, but are prepared to understand and even enjoy the age group.

There are certain difficulties associated with the middle school concept, aside from the challenges of working with the age group and some of the problems of junior high school that remain in middle schools.

- Smaller schools, or schools where options are limited by existing facilities, cannot always "house" or "schedule" middle school programs in ways that are entirely unique to the needs of the age.
- Under the same conditions, staffing presents problems because teachers often teach across two levels (elementary plus middle school, or middle school plus high school). This is frequently the case with "special subject" teachers, such as music.
- Again, the distribution of grades 5–8 across existing buildings rather than according to students' needs and program integrity has implications for implementing the middle school concept.
- Special resources are required, for example technology, guidance personnel, and smaller class size than in junior or high school.
- Involvement of teachers and parents in adopting and planning middle school programs makes these programs perhaps even more varied than junior high school formats based on high school models. Variability between middle schools makes transfer to a *new* middle school all the more difficult for students, and parental mobility contributes to the problem.

Special Problems for the Music Teacher

- Music teachers often teach across two levels and thus need to be able to adapt to the needs of each group.
- In very small schools, the teacher may cover K–12. This has the benefits of continuity over the years, and allows the teacher to see the final outcome of the program. But it requires the ability to "change gears" for each of the three styles of teaching. Scheduling can also get in the way. A teacher following a high school schedule may end up with periods of instruction that are too long for the attention spans of K–3 students.
- Staffing varies widely. Instrumental specialists find themselves assigned to a particular middle school building where they are expected to teach general music class. More typically, the "choral director" and the "general music teacher" are the same person, who therefore teaches both classes despite the different specialty involved.
- The curricular and instructional needs of chorus and general music are considerably different. Yet it is not uncommon for some general music teachers to make general music classes little more than a preparation for chorus. Students who fail to show interest or ability in chorus by middle school are, for all practical curricular purposes, overlooked in terms of their future musical needs.
- State and local requirements and practices concerning requirements for music instruction are often met in two separate ways: *either* by being in chorus, band, and orchestra, *or* by being in general music classes. This has several unfortunate consequences.

  First, the musical education of the students in ensembles is narrowly focused only on performance and only on the literature that group performs over the years in question. These students are thus denied the richer and broader musicianship and choices that only an effective general music class can develop. For example, composing and listening, though supposedly required by national and state standards, are typically given scant attention by ensemble directors with their eyes on the next concert.

Secondly, students who have developed no interest in ensemble participation by middle school are in effect 'dumped' in general music classes. Too many teachers see this group as musical "leftovers." These students respond to the teacher's self-fulfilling prophesy and behave exactly as the teacher expects, often making these classes a miserable experience for students and teachers alike. Teachers 'endure' general music and focus their interest and energies on chorus. Thus general music students' musical needs go unmet even though many are intelligent, and will become future doctors, police chiefs, business people, and the like.

- The social nature of ensembles and the social needs of early adolescents make ensembles particularly attractive at this age. Unfortunately, this can attract students to chorus whose initial intentions are often more social than musical—particularly, in middle school, since band or orchestra require prior skill at this age. But whether in chorus or instrumental ensembles, focused *musical* intentions regularly fail to develop because *the rewards students seek are more social than musical*. Large numbers of ensemble students regularly fail to "break 100 in music" when, if they had *also* been in a successful general music class, their choices and likelihood for further musicking would be enhanced. Even those who remain in high school ensembles have, for all practical purposes, little to do with music after graduation beyond the types of listening they would have done in any case.

- While it was common for general music class to be offered each year of junior high school, it is increasingly uncommon to find it offered at each year of middle school. Various reasons are given, especially the need to include evermore special subjects such as language and technology classes and high-stakes testing in reading and mathematics. However, many general music teachers willingly accept being "relieved" of this instruction because they can devote more time to chorus or their other ensembles. However, when general music is offered only at the sixth *and* seventh (or sixth, seventh, or eighth) grades there is a greatly reduced likelihood that "breaking 100" will ever occur.

THE GENERAL MUSIC TEACHER FOR 'TWEENS AND EARLY TEENS

A general music teacher needs to be especially prepared for the challenges of this age group.

A Desirable Musical Background Includes:

1. An effective background in music theory and composition for planning lessons that help students understand music's "innards," "how" and "why" it is created, and what it is "good for" in human life.

2. A rich background in the literature of world and other musics that can serve as a basis for meeting the needs of the age group and for enhancing their musical choices.

3. Skill on the keyboard and a performance range of other recreational instruments, such as (at least) guitar. Such performance skills must be of high enough quality to enhance students' skills and to serve as an adult model of recreational playing.

4. Aural skills for planning directed listening lessons—skills that should encompass a wide variety of musics.

5. A familiarity concerning current musical and other interests of 'tween-agers.

6. Understanding of the many praxial values of music, in addition to the "just listening" associated with concert music.

7. Active musical involvement outside of school that meets the teacher's own musical needs so that school is not the source of a teacher's own musical needs. Outside involvement also models that the teacher practices what is "preached" in class.

Necessary Professional Traits Include:

1. A functional knowledge of pre- and early adolescence that can be put into action successfully.

2. Interest in the special needs of this age, and the unique rewards of working with them.

3. "With-it-ness," an understanding of what is occurring concerning adolescent life and musical trends, is especially useful in convincing this group that the teacher is at least in touch with their values.

4. Ability and willingness to help students with personal and social needs, not just an interest in their musical learning.

5. Practiced skill in the modes of instruction and strategies most suited to the developmental needs of 'tween-agers (Part Two of this text).

6. Curriculum design, implementation, and evaluation that are fully cognizant of transescence and that adjust to the context of the neighborhood and community (see Part Three).

7. Competence with technology sufficient to enhance the means and ends of instruction.

8. Personal philosophy of commitment to general music and general music students.

SUMMARY

Given the important developmental variables of students in grades 4–8, and the unique conditions of a particular school setting, it is clearly in the teacher's and students' best interests to always take the factors covered in this chapter into appropriate consideration in curricular and lesson planning. These variables, as they apply to the particulars of a given teaching assignment, should therefore be kept firmly in mind in reading the next chapter, which deals with general considerations of planning, and in Parts Two and Three, which deal with specific kinds of lessons and other aspects of instruction.

CHAPTER THREE

PLANNING GUIDELINES

GENERAL ORGANIZATION OF PLANNING

Action Learning depends on basic guidelines that help organize the teacher's planning. These lead to lessons that, despite their variety, have an overall consistency. This unity within variety provides a framework that helps students organize their own learning. The guidelines also promote consistency between different teachers jointly responsible for a program, yet who have important individual differences. With a shared planning approach and vocabulary, individual teachers can "do their own thing" but still communicate and advance the general music program towards unified results.

> The *general* planning guidelines of this chapters are given *detail* in each of the chapter in Part Two according to the specific conditions of each musical praxis. Each lesson a teacher plans, then, should seek to advance each student's *functional ability* (the musicianship dimension) in ways that are *personally satisfying* (the attitude dimension) in relation to a *real-life kind of musicking* (the praxial dimension).

ACTION IDEALS

As was briefly explained in the earlier chapters, Action Learning focuses on real-life kinds of musical praxis. These constitute the **action ideals** that are the focus of an Action Learning curriculum. Action ideals for *curriculum development* are discussed in depth in Appendix A where a sample curriculum for Grade 6 is also provided.

To summarize for purposes of *daily planning*, a given action ideal consists of three parts: The first is the *praxial dimension*—examples of the kind of *real-life musicking* that curriculum and instruction are seeking to promote. The sample curriculum, for example, focuses its first action ideal on "Recreational Singing" (see page 260):

I. RECREATIONAL SINGING

Praxial Dimension

- Singing in community choirs
- Singing in musical theater productions
- Solo performance (community choirs, weddings, musical theater)
- Singing as a social or personal recreational activity

The second part of an action ideal is its *musicianship dimension*. This is concerned with developing the musicianship knowledge and skills needed *to be able to* do one or more of the examples indicated in the praxial diimension. The sample curriculum (page 257) includes:

Musicianship Dimension

- Matches pitch and sings in tune
- Utilizes healthy vocal production (breath support, proper phonation)
- Demonstrates vocal independence in ensemble singing
- Maintains an established steady beat
- Reads standard vocal notation using solfège
- Follows basic music symbols (dynamic levels, rhythmic values, pitches)

The third part is the *attitude dimension*. It focuses on the attitudes, rewards, and values of *present* instruction needed if the student is going *to want to* take part in one or more of the examples featured in the praxial dimension in the *future*. The teacher who wrote the sample curriculum (page 257) intends to nurture the following traits:

Attitude Dimension

- Enjoys singing for personal use
- Demonstrates self-confidence in regard to singing voice
- Sings comfortably among others
- Enjoys singing in ensembles
- Interested in improving singing by practicing healthy vocal technique
- Values the importance of music reading

Other Action Ideals in the sample curriculum focus on composing, listening, and playing instruments.

Action Ideals address the musicianship skills and attitudes students need if they are to be *able* to and *want* to take part in the particular models of musical *praxis* that are given focus by a lesson.

MANAGEMENT STAGING

Management staging "manages" or organizes instruction by breaking *individual lessons* into separate "stages" or *steps* (see Figure 3.1). It is the sequence of individual stages that are the small steps of a given lesson.

Management staging is particularly necessary with students of this age since they require *freedom, but within structure*. Without this staging into small steps, students quickly wander "off task" and socialize or misbehave. Management staging, then, provides the conditions for keeping students focused on *successive* small steps and it uses time efficiently and minimizes "fooling around." In terms of "teaching as coaching," management staging provides the realistic offensive and defensive strategies necessary for success

There are seven *management stages*, and each has its own requirements:

1. The *priming* of intentionality

2. *Transition* to lesson

Figure 3.1 Lesson Plan Format

Grade_____ Day/Time_____ Date_____
Performing___Listening___Composing___Moving___Other___ THEME_____

1. Priming:

2. Transition:

3. Stages and timing:

4. Crescendo of intentionality:

5. Culmination:

6. Evaluation
Reflection
Cognitive Strengthening

7. Connecting lesson:

_____

Comments:

_____

3. Body of the lesson: sequential **stages**

4. *Crescendo of intentionality*

5. *Culmination* of intentionality (i.e., the "pay off")

6. *Evaluation, reflection, and cognitive strengthening*

7. *Connecting* with next or a subsequent lesson

1. "HYPE" OR PRIMING OF INTENTIONALITY

Intentionality promotes the *meaning* or *relevance* that will direct students' willingness to learn. It is the *goal, purpose* or *value* toward which a student's mental and physical actions are directed. It is best summed up as what the student is mindfully "trying to" accomplish. In order for learning to be effective and musical, students must be "trying to" accomplish something *musical*.

After the action focus of the lesson has been decided upon, the first planning step is to *prime* or "hype" the lesson:

1. The *musical goal* or point of the lesson; what the lesson is "about" or going to advance

2. The type of *process* and *outcomes* at stake

3. The musicianship (competencies) to be advanced

4. The *personal reward* (i.e., interest, relevance, etc.) to be evoked

The term **priming** comes from cognitive psychology and is based on an analogy to pumps. You have to put something in most pumps before they work. Similarly, with students, in order to get them to work, study, or practice, you need to put something "in" them that was not there—in mind, or in the way the teacher wants—before the lesson began.

> Priming is the attempt to get into students' minds a *musical challenge, model, example, or temptation* they can find attractive and interesting enough to "try to" accomplish.

Years ago, teachers were taught to begin their lessons with "motivation." This typically focused on *extrinsic* values, such as that there would be a test; or it was so abstract or remote that no immediate *intrinsic* interest was reasonable. For example, one teacher began a "unit" on twenty famous composers and their most famous compositions with the motivation, "Someday, when you're at a party and everyone else is discussing music and culture, you'll be able to have something to contribute to the discussion." Successful priming, in contrast, will focus on the here and now of the upcoming lesson and the *present* possibilities for intrinsic interest.

This first stage is important at all levels of instruction. At the primary level, for example, teachers often demonstrate something musical the children are tempted to try to imitate (e.g., clapping back a pattern). But with preadolescents (grades 4–5) and early adolescents (grades 6–8), the need for hyping lessons is more specific and the strategy chosen is more crucial. Successful priming often involves one or more of the following considerations.

1. *Modeling or previewing* the forthcoming musical process and its rewards in short, simple, and attractive ways is an effective priming technique. For example, with guitar in hand, the teacher performs a new strum, or new chord for a tune the class already likes to play. Models present what the class can look forward to accomplishing today.

2. Priming can employ imaginative or fanciful *"gamesmanship"* or fanciful teasing that usually involves the teacher or anonymous adults. For example, the teacher plays a 30-second recording of a song or sound composition she composed that she (jokingly) says she might enter in a competition, and asks for class feedback and help. When they critique the tape (predictably, because the music is intentionally and humorously awful), the teacher is in a position to get the class involved in trying to do the same kind of thing better (e.g., see the second point under "transition to lesson," page 57). This kind of approach works especially well with a teacher who has a good sense of humor and whose rapport typically involves a teasing give-and-take with students.

3. *Story approaches* to priming can be effective, but only if the "story" is imaginative or amusing. For example, "If we were going to create a musical soundtrack of the video highlights of the basketball game last week when our team came storming back from behind and won at the buzzer, how would the music have to change?" hypes the students to do just such a composition. Or, (tongue in cheek) "I know this guy who wants music for his web page that advertises (name an fanciful product, such as deodorant for cows); what kind music could help sell the product?" primes a lesson with **brainstorming**.

4. The three examples just mentioned are *direct* approaches to priming. *Discussions* are good examples of *indirect* priming where the "point" of the lesson "unfolds" more gradually (but is not overly drawn out). For example: The opener, "I was watching MTV the other day—yes, me!—and wondered how the dancers know whether the music is fast or slow? Does fast music get over quicker, or what?" initiates a brief discussion that can lead to a sound composition where the challenge is to make the "A section" sound "fast" and the "B section" sound "slow" (or their choice of order), even though each is 20 seconds long.

5. *Focusing on common subjective feelings* or situations by reference to adjectives and other descriptions is another indirect approach. A show of hands on, "Who feels scared during a thunder and lightning storm? Of those of you who don't, what feelings *do* you have?" begins to develop criteria of a personal nature that can be turned to musical interest; for example to compose "storm music" that is expressive of each groups' choice of a feeling; or as a basis for comparing two different "musical storms" from recordings (e.g., the "storm" sections from Beethoven's *Pastorale* Symphony and Rossini's overture to *William Tell*).

The trick is for the priming to be inviting, tempting, and even natural feeling, not just announced in a bossy fashion. Thus, rather than the old-fashioned style of motivation, "Today we are going to listen and compare two 'musical storms' written by famous composers from the nineteenth century Romantic period in music history. . . ," the Action Learning teacher might use both possibilities mentioned in 5. that is, create a series of group sound compositions to particular "moods" in the previous class as a prelude to comparing their compositions and examples by famous composers in today's class. (This "sequencing" is called *readiness staging* and is discussed later).

Priming must be efficient. It is intended to *quickly* stimulate students' attention and intentions. But if intentionality is *not* successfully primed, it is all but certain that ineffective and off-task behavior or simply misbehavior will waste teacher and student time! Thus, it is probably better to ensure that priming is effective and then practice making the same priming more efficient in the future.

In general, this stage of the lesson should be as *student-focused* as possible in its attractions—even when the teacher or some other source is the immediate focus of attention, as in 2. stated prior.

2. TRANSITION TO LESSON

The lesson should seem to flow naturally from the priming stage. Many teachers ruin the effect of a good hype by abruptly announcing the lesson with "today we're going to. . . ." Without a smooth transition from the student-centered priming to the lesson, however, students become convinced that this is really a teacher-dominated class, or this is an authoritarian teacher, despite the hopeful beginning.

- Only a sentence or two is usually needed but it must be extremely well chosen, even "scripted" (but not simply read) to insure sufficient care and attention.

- The transition to the next stage ought to appear to be a logical or reasonable consequence of the priming strategy. Thus, for example, in the case where the priming involved a critique of the teacher's song or sound composition, the transition might be, "Well, then, if my piece is so bad, and you have so many ideas you think are so great, let's see if you can do it any better yourselves. Let's count off into groups of five and see how your compositions compare to mine, and to each others'." Similarly, a priming strategy that discusses the differences between "five minutes being drilled in the dentists' chair," and "five minutes before a good party will end" might be followed with, "Let's make a list of the kind of music that might have the same feeling for you as the dentist's chair or the party" as the transition stage to "Now let's experiment with and explore some actual sounds and sound combinations for each feeling" which is already the body of the lesson underway, and without any abrupt announcement that "today we're going to do a sound composition."

- Transitions—and directions generally—are best phrased in terms of "let's" (e.g., the sentence just stated). In other words, by stressing "let *us* as a class group try to . . . " the *teacher becomes a member of the group*. The teacher is "our" leader not the boss. Her *authority* (useful knowledge) helps "us" reach our needs.

3. BODY OF THE LESSON: SEQUENTIAL STAGES

The body of the lesson is set up in *small, separate, sequential,* and *timed steps.*

The *time* for each step needs to be approximated or calculated with some care. For example, if a recording takes 3 minutes to play once, and a listening lesson is going to require three hearings of the recording, that alone will take at least 9 minutes. Discussion time then needs to be approximated.

1. Given no time limits, students will drag a project on forever; furthermore, different individuals or groups will always be at different stages of completion!

   2. Students of any age will typically fill the time made available to them! Give them,
      say, 5 minutes to complete a stage, and they'll try to take at least 15 minutes. Know-
      ing this, give them somewhat less than 5 minutes to force them to remain on-task
      and to work quickly. You can always allow a little more time.

   3. Get them into the habit of working busily and steadily, with little time to waste.

   4. Nonetheless, since individuals and groups vary, *always prepare additional alterna-
      tives for those finishing early* (e.g., renotate the song neatly).

   5. Children in fourth and fifth grades invariably need *many short stages* of no longer
      than 1–2 minutes each. Some stages, such as deciding on a "mood" to compose to,
      should allow only 30 seconds. Students in middle school can handle stages of 2–3
      minutes and, as they learn basic lesson protocols, they can handle several short stages
      combined into one longer stage of 3–5 minutes.

   6. Teachers new to *action planning* usually do not break the lesson up into a sufficient
      number of small, sequential steps—particularly when group or individual creative
      work is at stake.

   7. *It is always better to have too many steps than too few.* Too many small steps can
      be skipped; students will do this, in any case, as they learn the process and thus an-
      ticipate the next steps. But if you have too few—that is, too many large steps of 5
      minutes or more—much time will be wasted, results will be ineffective, and behav-
      ior and conduct will progressively deteriorate. Thus rather than giving students, say,
      15 minutes to "practice a new chord" on the guitar, break it into small, timed steps:
      for example, 3 minutes to practice getting from the previous chord to the new chord;
      another 3 minutes for getting from the new chord to the next chord; 3 minutes for
      practicing the chord change in the metric context of a particular song, adding the
      strum pattern, and so on.

   8. Always *announce the time* for *each* stage in a loud, clear and firm voice: for exam-
      ple, "You have 3 minutes to do this, so get right to work!" or "Take 30 seconds to
      choose two contrasting feelings for each section of your composition."

   9. At the end of the announced time, it is necessary to have a **signal** that easily gets
      students' attention rather than having to shout or otherwise waste time getting the
      class to be quiet so they can listen for what to do next. A signal is easiest when the
      teacher can make it from anywhere in the room, such as clapping or a hand drum.

   10. During the time allowed, the teacher monitors students and, if needed or useful,
       makes brief remarks and suggestions, or restates or gives or new directions.

If more than a few students are confused, it is usually most efficient to signal for attention and then rephrase the directions for the *entire class!* Individuals or groups
with the same problems or questions are usually not alone in being confused.

   • The *sequencing* of steps ought to be carefully considered. Ideally each step ought to
     lead in some reasonable way to the next in a progression that gradually goes from easy

or simple, to more complex or complete (e.g., the example previously mentioned in no. 7).

- However, *there is no single or logical sequence of staging*; different teachers will stage the same lesson into different sequences with equal results (e.g., the example in no. 7 is not the only possible sequence).

- On the other hand, a stipulated sequence may not suit the learning of each student. Be alert to this and intervene, if needed, with an alternative sequence. Individual students, especially in skill practice, often profit from having different options. Older or more advanced students, in fact, ought to become increasingly able to and expected to *stage their own problem solving and practicing*!

4. CRESCENDO OF INTENTIONALITY; REPRIMING

Each step in its mounting complexity should maintain a *rising tide of interest,* as the conclusion gets closer to completion in the students' anticipation.

- Students usually require *repeated reference to the priming*—even frequent *repriming.* These reminders help maintain focus and are easily worked into the directions given for subsequent steps: for example, "For the next step in *our soundtrack for the video of our basketball teams' great comeback,* you have 4 minutes to. . . . " Sometimes more forceful re-presenting of the priming will be useful: for example, "I'm hearing some interesting possibilities, but I'm not so sure I'm hearing anything so far that is much better than my composition that you complained so much about."

- Generally, however, when stages are "stepping" toward holistic actions, there is some built-in progression of interest as the final "payoff" gets closer and thus activity or practice becomes more naturally rewarding (e.g., the new guitar chord is getting easier and more rewarding to play). If this isn't apparent, remind students that "we're almost ready to . . . " whatever the payoff for the lesson might be.

- Performances of any kind almost always benefit from a "dress rehearsal" where the individual or group "pulls it together" for a trial run. Sometimes it is useful to have such a step for each stage of a longer lesson: for example, where there is a separate "dress rehearsal" of section A of a sound composition, then later of section B and, finally, of A and B together.

- The dress rehearsal should be followed by the opportunity to **act adaptively**—that is, time to evaluate and make improvements. In general, such *reflective appraisals* should be mainly self-diagnoses, but this is also an opportunity for the teacher to make last-minute observations and suggestions for improvement and reminders of criteria.

Simultaneous dress rehearsals can be noisy unless the teacher takes steps to prevent such cacophony. For example, in the case of a simultaneous "dress rehearsals" of individual sound compositions or instrument practice, the teacher requires *less than final volume* "or else you won't be able to hear your own piece enough to evaluate it."

5. CULMINATION OF INTENTIONALITY

This is the "payoff" in more respects than one.

- The culmination ought to model some relevant portion of the Praxial Dimension (composing, performing, etc.) that is at stake in the lesson in a way suitable for the age-level and developmental skills and abilities of the class or individual.

- Any lesson that does not lead to a natural and effective culmination has not been musically authentic and *holistic* and, therefore, has not met one or more other qualifications of Action Learning. Whatever might have been "learned" will be abstract and **atomistic** and thus short-lived and musically meaningless.

- Typically, the culmination also should demonstrate that students now can do something new or better than before; in other words, that they have improved at an old skill or gained a new one. If such progress is not noticeable to *students* during a lesson, their intentionality will not have been rewarded! Without some sense of increasing mastery, their **need for achievement** also goes unfulfilled and any aspirations for "breaking 100" remain untapped.

- A successful culmination, however, should leave students wanting even more, better, or higher levels of fulfillment. It should seem like a positive step on the way to more and evermore satisfying achievement.

- The culmination stage is also important to the teacher's evaluation of the lesson itself—both the plan and its delivery. Culminating results—successful or not—provide the data (along with no. 6 that follows) for re-hypothesizing either the premise of the lesson (i.e., the *curricular* question, "What is worth teaching?"), or the teaching techniques (i.e., the *instructional* question, "How best to teach this learning?")—or both!

6. EVALUATION, REFLECTION, AND COGNITIVE STRENGTHENING

Every lesson needs a stage that elicits students' self-evaluation and reflection.

- As will be noted in the chapters in Part Two, some guided discussion or other forms of structured analysis should conclude *each* lesson.

- This **reflective abstraction** helps students focus critically and reflectively on their efforts and progress. This "summing up" focuses on the learning that was *demonstrated* and tries to identify important aspects for future growth.

- Discussion and reflection are extremely central to the process of **cognitive strengthening**. Much growth in musical functioning during a lesson happens precociously, spontaneously, or naturally; that is, new learning or progress comes about without students at first realizing how they succeeded. Reflection makes such natural discoveries or learning more apparent to them, and formal labels and terms can be applied to such informal learning for future use at this concluding stage (not at the beginning).

- However, the older tradition of reviewing or restating "what was learned today" is superfluous. Thus, summaries such as "today we learned to compose a melody by using steps, skips, leaps, and repeated tones to create interesting musical shapes that go up and down and sometimes stay the same" verbalizes what is meaningful only in action and emphasizes the words instead of the doing. It is something like exclaiming to the first-time bicyclist: "Well Johnny, today you learned how to keep your balance."

7. CONNECTION TO NEXT OR A SUBSEQUENT LESSON

While this is not actually a stage of the *present* lesson, it is an important to **readiness staging**, the sequential connection to subsequent lessons described next.

- Lessons do not necessarily connect like circus elephants in a direct line: $1 \rightarrow 2 \rightarrow 3 \rightarrow$, and so on. Sometimes the present lesson may be followed by a second that, for the time being, is not directly related; but the third lesson might connect the first and second in a fruitful way.

- Some lessons cannot be accomplished within a single class period. When resumed during the next class period, *priming needs to be repeated* and the previous stages reviewed or re-practiced before proceeding.

- A lesson begun last class and that concludes today need not take all of today's period. Thus, the transition to the next lesson for today's remaining time needs to be carefully planned—especially if it involves moving students or furniture!

- With fourth grade, and early in fifth grade, students still profit from several short, varied lessons within the same class period. Some "restless" middle school classes also benefit from such variety within the class period.

- Each lesson in a period needs to be management staged and transitions planned carefully.

READINESS STAGING

Lessons should not be freestanding activities—single, unconnected occasions of musicking. While such individual lessons might be fun (for a while), no *systematic* development of musicianship skills results. Learning is haphazard at best and doesn't build on previous skills to a state of musical independence that can be used in life.

Readiness refers to the conditions needed to profitably undertake new learning. It involves *cognitive* needs—for example, understanding meter as a basis for rhythm. Some readiness, however, is *developmental*; for example, Suzuki scaled down the physical size of stringed instruments to accommodate young children. Similarly young children are not developmentally 'ready' to learn abstractly.

What is here called **readiness staging** refers specifically, then, to the *knowledge and skill students need to succeed with new learning*; for example, students need to be able to keep a steady beat before they can strum a guitar properly. By means of readiness staging, then, the teacher *systematically sequences lessons* so that, over time, each new lesson (a) is based on learning developed in earlier lessons and (b) is itself a step or stage to a new level of learning. This *sequencing* of lessons provides a "scaffold"—a structure of support for future lessons—and thus the process is technically known in educational psychology as **scaffolding**.

> While management staging involves the sequence of *within* a given lesson, readiness staging is the sequence *between* lessons.

- At the heart of readiness staging is **transfer of learning**, the successful use of information or skill learned in one situation to a later and somewhat different context. Several types of transfer can be distinguished, though considerable overlap is often present.

GENERAL TRANSFER involves general principles, hypotheses, and concepts that, when learned in one situation, can be used successfully in a new situation; for example, a chord learned in relation to composing melodies is the basis for learning to play that chord on the guitar. Lessons devoted to general transfer are very efficient use of time because they have such wide applicability. They focus on *breadth* at the expense of depth or detail, however.

SPECIFIC TRANSFER involves facts, rules, and skills learned in one situation to future specific situations of the same kind. For example: Learning to play a given chord is different on a guitar than on a keyboard. Such lessons are specific to a particular kind of use and thus must be taught separately for each different use, which raises the problem of *depth* versus breadth.

POSITIVE TRANSFER happens when a particular learning *readily* connects to future learning. Because it was not oversimplified or presented out of context, such learning does not have to be recast, revised or updated for future use.

NEGATIVE TRANSFER, in comparison, hinders new learning; for example, "up" (for children newly entering school) refers to the space over their head or to the loudness of music ("Turn up the volume") and its metaphoric use in relation to *pitch* often confuses learners. Negative transfer also arises when new learning conflicts with earlier learning; for example, referring to a "pitch" as a "tone" in K–3 often creates negative transfer when "tone quality" is discussed in the intermediate and middle school in connection with timbre.

ZERO TRANSFER is learning that has no transfer to subsequent or other situations, particularly where two situations have nothing in common; for example, fingerings for certain toy instruments have zero transfer for recorder while recorder has positive transfer value for other real wind instruments.

HORIZONTAL OR LATERAL TRANSFER of learning allows students to apply learning acquired in one context to similar contexts. For example, learning to "hear" when to change chords can be used with guitar or keyboard.

VERTICAL TRANSFER occurs when earlier learning, information, or skill directly leads to or aids future, more complex applications. A **spiral curriculum** is predicated on vertical transfer.

The readiness staging of Action Learning relies on vertical, lateral, positive, and general transfer. And where specific musical applications are at stake—such as playing instruments—specific transfer is promoted, too.

- Readiness staging of individual lessons into effective sequences profits from the following conditions.

  CONTIGUITY OF LEARNING—Nearness in time between learning and its actual application enhances transfer of learning. Lessons violate this common sense principle when they do not apply learning (usually abstract concepts or memorized information) to models of the eventual praxial uses such learning is supposed to promote.

  SIMILARITY OF SITUATION OR CONTEXT—The more a problem and its context resembles previous problems and contexts, the greater the likelihood of transfer of learning.

The greater the similarity between in-class lessons and real-life applications of learning outside of school (i.e., throughout life), the greater is the likelihood of transfer of learning to life! This is the major premise of Action Learning.

PROBLEM-SOLVING STRATEGIES/FORMATS—These involve similarities between lessons, or general formats for lessons. The protocols in each of the following chapters promote such frameworks for students. In music, set practicing strategies are also important if students are to learn *how to practice* efficiently and effectively.

ADVANCE ORGANIZERS—These directions or reminders by the teacher specifically focus student attention on how a new situation is similar to and different from past situations. However, students need to progressively learn to diagnose certain advance organizers by themselves—for example, determining the meter and key of new pieces.

MASTERY LEARNING—This involves the need for each "stage" of a *progressive sequence* of learning to be "mastered" according to *mastery criteria* before proceeding to the next step. Students who do not meet the stated criteria are not penalized; they are given *corrective instruction* or *extra practice time*. Many musical skills, such as pitch matching, performing on instruments, and knowing basics of counting rhythms, should be predicated on mastery learning! Such instruction must provide (a) individual attention, (b) the criteria against which students learn to evaluate their own performance, and (c) in-class practice opportunities.

PEER TUTORING and *self-paced practice* should be promoted with transfer of learning in mind.

- The supporting structure—the scaffold—of past lessons, makes present learning more likely and subsequent transfer more probable: (1) the sequencing of lessons in an orderly progression incorporates and reinforces previous stages; while (2) simultaneously applying previous accomplishment to new (and evermore real-life) conditions, particulars, and complexities of achievement.

- Thus, the scaffold does not just go up one more level, unchanged, like a window washer's platform. Instead, it becomes stronger and more powerful—that is, *transferable to more and more uses*—as it becomes more complex and "real."

- There is *no one sequence* of readiness staging that is inevitable or absolute! There are many routes to the same destination, although some may be more efficient. However, some "stages" *are* prerequisite to others; for example, matching pitch is a prerequisite to vocal music reading. Otherwise, sequencing of lessons varies between teachers. But since not all learners profit equally from the same sequence, the teacher should be flexible and have alternative sequences in mind.

- A *spiral curriculum* returns frequently to certain knowledge and skills and expands and extends them to increasingly more complex, real life, and musically independent (functional) abilities. Action Learning "spirals" of transfer build ever closer to real-life musicking.

Because instruction focuses on likely models of such musicking, first focusing on their similarities, then accommodating their important uniqueness, learning is naturally holistic. *Planning for transfer*, then, basically amounts to choosing progressively more "realistic" musical tasks that students want to "practice" and accomplish, such as new literature that expands their technical skill and musical enjoyment.

No matter how much students enjoy a particular lesson, unless there is a suitable sequence of lessons provided by the readiness staging, learning will be haphazard and will fall short of developing effective musicianship.

USING GENERATIVE THEMES TO FACILITATE GENERAL TRANSFER BETWEEN INDIVIDUAL LESSONS

WEAKNESS OF THE "ELEMENTS OF MUSIC" APPROACH

General music teachers often teach the so-called *elements of music*—the "concept" labels of melody, harmony, rhythm, form, and timbre that are supposed to be the subparts of music. This "structure of the discipline" approach, however, does not naturally transfer to holistic musicking and, thus, has the same kind of problems as, for example, "experiencing" the parts of a guitar without actually learning to play guitar functionally.

- As conceptual categories, the "elements" do not adequately apply to contemporary or world musics where they are altogether missing (e.g., drumming music that has no "melody") or are treated in *praxis-specific* ways ("melodies" that are decidedly "untuneful"; e.g., free jazz).

- The vocabulary is abstract, misleadingly oversimplified, and often promotes *negative* or *zero transfer* (see page 62). For example, terms students learn when they are younger are first "experienced" with very simple children's music and later do not apply at all or in the same way to "real" music (e.g., the "melody" of a child's tune versus the "themes" of symphonies) or at all (e.g., world musics having no "harmony").

- Considerable time is spent teaching students the "elements" by merely exemplifying the *terms* through "experiencing" **atomistic** musical activities in ways that never quite add up to a functional understanding—the ability to do things with or respond more effectively to, for example, "melody."

- Focusing on separate "elements" thus obscures the *holism* of musical experience. Knowing that "melody is a sequence of pitches moving up, down, or staying the same" leaves out the contribution of rhythm/meter, harmony, and form and certainly falls far short of the realistic experience and value of "melody" in holistic and practical musical use.

- All the above contribute to problems of *proactive* and *retroactive interference* with transfer of learning (see *negative transfer*, page 62) where early learning interferes with later learning (e.g., world musics where "melodies" are not tuneful or do not have "form"). "Unlearning" or "relearning in new terms" is not only inefficient, but is often confusing and thus impedes learning.

The "elements of music" approach misrepresents music—both its holism and the differences involved in various musics! Furthermore, its emphasis on abstract verbal concepts too often falls short of meaningful *use* in realistic circumstances of musicking and fails to impress students with what music (and musical knowledge) is "good for" in their lives.

GENERATIVE THEMES: THE ACTION ALTERNATIVE

Generative themes are very general organizational categories that promote the likelihood of *transfer of learning* between lessons, particularly over time (e.g., from simpler children's music to more real-life musics studied in middle school) and between musics that are unique. Using generative themes to organize curriculum at various levels and to promote readiness staging and *general transfer* of learning avoids or minimizes most of the problems of "teaching the elements of music."

To review: *General transfer* involves general principles, hypotheses and ideas that, once learned in a particular context, can be used successfully in new contexts. Lessons organized along the lines of general transfer are efficient (because they do not require new teaching or reteaching) and effective (because they have such wide-ranging application).

Generative themes, by definition, also "generate" new learning, new interests, new meanings, and new musical relevancies. The generative themes suggested here fall into four groups, concerned respectively with:

- *Materials of music*: what music is "made of" or "made from."
- *Structure*: how music is constructed, or put together.
- *Music "in" life*: issues of musical praxis in relation to its use.
- *Musical values*: what music is "good for" and what, in consequence, goes into judgments of "good" music and performance.

These groupings are not, of course, mutually exclusive. Natural and reasonable interactions arise between groups (e.g., where structure is determined by use). However, it is best to *focus on* one theme as the major conceptual organizer for a given lesson and let the other connections make their natural appearances. This natural interaction is a particularly useful focus for the sixth step of the management staging explained earlier (Fig. 3.1, and page 60), *reflection and discussion*.

The bulleted subtopics in the following table are suggested for "generating" more in-depth or complex musicianship, as befits the praxial dimensions at stake in the curriculum. Thus individual lessons that focus on a subtopic develop it under the umbrella of the overall theme which, in turn, relates the lesson to other lessons based on that overall theme.

Generating a Student's Personal Theory of Music

The generative themes outlined here should guide planning. One of the numbered themes (1–10) should serve as the **primary focus** for a given lesson! It functions as a question or is-

GENERATIVE THEMES

A. Materials of Music

  1. Time: created experience of time "made special" by passing faster or slower, quickly or slowly.

  - **"good time"** as opposed to less interesting "time" in, or from, music
  - impression of musical movement "through" time
  - feeling of progression, evolution, change
  - augmentation—expansion, slowing or drawing out of time
  - diminution—shortening or compacting time
  - speed—pace of time passing or moving

  2. Sound and silence: the raw materials of music's time.

  - musical "tone," as opposed to merely "noise"
  - relativity of pitch levels
  - relative loudness, intensity, dynamics, amplitude
  - quality—type, distinctiveness, attractiveness, interesting features of sounds and silences
  - "color"—source and the unique tone quality
  - "weight"—heavy or light
  - "frame" or envelope—nature of onset, sustaining sound, decay
  - expressiveness—feeling, mood, and so on, a sound (or silence) can be "expressive of"

B. Structure of Music

  3. Linearity: a "line" of musical thinking that carries musical interest in relation to other "lines," or that attracts musical interest in relation to "blocks" of simultaneous sounds.

  - "voice"—an easily followed part or layer
  - "voicing"—creating an easily followed part or layer among others
  - melody, tune, theme
  - motifs, their combination and "development"
  - shape, expressiveness, direction of musical "line"

  4. Simultaneity: musical results conveyed by sounds that occur at the same moment.

  - "blocks" of sound-silence
  - chords, harmony as relative to a praxis
  - consonance-dissonance as relative to a praxis
  - active versus static nature of combinations of sounds

- expressiveness (of vertical sonorities)
- texture—thickness and thinness

5. **Organization**: giving sounds, silence and other musical values structure (i.e., *meaning*) through intentional types and degrees of relation to each other.
   - "making sense" of, or "in-forming" (inwardly "constructing") music
   - relationship of organization to a praxis
   - patterns of similarity-contrast, unity-variety
   - order-disorder as degree or type of pattern, predictability
   - role and consequence of notation versus improvisation
   - organization by chance versus controlled design or pattern
   - sections versus continuous evolution or unfolding
   - "development," or working out or unfolding of musical ideas

C. Music in Life

6. **Play**: personal re-creation (recreation), self-actualization, meaning-making and "good time" through music.
   - "breaking 100" in music as "good time"
   - creativity, invention, imagination employed or shared through music—"playing" with and through sound
   - "good time" or events and actions "made special" via music
   - fixed musical rules, variable musical results
   - **practicing-in-action**
   - music in the "active life," or "life worth living"

7. **Expression**: Most people experience music as **"expressive of"** feelings. This means, simply, that listeners "read into" their musical experience certain kinds of feeling states. The feelings are not "in" the music; they are "in" the listener in the same way an "angry sky" is a feeling projected on the pattern and movement of clouds.
   - affect, feeling, moods as variable **affordances of music**
   - interpretation as personalizing musical performance, composition, and listening
   - extending, developing, heightening, exploring, refining of feelings through music
   - transitions, alternations, and contrasts between musical feeling states
   - giving "form" to un- or disorganized "raw feelings"
   - "feeling good" and "good time" in connection with music, even when the feelings at stake are sad, angry or the like
   - "making special" of feelings via music (e.g., wedding music)

8. **Style**: a special and recognizable manner of handling musical ideas and materials that is unique to an individual composer or performer, a historical context (time or place), a musical medium or praxis, or a cultural group.

   • particular musical practices: types of music in relation to use, era, group, instruments, and so forth
   • popularity, fashion, and fads versus individuality, uniqueness, and consistency
   • trends and "progress" in music: Is new music "improved" or "better"?
   • "classics" of any music over time: How does some old music stay relevant?
   • categories of music according to similarities
   • musical idioms; being a type of music
   • multiplicity of styles in relation to multiplicity of uses and meanings
   • coexistence of competing styles
   • being "stylish" and "classy" through music: Musical tastes as personal or group identity
   • relation of style to use, needs, expressiveness, and so on

D. Musical Valuation

9. **Quality**: musical distinctiveness that allows differences concerning value, excellence, goodness.

   • creativity: effectiveness of music for a particular practice; that is, "good" in terms of "good for"
   • action dimension—the "making special" of practices that music is "good for" in life; for example, celebrations
   • competency dimension—music is "good music" when it is "good for" the "good life"
   • praxial dimension—how or why music is used to serve human "goods"
   • "sensibility"—perceptual and sensory delights, interests, and meanings in addition to praxial suitability
   • "musical qualities"—qualities that allow sounds to be regarded as "music" or musical (as opposed especially to "noise" or nonmusical "sound")

10. **Technique**: practiced refinement of musical skill that is predictably "good" and repeatable.

   • composing techniques—methods, processes, systems
   • performance technique—delivery, execution
   • listening technique—accuracy, discrimination

sue that is *explored by* the lesson. Use the space provided for "THEME" on the format suggested in Figure 3.1 to indicate the theme chosen for focus. Returning to the same theme, but in terms of new and specific subthemes (i.e., the bulleted topics in the table), promotes general transfer across a wide variety of lessons and musics, and a spiral curriculum.

- The individual themes and their subthemes or refinements are *not* presented as definitions to be taught as abstract concepts. They provide the framework by which students *construct their own personal theories of music* and of musical value.

- Note, too, that the themes are not initially or necessarily presented in terms of technical jargon. Rather, they draw upon common words and ideas that *can* take on a more "technical" musical meaning; for example, "expansion" of time, can give way to "augmentation."

- Thus, *terms* are rarely "introduced" in the abstract beforehand as a condition of a lesson. Instead, the theme or bulleted subtheme at stake is evoked in existing, often nontechnical terms (AB "organization" eventually can be called "binary form"). Only later in the lesson or in the curriculum might a word be used *as* a term. And, even then, the use is often very casual and might be given at first as a synonym. For example, a lesson predicated at first on "fast versus slow music" might end by referring to "the speed—or *tempo*—of the music." "Speed" and "tempo" might continue to be used interchangeably in the next several lessons. Eventually "tempo" can be used as the preferred term.

- A "vocabulary" of "concepts" or "themes" is not itself useful beyond giving directions or discussing music. Since terms are not taught, then, for their own sake, *meaning and relevance are seen in use*, not on vocabulary tests. Terms that have no use, or are put to no use, will remain empty abstractions and will soon be forgotten.

- Generative themes provide focal points or highlights around which students can organize their own thinking, responding, problem solving, and creation. They function as familiar "landmarks" that help students construct their own conceptions and perceptions. Yet because they are the basis for ever new and changing musical situations, contexts, and problems, they also provide a stable base for *transfer of learning* and help organize *readiness staging*.

A major purpose in using generative themes is to create new interests. Because they are approached as "generative" issues or ideas, they "generate" ever new musical curiosity, connections, and thus possibilities. The connections they make possible between widely different kinds of musical praxis enrich musical interests and promote various musical "discoveries" and meanings.

TEACHING VERSUS USING THE TEACHER'S UNDERSTANDING

Quite early in his pragmatic philosophy of teaching, John Dewey pointed out that teachers should not *directly* "teach" their mental "maps" (i.e, *their* "concepts") but, rather, should "use" their understanding to *indirectly* help students construct *their own* mental "maps." The

Using, Not *Teaching*, Your "Musical Maps"

In Dewey's analogy, general music teachers *use* their own mental maps of the musical territory to lead classes through selected "musical terrains" to rewarding locations students will enjoy returning to *on their own,* thus "breaking 100 in music." The trip (the instruction) should always be carried out with this end in mind. Thus, teachers will not just be happy to have led (or dragged) students to these destinations, but will help students develop mental maps, knowledge, and skills that are sufficient to being *able to* take their own independent trips to similar locations throughout life. And, finally in this analogy, the good teacher, like the good scout leader, will lead in ways that make it more likely that students will profit and enjoy themselves and thus will *want to* return again and again by themselves to the same or similar musical destinations.

musical "territory" the teacher has covered (formally or informally) informed the teacher's personal musical map—namely, the teacher's personal construction of knowledge, skills, attitudes, and values. The teacher's musical map provides the "landmarks" and "coordinates" that allow the *teacher* to return again and again with benefit to the same and similar musical "territory"—not unlike using a real map to visit a locale over and over again during different seasons or for different reasons.

However, much of the teacher's musical learning goes well beyond what the average well-educated general citizen can ever know or needs to know, or be able to do in order to enjoy the fruits of musicking. In fact, *some of the teacher's training has negative transfer value*: It can make us more critical; for example, trained musicians who are so caught up as listeners with a performer's *technique* that they seem to miss the *music.*

However, the richness of the teacher's map promotes the insights the teacher draws upon in planning and organizing instruction. The more "territory" the teacher has covered, the more interesting and relevant instruction can be.

The teacher-leader thus uses his or her personal map to organize interesting and profitable "treks" or "explorations"—individual lessons—through various "musical territories" at levels of involvement suitable to the age group. Teachers whose backgrounds are narrow and limited will end up being like scout leaders who lead scouts to the same few locations by the same and progressively boring and unprofitable routes. Teachers with a wealth of background will be able to choose from a wealth of potential locations and will make the process of getting there interesting and rewarding, as well.

Obviously, the teacher cannot teach the map in the abstract—without actually going to real musical "territories." And teaching it *directly* uses only a rote, "follow the leader" kind of example. Once the limited territory has been "covered" (or the limited repertory of music and skills has been learned by rote), there is little further interest or benefit to entice the students to *want to return to the territory on their own.* In fact, even if they were so inclined, the "follow me" kind of learning does not help students find their way back without help. When help is not at hand (i.e., no teacher) and there are no more "trips" (i.e., required music classes), they take trips to other locations in life that are of more interest, and where they can get there on their own.

SUMMARY

- *Action Ideals* focus teachers on real-life musicking as the bases for promoting competence and positive attitudes.

- *Management staging* effectively organizes each particular musical "trip" or exploration of a particular musical "territory" (i.e., praxis).

- *Readiness staging* helps base each new trip on previous trips for sequential growth of knowledge and progressive skill development (i.e., transfer).

- And *generative themes* are the reiterated landmarks, focal points, coordinates, and common highlights used on individual trips to help students progressively learn more from their travels and, over many such trips, to develop their own musical maps for future trips on their own.

CHAPTER FOUR

TUNES BY 'TWEENS

INTRODUCTION

Seasonal songs, religious music, music in movies and television shows and, most importantly, popular music of the time are all typical examples of the kind of music pre- and early adolescents have in their "ear" as a part of growing up. They "know" and respond to it with precocious competence; however, they are indifferent about and, thus, inattentive to musical details.

They "soak" up this musical "language" in informal and **tacit** ways just as their precocious competence with the spoken language is developed without acquiring the technical details of grammar, syntax, and the like. Schooling sets in motion a formal process where they learn to read, write and spell words, to compose sentences and to organize them into meaningful ideas, and to listen to and comprehend spoken language. By the end of elementary school, students, teachers, and parents know that tangible progress in language skills has taken place.

General music classes should perform the same function for music! Students who learn formal musicianship skills will have control over their musical actions and choices for life. They gain this control by learning to read and notate music, by organizing musical ideas into meaningful wholes, and through practice listening to and comprehending evermore complexly-organized music. And by the end of general music classes, their improved competence and its tangible benefits should be as apparent to students, teachers, and parents as their progress in other school subjects.

General music class thus becomes a *musicianship laboratory*, not a buffet that simply samples and surveys music "in general," or that teaches isolated skills and abstract concepts of the musical discipline for its own sake. Science "labs" conduct experiments that investigate scientific theories about how the world works. Similarly, then, a laboratory for developing *general musicianship* engages in experiments, explorations, discoveries, and other active learning concerning how music works.

Teaching general music as a "musicianship lab," therefore, does not feature simple trial and error experiment, directionless discovery, or 'anything goes' creativity. Instead, lessons are *practicums* for learning the "rudiments" of functional tonal theory, standard musical notation, and the aural skills associated with both. Action learning is an apprenticeship in *applied* musicianship, and aural skills and experiences are a major focus because music is an aural art. Just as putting the would-be sailor in a boat on the water creates the realism and holism of a successful practicum, so putting the general music student in an aural environment engages the realism and holism necessary to any musicking.*

---

*Aural skills in relation to melodic composition and tonal theory are developed by listening to student compositions and by devising separate listening lessons that promote criteria for students' own melodies. At the end of Chapter 6 an "ear training" format is detailed that specifically helps students aurally process melodic movement and shape.

The protocols in this chapter provide **primary focus** on, and thus promote, the following generative themes:

- *Time*—what musicians call "meter," "rhythm," "tempo"
- *Sound and Silence*—planning and control of "pitch" and "rests" via eye (notation) and by ear
- *Linearity*—"shape," "direction," and "line" in terms of "tunefulness" of a melody
- *Simultaneity*—interaction of chords, harmony and chord construction, chord "progression" and harmonic variety on melody
- *Organization*—patterns of similarity and contrast and how basic musical units ("phrases") are combined or "developed" into larger, more interesting units (i.e., "small part forms")
- *Technique*—compositional practices and aural skills

However, because lessons are holistic, the other themes and subtopics are inevitably noted as secondary considerations. Thus, for example, the "shape" of a melodic line and its underlying chord progression both have important implications for musical *expressiveness*. Such holistic details are central to what a tune is "good for" and are important in evaluating a "good tune" in terms of the type of musical praxis at stake. A love song and a beer commercial will differ considerably according to how their tunes incorporate the details of harmony, line, and the like.

MELODIC FOCUS

Melodies, of course, can be notated or improvised by ear. Both approaches are important.

- The tonal theory learned by composing notated melodies develops **readiness** for visual analysis and performing (Chapters 8 and 9).
- Improvised melodies develop "ear training" readiness for all kinds of listening (Chapter 6) and for improvised music.
- Composing notated melodies provides cognitive criteria and musical ideas for improvised melodies and improvised melodies help students "hear" musical ideas that can then be notated. Readiness staging that continually relates notated and improvised lessons is central.

Because planning notated lessons is more detailed and involves more formats, they are presented here first.

NOTATED FORMAT FOR COMPOSING MELODIES

These "experiments" focus on the relationship between the pitches of a melody and the scale that provides the tonality or key center. Lessons focus at first only on the most basic of criteria for selecting pitches. Rhythm and meter are "given" by the teacher, leaving strictly melodic pitch relationships as the main variable for focus. (Rhythm is given its own primary focus later in this chapter; for now, it takes on a secondary role, although it still has a holistic presence.)

Early lessons focus largely on the process of putting pitches together in terms of how they "look." How they "sound" is progressively developed in conjunction with having students perform their own tunes (see Chapter 8). Notated tunes are at first only 4 measures in length, but quickly expand to 8 and 16 measures. Middle school students can compose melodies of 32 measures, especially if these lessons are begun in grades 4 and 5.

Basic Strategy

The scale of a given key, usually C major at first, is given in the treble clef.

1. Prepare a handout that has the scale notated at the top of the page, and placed on the treble clef, with scale steps numbered above and pitch names (or solfege syllables) shown below.

Example 4.1

2. Beneath that should be several empty staves (the number depends on the lesson). (a) Each staff should have a treble clef sign and an arrow pointing to the G line. (b) Above each staff should be an interesting rhythm using only eight rhythmic indications (since, at first, students are going to be using *each tone of the scale only once*). (c) Under the last note of the rhythm should be a 1 or 8 to make sure the tune ends on the tonic:

Example 4.2

3. Prepare several transparencies from the handout, and make copies of the handout for the class. In composition lessons, *always have several students compose on transparencies.*

Management Staging

1. By suitable *priming*, focus student intentionality on composing their "first" notated melody. For example, it can be compared to writing their first sentence.

2. For the *transition*, the teacher directly models the composing process for the whole class by involving the class.

a. After passing out the handout (and several transparencies), demonstrate the process of choosing *one* pitch from the scale and placing it on the proper staff line under the first note head of the rhythm, and in the same rhythm.

b. Ask individual students to suggest the subsequent pitches (by name or number) until all eight scale steps are used.

c. Cross off each pitch of the scale as it is used.

d. Copy its scale step number and name underneath.

Example 4.3

For b. it is useful to pose the choice in terms of "Do you want to choose the next note to be close to the note we already have, or far away?" in order to start making clear that criteria exist. Only the teacher notates the choices on the overhead projector. The scale *step* (a less confusing term than scale *degree*), and the *pitch name* are always indicated.

3. "There, now that we have composed our first song as a class. Now let's each compose our own." Give specific directions and staging time limits.

- Make sure students copy scale step and pitch names for each pitch they use. To avoid using a step more than once, make sure they cross off pitches on the scale as they use them.

- As students work, look over their shoulders, helping if needed. Pay particular attention to students composing on transparencies!

- Collect those, because they were "previewed" and you will have some idea of what (and how) to discuss for the benefit of the rest of the class.

4. Discussion should focus on analyzing what the overall "shape" is of each melody. (Does it generally go up, down, or change direction frequently?)

⇨ This can be aided at first by connecting the note heads with a segmented line:

Example 4.4

⇨ *Play each example* and compare its "sound" to the "look" of its line: Is it smooth, or rough? Does it sound like a question ending on an upward inflection, or downward like a command?

5. Provide the opportunity for acting adaptively and cognitive strengthening: On a remaining staff—set up just like the one previously used—have students compose a *second* "improved" melody that applies what they learned from comparing their melody to those analyzed from the transparencies.

   • Proceed as in 3.

6. Plan a stage where students make any last minute corrections or changes, then have them copy their work neatly according to teacher directions and models.

   • Younger students can take these home, or they can be displayed on a bulletin board or on the wall outside the students' own classroom.

   • Middle school students can put these in their folders for later use.

   • Either group can include them in evaluation portfolios.

Readiness Staging for Future Lessons

The basic format just provided usually needs only several follow-up lessons using different meters. However, devote more attention in each subsequent lesson to analyzing the melodies (visually and aurally) and developing criteria for melodic movement and "line" (shape). Later lessons—especially the other formats that follow in this chapter—build upon this readiness by adding new possibilities for organizing pitches (e.g., based on harmonic and rhythmic criteria). Melodies then become progressively "tuneful" and musically satisfying. Some suggestions teachers find useful:

1. As soon as students have mastered (see **mastery learning**) the basic strategy of using each scale step only once:

   a. Expand the number of measures by extending the given rhythm pattern, and give students the choice of using any given tone two or three times—in a row, or at points throughout the melody (e.g., by modeling 4.5):

Example 4.5

   b. Focus more on the shape of the melodic line. The goal is to develop *cognitive criteria* by which students select the pitches of their melodies. These criteria are the focus of follow-up questions, reflections, and adaptive actions.

SMOOTH

JAGGED

Example 4.6

⇨ Is it smooth or jagged?

⇨ Does it have an interesting design or direction?

⇨ How and where does it use steps, skips, repeated tones, and leaps?

⇨ "Steps" involve any two adjacent steps of the scale:

Example 4.7

⇨ "Skips" skip over the next higher or lower step leaving the note in between out and thus creating a narrow melodic "space" or "interval":

Example 4.8

⇨ "Repeated tones" immediately repeat a tone one or more times:

Example 4.9

⇨ Or repeat tones at different points in the melody:

Example 4.10

⇨ "Leaps" are "intervals" ("spaces" between pitches) larger than a skip.

Example 4.11

   c. Transpose a treble clef composition into the bass clef (use an arrow pointing to the F line).

- Later, compose some melodies in the bass clef.
- As soon as the association between the clef sign and the G or F line has been made (by sheer familiarity), have students practice recalling lines and spaces without the arrows.

- The names of lines and spaces are learned simply by frequency of use in composing and analyzing! *This is an important readiness stage for music reading in connection with performance.*

  d. Use a variety of different common meters.

  - Meter and rhythm are still given; however, students will gain competence with common patterns they use over time.

  e. Use typical rhythmic motives and relations and investigate their effects on pitch selection, tunefulness, and interest.

Example 4.12

    f. Focus on the different effects of melodic direction, particularly at the cadence when ending on scale step 1 in comparison to step 8.

Example 4.13

    g. Set up problems where students compose *contrasting* and *repeated phrases.*

        ▷ Contrasting: The second phrase is significantly different and unique and this type of melody is typically represented as AB.

Notice, though, that the rhythmic organization is A A' , and that each phrase ends on a tonic chord.

Example 4.14

  • Repeated: The "answering" phrase is a literal copy of the first, or is extremely similar. It is typically represented as AA.

Example 4.15

  h. Combine groups of phrases into longer melodies, such as AABC, AABA, ABCA, and so forth. Base these groupings on examples chosen from songs students like. Analyze these before beginning to compose similarly organized melodies:

Example 4.16

  i. Always perform many examples of students' tunes, analyzing visually and aurally. As performing skills develop, students should perform their own melodies and make improvements based on what they hear.

  j. Transpose melodies from one key to another by renotating an existing well-known song using another scale provided on a handout. Students who play transposing instruments can learn how to do the particular transposition needed for them to play a melody, for example on the trumpet, along with a piano or guitar.

    • Transposing known tunes—their own and "real" tunes—to new keys is a way to teach new fingering since students already have the tune, meter, and rhythm in their ear.

 2. Frequently analyze melodies (themes) featured in listening and performing lessons for ideas students can use in their own compositions.

3. Compose melodies to words using the protocol for SONGS discussed later in this chapter.

4. Compose melodies that feature a particular multicultural "feel" or influence.
   - Be sure to work on "blue notes" (the in-the-cracks flatted third and fifth degrees of a *blues scale*).
   - Consider introducing some basic notation for jazz inflections:

Scoop   Slide   Drop   Turn   Flip

Example 4.17

5. Composing tunes for purposes that are amusing or off-beat develops intentionality, such as:
   - advertisements for peculiar, even fanciful products
   - themes or songs for certain kinds of television shows or movies
   - themes or songs for, or involving their feelings about friends parents, relatives (particularly grandparents), or idols (movie stars or sports heroes); "Valentine songs" promote high intentionality
   - pep songs and tunes for school sports teams
   - environmental and other social or philosophical "causes" of current relevance
   - "occasional music"—songs or themes composed for special occasions, such as a wedding or birthday or celebrating a local or world event (e.g., a space walk, etc.)

6. Students profit from composing in **cooperative learning** groups of two or three students. This takes more time so management staging must be strict!

7. Students can learn to use composition software to compose and hear their melodies.

8. Software can also be used to notate compositions so they look "professional."

Nuts 'n' Bolts 'n' Cautions

- Use pencils so students can erase. Always have a coffee can of pencils for students to use.
- Stress that notation is comparable to writing words and is most valuable when it can be easily read.
- Students in grades 4–5 need staff paper with wider spaces than do middle school students.
- Students who compose on transparencies need felt-tip pens or china-marking pencils and a paper towel to use as an eraser. Students who compose on transparencies can either recopy their tunes onto paper for keeping, or the teacher can photocopy them.
- Chairs are best set up so the teacher can walk behind students, looking over their shoulders as they work.

- Students should eventually check their own melodies by playing them; otherwise, the teacher needs to play them quickly for individuals.

- If individuals have trouble seeing a melodic "line," put a blank transparency over their tune and have them draw a line that connects each note head (see also no. 19, Chapter 6). Then study the resulting line on the transparency. This is also useful as a separate management stage for fourth and fifth grade classes at early readiness stages.

- Steps, skips, leaps, and successive repeated tones can profitably be labeled "ST," "SK," "L," and "R," respectively until the students recognize the intervals automatically.

Also see - 4.7, 4.8, 4.9 & 4.10

Example 4.18

- Compositions should be treated as "serious" products; for example, put on display or included in a class folder or portfolio. If most are just discarded, students will fail to take new lessons seriously.

- Grading compositions and other creative efforts can be detrimental to mastery learning and to creativity. However, evaluation and diagnosis are necessary and useful. Thus the teacher should periodically collect students' efforts for comments and suggestions.

- If grading is desired, it should take place only at periodic points in the learning process and should summarize students' strengths and weaknesses. It is best *not* to announce in advance that a new composition will be graded; just carry out the lesson as usual, then collect and grade the melody. Suggestions and encouragement should be given, nevertheless.

- Progress depends on careful readiness staging! Students who fall behind will be increasingly disinclined to compose if they don't receive help.

- Compositions can also be structured as **homework, independent, individualized instruction, and goal cards.** These formats are particularly useful in helping transfer students, or those who are learning at slower or faster rates.

MELODIC IMPROVISATION FORMAT

These "melodic" pieces (as opposed to "melodies") usually end up being "free form" and considerably more musically adventurous because they are worked out "by ear." Pointing out their similarity to the "works" of most popular recording groups—where, instead of a score, only the recording exists—is a useful way of priming such lessons.
Particular considerations:.

- Many melody instruments are needed that students already know how to play, or that are easy to play with little formal practice. Orff, keyboards, and pitched percussion instruments are typical, but guitars and other stringed classroom instruments should not be ignored.

- Simultaneous composing can get loud. This can be distracting to some students, especially those with ADD! Use adjacent practice rooms and spaces (e.g., instrument storage rooms, etc.) if possible, otherwise management staging must anticipate cacophony and its distractions.

- Tight management staging and the promise of the "live" performance, recording and discussion, usually "motivate" students to complete the problem in the time allotted.

Basic Protocol for Improvised Tunes

1. After appropriately priming the lesson, establish the primary focus. Examples include:

   - A melody that is expressive of two clearly contrasting moods: A | B (highest contrast in the middle)

   - A melody that begins with one feeling and very gradually "develops" and ends in a contrasting mood: A → B (highest contrast between beginning and ending)

   - A complex melody with a recurring "theme" alternating with certain contrasting sections: ABACABA, and so on

   - A melodic composition that might be "good for" a certain kind of scenario, commercial, video, film, or slide show, for example, lovers strolling romantically along a beach; then a choice of contrast (e.g., running, skipping, swimming, water fight, etc.); then the opening scene returns

   - A "theme" and variations, or a set tune followed by a "jazzy" improvisation

---

If twenty-five or thirty compositions must be heard, they must be brief. So many performances lead to increased memory problems for the later performers, not to mention audience fatigue. Small groups are a manageable compromise. Then, melodies can be accompanied (e.g., by rhythmic or sound composition background), or several melodies can be combined (e.g., as in polyphony, or Dixieland jazz).

---

2. Set a specific time length for the melody (e.g., lasts 30 seconds or 1 minute).

3. Have a very tight management staging plan. *Reproduce it as a handout or write it on the chalkboard or overhead.* Refer to it often: Use a **signal**, then "Now you should be at step . . . ."

   - Individual stages need to account for (a) generating melodic ideas, (b) choosing which ideas to actually use, (c) practicing those ideas individually, (d) combining them into longer melodies and compositions, and (e) several chances to attempt then improve the overall composition.

   - If circumstances allow, let students "prerecord" their pieces so they can listen and improve them before the "final recording session."

   - The specific manner in which compositions will be performed needs to be carefully considered in terms of (a) the time needed for the total number of performances; (b) how the recording will take place (e.g., for the "live audience" or in a separate "recording studio"—a side room set up for that purpose).

   - Discussion, aural analysis, reflection, and cognitive strengthening all need specific planning to maximize the results. Focus should be on (a) how, and how well, the *primary focus* was addressed; (b) particularly strong or unique musical ideas (at least per each individual or group); (c) specific suggestions per each individual or group; (d) general weaknesses or "food for thought" that can benefit everyone.

- Discussion and analysis needs to be thorough but not repetitive, matter of fact, or boring. Remember, the need for a *crescendo of interest* and a sense of satisfying *culmination* are the concluding stages of any good lesson.

Readiness Staging for Future Lessons

Improvised melodies take a great deal of time and cannot be used as often as the notated format. Therefore, they are best used to build aurally on learning addressed in notated melody format.

1. Specifically relate the primary focus of these compositions to similar focal points addressed through *sound compositions* (see Chapter 5). For example, most of the suggestions included in the first point of the basic protocol (see page 73) can also serve sound compositions. Results should be compared in order to enhance transfer of learning.

2. Incorporate improvised tonal and melodic elements into sound compositions and, similarly, incorporate sound composition and rhythmic effects and accompaniments into the "by ear" melodic compositions.

   - For example, improvised "themes" can be introduced into sound compositions, and sound compositions can accompany or enhance melodic compositions.
   - In either case, whichever is the *primary focus* should clearly dominate. Thus, a "melodic piece" with "sound composition accompaniment" ought to *stress* the melodic aspects.

3. Relate melodic compositions to listening lessons (see Chapter 6), and vice versa. Aural skills developed in one type of lesson are cognitively strengthened when applied to a different praxis. For example, a particularly "romantic" melody from a listening lesson can be used to prime students' own "Valentine songs."

4. Consider combining separate melodic compositions into different "movements" or sections of longer compositions, for example, as "ballet music" that individual students in class (or in local dance classes) might actually enjoy moving to.

   - These should be videotaped. Students find them especially rewarding to view.

5. "By ear" melodic pieces can be developed in the style of a particular multicultural or world music.

   - The point is especially to focus on the melodic character in relation to the use-conditions of the praxis in question (e.g., *Shakuhachi* flute music for Zen meditation).

Nuts 'n' Bolts 'n' Cautions

- Because audio (and sometimes video) taping are crucial components, the equipment must be set up and ready to go. Students enjoy running the equipment, too.
- "By ear" melodic compositions are longer, more complex, and more demanding of aural discrimination and aural attention than students' notated tunes. They are extremely beneficial since listening is the most accessible musical praxis for to the general population.

For the same reasons, the class as an "audience" must be primed to listen. Thus, the same kinds of *listening directions* are needed for these lessons as for the **directed listening** described in Chapter 7! In fact, it is usually necessary to plan the listening phase of improvised melody writing lessons *as a separate listening lesson,* with its own staging.

HARMONIC FOCUS

Plenty of music in the world consists of unharmonized melody. However, lessons that focus on melody construction are not as musically satisfying to 'tweens as melodies that contain an interesting harmonic accompaniment.

Harmony is also central to tonal musicianship. Effective performance on chording instruments (see Chapter 8), for example, benefits from understanding the relationship between melody, scale (tonality), and chords. Also, the organization of tonal melodies is influenced by the harmonic implications of cadences, melodic skips and leaps on chord tones, and the like. As soon as possible, melodies should be composed in terms of harmony.

This entails the following musicianship skills:

- creating scales
- building chords from scales
- understanding the relationship between strong and weak chords; that is, the idea of "chord progression"

Action learning seeks to develop such knowledge of tonal rudiments without abstract skill drill; in other words, *in context* as much as possible. Therefore the following approach is recommended as an intermediate step for progressing from monophonic to homophonic melodies.

TETRACHORD BASICS

In traditional jargon a *tetrachord* was a series of four *scale steps* within the interval of a perfect fourth. However, young students easily confuse the "chord" in this ancient term with triads. Thus the term "scale pattern" or some other such expression should be used until students are capable of more advanced learning.

The arrangement of "whole step–whole step–half step" is the basic pattern used for both the upper and lower halves of a *major* scale (see 4.21) with a whole step between the upper and lower tetrachord.

The basic strategy starts out with a teacher-led investigation using leading questions, follow-up questions and clarifications, and brief discussion.

1. Make a handout and transparency with Example 4.19 on the top half of the sheet. The second graphic (see 4.20) will be the bottom half of the full sheet. Have students fold their sheets in half, thus exposing only the top half at first (so they're not distracted by what is to come).

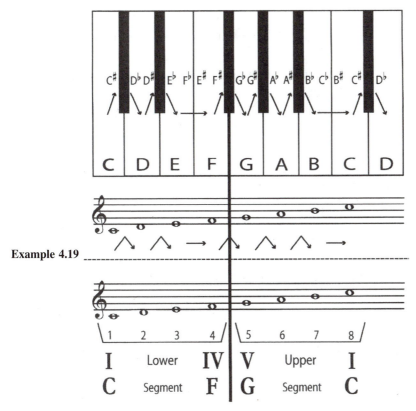

Example 4.19

Example 4.20

Mastery of names of diatonic pitches on the piano keyboard, tone bells, or Orff instruments is assumed. Thus *this kind of lesson cannot proceed without adequate readiness staging concerning at least the pitches of a C major scale.* This readiness must be developed first using the notated melody protocol described earlier. The use of sharps and flats and other keys, however, is eventually learned when scales other than C (usually G or F) are learned in connection with the tetrachord strategy.

2. Visually analyze the relationships between steps and half steps on the keyboard and their appearance on the staff by asking leading questions, *followed by an action*; for example:

"If (while pointing to each) there is half step from C to C♯ and another half step from C♯ to D, what is the distance or 'interval' between C and D?"

"Right, a whole step. So write a 1 on the 'interval' identification line between C and D on your staff."

"Notice how this line has two sections, like the top of a triangle. This reminds us that there are two half steps involved in one whole step. It even looks like the arrows on the keyboard drawing that go from from C to C♯ and from C♯ to D."

"Now, what is the interval from D to E? Why? How can you tell?"

"OK. Write a 1 on the interval identification line between D and E on your staff."

"Now, what is the interval from E to F? What is missing between these two white keys? How many arrows are there?"

"OK. Write a $\frac{1}{2}$ on the interval identification line between E and F."

"Notice how this interval identification line has only 1 section. This tells us that there is only a half step for this interval."

"Do half steps and whole steps *look* different on the staff?" (Discuss that they do not look different.)

"Good. We've already completed the *bottom half* of our scale. Now let's see if you can figure out the *top half* even though I have not provided you with the interval identification numbers."

3. With younger or less advanced students, the teacher should lead the class through the next half of the scale in a similar manner. But most middle school students can figure out the remaining segment on their own.

4. Now have students turn to the bottom half of the handout (see example 4.20).

5. Briefly discuss the Roman numeral chord symbols that "some musicians use," and the capital letter style chord symbols that "pop, rock, folk, and jazz musicians use." Focus on the obvious relationship between scale step and Roman numeral chord number, and the pitch name of a scale step and its chord name (e.g., the relationship between "c" as the first scale degree, the I chord, and the "C chord").

"Here's how musicians build chords." Demonstrate building the I/C and IV/F chord (as per the model at the top of 4.23).

6. Before actually beginning to compose, explore the following topics:

"Which scale steps in a tone block got a chord?" [The first and last.]

"Are there any pitches in common between the first and the last chord of each segment? "(Focus, for example, on the fact that the top pitch of the IV/F chord (c^8) has the same name as the bottom pitch of the I/C chord (c^1).

Later, the fact that the first and third chords built on a tetrachord share two pitches, as do the second and fourth, can be addressed as preliminary to using such "secondary chords" (chord built on the second and third steps of a tetrachord) as *chord substitutions* for the "primary chords" (especially ii as a substitute for IV and vi as a substitute for I). For now, establish only that the I and IV (C and F in C major) are *primary chords* because they occupy the strong positions at the beginning and end of each tetrachord, and that primary chords are therefore the most basic.

The following graphic should be made into a large poster displayed in a prominent location:

MAJOR SCALE

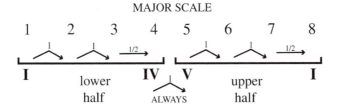

Example 4.21

7. Begin composing using primary chords, following the basic strategy of the Harmonic Format on page 89.

READINESS STAGING FOR FUTURE LESSONS

The tetrachord strategy (4.19–21)—by whatever name—is used to teach new scales, keys, and chord substitutions, even modulation and transposition.

1. New scales and keys, usually G or F major.
   - Have students notate seven pitches starting from a given tonic.
   - Then, using the poster (4.21), have the students calculate the proper intervals, selecting an F♯ or B♭ (depending on whether G or F major is utilized) in order to get the appropriate interval pattern for each of the two scale segments.
   - Present *key signatures* as the efficient alternative to having to use individual *accidentals*.
   - Discuss the continuing usefulness of the Roman numeral labels: that is, the idea that the I, IV, and V labels tell chord *relations* in any key, but their names change according to the key so that a I chord in C is a C chord but a I chord in G is a G chord, and so on.
   - Use the words "lower" and "upper" to refer to the different segments of a scale in preparation for later lessons on *modulation* to closely related keys (see 4.22).

2. Chord substitutions.
   - After composing a melody that uses several IV chords, go back and substitute ii chords in several likely locations. Take special note of the similarity between the IV and the ii but note that the IV is a *primary chord* (see the box under 6. in the previous list) and thus "stronger."
   - On another occasion, go back and substitute the vi for the I chord (except at a final cadence).
   - Later, compose pieces that use primary and secondary chords from the first for variety.

3. Modulation. Pieces that modulate offer additional interest. Using the tetrachord format, modulation to closely related keys is not difficult to teach.
   - Prepare a handout that shows how two scales/keys are closely related due to *sharing a scale segment.*

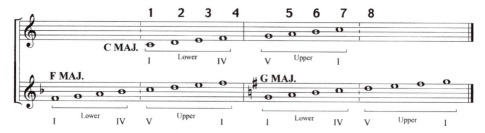

Example 4.22

- Identify *common chords*; the V chord in C major has the same pitches as the I chord in G major.
- Prepare a handout for composing in the Harmonic Format (see page 89 that follows) that employs a *common chord modulation*.

4. Transposition. Transposing a composition, along with its chords, to a different key is especially useful where guitars and such accompanying instruments are included in the curriculum as models of recreational performance (Chapter 8).

- This is especially recommended for sing-along tunes so students can play them in more than one key simply by understanding the relationships between the primary chords of different keys (i.e., that I, IV, V, I have the same function but different "spellings" in different keys). This relationship is easily illustrated and taught in connection with Examples 4.19 and 4.20.
- Students who play transposing instruments in band, or who want their compositions played on a transposing instrument but accompanied by an instrument in another key (e.g., a trumpet or clarinet solo accompanied by piano) can be shown how to transpose using the tetrachord process.

5. Minor keys. Minor scales come in several varieties and this presents a problem. However, if the curriculum includes teaching minor keys, stress the pattern of half and whole steps involved with the *entire* minor scale in question instead of using the two tetrachords format.

- *Natural* and *harmonic minor scales* are basic.
- Decisions concerning minor melodies can be handled first by ear, then working backwards (if at all) to the *melodic minor scale*.

Nuts 'n' Bolts 'n' Cautions

- When primed in terms of "learning how professional musicians know how to use scales and keys, chords, and harmony," 'tweens are often keenly interested in the technical information—but *only when it is learned through composition.* Thus it is imperative that these classes not devolve into "theory" lessons.
- The teacher's role here is to "lead" students to conceptualize tonal theory in their own functional terms. The tetrachord format is a very simple, straightforward model for visualizing much otherwise very technically abstract information.
- "Tests" of their comprehension and skill should be seen *in compositions*, not on abstract tests.
- Grading, if used at all, ought to reflect the competency demonstrated in composing pieces where melodic and harmonic relations and organization are technically accurate.

- The "bottom line" for these lessons is to teach musicianship rudiments *through* composing pieces in which harmony is the focus (see the Harmonic Format following). If students are to ever be able to compose "real" music for their garage bands, for example, they will have to be functional with chords and the relationship of harmonic structure to overall melodic organization (not to mention, yet, rhythm).

HARMONIC FORMAT: HARMONY-BASED MELODIC COMPOSITIONS

These lessons teach students how chords relate to melodies. All the basic considerations of melodic organization developed in conjunction with lessons focusing on melody alone—questions of line, shape, direction, and so forth—are applied now to the framework provided by chords. Thus plenty of skill composing melodies using the Notated Melodic Format (page 73) should precede first attempts with the Harmonic Format.

Basic Strategy

1. Begin with a handout prepared that looks like this:

Example 4.23

- The scale is provided and the chords to be used are built upon it. Scale steps and both Roman numeral chord symbols and chord letter names are labeled. The arrow pointing to the line appropriate to the clef in question is provided until students can be weaned from needing it.

- Notice, too, that the meter and rhythms are given. However, because the emphasis is on pitches organized in relation to chords, *rhythm is not the primary focus*. Thus students' thinking and aural perception are focused on the relevant harmonic variables.

2. Once again, prepare handouts and transparencies, one of the latter for the teacher to use and several for student use. As before, the entire class, for application to their own work, will analyze the compositions some students do on transparencies.

3. Proceed by composing the first four measures with students, for example:

"In our first measure we need pitches from the I or C chord."

"Look up at the top and you'll notice the C chord. What three pitches does it contain?"

"Waldo (call on a cooperative student by name), what pitch would you suggest we use first?" (Notate it on the transparency in the correct rhythmic value, directing the class not to write anything yet on their staves.)

"(Calling on another student by name) what do you want to use next from the C chord? The same note, or one of the two other pitches?"

And so on for the first four measures.

4. Play the result. Ask for suggestions and alternatives that might help the line or shape of the melody according to those criteria developed in earlier compositions where melody alone was the sole focus. Make some improvements that seem most productive of a "standard" tune, such as fewer changes of direction, and so forth.

5. Now that the process has been modeled, have students complete the next four measures on their own.

- Set a time limit for completing this stage.
- Analyze the compositions of the students who have worked on transparencies, focusing (a) on whether they have chosen correct pitches according to the chords given, then (b) on matters pertaining to smoothness of line, changes of direction, and overall contour.
- Play their tunes *with the supporting harmonies*, at least as block chords. An interesting accompanying pattern helps prime interest.

6. Compose a new 8-measure melody using 2. provided on the handout (Example 4.23).

- Again hear and analyze the completed examples of the (now different) students composing on transparencies.
- Give students a chance to *revise and improve* any features they want or need to improve as a result of the discussion.
- Aside from focusing on the accuracy of pitch selection in relation to chords, be sure to stress the most basic features of melodies that were learned in previous lessons where chords were not used.

Readiness Staging for Future Lessons

The basic strategy should be expanded progressively in the direction of longer and more "authentic" models of good melodies studied in listening lessons (Chapter 6) or used in performance (Chapters 7 and 8). In particular:

1. Eventually students should be given just the scale, a choice or scales, or construct their own scale, then build chords on it.

2. Structure problems that involve different cadences, their relationship and effects. Especially:

   • In particular, explore the differences between a *parallel period* (AA′ where A ends on IV or V and A′ on I) and *repeated phrases* (AA where each A ends on I): For AA′, the ends of the phrases will vary melodically because of the different chord.

   • Also investigate the differences between *contrasting periods* (AB where A ends on IV or V and B on I) and *contrasting phrases* (AB where both phrases end on I).

   • Find, analyze and listen to examples of both from various repertories.

3. Various typical small part constructions should be explored and experimented with concerning their advantages and differences. For example:

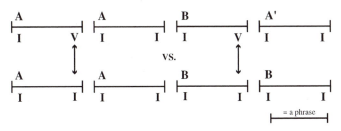

Example 4.24

4. Take chord *progressions* from songs the class already enjoys and compose new tunes in the same keys to different rhythms and meters.

   • Compare student compositions to the originals.

   • Focus especially on *chord progression* basics.

   • Be sure to compose some "classic 12 bar blues":

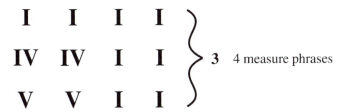

Example 4.25

   • And compose some not-so-classic 12 bar blues where V "progresses" backwards to IV before returning to tonic.

Example 4.26a

- A chromatic *passing chord*—labeled just PC—between V and IV provides a familiar sounding progression. Students can play this passing chord easily on keyboards, but not as easily on guitars, and the like.

Example 4.26b

5. Eventually make V chords into V_7 by adding a fourth chord tone on top of the basic *triad*. Use a graphic example to demonstrate where the "7" comes from:

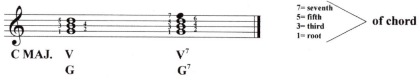

Example 4.27

- If vocabulary of chord construction is a part of the curriculum, this is the time to begin to regularly use the terms "root," "third," "fifth," and "seventh."

6. There is no particular reason to teach labels for "root position," "first inversion" (i.e., where the third is on the bottom) since these can be confusing and have no practical use in compositions by students at this age.

- Where such variables are relevant (e.g., for performance interest), simply refer in nontechnical descriptive terms to the "chord with the third as the bottom," and so on.

7. The appearance of *major* and *minor* triads (in both major and minor keys) can be addressed quite late in the game, if at all. Using other modes (and their derived harmonies) can add interesting possibilities at later stages. With such modes, melodic movement and chord progressions are often unusual and allow considerable freedom of choice as long as confirmed by the ear.

8. As soon as students can handle skips of chord tones predictably well, set up problems that involve *nonchord tones* in the melody.

- *unaccented* nonchord tones (i.e. not on a strong beat), especially upper and lower *neighbor* and *passing* tones:

Unaccented non-chord tones

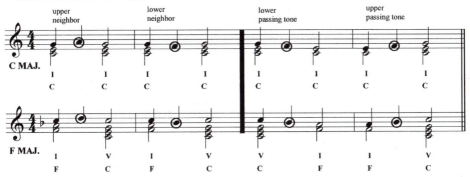

Example 4.28

- *accented* nonchord tones (i.e., on strong beat) that resolve to chord tones:

Accented non-chord tones

Example 4.29

Nuts 'n' Bolts 'n' Cautions

- As harmony enters the picture, performing these compositions becomes more difficult. The teacher who can play both the melody and chords at sight with an improvised and attractive accompaniment has a real advantage!

- **Dyads** of students can perform each other's tunes. Since the chord progression is set, it is easily played using the chord functions of electronic keyboards and some built-in rhythmic accompaniment. Once they can each play their own melody (for example on keyboard, recorder, and the like), then they can play it while accompanied by the other student. They can also learn each other's tunes. Two students per keyboard is often the simplest approach.

- Harmonized tunes start to sound "real" and become more musically satisfying. Thus performances can be recorded. In fact, it is useful for each student to have a cassette tape that is his or her "personal album." These can be used in future lessons, displayed to family and included in a student's portfolio.

- Learning to place chord symbols promotes new intentionality when using notation software.

- These pieces take much longer to complete, and especially to practice and perform. Planning must take into consideration not only the kind of management staging necessary to keep students on-task, but how many compositions of this type are affordable in terms of the time available.

RHYTHMIC FOCUS FORMAT

Lessons that stress the rhythmic organization of good tunes depend on readiness staging lessons that develop mastery with the basics of meter and rhythmic notation.

Readiness Staging for Rhythmic Emphasis

1. Absolutely basic is knowledge of note values in relation to given meters.

   - Have students compose "x" number of measures of different rhythms to given meters (using 4.30 as a poster for student reference) and (a) combine them into interesting phrases, then (b) perform them.

   - Find the same, similar, or other interesting patterns in familiar songs and sing the songs using rhythmic counting (or the teacher's choice of rhythm syllables).

METER

Simple   Compound

*The teacher's preferred rhythmic syllables should be used

Example 4.30

   - *Meter signatures* are best presented at first with the number of main beats on the top and the type of note getting a "main beat" actually shown. Thus *simple* meters (i.e., where each main beat is divided into *two* counts) are first shown as [Example 4.31] long before [Example 4.32]; and compound meters are shown as [Example 4.33] long before [Example 4.34].

Example 4.31

Example 4.32

Example 4.33

Example 4.34

Notice that 4.30 shows both ways of notating a meter signature. When both systems are used, through sheer frequency, students easily associate the type of note getting a "main beat" with the proper bottom number of a meter signature. Furthermore, they will understand that in compound duple meters (e.g., 6/8) there are not *six* "main beats" in a measure but *two* "main beats" with six counts.

---

2. Students also need to be able to "see" and analyze *rhythmic* patterns without being distracted by *pitch* patterns. Students who are **field-dependent** will naturally have more problems with this than students who are **field-independent** and need more encouragement and a little more practice.

- Notate just the rhythms of familiar tunes. Then perform them as a class and "name that tune" simply by its rhythm. Analyze some examples and help students "pick out" the different rhythmic patterns or motives by circling and labeling them in various ways (e.g., using "a," "b" etc., to label each different pattern or "motive"). Start using the words "pattern" and "motive" (or "motif") interchangeably with regard to these basic units of rhythmic organization.

- Then, in another lesson, reverse the above process: Start with a familiar tune, and "pick out" its rhythmic patterns by circling and labeling as before. Then perform its overall rhythm without the pitches.

- Study how favorite songs are organized rhythmically. Renotate their rhythms on a separate staff (i.e., without pitches) and analyze their relations and organization. The point is to understand that (and how) rhythmic organization contributes to the overall melodic organization and effect.

Performing rhythms as a class by clapping is notoriously inaccurate, especially for younger students. Instead, the following are strongly recommended:

- Chant the rhythms on "tah"
- Use rhythm syllables

With this kind of readiness, older students can usually play rhythms on one pitch (e.g., on tone bells or Orff instruments). Clapping, if used, should be done properly: Hold one hand stationary (like a drum) and "clap" it with the other hand using only a little controlled wrist and forearm movement. Avoid large movements from the shoulders and moving of both hands.

Basic Rhythmic Format Strategy

Provide students with a four measure rhythmic pattern (eventually working up over several lessons to eight and sixteen measures), any one of which exemplifies different kinds of rhythmic organization and interest.

- *Option:* Use the rhythmic patterns of songs in various meters the students already enjoy.
- *Option:* Gives students a choice from among patterns so there will be variety in the results.

1. Set up a handout accordingly based on those patterns.

2. Students compose tunes using either the basic Notated Melodic Format (page 73) or the Harmonic Format (page 89).
   - Each individual (or cooperating group) composes a melody to its assigned (or chosen) rhythm.
   - Results are heard and analyzed as discussed earlier for each of those basic formats.

3. Analyze the rhythmic organization of melody by stressing how *repetition and contrast* of rhythmic patterns or "motives" contribute to (a) rhythmic and (b) melodic *unity and variety*; that is, how rhythmic and melodic patterns work holistically.
   - Approach *repetition* as leading to *unity*, which helps the melody be understood as a "unified whole." *Contrast* leads to *variety* and promotes "interest."
   - Pose the problem of balance between the two: "How much unity is enough to help our ear and brain organize the tune, and how much is too much and therefore boring? How much variety is needed to provide interest, but not too much to sound disorganized?"

4. *When composing to the rhythms of songs students already know,* compare students' melodies to the originals.
   - Because their melodies have the same rhythms as the originals, the words of the originals can be used to sing their compositions,

Readiness Staging for Future Lessons

1. Students compose eight measures of rhythms as the basis for compositions that proceed according to the basic strategy of either the Notated Melodic Format, or the Harmonic Format.
   - Attention should focus on rhythmic unity and variety.

2. Assign longer compositions that place a greater premium on the *need* for rhythmic unity and variety.

3. With older students (i.e., at least by late middle school) or advanced students of any age, begin to focus on the importance of *rhythmic organization* for *melodic organization* and interest.

   • Question: "How do pitch organization and rhythmic organization work together to create unity and variety?"

   • Where chords are being used as the basis for pitch selection (Harmonic Format), investigate the role of harmony (and especially modulation) in relation to rhythm (i.e., **harmonic rhythm**).

4. Analyze successful models of rhythmic organization and interest (i.e., unity and variety) chosen from an assortment of scores, and/or aurally.

   • Or, compose examples of your own as straightforward models of new techniques. Then have students use those examples in their own pieces.

5. Proceed as with 4., but choose examples that feature some interesting interaction of melodic, harmonic, and rhythmic organization (e.g., Examples 4.12–13, etc.).

6. Compose some strictly rhythm score compositions for "percussion ensemble" where the entire organization and interest comes from rhythm, meter, and the tone quality of the instruments. Do not ignore the rhythmic possibilities of nonpercussion instruments (e.g., using single pitches or chords on pianos and guitars) and especially nontraditional "instruments" (e.g., brake drums, etc.).

The professional percussion ensemble *Stomp* has toured the world to popular acclaim. This group mixes dance and theater with the rhythmic use of everyday objects to produce a musically exciting and entertaining result that young and old enjoy. A video of this group is available.* It contains many individual works with considerable of potential to inspire 'tweens. Use selections from the video to *prime* these rhythm pieces *and* the sound compositions described in the next chapter!

———————

*"Stomp Out Loud" (HBO Home Video).

Using the model of "Stomp," compose and notate rhythms that can be combined in preplanned ways into longer compositions.

   • After inventing rhythms according to certain given criteria (for example, concerning the number of different meters and their combination as polymeters), assemble these into a longer composition *that can be repeated* by the composing group (even though not every rhythm is notated).

   • Have students bring in everyday objects to use as rhythmic sources. (It is best to avoid the "dance" aspects of "Stomp" in the interests of classroom decorum and control. Students can be encouraged, however, to come in after school to make their own "Stomp"-like videos.)

7. Compose in changing meters.
  - Study some examples (e.g., from current musical theater or pop music groups) as a basis for the intelligent and musical use of changing meter.

8. Renotate well-known "sing-along" kinds of tunes in different meters, or in changing/meters *that make musical sense*. Compare different student solutions.

9. Study favorite songs and melodies (aurally and visually) for interesting examples and models of *syncopation*.
  - Upon such bases, compose melodies that gain interest from syncopation.

10. Listen to examples of melodies that are performed strictly as notated, and the same melodies as "swung."
  - "Swing" selected examples of student or other compositions "by ear."
  - Learn the notational convention for "swing":
  - Compose melodies that use both "straight" and "swung" notation.

Example 4.35

11. Use models or influences from multicultural or world music.
  - Models such as rap can be used in simplified forms early in the readiness staging process. These models may focus on, for example, the rhythmic interest of words. However, these musics are often of considerable subtlety and deserve not to be so oversimplified as to misrepresent their value as music.

Drumming groups are often popular with this age. However, the same differences mentioned earlier between improvised and notated melodies and notated rhythms apply here. Thus drumming group lessons should be clear as to which focus is at stake: (a) lessons performing from notation should stress *accuracy* in connection with notated complexities (including multiple parts) in the spirit of a traditional percussion ensemble; (b) lessons that are improvised or performed by ear from a "leader's" example or directions stress the "feel" and importance of rhythm as its own musical interest.

Nuts 'n' Bolts 'n' Cautions

  - All the aforementioned possibilities depend on previous readiness staging of basic metric and rhythmic notation.
  - More time and practice are often required for student performances of rhythmically-oriented pieces.
  - Performance of rhythmic compositions lends itself to "fooling around" misbehavior with percussion instruments. This needs to be anticipated and minimized.

- Because of the preliminary readiness involved with both rhythmic notation (and its arithmetic) and performance, *newly arrived transfer students and mainstreamed students often need individualized help, or even independent learning.*

- Discussions should aim toward the progressive understanding of how *rhythm and pitch are inseparable in melodic organization and interest.* Without understanding this interdependency, student compositions will fall short of musical authenticity and interest—although students, particularly younger students, will still find their achievements to be satisfying.

- On the other hand, drumming and "Stomp"-like projects can motivate interest in rhythm as its own musical value, especially in regard to various ethnic and world music drumming traditions.

SONGS

Songs have words that add a new dimension to melodies and, for this age group, create special interest in composition. To the degree that the words are relevant or interesting to students, musical intentionality is all the more energized and focused. On the other hand, words add new difficulties and thus pose new learning opportunities.

First, music and words should "fit" like a hand and glove. Songs are not a melody *and* a poem, but a synthesis of the two. Compositionally, words make certain musical demands, and the music carries important consequences for the handling of the words. 'Tweens somehow get the idea that melodies are written first, then words added after the fact. However, it is important to stress that many successful songwriters, including those of popular and show tunes, art songs and opera, consider both words and music from the first.

The protocol here simplifies the process, at least for beginning purposes. While "creativity" is a welcome result, the first and foremost consideration is to help students understand:

- Why composers write songs to begin with.
- How the composition process can be organized so that the song is orderly.
- How the music can become expressive of the words.
- What constitutes a rich and competent song from the musicianship point of view.

> For the purposes of general music class, the "craft" can be considered separately from the creative "artfulness" involved. General music teachers need to be sure the former is accomplished as the basis for the latter. The "bottom line," then, is for students to learn how songs are "put together" by demonstrating the craft of composing songs that fulfill basic conditions of musicianship.

Basic Strategy: Song Format

1. Of foremost concern is the choice of words (or "lyrics" as the teacher may want to refer to them in 'tween jargon).
   - Poems need to be of compelling interest for the age.

- Strongly metric poems are preferred, as are poems that have simple structures.
- First efforts need to be short, resulting usually in at least 8-measure melodies; 16 measures are ideal for first attempts.

2. Reproduce the poem on a handout with words divided into syllables with individual words and syllables evenly spaced:

When   I   am   old - er   and   al - so   much   bol - der

Life   will   go   I   know   not   where.

Now   as   a   rule   I'm   main-ly   in   school,

Not   yet   sure   how   I'll   get   there.

Example 4.36

3. Provide students with copies; as usual, several should work on a transparency and the teacher should use a transparency throughout to read and refer to the poem.

4. Read the poem to the class at least *two* times, with a consistent meter, *overstressing accents the second time.*
   - Have the class read it in unison at least two times, stressing accented syllables.
   - Have volunteers read it individually, or assign different individuals to read each line.
   - The point is to use repetition to solidify the meter in the ears of the students.

5. Have students put a line under each word or syllable that is stressed.

When   <u>I</u>   am   <u>old</u> - er   and   <u>al</u> - so   much   <u>bol</u> - der

<u>Life</u>   will   <u>go</u>   I   <u>know</u>   not   <u>where.</u>

<u>Now</u>   as   a   <u>rule</u>   I'm   <u>main</u>-ly   in   <u>school,</u>

<u>Not</u>   yet   <u>sure</u>   how   <u>I'll</u>   get   <u>there.</u>

Example 4.37

- With the entire class, model the process of adding lines under stressed syllables for the first line.
- The students copy each line and then complete the remainder of the poem on their own handouts.
- Analyze the work of the students who worked on transparencies.
- Obtain a show of hands of those in the rest of the class whose work was correct.

- Ask the others what they had that was "different" and, for the entire class, clarify the confusions. Often this requires only getting these students to read the poem *aloud* with the proper accents.

6. Have students place a vertical "measure line" before each underlined syllable:

When | I   am | <u>old</u> - er and | <u>al</u> - so much | <u>bol</u> - der |

| <u>Life</u>   will | <u>go</u>   I | <u>know</u>   not | <u>where.</u> |

| <u>Now</u> as a | <u>rule</u>   I'm | <u>main</u>-ly   in | <u>school,</u> |

| <u>Not</u>   yet | <u>sure</u> how | <u>I'll</u>   get | <u>there.</u> ||

Example 4.38

- Proceed as in step 5.
- Place a double line at the very end (see 4.38).

7. Read the poem again to determine whether the words "move in a pattern of two or of three."
    - Have students tap a steady pulse while the poem is read correctly.
    - Get students to focus on discriminating whether the poem is, to use musical jargon, in *simple duple* or *simple triple* meter (i.e., is read with either 2 or 3 beats per measure).

Be aware that most poems can be read in either meter but one usually feels more natural. Thus choose the meter carefully and be consistent in step 4.

    - Decide as a class on a meter of 2 or 3 (simple duple or triple meter), while clearing up any inconsistent or confused conclusions.

Students might either guess the correct answer or get the correct answer for misguided reasons. Thus the process of dealing with wrong conclusions usually helps students who got the correct answer without really understanding why they were correct.

---

8. Write the meter number (a large 2 or 3) at the beginning of the poem and under the text, have the class number the main beats using the chart shown as Example 4.43:

3 When | I am | old - er and | al - so much | bol - der |
3 | 1 2 3 | 1 2 3 | 1 2 3 | 1 2 3 |

| Life will | go I | know not | where. |
| 1 2 3 | 1 2 3 | 1 2 3 | 1 2 3 |

Example 4.39

- When asked whether a word or syllable receives 1 count, some students will put a 1 under each beat.

3 | Now as a | rule I'm | main-ly in | school, |
| 1 1 1 | 1 1 1 | 1 1 1 | 1 1 1 |

| Not yet | sure how | I'll get | there. |
| 1 1 1 | 1 1 1 | 1 1 1 | 1 1 1 |

Example 4.40

- Thus, before beginning, the process, it needs to be demonstrated that the first count is labeled "1," the second count "2," and the third count "3," then starting a new measure with "1," and so on.
- When a word or syllable is held for more than a count, use a tie to connect them. The tie symbol will eventually transfer to tying together two notes (e.g., two quarter notes) as readiness for the next larger note value (e.g., half notes).

3 When | I am | old - er and | al - so much | bol - der |
3 | 1 2 3 | 1 2 3 | 1 2 3 | 1 2 3 |

| Life will | go I | know not | where. |
| 1 2 3 | 1 2 3 | 1 2 3 | 1 2 3 |

| Now as a | rule I'm | main-ly in | school, |
| 1 2 3 | 1 2 3 | 1 2 3 | 1 2 3 |

| Not yet | sure how | I'll get | there. |
| 1 2 3 | 1 2 3 | 1 2 3 | 1 2 3 |

Example 4.41

9. Assign or decide on what note value will receive one beat. A quarter note is a common beginning point. Place the note under the meter number:

3 When | I   am | old - er and | al - so much | bol - der |

3 | 1 2 3 | 1   2   3 | 1   2   3 | 1   2 3 |

| Life   will | go   I | know   not | where. |

| 1 2   3 | 1 2   3 | 1 2   3 | 1 2 3 |

| Now as a | rule   I'm | main-ly   in | school, |

| 1   2   3 | 1 2   3 | 1   2   3 | 1   2   3 |

| Not   yet | sure   how | I'll   get | there. |

| 1 2   3 | 1 2   3 | 1   2   3 | 1   2   3 |

Example 4.42

- Provide a chart on a transparency or the chalkboard that shows students their rhythmic choices.

♩ = 1 Count

1

♩ = ♩♩ = ♩ + ♩ = 2 Counts

2   1   2   1 + 2

♩. = ♩♩♩ = ♩ + ♩ + ♩ = 3 Counts

1 2 3   1   2   3   1 + 2 + 3

or

♩ ♩ = ♩♩♩ = ♩ + ♩ + ♩ = 3 Counts

1 2 3   1   2   3   1 + 2 + 3

Example 4.43

- Have students refer to the chart as they notate the rhythm of the poem (as read) by placing the appropriate metric values over the word or syllables.

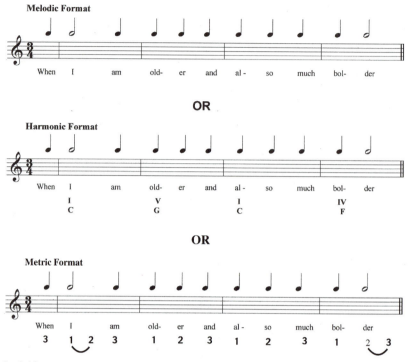

Example 4.44

  • Analyze student work and clarify any confusions or errors.

10. Using the correctly notated rhythm of the words, proceed to compose the song according to either the Harmonic or Metric Formats (both are shown in 4.44).

Readiness Staging for Future Lessons

1. *Composing songs should be deferred until readiness has been developed* via the Melodic, Harmonic, and Rhythmic Formats (see pages 73, 89, and 96)!

   • However, meter and rhythms can be derived from words with the Basic Rhythmic Format.

   • Ultimately, songwriting serves well as a culminating kind of project; it "summarizes" and synthesizes learning developed with the earlier formats. This way, students find songs are more satisfying and they provide the "payoff" of student intentions that makes the whole process worthwhile.

2. As soon as students can independently set a metered poem to rhythm, then poems in less strongly metric, or even free verse can be used. The rhythmic setting will be more fluid and thus the choices more complex.

   • Students need to practice reading such a poem aloud consistently in the desired manner. Then they should notate the meter and rhythm by proceeding as in the basic Song Format (see page 99). If they cannot, the problem is lack of mastery of the basic format and that needs to be reviewed.

   • Stress the *natural accentuation of syllables.*

3. Quickly expand from 2 to 4 beats by confronting the problem of *primary* and *secondary* accents.

   - Take a piece they have already composed with 2 beats per measure and, after considering the difference between 1̠ 2 1̠ 2 and 1̠ 2 3̠ 4 , renotate it using 4 beats per measure.

4. Eventually 3 "main beats" (a simple meter) should be combined into a meter having 6 "counts" but only 2 "main beats" (a compound meter). Example 4.45 produced as a poster (or overhead) is useful studying the difference between the pattern and effects of each and for setting specific compositional problems that focus on composing a piece in 6/8.

   - Compare the different "feel" when the same familiar melody is performed in both patterns, say in 3/4 and 6/8.

   - A listening lesson using a strong waltz pattern helps stress the difference between 1̠ 2 3 / 1 2 3 and 1̠ 2 3 4̠ 5 6.

Meter

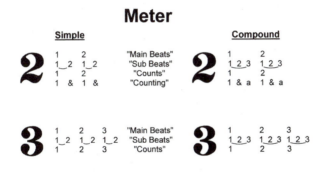

Example

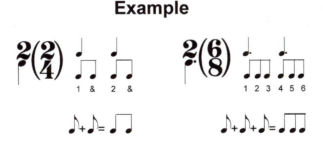

Example 4.45

5. As students gain mastery over these technical variables, further emphasis is given to:

   - melodies that are expressive of how the composer (or group) feels about the words.

   - refinements concerning phrase structure and cadences, rhythmic structure and interest, and modulation and other uses of accidentals. These compositions are best approached through study of good models.

- focusing on rhythmic-melodic motives and their musical "development." For example, after considering the model of, say, the motives of "Do-Re-Mi" from the *Sound of Music* (or the second examples of 4.12–13) students can then compose their own pieces using their versions of a similar *figure and sequence* approach.

All the points noted can serve as the focus of specific compositional problems, but are best prepared by visual and aural analysis of models. *Readiness staging via listening lessons* should focus on developing lists of criteria and guidelines that students can use in their own compositional efforts (which, therefore, should follow immediately on the heels of such listening lessons).

---

6. Songs can eventually be composed "by ear" in the sense that students sing or play their ideas and correct or improve them "by ear," then notate them.

7. Younger students, or middle school classes where the act of singing is like "pulling teeth," can also profit from "improvised songs."

Since it is often difficult to get *each* student in a class to improvise an entire song (which in any case is time-consuming), "improvised operas" or "musicals" can be created along certain musical and interpretative guidelines: for example, a "blues opera" complaining about too much homework that is 2 minutes long, in a 'bluesy' style where every member of the group participates in improvising a recitative, or an "aria" (song), *or* participates in a duet or chorus. This is the best way for helping students learn what the components of an opera or musical theater piece *are* and are "good for." It is best undertaken in connection with listening or viewing such a work for the purpose of generating ideas for "our own" opera or show.

Nuts 'n' Bolts 'n' Cautions

- Step 10. of the Basic Song Format strategy (page 104) is greatly enhanced if a new handout is provided on which students find what they have been previously working on *already recopied neatly and correctly* by the teacher, rather than to have them re-copy—which wastes time and is often inaccurate!

- The original handout can be presented with the text already under the staff, though leave adequate space for the rhythms (above the staff), the counts (between the text and melody), and the chords (under the text). However, the staff and other mechanics can distract younger (or field dependent) students. Thus first efforts should use only the poem that is later transferred in rhythmically notated form to the staff on a separate handout for the actual composition process.

- Notes held or tied for several counts, especially whole and half notes in certain contexts, introduce the idea of *rests*. Held notes at the ends of phrases are particular good places to suggest using rests as literal "breathing" points (e.g., a rest on the last beat), and as a way of emphasizing the words that follow (for example, beginning new sentences or lines of a poem). Models should be studied from among songs students enjoy.

- Once students can perform their own songs on instruments (Chapter 8), they can play and make improvements to their tunes. This is encouraged especially by including any such compositional work in their folders or portfolios with the understanding or expectation that the melodies should be improved before presenting the collected work for final evaluation.

Students will often practice their own tunes with more interest and dedication than many of the tunes typically used to teach an instrument. Use this to instructional advantage by composing melodies that students then practice in their separate performance lessons. However, as a rule, do not have melodic composition lessons *always* lead into performance lessons. Melody composition should sometimes lead to sound compositions (Chapter 4) that involve similar generative themes (e.g., organization, expression) and to listening lessons (Chapter 6) that focus on melody.

- A class album of songs (or a "song cycle" composed to related poetry) makes a good group project. Similarly, some teachers make simple two- and three-part arrangements and have the school choir perform particularly successful songs, even in concert. This is a prime way of "going public" with the benefits of general music class, and of inspiring and rewarding especially advanced students.
- Songs can be composed through **cooperative learning**. A group of students of equal ability will often generate far more good musical ideas than any one of them individually.
- Notation software can be used (i.e., " . . . as though you were sending a copy of the score to a publisher to follow while listening to your 'demo' recording."). Even if done by hand, renotation is an opportunity to teach *manuscript* and *calligraphy* basics.

Teachers are of different mind on the value of using general music class time for students to write their own poems. Many avoid this because they do not feel competent to lead students effectively through such a language arts activity; or because they prefer to spend the limited class time mainly on music. Options: (a) a joint undertaking with the English or language arts teacher where students write their poems in that class, and then compose their songs in general music class; (b) these same teachers can help you select poems that students can understand and enjoy; (c) students can chose a poem from among given options.

CONCLUSION

If begun in grades 4 and 5, all students can acquire significant musicianship skills in the rudiments of tonal music by the end of middle school.

The use of the **rubrics** described in Appendix B is highly recommended to develop a functional understanding of tonal music via the protocols described in this chapter.

With a little extra help from the teacher, and peer tutoring, transfer students can quickly catch up with the students who have been developing these skills since fourth grade.

Without developing this kind of basic musicianship by the end of middle school, there will be little tangible evidence for claiming that students are "generally well educated" musically. If music is to be "basic" in any pragmatic sense, then students need at least the "basics" of tonal music promoted by the melodic composition formats suggested in this chapter as a basis for the listening and performing stressed in later chapters. Even though instructional time is less, in music class, progress developing basic tonal musicianship can be as noticeable as improvements students make in their other subjects. And if tonal composition begins in grade 4, by the end of middle school students will have solid musicianship skills.

CHAPTER FIVE

THE SOUND
COMPOSITION LABORATORY

When students compose, they not only learn *how* music is put together but also *why* it is created in the first place—that is, what music is "good for." This is important to praxial theory because it emphasizes the *pragmatic* relevance of music. Whether or not they ever compose again, by listening to their own works and those of their peers, students learn how to listen; that is, *what* to listen for. Because they perform their own works, performance skills are also advanced. In addition, they learn how important performance technique is to the overall musical result. Finally, composition is an important musical praxis and it needs to be directly modeled in an Action Learning program.

The composing formats in the previous chapter addressed important rudiments of traditional tonal theory. This chapter focuses on longer compositions and, therefore, a much larger spectrum of musical possibilities is at stake than can be addressed in composing short tonal tunes and songs.

Planning sound composition lessons does not usually require as much development and reproduction of handouts and other learning materials as do other lessons. Rather, planning focuses mainly on *management staging*, so that class time is used efficiently and students remain on-task and orderly. *Readiness staging,* too, becomes of major importance; *sound compositions should typically lead into or follow up listening lessons.*

The following *generative themes* should receive **primary focus**:

- *Time*—"creating" the feeling of different qualities of time and of organizing ideas in and through time.
- *Sound and silence*—the role of timbre (tone quality) and the expressive and formal roles of silence.
- *Linearity*—ideas of "line," "voice," and the like are employed in the absence of a "tune" or "melody"; the "development" of musical "ideas" into a "line" of musical thinking.
- *Simultaneity*—issues of texture, tension-release; also the formal and expressive implications of combinations of musical ideas.
- *Organization*—unity and variety, the role of notation, and the degree to which composers help listeners organize perception into aural structures that have unity and interest.
- *Play*—the variables influencing musical "good time."
- *Expression*—the feeling and subjectivity of music is a particular focus, particularly the many compositional variables responsible for different kinds of musical **affects**.
- *Style*—addressing "old" styles of music through sound compositions; everything from "Dixieland" to "romanticism" can be addressed through such lessons; differences of "style" between composers are also addressed.

Advantages of Sound Compositions for Students and Teachers

Learning Conditions

- Sound compositions are not limited by tonal theory—although tonal elements can be included, thus enhancing and extending *transfer* of learning.

- They are *summational*; they tend to summarize and synthesize past learning from a wide variety of other lessons in holistic ways.

- The different ways in which student composers solve the same or similar problems advance understanding and skill.

- The *individual constructivism* activated by sound compositions personalizes learning in functional, long-term ways.

- Similarly, *discovery* and *problem-based learning* are at stake, and these are a major focus of the middle school philosophy.

- These compositions are extremely *holistic* and thus educationally efficient: They always involve all three major types of musical praxis, composition, performance, and listening.

"Modern" and World Music

- Sound compositions explore the possibilities and satisfactions of **atonal** and contemporary musics.

- 'Tweens are especially receptive to such music because it is of and for their own time. This contemporary focus shows students how the past relates to the musical present and future.

- These compositions allow endless possibilities for exploring the musical practices of other musical cultures.

Readiness

- Students need no background of notation skills, yet learn to appreciate the role, contribution, and limitations of notation.

- When notation *is* made a focus, students "discover" (a) why notation exists, (b) what it is "good for," and (c) what can and cannot be adequately notated.

- Sound compositions are particularly advantageous in dealing with the predictably varied readiness levels of students—especially when several elementary schools feed into a middle school.

- Mainstreamed and other special students are also accommodated, as are transfer students. Even non-English speaking students can participate meaningfully.

- Musical "problems" undertaken by "real" composers can be explored through sound compositions, thus students become familiar with many of the most important techniques, practices, and possibilities of the standard literature.

- In fact, such musicianship develops as a condition of such lessons and has its natural application in listening lessons (Chapter 6).

Age-group relevance

- Aside from the musical rewards, the easily gained and tangible successes of sound compositions tend to reinforce students' *need for achievement.*
- Sound compositions also give greater scope to students' creative invention and spontaneity in immediately tangible ways.
- Results vary widely, yet all can be successful in differing ways. Such *variable results* model one of the prime attractions and benefits of musicking and are essentially humanizing in a school where uniformity and conformity are the rule.
- The process is almost always carried out in small groups. Cooperative learning is attractive to the social needs of this age group. Since developing personal responsibility is a focus of schools, general music teachers need to address this developmental need, not avoid it.
- With groups there are fewer compositions; thus all can be heard and directly compared. *Comparison* is a major variable in *social constructivism* and also influences each student's sense of accomplishment and thus self-concept.

Musical expression and satisfaction

- Contemporary graphic notation is used and when compared to such "real" models their work seems all the more of a realistic achievement to them.
- Not being limited by standard notation allows students to focus on expressive and formal elements with more attention and nuance than in their tonal compositions.
- Sound compositions are therefore often more musically "satisfying."

- *Quality*—exploring the variables that contribute to *musical quality* (as opposed to noise, sound effects, etc.), and to the perceptual delight and cognitive interest afforded by sound.
- *Technique*—composition, performance and listening techniques are "practiced" in every lesson; also, the realization that a poor performance can wreck a good composition is promoted.

Overlap of generative themes between melodic compositions and sound compositions contributes to transfer of learning. Elements of each kind of lesson can be used in relation to the other; for example, where tuneful motives are featured in a sound composition or where sound compositions "accompany" improvised melodies. Sound compositions should regularly be used as *readiness staging* for generative themes to be stressed in listening lessons, and listening lessons similarly provide readiness staging for generative themes addressed through sound compositions.

A Praxial View of Sound

Viewed praxially, sound becomes "music" when it is organized for particular human *uses*, such as listening, dancing, celebrating, worshiping. The social praxis for which sounds are created, selected, or organized is a major determinant, then, of what music "is" and thus is "good for." Similarly, and just as important, the "music" thus created shapes or creates the event in important ways that depend on the music; for example, the way music used in a wedding or ceremony gives "form" to the event.

Whether such a praxial use is mainly intellectual contemplation (e.g., "just listening"), or celebration or advertising or socializing of various kinds, to name a few typical uses, the sounds and silences involved derive a considerable part of their meaning from the **situatedness** of the moment. A certain organization of sounds in one situation has a meaning that is importantly different than those same sounds in another context. Thus, for example, a secular love song used in a church wedding takes on a religious meaning in that praxis.

This relationship between sound—its praxial use and situatedness—and "music" needs to constantly be stressed. In world musics, for example, the sounds available to the culture need to be related to the "goods" which music serves in that culture. To say that music and musical sound is *relative* to such situated use is, in the praxial view then, not the same as claiming that "anything goes." Rather, the *sounds chosen and their organization are relative to the praxial purposes and criteria they serve*, and these, in turn, vary between cultures!

On the other hand, however, sound has some universal traits. In addition to the acoustics of sound in relation to the physiology of hearing, some factors transcend cultural differences and give testimony to the worldwide appeal and cultural importance of sound made into "music." It is important to note, however, that in some cultures music is so wed to use that there is no word that distinguishes "music" from dance, worship, and celebration.

One important transcultural trait is that sound itself triggers certain affective and subjective *sensory* qualities that influence a certain state of consciousness by themselves. This **embodiment** of sound—and thus of music—is unique in comparison to the other senses and arts. This "sensuous," affective or expressive or pleasing quality of musical sound is sometimes loosely referred to as "aesthetic" with no particular harm. However such "sensibility" is different than the claims of orthodox aesthetic theories that musical meaning and value are absolutely good and that musical "works" are thus autonomous of time and place and "for their own sake."

Praxial theory, instead, stresses the situatedness of meaning and value and as thus being linked to the human needs of a particular time, place, and individual or collective praxis—only one possibility of which is "**just listening**" to music contemplatively. Thus sound, itself carries a certain value that is (a) unique to hearing, (b) unique to a sound source, and (c) unique to the social praxis involved. The sound as organized for its situated use, then, not the existence of a *score*, a titled work, or the like, is "the music." Music, therefore, is understood in terms of the total conditions of the situation and human use in and for which it exists.

Silence is a "frame" around sound, and provides its punctuation. Silence gains its own expressiveness by the sounds that precede and follow it. Silence gets its meaning, its "drama" or expressiveness, in conjunction with sound, and contributes to the expressiveness of sound. Silence, however, is only the comparative presence or absence of audible sound, which is relative to hearing capacity, acoustics, and the like.

Praxial theory stresses the special importance of focusing students' attention on the values and qualities of sound and silence and, in particular, on *how sound becomes "music."* All lessons also need to stress the praxial nature and conditions of sound that has become music. Whether listening, composing, or performing, it is useful to attend to what is loosely called "form" and "expression." Sound compositions really zero in on these by leading them to consider whether or how their compositions are "music" rather than just sound effects or collections of sounds.

SOUND COMPOSITIONS

BASIC SECTIONAL FORMAT

Early exploration and "experiments" focus on the expressive and sensuous qualities of sound by setting up very simple compositional problems that get students to select and organize contrasting sections or blocks of sound. Such sections do have a basic "part form" (e.g., AB, ABA), but "form" as such is not the concern at first.

The primary purpose of these very first sound compositions is to focus intentionality and thus attention on the sensuous, *expressive qualities* of sound and their value for music. The secondary focus is to model the basic process of sound composition, including its pleasures. Thus the sectional organization is, at first, a given. However, "sectionality" has considerable impact in later readiness staging when *formal organization* as such does become the primary focus. Then the previously informal presence of sections and their relationship becomes the primary focus.

Basic Strategy

1. Begin by **priming** students into identifying, for example, two decidedly contrasting moods they associate with two clearly contrasting common life situations. Begin with a graphic such as this on a transparency or the chalkboard:

SUMMER VACATION	SCHOOL IN SEPTEMBER
A	B

Example 5.1

2. From students, elicit a list of descriptions for each of the contrasting situations or "moods" and place these on the visual:

SUMMER VACATION	SCHOOL IN SEPTEMBER
A	B
fun	*sitting*
play	*dread*
free	*boring*
outdoors	*work*
running	*pain*

Example 5.2

3. As a transition to their composition, briefly discuss each "mood":

"What kind of music could we compose that is **expressive of** how those two situations feel?"

"If we were making a movie of you in those situations, what musical differences would be apparent in the sound track between sections?"

"Describe the kinds of sounds that could be used for the first section? For the second section?"

4. Jot an informal list of the *more likely suggestions* on a second copy of the first transparency (5.1). Keep the second transparency—such as in 5.3—to use again when they begin to compose and later for the discussion of student's compositions.

- As the students make suggestions, the teacher selects those having the most potential. The teacher should feel free to "translate" any one or group of similar suggestions into simpler or common terms: for example, "Let's call those three ideas, 'tense sounds.'"

5. After a transition (such as, "Let's see how well we can compose a sound track for such a movie scene") divide the class into groups of (usually) 3–5 and have them physically move to locations in the room where they are sufficiently separated from other groups.

- Limit the length of each section to, say, 20 seconds—thus a 40 second total length.

A	B
lively	*tense*
fast	*dragging*
energetic	*slow*
relaxed	*tired*

Example 5.3

6. Depending on vastly individual different circumstances (e.g., the availability of class-room instruments and other sound sources), focus groups on identifying the most likely sounds for the *first section*: one sound (instrument) per group member. For this and each subsequent management stage, be sure to announce appropriate time limits: for example, "You have 2 minutes to come up with your ideas for instruments for the first section of your movie sound track."

- When Orff and other classroom instruments and sound sources (e.g., wind chimes, brake drums, etc.) are easily *seen* on shelves, selection does not depend on memory.

- Students (particularly in middle school) can also use "instruments" they have with them: books, ring binders, pens and pencils, spiral bindings on their note-books, and so on, and other sounds within reach, such as chairs, radiators, waste-baskets, and the like (obviously with proper forewarning and cautions).

- Some teachers provide each group with a preselected collection of instruments that provides a range of possibilities from which to choose.

- The point of the activity is to have groups think about and hypothesize in ad-vance the 'instruments' they want to try, *not* to simply start experimenting wildly and blindly.

7. Now have them experiment and choose the instruments they actually want to use. Again, announce a very strict time limit.

- Remind them that the instruments they select must serve the contrasting music of *both* sections.

8. The next stage is: "You have 3 minutes to create and organize your A section so that it sounds the way you want to musically interpret those feelings."

   • Remind them that efforts must be at less than full volume if "we're going to be able to hear ourselves compose."

9. Before going on to the B section, have a hearing of the entire A section, then allow groups to improve anything they were not satisfied with.

10. Repeat stages 6–9 for the B section.

11. This is followed by a "dress rehearsal" where sections A and B are combined for the first time. Again, allow time for making refinements.

12. Perform all compositions.

    • Always have the class *applaud* for *each* performance!

    • Stress good listening habits and etiquette on the part of the "audience" because "you will want a quiet audience when you're performing."

    • Direct audience attention to the criteria developed earlier (see Example 5.3) as a basis for their listening and for the discussion.

    • *Always record* each sound composition as though doing a "take" in the recording studio! Announce the title of the composition and the number (group 1, 2, etc.) or name of the group (they choose a name), or of the group members. This makes it easier to locate for future auditing.

Recording increases the chances for a quiet audience and increases the desire to "perfect" the performance. It also demonstrates the problem of excessively soft or loud sounds.

Readiness Staging for Future Lessons

The basic strategy above is easily and profitably expanded in subsequent classes. Focus is still on the expressive and sensuous qualities of sound, but attention should be increasingly given to the selection, arrangement and combinations of sounds and sound patterns.

   • Focus, and thus learning, is structured by the *conditions* and *limitations* you pose—for example, in the example given, two contrasting sections, their titles, and the choices of instruments.

Often no more than two or three such basic "block" compositions are needed before for students become familiar with the basic format. Then focus can turn to the musical ideas students create and their combination or arrangement.

1. Once students are familiar with the basic format, increasing focus should be put on the *musical* effectiveness of the sounds chosen.

   • While sound quality is never taken for granted, it does stop being the primary focus and is considered instead in terms of its role in creating *unity* and *variety*. However, the occasion often arises when some really interesting or effective sound (or combination) should be noted by itself.

2. A sound source should be analyzed increasingly in terms of those qualities that make it an effective "musical instrument."

- Many interesting sounds cannot easily be repeated (e.g., ripping paper), for instance, others are messy (e.g., pitched water bottles). Discussions should focus on the criteria composers need to keep in mind for pragmatic sources of musical sound.

3. Sounds recorded from nature and prerecorded fragments of existing music and electronically generated and sampled sounds (including from electronic keyboards, such as background rhythms, etc.) can also be used. This adds a technical problem to the live performance, however.

4. As soon as possible, restage an existing AB composition as an ABA composition (e.g., summer, back to school, next vacation). Aside from adding length, it adds the problem of repeating the "A section" recognizably (ABA').

- This provides a natural readiness stage for the first ABA composition where students know from the first to compose their A section with that criterion in mind. (e.g., the two summers are different).

5. Use other typical patterns of sectional compositions.

- ABACA
- "Theme and variation" A^1 A^2 A^3 A^4
- A jazz improvisation on a given "theme."
- An AB composition where instead of the highest contrast being in the middle (A | B) it is at the very beginning and very end (A $\rightarrow$ B). Students then need to evolve gradually from beginning to end so that there is no clear end of the first section.

6. It is natural and quite easy to focus first on feelings and moods. However, other criteria should progressively serve as the "tangible" bases inspiring musical decisions for different sections:

- Programmatic themes (e.g., thunderstorm/calm)
- Colors (e.g., fiery red/funky blue)
- Textures (polyphonic "lines"/solid blocks of sonorities)
- Different TV shows or characters
- Adjectives other than moods or colors (e.g., bright/dark; light/heavy) that develop "discriminating" vocabulary for describing music
- Animals (e.g., lion/swan)
- Abstract ideas (e.g., pride/defeat)
- Time (e.g., 30 seconds that "sound fast" / 30 seconds that "sound slow")

7. *Transfer of learning* is increased when sound compositions are readiness staging for listening lessons and when listening lessons are readiness staging for sound compositions. For example:

- The "thunderstorm" section of Beethoven's *Symphony No. 6* ("The Pastoral") can provide readiness for a sound composition expressive of a thunderstorm that, in turn, can be followed by a listening lesson on the "storm" from Rossini's overture from *William Tell*.

- A sound composition with contrasting sections expressive of a lion and a swan serves neatly as the readiness staging for listening to the two sections by those names from Saint-Saëns' *Carnival of the Animals.*

- Two jazz or rock pieces, one "red-hot" and the other "laid-back blues" are chosen and analyzed for the musical qualities contributing to such descriptors. A sound composition follows where the problem is to achieve similar moods in a sound composition.

- Multicultural and world music recordings can also be related to sound compositions; for example, sound composition music suitable for Zen meditation or for different kinds of traditional dancing.

Nuts 'n' Bolts 'n' Cautions

1. Avoiding off-task behavior

    - *Priming* is central; it must focus student attention on the musical matters at stake and away from competing interests, such as socializing, showing off, and so on.

    - Transitions between stages must be smooth. Give directions for each stage TWICE, in *different words*: for example, "You have 3 minutes to create musical ideas that are expressive of a lion. *In other words*, the music should sound like a lion—how it moves or acts. Go!"

    - Announce time limits and stay reasonably close to them.

    - Have an audible and easily given **signal**. Several groups working at once create more noise and your signal must be easily heard. You need to "train" students to respond *instantly* to the signal or else it is useless! "Instantly" means *total silence, no movement and full attention within just a few seconds.*

    - If groups have trouble with a given stage, stop and deal with the issue as though the whole class has the same problem. All can profit from the extra clarification.

    - If something was left out or not anticipated, *stop and restage* accordingly. Don't try to "fake it out" to the end of the lesson.

    - The need for a *crescendo of interest* is best met by *frequently restating the priming strategy* as part of the directions for the next stage (e.g., "For the next step toward *our film score*, we need to . . .), and by frequently reminding the groups how much closer they are to the performance. Restating should also be used to lead wayward groups back on task.

2. Forming and locating groups in the classroom

    - Groups can be formed *randomly, preselected,* or according to *student choice.* An unpredictable but reasoned mixture of all three is recommended.

    - *Best friends* always want to work together but often socialize too much. However, when management staging controls socializing, groups of friends often produce the best efforts.

    - But since some students have no best friends in class, not all groups can be of close friends and *random groupings* puts students in contact with others in a cooperative working relationship.

> ➪ Counting off is the quickest way: If you have 25 students in class and want groups of, say, 4, count off by 6 and each group will have 4, and 1 group will contain 5.

> ➪ Be aware that this age can cruelly reject a classmate they do not like. Without fanfare, place such students in the most responsible or caring group. This will not solve the social problems involved, but it avoids hurtful comments and gets the lesson going smoothly so the student in question has some chance of getting involved.

- *Preformed* or *preselected groups* are made when a careful grouping of students is needed; for example, **jigsaw groups** and certain types of the other formats listed in the glossary under **cooperative learning**. Students in a group can be prelisted on the chalkboard.
- *Separation between groups needs to be as great as space permits.*
- In moving from normal seating into groups always remind students to move "quickly and *quietly.*"
- When preselected groups are involved (and a lesson begins at the start of the class period), chairs can already be pregrouped with the names of group members given on a card.

3. Group size

- Groups of three to no more than five students are ideal. Smaller than that and compositions tend not to be as interesting and satisfying. Groups of more than five tend to allow individuals to "get lost" doing nothing, to musically "hide," and their contribution gets swallowed up in anonymity.
- The number and size of groups is relative to (a) the physical size and layout of the classroom or adjacent spaces (e.g., instrument storage room, practice rooms) that can be used; (b) the size of the class and therefore the total number of performances that will result.

4. Classes not yet ready to work in cooperative groups (e.g., too young, too disorderly, etc.)

- Do the same composition problems *as an entire class*, with you as "group leader" and "conductor" of the whole process.
  - ➪ First attempts in fourth or fifth grade should proceed in this manner (then gradually introduce small working groups).
  - ➪ Management staging needs to be adjusted and the process takes much longer.

5. Choosing and returning instruments

- It is best when "instruments" are easily seen from anywhere in the room and are just as accessible.
- If instruments must be stored in a cabinet or room, or cannot be relocated in plain view or preselected by the teacher before the class arrives in the room, plan to avoid a traffic jam when students all go to the same location at once.
- When different groups want a single instrument at the same time, the teacher should ask about the intended use, and choose the group with the most crucial need (explaining the reasoning and—most importantly—suggesting other alternatives).

- After each performance, give each group in the *audience* 1 minute to discuss, as a group, the performance in terms of the criteria at stake. During this minute, performers put their instruments away quietly.

6. Noise levels

- Depending on class size, room size, and room acoustics, it is seldom possible (or in any case, seldom a good idea) to let students explore and practice at full volume. If need be, persistent violators must surrender their instruments and watch. Their assignment will be completed after school.
- When a class has a recurring problem with too much noise, restrict their compositional efforts to the same dynamic level (e.g., an entire piece that is soft; see example under 7. following) or limited range (no more than very soft to moderately soft).

7. Compositional criteria

- Teacher-set *criteria* do not *limit* students' creativity they *focus* it! A composer who composes a string quartet cannot use timpani or tuba. Attention gets focused, then, on remaining possibilities. When students are limited in, say, the use of only a soft volume (e.g.: "A sound composition lullaby to keep a man-eating lion asleep: wake him and you're dead!"), they explore and learn other variables. In this case, they are challenged to create interest (variety, contrast) by means other than dynamic contrast—or excess!
- Problem solving and decision making are controlled by the limitations set by the teacher. That is what **problem-based learning** is all about: The problem a teacher chooses directs and controls the learning potential of a lesson.
- Compositional problems should focus on *generative themes* that have high potential for transfer to other lessons and circumstances.

8. Sound composition performances

- Although the "look" of a performer is often relevant in "live" performances, students predictably try to make the *visual* aspects of performance suggest the expression the *music* should create. Accordingly, for example, they will express a happy mood more by their faces and bodies than from the sounds! To avoid this, have the audience face away from the "stage," or discuss the *recordings* after the visual clues have been forgotten.
- Each performance can be discussed immediately afterward, which is the most thorough way. But such discussions can get *repetitious*. Each successive discussion needs to create new interest yet address the same criteria.
- As an alternative, performances can all be given in succession, followed by an overall discussion. However, this relies progressively on memory, and that fades quickly.
- Some students will predictably "show off" while performing. There is no easy solution to this, aside from stressing repeatedly how such behavior detracts from the *musical results*.

9. Listening and discussion

- This management stage needs to be planned with almost as much care as a freestanding listening lesson (see Chapter 6), and should use those formats and guidelines.

- Aural analysis and **reflective abstraction** by students provides most of the lasting value of the lesson for most students. It is the major means by which students **cognitively strengthen** existing or proto-concepts (i.e., *assimilation*), alter old hypotheses (i.e., *accommodation*), and construct new ones (i.e., *constructivism*). Reflection develops and otherwise strengthens the **cognitive** criteria of musicianship that should influence their musical choices in the future, in and out of class.

- The remaining value for students is in the pleasures, satisfactions and sense of achievement.

10. Differences between "music" and "sound effects"

- *Never ignore this distinction*—particularly in connection with programmatic and other topics where imitating the sounds associated with the thing or event is tempting.

- One way to confront the problem directly (and early, beginning in grade 4) is through an AB composition where one section consists largely of sound effects associated with, say, an animal, and the other section deals with a musical interpretation of how the animal moves or how we feel as we think about or watch that animal.

- Another way is to always discuss whether the sound "quoted" life or was **"expressive of"** life.

11. Busy minds and bodies

- When students are actively exploring, composing and performing, the class can *look* disorderly when, in fact, it is *highly structured* by management staging. This needs to be made clear in advance to administrators. However, when hustle-bustle (however productive) becomes distracting to *students* (however few), it needs to be tamed!

NOTATED SOUND COMPOSITION FORMAT

These compositions teach students important lessons about notation—both traditional and contemporary—but also allow for longer or more controlled and detailed musical results.

Basic Strategy

The basic problem involves introducing the *need* for notation. Such a need comes into play when (a) a composition needs to be repeated (in whole or in part) with considerable accuracy; (b) or when others—rather than the composer(s)—will perform it.

1. Have students invent symbols (and/or borrow those that can be used from standard notation) for the sounds they are going to use.

- Younger or otherwise inexperienced students will often draw simplified pictures of the sound source: drawing of a hand for a clap, and the like. This is cumbersome and usually ineffective for complex musical ideas. Sooner than later require the use of abstract symbols of various kinds to represent particular sounds by constructing a "key" for the piece:

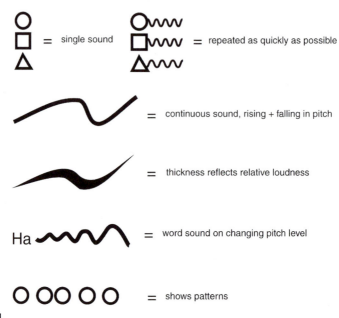

Example 5.4

- Compose a short notated sound composition of your own that uses examples of contemporary graphic notation and perform it as a class. Students will readily use the same symbols and similar variants they invent.

2. A "grid" format is often an efficient way to begin. The grid has two dimensions: down the left side is a provision for each performer, with different possibilities across the top.

   - One choice across the top can be a provision for "time blocks" (or "measures" as they should increasingly be called) and the relative timing per "block" or "measure."

     Groups perform by watching the second hand on a clock; "measures" are often best done in units of 5 seconds.

   - Another possibility is to number the "measures."

     These numbers represent a conductor's "cues." The *conductor* (usually a group member but sometimes the teacher) watches the clock or a wristwatch and gives a "cue" for the beginning of each new measure.

   - Eventually the numbers can organize "measures" whose length is controlled by various numbers of beats or counts, and the conductor can "beat" a pattern to at least coordinate the performance tempo.

This option is, of course, excellent for (a) *teaching standard beat patterns* so that every student can "lead" not only sound compositions but also recreational or church singing, and (b) for demonstrating the important *function of a conductor* in any large group performance using a score.

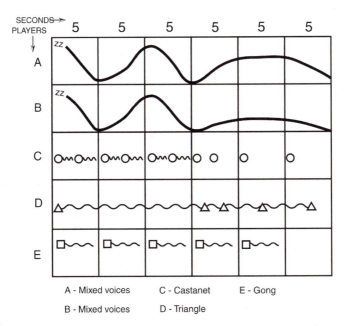

A - Mixed voices   C - Castanet   E - Gong

B - Mixed voices   D - Triangle

Example 5.5

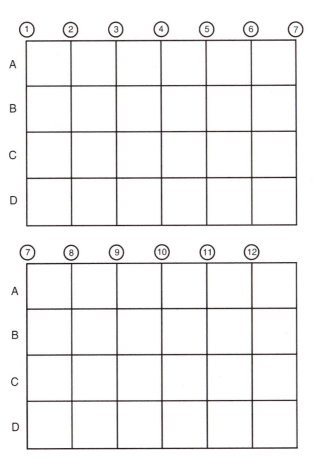

Example 5.6

3. Considerable extra staging is needed for student composers to practice performing their compositions to their liking.

Readiness Staging for Future Lessons

1. Notation is usually not an all-or-nothing criterion. It is best introduced as a part of an otherwise improvised composition.

2. Combine traditional notation and contemporary graphic notation in the same pieces.
   - Notating rhythmic and melodic features in sound compositions enhances skills with traditional notation while the sound composition format extends the expressive and formal possibilities.

3. Rhythm pieces, similar to those discussed in the previous chapter (pages 94–98), should be staged as notated sound compositions. "Measures" can be shown in a modified grid:

Example 5.7

4. When students are assigned to compose a piece that will be performed by another group, they learn the value of making the score as detailed as possible. Start with very simple attempts.
   - After groups have attempted to perform each other's scores, return the score to the composers for further improvement. Never allow them to demonstrate or describe the results! Prod them, instead, to notate their ideas as fully as they can.
   - If circumstances permit, have the composers *secretly* prerecord their piece so the recording and live performance can be compared.

Nuts 'n' Bolts 'n' Cautions

1. Notated sound compositions take a considerable amount of time. Thus management staging must be very detailed and tight.

2. Because they consume several class periods such projects will be few in number and should be chosen and planned carefully for maximum transfer and readiness staging.

3. When a lesson spans two or more class periods: (a) the most logical points in the management staging must be chosen to stop; (b) resuming always requires some recapitulation of students' work; and (c) the project needs to be *re-primed* to refocus intentionality.

4. Notated sound compositions require poster paper or large rolls of paper to use for the "scores," and marking pens, rulers, colored pencils, and so forth.

- An alternative is to compose on and perform from a transparency. This way the class can "follow the score."
- Either way, first efforts usually produce a very sloppy score. Thus, it is often useful to recopy the "final score"—if possible, outside of class time—for inclusion in portfolios.

SECTIONS WITHIN SECTIONS FORMAT

Using this format, large sections have their own subsections. These add complexity and interest throughout long compositions.

Basic Strategy

Early sound compositions stress broadly uniform sections.

1. Important gains are made, however, when composition problems are structured so that sections have subsections. For example:

A	B	A
a b a	c d	a b a

2. This poses the problem of *variety in unity*, where subsections provide variety and as a result interest, but within the unifying conditions of the overall section.

- Thus if A-B-A is predicated on "vacation time-school days-vacation time," the A and B sections themselves need two contrasting moods in the indicated arrangement.

Readiness Staging for Future Lessons

1. Musical techniques that can become the focus of such lessons are literally endless and are governed only by the teacher's own creativity and curricular intentions.

- Refer to examples from "real" compositions (especially prior listening lessons) to find ideas and models for students' efforts.

2. Given the importance of the "sonata principle" in Western art music, it is useful to predicate some sound compositions on that organizational strategy, if only as a means of preparing students to be able to *listen* intelligently to such music.

- Have students create a simplified "sonata form" where a' and b' "develop" the two contrasting "themes" from the Exposition and where the "themes" are restated at the end. The Exposition and Recapitulation can be notated (or practiced until recognizably similar) and the development treated improvisationally.

Exposition	Development	Recapitulation
A	B	A
a b	a' b'	a b

The "development" of musical ideas—the notion that a rich musical idea is capable of generating further (though related) musical interest—is an important feature in much of the world's music. Only by getting students to "develop" musical ideas compositionally (or improvisationally) can conceptual thinking begin to hypothesize what developing a musical idea *means* and *entails*, and why anyone would want to do it; that is, what "development" in music is "good for." Such learning will *cognitively strengthen* the role of this important musical resource in **subception** for all kinds of future listening. For example, improvisation in jazz and rock can be heard in terms of "developing" the given tune.

Nuts 'n' Bolts 'n' Cautions

1. Do not teach "form" for its own sake. Always relate the idea of "variety within unity" to *life* through the kinds of priming that serve as the focal point or "inspiration" for composition.

   - For example, in a sound composition that deals with "how time feels as it passes when you're waiting in the dentist's outer office versus being 'drilled' in the chair," an overall AB section form is natural. For the first section [A] pose a scenario for subsections; for example, "[a] As you are waiting, and are for example, bored, tense or fearful, a really good-looking guy or girl comes in the office to make an appointment and [b] your interest perks up while they are there; but they leave and [a] you return to being bored, tense, or fearful." A similar scenario for subsections can be suggested for the next section, (e.g., [a] drilling pain; [b] fainting), or students can be allowed to invent their own.

2. Similarly, avoid teaching "variety in unity" as an abstract concept. Focus on common life situations involving variety within unity is.

   - Architectural examples (good and bad, real, or fanciful) are useful points of departure for discussion, as is discussion of variety in unity in current clothing fashions (chosen from teen magazines).

THROUGH-COMPOSED MUSIC

Rather than repeating new verses to existing melodic material, *through-composed* music creates a perfect fit with the text. The problem posed in such compositions—with or without text—is again the need for variety within unity, but where unifying the everchanging musical ideas creates special challenge.

Basic Strategy

1. Begin with a narrative poem, short fable or popular tale.

2. Read it for, then with the class and discuss, for example, at least the following, making a *list* of each:

   - The overall "mood" or feeling of the story line or poem.
   - Sequential changes within the overall mood or feeling that would be expressive of the evolving parts of the story or poem.

3. Stage a sound composition lesson that begins by (a) selecting and organizing sounds that "fit" the overall interpretation chosen for the first list; then, focusing on the second list, (b) make suitable variations within the overall mood that are expressive of the narrative changes.

   - "Fit" or "time" these specific changes to coincide with the identified moments, but otherwise continue the overall mood or general impression throughout the reading of the poem or story.

4. "Accompany" the reading of the poem or story with the music and record it.

5. Listen, reflect, and discuss the various solutions and draw musicianship conclusions for subsequent use.

Readiness Staging for Future Lessons

1. Carry out another lesson along the same lines, but perform it *without* the story or poem being read aloud. Instead, as a kind of "score," one student (or the teacher) points to the words of the story to guide the performers in knowing where they are in the story line and, accordingly, when to do what. Record and discuss the musical interest of the composition without the words that inspired it.

   - All groups can compose to the same story line (thus providing comparisons of ideas and solutions) or to contrasting scenarios (thus generating a wider range of musical ideas and solutions).

2. The *melodrama principle* is at least familiar to students in connection with TV shows (particularly soap operas) and movies. It involves spoken text, dialogue, and action enhanced by musical accompaniment.

   - Play a recorded scene from a film or TV without its sound track; stage a sound composition "sound track" that is performed with the (still silent) video.
   - After all are heard, analyze the original sound track of the scene.

3. Similarly, *"sound tracks" for documentary videos*, real or imagined, usually depend on through-composed principles.

   - Make some videos of school scenes as a basis for composing; for example, a student (the "theme") in different class contexts (the "variety"). The same idea can be applied in sectional compositions: for example, a video of students reading silently that quickly switches to cafeteria bedlam.

4. *Improvised operas and musicals* can also be "composed" where the singing is done as *Sprechstimme* (literally, "sung" or intoned speech), accompanied by sound composition. Keep the plot (and correspondingly the length) simple and short.

   - Try to incorporate at least: (a) *recitatives* that tell the story and carry out dialogue; (b) *arias* or songs where main characters reflect on the action; (c) *choruses* or ensemble numbers that comment on the action or "moral" of the story.

Nuts 'n' Bolts 'n' Cautions

1. Plenty of time is needed for experimentation and improvement of ideas.

2. Students also need extra time to rehearse.

3. Sound effects are especially tempting here, (e.g., the happy character who "laughs" aloud in a real rather than a "musical" laugh) and should be restricted in advance.

4. These lessons can span several periods, thereby consuming much class time. Management staging must be very tight and segmented lessons (that continue over more than one class period) must be planned as described earlier in Chapter 3.

POLYPHONY AND COUNTERPOINT

Every class should create at least one composition where individual "layers" or "voices" of linear interest are combined, yet can be followed separately.

Basic Strategy

1. Sing or listen to a round or canon that has "up-beat" words.

   • Create new (humorous or otherwise relevant) words to an existing round and perform it with these new words.

2. Then, as a class, perform the words in rhythm as a two-part canon or round *without the tune*. Advanced and middle school students can perform three- and four-part rounds.

   • Instead of using a tuneless round, start with strongly rhythmic poems (e.g., 5.8) performed as rounds.

Spending Time

Time is something you can share,
and quickly comes and goes.
Yet when you think you have some time,
there's really nothing there!

Example 5.8

   • Focus especially on having each "voice" (part) *rehearse* the words with expressive, interpretative inflection, dynamics (mark them in), and in a crisply articulated and *uniform* rhythm, until all on that part are, in fact, one "voice."

   • Informally (i.e., without lecture) use the term "voice" in referring to the "parts," making it clear in context that a "voice" is a "line" and thus singular, regardless of how many "voices" are performing it. When words are dropped, the word "voice" will be applied to *nonvocal* contrapuntal "lines" as well.

3. Where classes have achieved musical **readiness**, repeat step 2. in small groups having two or three performers per "voice" (for example, a three-part round would require perhaps six to nine students per group).

   • Or have one half of the class perform for the other half, which acts as audience and "music critic."

4. Now, perform the poem's *word rhythm* (by ear) using instrumental, vocal, or body sounds.

   • Each part needs a distinctive timbre. Thus, one group might use metallic sounds for one "voice," wooden sounds for another, and drum sounds for the third— usually sounds that are very similar in pitch level, and so forth.

5. Practice and perform what are now entirely polyphonic instrumental pieces.

   • Expect the performance of any "voice" to observe the proper rhythm and dynamics.

6. Discuss and reflect on the pieces, especially in term of the musical differences, and benefits, of a polyphonic texture consisting of separate "lines" of interest.

Readiness Staging for Future Lessons

1. Repeat the basic strategy with a longer or more rhythmically complex set of words.

2. Move away altogether from words and prepare a strictly instrumental piece.

   • For example, after an appropriate prior lesson involving Dixieland jazz (i.e., as readiness staging), create an ABA piece where A = set "thematic" material (i.e., that is learned and repeated by all in the group) and B = simultaneous improvisation, finally returning to a "restatement" of A.

   • *Counterpoint*, as distinguished from polyphonic texture, will come into play to the degree that students can be brought to *interact intentionally* with the other parts.

3. Nothing can help students understand the fugue better than composing a *sound fugue*. However fugues need plenty of readiness staging because they combine several generative themes learned in other context.

   • Use a canon or round as the "exposition" of the fugue "subject" (as the main "theme" will now be called).

   • Then, "develop" (vary) the fugue subject and explore its musical potential within the polyphonic texture. Have performers (and audience alike) concentrate on the musical *interaction* of separate lines, not simply the fact that there *are* separate lines.

   • End with a *stretto* where the original fugue subject should "pile up"—usually a process involving shortening of rhythmic values: for example, progressively changing, say, from a feel of the quarter and half notes of the fugue subject to the eighth and sixteenth notes of the stretto. This "piling up" process should have the effect of a building up to a grand and exciting climax.

   • A teacher-composed example, or contemporary model encountered in a listening lesson, usually serves well as readiness staging.

Nuts 'n' Bolts 'n' Cautions

1. For fugues, aural attention should be focused on the interaction between separate "voices," and on the overall effect of "spinning out" or "developing" the fugue subject, not on the fugue as though it were a "sectional form" (which it is not!).

2. Similarly, avoid teaching "the fugue" as a generic or diagrammed "form." Rather, stress the fugue *process* (i.e., "fuguing") and the interest created by the interaction of intertwined lines.

MORE READINESS POSSIBILITIES

Each of the following is its own "basic" strategy that can be extended simply by changing the requirements to evermore challenging and therefore, realistic musical problems.

   1. *Timbre pieces* focus particularly on combinations of tone qualities.

- Since "orchestration" or "instrumentation" is a major variable in any musical setting, it is worth concentrating on in diverse ways. For example, dictating the use of assorted timbres (wooden, metallic, drums, vocal, and body sounds, such as clapping, tapping, etc.) requires unity while restricting a group to the use of, say, wooden sounds, puts premium on variety.
- One "instrument" no classroom should be without (if possible) is an old out-of-tune, "junk" piano (i.e., fit for the junk yard), with the insides exposed. This allows students to strum and strike the strings, use the pedal to "catch" other sounds and generally to explore the many reverberating possibilities of the soundboard.
- Electronic, computer generated, and recorded sounds can also be used.
- "Found sounds" (e.g., from objects such as pieces of metal, etc.) are particularly popular. In fact, one common way to "outfit" a class with a wide range of "instruments" of different timbres is to assign **homework** where students construct or bring in such instruments: for example, a piece of pipe hanging from a wire, keys suspended on strings and strummed like wind chimes, garbage can lids that function like gongs, and the like. Such a project is best "inspired" by first (a) modeling some possibilities and (b) discussing other important criteria, such as durability, portability, ease of use, and so on.

> The video of the percussion group "Stomp" cited in the previous chapter (page 97) is especially beneficial in inspiring interest in the musical potential of common objects. No unsafe "instruments" (e.g., sharp) should be allowed, however, and students should be reminded to get permission (from parents or whomever) before bringing anything to class. Objects that can become part of the classroom "collection" are ideal.

   2. *Idiomatic pieces* explore the musical potential or "idiom" that is unique to a particular instrument. Students who play instruments at home can be allowed to compose for those. Orff instruments (including drums) and guitars in the classroom are suitable for the remaining students.

- Assign students to explore *all* musical (sound) possibilities for an instrument, not just traditional uses.
- Teachers who are aware of the many ways in which contemporary composers use instruments for unusual sounds will have little trouble modeling some possibilities as a starting point for student exploration and composition.
- The intention is to model the satisfactions of compositions that students can do *by themselves* outside of school.

3. *Dance compositions* are highly rhythmic sound compositions composed especially for dance.

   - An "MTV" sound piece that just about anyone in the class could dance to, or a class "ballet" (modeled, for example, by a segment of Aaron Copland's *Billy the Kid*) can be composed.

   - Attention is directed first to the basic mood (or pattern of mood changes). Then suitable dance movements are planned and music composed for those movements. Put a premium on composing music that has strong interest of its own when heard without the dancing!

   - Videorecord performances, but discuss the recordings with a focus on the music, *not* the dancing.

   - Such dance composition-performances can be included as "interludes" between groups on concerts and assembly programs (the latter, e.g., when the middle school chorus puts on a program for elementary school students).

4. *Multicultural pieces* are sound compositions that borrow elements, influences, or musical materials and instruments from ethnic, folk, and world-music sources.

   - The challenge is to use these ideas in ways that *respect and honor the source*, but that use them in newly creative ways.

   - Make sure students demonstrate a competent understanding of the sources rather than just "messing around" with various *effects*.

     ⇨ Each group should work from a list of characteristics of the source music in question. Such lists should also be the criteria for discussing the compositions.

     ⇨ Lists of characteristics can be "researched" as **cooperative independent learning** projects, in or outside of class. Preliminary study should primarily focus on listening examples the teacher provides.

     ⇨ This study and making of lists can also be developed in connection with prior listening lessons, preferably in *students' own terms*.

   - Such a sound composition approach in connection with listening can be a useful way of investigating various world and ethnic musics in personally relevant and musical ways, rather than just "covering" a menu of them superficially in listening lessons.

   - In particular, have students investigate the music of their own ethnic background as a basis for such composition. Having students utilize musical influences from the local community *other than* of their own ethnic background is also valuable.

5. Most of the sound composition problems suggested in this chapter can be approached using computer software programs.

   - Given the compelling interest most students of this age have in computers, general music teachers should stay up-to-date about the availability of software—which changes faster than texts like this are printed. Even if the classroom doesn't have the capacity to offer instruction on computers, students should be advised of the existence of such software for their home use.

> At the beginning of the year, have students make lists of the type of audio and video equipment, electronic keyboards, pianos, other musical instruments, computers, MIDI, and so on they have at home, and of any musicking (e.g., in church, caroling, etc.) done by their family. Such lists are also useful in understanding the musical life of the home and therefore of the student's musical background.

- Students who have MIDI and other computer possibilities at home can be turned on to a lifetime of "recreational composing" (or might, in high school, develop a more focused career interest).

- Make available single copies of such software for student exploration after school, with the hope the interest will expand to that student's personal system at home. If possible, order such software as part of the school's "computer lab" budget rather than from the "music department" budget.

Nuts 'n' Bolts 'n' Cautions

1. These more advanced lessons consolidate and synthesize in holistic ways a great deal of knowledge and skill developed in the previous lessons. They also function as *benchmarks* or "mile posts" that, expressed as **rubrics**, help indicate and acknowledge student progress.

2. Timbre-based criteria are frequently posed as factors in just about any sound composition problem—primarily because (a) such criteria are central to any discussion of the *sensual and expressive* qualities of sound itself, and because (b) contrasts and similarities of timbre are always key ingredients in matters of *unity and variety*.

3. Don't overlook the many possibilities for approaching sound compositions as **independent study**, or **individualized learning**, or as a **learning station** lesson done by groups in sequence by the entire class.

CONCLUSION

Sound compositions are a major tool for developing *functional* and *independent musicianship*. They are holistic and thus efficient because they always involve students in composing, performing, and listening. They are exceptionally well suited to the need of this age group for *concrete* learning. And the tangibility of results effectively serves as the basis for progressively developing the *reflective abstraction* that leads to the formal operational thinking of adolescence. Such compositions easily progress along the natural lines of approximating evermore "realistic" contemporary musical models and thus progressively demonstrate "what music is" and "is good for."

These pieces build on the specific learning associated with tonal music composition, yet extend it to larger proportions (i.e., shape and control musical "time") and deal with complexities that, due to the problems of tonal harmony and notation, cannot otherwise be addressed "in action" in a general music class (e.g., jazz).

Most importantly, sound compositions have definite and direct transfer value that applies to any and all listening! This is one reason why the listening phase of such lessons is stressed, and why *readiness staging* for sound compositions should frequently involve *prior or follow-up listening lessons*.

CHAPTER SIX

THE LISTENING LABORATORY

INTRODUCTION: "JUST LISTENING"

Listening is the heart of music. However, listening as a performer is considerably different than the aural purposes and processes of audience members. Furthermore, the audience at a concert is engaged in a musical praxis that is notably different from, for example, the actions of indigenous 'audiences' around the world who are actually involved in and contribute to the musical rituals, celebrations, ceremonies, or worship at stake.

In similar ways, listening plays an active personal and social role in the lives of 'tweens and teens. Rarely do they just sit and listen to it, even at rock concerts. Instead of **"just listening,"** then, for teens music is a praxis that diverges from the *pure contemplation* associated with the last 150-plus years in the Eurocentric concert music traditions. Youth (and most adults) today are accustomed to doing "other things" while listening. Their listening is an accompaniment to these other pursuits and involves nowhere near the kind or degree of perceptual focus as listening attentively to concert music.

"Just Listening"

The 'ordinary listening' of youth and most adults is not unlike audience praxis prior to the nineteenth century when music was a praxis that served the socializing of royalty and aristocrats. Mozart's *divertimenti*, for example, were "divertissements" very similar in purpose to what today is called "cocktail" music. As the middle class acquired wealth and aspired to the "classy" stature of the aristocracy, the new aesthetic philosophy of the late Classical and early Romantic periods led to the rise of public concerts and thus to an increasing number of professional musicians. The rise and deification of the virtuoso is another result—including, the virtuoso conductor. Audiences at first socialized and critiqued the music while listening, but professional musicians increasingly demanded quiet, attentive audience etiquette.

Early audiences attended concerts to hear *new* music. But as instrumental pieces became longer, "form"—particularly the sonata principle—helped provide certain aural outlines that aided the audience to perceptually organize music they had not heard previously. Regardless of audience preferences, however, professional musicians increasingly selected music they found interesting to *play* and this meant playing "works" that audiences had already heard. "Discriminating listening," then, involved being attentive to the interpretive differences between one performance (and performer) and another. Listeners were increasingly expected to be familiar with "masterworks" that (according to the musicians) deserved to be interpreted and, as a result required and satisfied "good taste" and connoisseurship.

Composers at this time were influenced by what today is called **modernism**: the eighteenth-century idea that science and rational thought would promote *progress* and the general advancement of life. With Darwin's "theory of evolution," fine art came to be seen as "evolving" historically from the praxial music of early centuries (e.g., masses, motets, dance suites, aristocratic uses, etc.) according to the newly-influential aesthetic theory that had been invented as the "science" of the "Beautiful." Romantic era ideals of "creativity" also led to the idea that the composer was a God-like figure; a genius in whose hands "creativity" took on metaphysical dimensions and meaning.

A result was the idea of "great music" and the standard repertory of supposedly timeless masterworks called the **canon**. The modern discipline of music history also arose at this time. It analyzed music as evolving from its early praxial roots to a purely aesthetic (contemplative) fine art that was listened to and performed *for its own sake*. Musical "rationality"—the theoretical, conceptual, and intellectual capacity involved in composing, performing, and listening to the canon of classics—became increasingly demanding as compositions became even longer and more complex in the later nineteenth century. Tonality and meter were enriched by leaps and bounds. New instruments were invented and existing ones improved. And virtuosity in both composition and performing outpaced the ability of even talented amateurs to approximate the competence of the professional.

Contemporary Listening

Such "progress" had some unfortunate consequences, however. One is that modern audiences (and many professional musicians) resist new music and prefer the familiar "classics." Another unfortunate consequence has been the demise of amateur performance. As late as the early twentieth century, making music in the home as a family or recreational activity was still a central feature of middle-class life. However, the canon demanded virtuosity that most people had neither the time nor energy to acquire. The consequence has been audiences of listeners who rarely make music any longer.

The advent of radio and recordings advanced this tendency. Listening to recordings also changed the process of "just listening." Recordings people own become so thoroughly familiar that musical form no longer is needed to organize aural perception, and one particular interpretation becomes ingrained unless recordings by different artists are purchased—a costly alternative to owning one recording of a variety of pieces.

Concerts of all kinds are also expensive and available mainly in cities. Increasingly, only the affluent can reasonably avail themselves of "live" performances. And aside from outpricing what the average person can spend on a single event, concerts of the classical canon also have an "exclusiveness" associated with dress and etiquette that are uncomfortable for many people. They spend their hard-earned money on recordings of the "classics" of favorite genres that they listen to over and over in the convenience of their homes.

Everyday Listening

The musical, social, and economic developments that have led to the "commodification" of music—a "consumer culture" of music and a "music industry" of recordings and recording artists in all genres—have brought profound changes to the listening habits of most people. The average individual who listens at home is typically *not* "just listening" while staring at the speakers. Listening, then, has become connected with adding **"good time"** to other activities. And, of course, it is also a major ingredient for social events like weddings, parades, worship, and ceremonies of all kinds.

That self-proclaimed "music lovers" today are rarely "just listening" is not being recommended here! There is certainly reason to be concerned that the decline of amateur performing means that listeners no longer have criteria for listening that used to be promoted through their amateur participation. Hence critics—and many general music teachers—believe that students need to be taught "music appreciation" in order to aesthetically contemplate "good music." However, the informality or effortlessness of contemporary listening habits is, in large part, a result of the widespread presence in life of music from recordings and the media; these habits have become so pervasive they cannot easily be changed.

Cultural Dynamics

'Tweens and teens, for example, resist being coerced to "just listen" to the "good music" recommended by adult authorities. Instead, teen music has come to define teen culture. Therefore, they *use* it to rebel against (or at least test) dominant social values. Teens further establish their identity in terms of membership in "taste groups" that form around certain performers or genres. As a result, unlike most academic studies, in their musical classes they often actively resist what social theorists call *enculturation*—the process by which a *dominant* culture attempts to convert a less powerful cultural group to its values. Enculturation often results in tension; in this case, between the cultures of "youth music," other "popular" musics and so-called "good music"—the "classics" of any genre.

Such tensions are reflected, as well, between socioeconomic groups and are even more evident in pluralistic societies where multiple cultures (thus *multi*culture) are the rule not the exception. Not only does the minority (or even "lower class") culture risk being acculturated by the dominant (or "classy") culture; the dominant culture also sees itself as threatened by the cultures it seeks to influence—for example, complaints about "pop" musics in school classes and concerts! In pluralistic societies, assimilation and acculturation are typically resisted (e.g., Afro-centrism). Some minority groups compete with the dominant culture—or even with other minority cultures—to get "their" music into the schools. And, of course, most of the musics favored by such groups are intended for social use rather than "just listening."

Because music features prominently in any effort to achieve the pluralism advanced by advocates of multiculturalism, the public school has become the "trenches" of this cultural battleground. Not only do racial, ethnic, and gender issues come into play, but the musical subcultures of geographical regions are also involved. All these issues lead to the *politics of music curriculum*—that is, the question of *whose music* to include in instruction. Subsequently, general music classes involve social tensions in ways that many "academic" classes do not.

LISTENING IN THE GENERAL MUSIC CLASS

Listening is the most accessible of all forms of musical praxis, yet listening lessons face a host of special challenges and considerations.

1. Pre- and early teens are simply not used to just sitting quietly, listening attentively for abstract, cerebral, and autonomous meanings. Even if convinced that such meaning exists, or is of value, they naturally tend to group it along with all the other "merely academic" subjects—of little interest to them—that schools and teachers nonetheless think are important.

   - Students need to be shown how the social (i.e., praxial) dimensions of listening to music are personally meaningful in ways they cannot at first imagine.

     Stressing the personal and social **affordances** of any musical praxis should be a key factor in advancing "just listening" as its own praxis. Music's "meanings" and "goods" are social, even when made or listened to alone. Individuals are "socially constructed" beings and the music of any social group is a major means by which culture shapes the individual being. Music cannot "communicate" personal subjective life and feeling directly the way language does, but it is typically regarded to be **"expressive of "** life. With this in mind, listening lessons with pre- and early teens should stress the connection of "just listening" to the heightened experience of everyday life.

Given their interest in self-actualization, the connection between the social role of music and students' inner lives can be explored favorably to the benefit of both. Because of their interest in the solitary Self in relation to the social Self, the endless ways music reflects social and therefore shared meanings should be a primary focus. Thus, for example, that music can be relaxing versus energizing for an individual is an **affordance**—a possibility—conditioned as much by social as by individual variables.

Social Uses of Music to be Emphasized as Generative Themes:

- *Play, Enjoyment, Entertainment*: Music serves leisure time in important ways—including, for some, the rarefied pleasures of refined taste and intellectual interest.
- *Personal and Cultural Identity:* Music brings people together but also serves the individual—sometimes in antisocial ways (e.g., music as rebellion against dominant norms).
- *Communication and Expression*: There can be no question that people report experiencing feelings, ideas, and other subjective meanings in connection with music.
- *Political, Social, and Ideological*: Music reflects political and social differences and is used to advance political, social, and nationalist views and agendas.
- *Pragmatic*: These include commercial functions and economic uses (e.g., music industry), didactic uses (e.g., teaching), and praxes such as work songs, lullabies, love songs, and "mood music" (i.e., used personally to alter mood, or socially to create a mood; e.g., for dinner or cocktail gatherings), and so on.
- *Ritual, Celebration, and Worship*: Music's most common praxial function is to "make special" a long list of common social practices.
- *Physical Response and Activity*: Dancing and many other forms of physical activity (e.g., aerobics) rely on music.
- *Therapy*: The therapeutic values of music have been known in Western culture since at least the Greeks, and are present in most indigenous cultures.
- *Everyday Uses*: These, too numerous to list, involve everything from film and TV music, music that "accompanies" everyday activities (e.g., while ironing clothes, jogging), listening while driving the car, and the like.

  The purpose is not to teach students this *list* of music's functions but to *model the "goods" of these uses* and accordingly to demonstrate the relevance of many of these kinds of musical praxis for their own lives.

2. Students are apt to assume that listening is a passive matter of "receiving" musical meaning that is "in" the music, or of needing to "decipher" it, as though hidden in some kind of code. Do not reinforce this mistaken tendency by treating the "goodness" and meaning of music as abstractly pre-given in the score and thus as autonomous of time, place, use, and user.

> • Instead, students need to be helped to understand listening as an active and "creative" praxis by which they construct their own responses, values and meanings!
>
> The interest and meaning of music is not built-in the music any more than a typical sentence has a fixed meaning. Language, even an individual word, gets its meanings from how and why it is used in particular situations. And just as the mind constructs concepts from experience, it also constructs meaning from musical sounds in terms of both personal factors (particularly the user's *intentionality*, personal *life-world* and musical background) and sociocultural variables (particularly the praxis at stake and even the physical and acoustical setting).

Musical meaning is not something that music "has" but something that it "does" for situations and individuals. It "makes special" the social praxis at stake, creates "good time" for the individuals who occasion the praxis and otherwise shapes their "being" at the moment.

The "problem" presented in a listening lesson, then, is not a matter of "finding" meaning that is already there, "in" the music. Rather, listening is a "doing"—the mental "in-forming" (inward "forming") of sound by aural sensibility, conception, feeling, and so on, as guided by intentionality. "Doing" listening, then, is an action-oriented process of *meaning making*. It is a process by which the individual brings musical values into being, in this present situation, as the "good time" of this moment. However, the grammar, syntax, and uses of music meaning are, like verbal language, social constructions and thus they involve social criteria and implications that rule out the possibility that "anything goes."

---

3. Some cultural clash or tension between the music of *any* culture and youth culture is likely. Imposing "good music" on them is seen as reducing their autonomy, sense of identity, and freedom to choose. Such teaching is typically resisted by either open rebellion and rejection or by subversively "going along" while "tuning out" the music.

> • Students' current tastes and interests should be accepted as valid, but not as the only options available to them.
>
> General music class should not be seen as rejecting "their music" in favor of acculturating them with "good music." Furthermore, since they rarely appreciate adults (mis)appropriating "their music," it is usually not wise for a teacher to try to teach them "their" teen music from a technical point of view.

When listening is treated as a matter of exploration of new musical possibilities, not as the imposition of a dominant and domineering institution, middle school students will adopt more open-minded and positive attitudes toward varied listening choices and tastes.

General music class should increase the students' awareness of musical options in addition to their current preferences. In particular, a major goal of instruction should be to *sample a wide variety of musics of potential interest* that students would not otherwise encounter informally in the home or through the media! When such music is explored (not imposed), students often discover interests and develop tastes that would not have been possible without general music class.

4. Students who have no experience with, or models for, "just listening" have little way of knowing what focused listening is "good for." It is not just that they do not know *how* to listen: They do not know *why* people find it valuable.

   • General music class, then, needs to help students know why and how to listen when certain different kinds of musical praxis are involved.

   This means being able to take into consideration the *situated particulars* of any praxis—that is, the contexts and uses that shape musical meaning. For example, listening to sacred music in church and in a secular concert involve different use-intentions and conditions. Similarly, when concert music is also used in film, each different *use* involves a unique praxis and offers diverse musical potentials. Listening cannot help but be affected by such variables.

The type of listening required is also influenced by the praxis. For example, listening as a jazz band "reads" the "chart" is different than the kind of listening done during the improvised solos. Various multicultural and world musics also require different ways of, and reasons for, listening. Rather than presume to "cover" superficially the music of this or that culture or praxis, the general music class instead models what listening is "good for" and illustrates when it is best to listen in one way as opposed to others.

5. This also raises the problem of deciding which music from which cultures is worth addressing in a curriculum. In general, this is a problem of "breadth" versus "depth." But, more specifically, there is always more that can be taught than there is time or resources to teach it *effectively*—meaning, in a way and to an effective degree that makes a functional difference in students' musical lives.

   • A general music program predicated on praxis will explore the many similar ways in which music is used across different cultures rather than present a superficial survey of musical cultures, styles, eras, or genres.

   Depending on the teacher's own background and the available resources, all common uses of music can be modeled by examples of ethnic and world musics—most of which also have present value and interest in contemporary music that is worth listening to in its own right.

Isolated lessons cannot do justice to the music of a culture. Even studying multiple examples from a culture still barely scratches the surface and takes much of the limited time available. Classes should focus instead on *how musicking serves the same (or similar) basic needs across various cultures.* Then music becomes a *lens* for viewing human nature, a *mirror* that reflects human qualities, and a *lamp* that illuminates important particulars of the universal human condition.

6. Given the "casual" approach to listening that is natural for students, the general music teacher needs to have students focus intentionally and intently on the "innards" of music. Otherwise they are so fixated on the forest that they miss attending to the delights of individual features.

- Increasing the capacity and accuracy of aural discrimination enables students to simply hear more features and thus achieve enriched results.

  Rather than assume to force "good music" down their throats, representative examples of successful music in a variety of types and styles from a range of cultural contexts should be selected that use music in the ways suggested under point 5. With this breadth, the "depth" or refinement addressed produces an improvement in perceptual and conceptual processing or acuity.

Students will necessarily miss the *nuances* of musicianship needed to be fluent in a particular musical culture. Such fluency takes more study and practice than time allows in any general music class curriculum. But *functional aural perception* can be greatly improved in the general music class by listening for, say, polymetric structures in several different musics. Musicians highly trained in one kind of music will hear *more* in connection with just about any music.* This empowers students to be able to "get more out of" just about *any* listening situation and thus to choose and pursue their "tastes" with more discrimination to details. With this background and interest, they can meaningfully become an *aficionado* of a particular music.

---

*Sometimes, however, training in one hampers listening in another. For instance, developing an "ear" for the Western chromatic scale makes it more difficult to listen to microtonal musics predicated on dividing the octave into more than twelve semitones.

7. The final challenge is simply to get students to sit still, be quiet, and to focus all of their aural attention on the music. In other subjects, students may "pay attention" but still may not be much *interested* in what they only *understand* better. This kind of result in general music class falls short of Action Learning.

- The general music class needs to model the option of "just listening" in connection with the kinds of music that are particularly "good for" that use.

  One prime way in which this is accomplished is to build on the interest they have in listening to their own and classmates' compositions—particularly sound compositions! This intentionality can transfer to listening lessons that are predicated on the same or similar variables that students have addressed in their own compositions. Similarly, music they relate to and enjoy serves as a starting point for "spiraling" up (see **spiral curriculum**) to more complex musics. For example the "blues" of R & B, or the rhythmic and improvisatory aspects of rap can be expanded in the direction of jazz.

The basic challenge for the general music teacher is to carefully select music for listening in terms of its suitability: (a) for the characteristics of the age group and, particularly, (b) for the potential that students might become interested enough to choose to listen to it outside of class—actually listen to it!

Aural focal attention needs to be directed toward aspects students would otherwise not notice and thus would not appreciate. They need to be helped, then, to create the kind and degree of personal meaning from listening that inclines them to see music as "good for" listening—all by its self! This is more likely when *listening is stressed in connection with all lessons.* Even if not "just listening," students' heightened perceptual skills allow them to hear more from all kinds of listening.

BASICS OF LISTENING LESSONS

The reasons for listening are so multiple and varied that listening lessons require a wide variety of formats. All should involve, however, certain basic principles.

1. **Directed listening**—All listening must direct **focal awareness** toward certain musical features or effects. The teacher cannot simply say "listen" and expect students to attend to features that they are unaccustomed to focusing on (or that they do not even know exist).

    - Directed listening develops *selective attention* by focusing perception on the particular musicianship variables the listening selection has been chosen to advance. Directed listening, then, is a particular type of **priming**. It depends on students *intending to focus their aural attention* in a way that is not at first "natural" for them.

    - Directions for listening should relate to the *generative themes* described earlier, individually and in certain combination or succession.

    - Directions that focus on too many or too few musical features are confusing or unchallenging.

    - Directions that result in **high order** responses are subjective or open-ended and have no single correct response—although a response can be more or less adequate: For example, a high order question might ask about, say, tension at a certain point. An answer such as "I thought it felt tense because the trumpet was blasting so loud" is not adequate if the instrument was a trombone. However, the association of "tension" with "loud" can still be appropriate. **Low order** directions point to objective features and have correct answers: for example, "What instrument plays the theme?

    - Too many low order directions make a listening lesson seem like a "test" and, in any case, do not permit discussion.

- Too many high order directions make it seem like any answer is as good as another. Students rightly wonder, then, about the point of the lesson.
- Depending on the piece, a 60/40 percent balance between high and low order directions is often best.
- High order responses *always* need to be probed for low order bases (e.g., the trumpet versus trombone distinction in the previous discussion). Thus a high order response is judged appropriate not by agreeing with the teacher or the class, but in terms of the accuracy of the perception that supports it (or not) it and that is thus revealed in the discussion.

2. **Attensive** qualities—These are the features that are most likely to "stick out" for listeners. This term from perceptual psychology combines the meanings of *atten*tion and in*tensive*. Thus attensive qualities are intensive enough to be attention grabbing once they are pointed out.

   - Attensive qualities vary according to the observer's interests, experiences, and intentionality. For example, a French horn part will be more naturally attensive to people who play that instrument.
   - Some general qualities—for example, "its got a good beat" or a "pretty tune"—will be naturally attensive to many listeners. These and most culturally "taken-for-granted" qualities are what students are likely to "hear" without much instruction.

     ➪ The point of listening lessons is to go beyond such general observations.
   - Music that has "striking" features and contrasts tends to be more naturally attensive and is more suitable. Music that is very subtle, understated, and lacking conspicuous contrasts—that is, "impressionistic" music of any kind—fails to have the kind of clear-cut attensive qualities this age group needs. Such subtlety is attensive only for experienced listeners who are already attracted to such nuance.
   - Since even avid concertgoers can find their attention wandering, listening lessons are thus most successful when student attention is directed to either attensive qualities that (a) are spaced evenly with no long "boring" interludes in between, or (b) are at stake throughout the entire piece (e.g., listening throughout for changes in levels of tension).

     ➪ Some combination of both kinds of direction is typical and desirable.
   - The specific point of any listening lesson is to focus on features in the music that will become *more attensive* for listeners in the future. By getting students to listen "for" these features, the teacher helps the perceptual skill *transfer* to other listening, in and out of school.

3. **Cognitive strengthening**—Conception and perception interact! What we *know* influences what we *perceive*, how we *feel* about it and, thus, how we *respond* to it. To influence and improve perception, therefore, it is necessary to help students learn of musical features that are worth perceiving.

   - Occasionally cognitive strengthening is instant: The teacher directs students to a feature that will be more attensive for students in the future.
   - Most typically, however, cognitive strengthening is like muscle strengthening: it requires exercise (i.e., repeated practice!).

- In particular, because musical features of a certain kind can vary so drastically according to the praxis, the cognitive strengthening of attensive qualities is particularly dependent on transfer of learning from one situation to new and different situations—that is, a *spiral curriculum*.

4. **Subception** and **subattentional** processing—The mind is perfectly capable of, in computer jargon, "parallel processing" of different, even competing, sources. We typically "do" several things at once without conscious attention to each. Therefore we can drive a car while listening to music or conversing. Subattentional processes of the brain somehow monitor our driving without it being in focal attention or awareness (at least while things are routine). Some aspects subception are so subattentional (or are so routinized) that they are not even in our **subsidiary attention**—unless something changes the "background" of subception to the "foreground" of cognitive focus; for example, an animal darts in front of the car.

   - Music depends heavily on this "background" of subattentional processes, especially as it become more and more complex. Counterpoint and polyphony are good examples of the process at work, but so are the interaction of melody and its rhythm, or melody and its harmony. Teaching "elements of music" in lockstep isolation misses this **synergy**.

   - Subception is necessarily holistic and thus involves complex interaction of parts and wholes. **Atomistic** teaching works against such holistic learning and application.

   - Subattentional processes are **tacit**, and as a result cannot be verbalized in the fullness of their interactive complexity.

   - Similarly, they are praxial: The only way to "understand" such matters is by "doing" them.

   - Generally, then, attensive qualities that have been cognitively strengthened will become progressively operative and influential in musical perception via subception.

   - Depending on the listener and the situatedness of the praxis, focal attention typically shifts rapidly in time from one attensive quality to the next; for example, from the tune to its rhythm or harmonies, or to the effects of orchestration and dynamics.

   - At any moment, features and qualities not in the foreground of attention provide the richness of the holistic musical background against which the attensive quality of the moment is highlighted—only to have another quality take precedence while the previous attensive focus withdraws to subception.

5. **Constructivism**—Listening is an active process of constructing a response, not of passively receiving a set or given meaning. Mental *action* is required to "in-form" (inwardly construct) a musical response. Listening is not a matter of the stimulus creating or "communicating" a set response.

   - *Listening* then, can be distinguished from simply *hearing*. The former is an active process of aurally reaching out—of listening *for* something—and then processing the results in ways that are determined by that intention. Hearing is correspondingly passive—although sometimes musicians use the word "hearing" as a noun form to refer to an overall occasion (e.g., "On second 'hearing,' I was more interested.") or to refer to the *results* of listening (e.g., "I listened carefully and 'heard' more detail").

- The type of mental action required by listening differs according to the praxis. Listening while performing, for example, involves different mental *action patterns* than when "just listening" as an audience member, and listening to a live jazz improvisation involves different processes than, for example, listening again and again to a recorded improvisation.

- Because students are physically inactive when "just listening," mental activity must compensate.

6. Repeated listening—While there are occasions where a teacher might play something once as an example, these are not listening lessons as such. In order to make certain qualities more *attensive*, and to *cognitively strengthen* them through *active mental processing*, students need to listen to a piece several times.

   - *Listening a minimum of three times is recommended.* The first time students become acquainted with the musical "whole"—in terms of the selective attention that has been evoked through the teacher's directions.

   - With this holistic impression in mind, the second time involves "listening *for*" the attensive qualities to which the teacher's directions point; that is, students really "stretch" their aural discrimination by focusing on the "parts" or details.

   - The third time they "listen *to*" the "parts" back in holistic context. With the synthesizing function of subception, the "parts" isolated in the second listening function in a more naturally appealing and rewarding way.

7. Length—The length of the listening selection is crucial. Long pieces allow too much time for student's minds to wander.

   - Long pieces—for purposes of this text, anything over 3–4 minutes—are either (a) too complex in their frequently changing attensive qualities or (b) are "boring" because the attensive qualities are too subtle or too few for the present perceptual and conceptual interest and capacity of this age group.

   - With three listenings, long pieces also make for very long lessons. A 5 minutes piece will require 15 minutes just of playing time, exclusive of the priming, directions and discussion.

     ⇨ Whole period listening lessons are extremely risky!

   - Some longer pieces—especially if they have words—can sustain student interest if the attensive qualities are *clear, interesting,* and *frequent.*

8. Overt responses—Aesthetic approaches to "music appreciation" seek to improve aesthetic responding. However, by definition, aesthetic responses are private. Consequently, they cannot be observed and the teacher has no evidence that aesthetic experience has been improved (or even occurred)! In contrast, because the praxial approach simply attempts *to improve aural perception*, enhanced discrimination *must* be observed in order to evaluate teaching and learning!

   - Overt indicators are used by the teacher as direct evidence of low order responding and to infer the status of high order responses. (Review the last point under 1.—directed listening, page 141).

- Such observable responses are not, however, intended to model that "just listening" is *supposed* to have overt consequences. Such actions are sometimes the case, as in toe tapping. Overt responses in class are only tools to externalize responses so they can be evaluated and discussed. They also add tangibility that contributes to cognitive strengthening and **reflective abstraction**.

- In cases where uses of listening other than "just listening" are presented for example, dancing, marching—overt actions are perfectly acceptable.

- However, the general music teacher has a special responsibility to nurture "just listening" as an alternative to the participative listening that is the typical student's usual practice. Thus, an effective balance needs to struck between the two, making sure in particular that "just listening" is not shortchanged just because, from the instructional point of view, it is predictably more difficult to achieve in class.

9. Discussion—Each stage of a listening lesson (of which, we have already seen in no. 6, there are three) has certain requirements and purposes.

  - After listening once, the teacher should address any confusion concerning what students are supposed to be listening *for* and how they are expected to overtly respond.

  - After the second listening, however, all the directions or "questions" the teacher has posed and primed for students' attention, need to be discussed *individually* and *in depth*.

    ⇨ Elicit answers or responses from *several* students for *each* direction.

    ⇨ For a given lesson, eventually involve *all* students in such discussion and reflection.

    ⇨ Lessons predicated only on *low order* responses leave little possibility for discussion.

    ⇨ Directions that focus only on *high order* responses can be endlessly circular unless they are based in part on low order cognition. In either case, "wrong" low order responses or bases for high order responses need to be corrected and clarified (see point 1. covered earlier).

    ⇨ Try to inspire new interest for the third listening. For example, "Some said this section was light and happy, but others thought it was bright and intense: This time let's try to hear it from the other point of view and we'll discuss how and why someone else might hear it that way."

  - The final (usually the third) listening also requires discussion and reflection that arise in connection with any loose ends, changes of perspective, or the like. It is especially good to have the students draw conclusions in their own terms.

10. **Readiness staging** and **transfer**—A lesson should always relate to past and future listening, composition, and performance lessons.

  - Though listed as the final point here, readiness staging is actually the teacher's *first* concern in all planning! It considers *why* the attensive qualities under consideration are musically and educationally important to begin with and, thus, *how* they build on or lead to other lessons.

- While listening lessons should not be treated only as a means to other ends, students *do* need to be told how the attensive qualities the teacher has in mind build on earlier lessons. This enhances transfer of learning.
- The potential for transfer of learning to life outside of class should always be made clear. This should be done not in terms of "Someday, when you're an adult, you'll want to use this . . . ," but through references to "When you're listening at home . . . ."

BASIC LESSON FORMAT

This protocol incorporates the prior ten basics and places them in a more easily grasped context in relation to each other.

1. Choose an appropriate selection.

- Such a choice represents the teacher's *hypothesis* concerning the attensive qualities of the music: (a) that students will find the music to be noteworthy and at least interesting; (b) that the hypothesized attensive qualities will be cognitively strengthened and lead to other lessons having a similar focus; (c) that the hypothesized attensive qualities are clear and distinct, yet subtle enough to challenge and therefore advance perception and cognition; (d) and that suitable directions can be formulated that effectively invite and guide students' attention *throughout* the piece
- The lesson, in part, is a "test" or "experiment" of the above four-part hypothesis. Failure of any part will produce some problems. Sometimes (a), (b), or (c) can simply be faulty judgments. However, weaknesses with (d) alone can doom an otherwise appropriate selection and should be improved for future use.

2. Next, **prime** students to focus on the attensive qualities in question. (Review priming on pages 55–57)

- Even assuming the four hypotheses above are effectively conceived, a listening lesson will not usually even stand a chance of succeeding if students do not have effective intentionality for "just listening."
- In general, student intentionality is primed most effectively when the music is related imaginatively to (a) their own lives (especially their 'feeling' lives) or (b) "What if . . ." kinds of real-life possibilities.

---

(1) For example, "If this music was expressive of a common experience in your life, what kinds of feelings would be involved? *Let's see how well* the music 'fits' or 'feels like' this kind of common time and whether musical feelings are different or any more 'special' than they are in ordinary experience."

(2) For example, "What if this music was being considered for its commercial possibilities? *Let's listen to it as if* we were employed by a record company and rating certain features of the music according to how easy they are to hear and how interesting they are."

Note: The second statement italicized in each example is a *transition* to the next stage of a listening lesson.

3. The questions and directions are given—according to the formats suggested later in this chapter—and previewed to make sure students understand what they are supposed to be trying to do.

   • Directions often take the form of questions that evoke a verbal reply. They can also direct students to "do" something, such as to conduct the meter or to draw something.

   • Directions are either (a) *sequential*, so that the first refers to an attensive quality right at the beginning of the piece, and the last to one at the end; or they are (b) *holistic* and should be placed first so students can monitor them throughout the piece. Questions that reflect on the whole piece are obviously given last.

4. During the first listening, students are usually directed to "just listen" and not yet "do" or "answer" anything.

   • This is just an "overview" and, in part "tests" how well they understand the directions.

Not only do *students* not talk while listening: As a rule the *teacher* should avoid interrupting listening by talking over the music!

---

5. After the first listening, discuss any questions or confusions about the directions and what students are supposed to be doing.

   • Also, *repeat the priming* in some way as preparation for the second, more focused listening about to occur.

6. Play the selection a second time.

   • Look over their shoulders to preview the kinds of responses students are making.

   • Be alert for likely people to call on because their responses will generate constructive discussion.

7. Discuss each question or direction in depth, with frequent reminders of the *priming* involved.

   • For example (1) in the box on page 145, this might be, "How does your 'life' feel at this point in the music?" or, "You say this sounds like a sad experience in your life, but how can you tell that from the music?"

   • For (2), reference might be made to, "Now if you're the average listener this company wants to sell records to, do these features stand out clearly?"

   • Leave some issues unresolved (or stir up some controversy) in preparation for the third listening.

8. Play the selection a third time.

9. Discuss any remaining issues and help students to draw conclusions in their own terms.

10. Afterwards consider:

    • How much interest students had in the music and the lesson—especially whether the priming worked.

- How well the lesson succeeded in terms of the curricular focus on the attensive qualities at stake.
- Whether the attensive qualities were challenging without being too subtle.
- How clear, balanced, and varied the directions were for the student.

SUMMARY

1. A listening lesson is not a "stand alone" lesson; it should set up a subsequent lesson or build on a previous one.
2. Music must consider the likelihood of its appeal for the age group and the nature and number of the attensive qualities suitable for that group.
3. Carefully prepare directions and questions that can evoke responses that at least indirectly are observable.
4. Direct students' focal attention to the attensive qualities that are the reason you chose the piece.
5. Discuss and otherwise determine whether or to what degree students are now newly aware of the qualities in question.
6. For future planning, evaluate the students' learning, their interest in the lesson (and music selected), and the overall effectiveness of the lesson.

TYPES OF LISTENING LESSONS

Several specific types of listening lesson formats are described in this section, each with its own advantages and requirements. They cannot be properly used without understanding the introduction and "basics of listening lessons" sections of this chapter, and the general planning basics provided in Chapter 3.

The pieces used in the examples that follow are from the standard repertory because the reader is most likely to be familiar with them and can thus understand the process better. However, music from all eras and genres, including multicultural music and music by women composers, can and should be used in developing the teacher's own listening lessons based on local curriculum decisions.

I. Standardized Lessons

These lessons involve a handout that applies to only one piece. Therefore they are time-consuming to develop but, once "perfected," can be reused.

1. Question and Answer Format
2. Graphic Scores

II. Reusable Formats

These blank forms are easily adaptable to a wide variety of selections. For that reason, they tend to be the most efficient use of the teacher's time. A large stock of each can be run off in advance. The time saved is given to planning the priming strategy and the discussion.

   3. Instrument Checklist Form

   4. General Broad Characteristics Survey

   5. Feelings/Instruments Response

   6. Continuum Chart

   7. "What I Hear/Feel"

   8. Comparison Ratings Graph

   9. Color Response Form

   10. Adjective Circle

III. Informal Lessons

These are short, to the point and are quite flexible in adapting to a particular repertory. A handout might be used; but the lesson is not an extensive undertaking.

   11. Familiar Songs

   12. Short Instrumental Compositions

   13. Class Performances

   14. Videos

   15. World and Multicultural Music

   16. Picture and Stories

   17. Readiness Staging

   18. Listening with Composition Lessons

   19. Ear "Training": Melodic, Harmonic, Rhythmic

I. STANDARDIZED LESSONS

1. QUESTION AND ANSWER FORMAT

This format is characterized by directions that take the form of questions that mainly proceed sequentially through the piece. Thus the first question pertains to the first attensive quality, the second to the second, and so on.

Directions are spaced or paced carefully so students have time to read each, focus aurally on the attensive quality in question, and then respond.

Questions are reproduced as a handout (Example 6.1). Student answers are the bases for discussion.

> In *any* listening lesson format, when a handout is used that students *write on*, typically give several students overhead transparencies to work on instead. This allows their answers to be used as a partial basis for discussion.

Students should keep these handouts in their folders or portfolios as a record of progress. They can also be collected for evaluation and written comments. Since they are intended to explore and to extend aural acuity, it is best not to grade them on a regular basis.

This composition begins with an INTRODUCTION that sets the mood. Then a slow MARCH begins that develops the mood.

Read the directions below so you can follow them easily as you listen. Ask any questions before we begin to listen.

1. Which design do you think describes the beginning of the INTRODUCTION? What do you hear that sounds like the design you chose?	1. a. ⬆️⬇️⬆️⬆️⬇️⬆️ b. ⬆️⬆️⬆️⬆️
2. Which line has the same feeling for you as the music that <u>follows</u> the INTRODUCTION? Why do you think so?	2. a. ——— b. 〰️〰️〰️ c. ∿∿∿ d. ?
3. Which color has the same feeling for you as the music now? What are your reasons?	3. a. red b. blue c. yellow d. green e. purple f._____
4. Which is the MARCH THEME? How could you tell <u>IDEAS:</u>_____	a. 🎵 b. 🎵
5. Which instrument plays <u>the beat</u> of the MARCH THEME in addition to the drums?	5. a. clarinet b. trumpet c. tuba d. flute
6. Which <u>family</u> of instruments plays the <u>melody</u> of the MARCH?	6. a. brass b. strings c. woodwinds
7. Do you think the marchers get <u>closer</u> or <u>farther away</u>? How can you tell?	7. Closer? Farther away? <u>IDEAS:</u>_____ _____
8. Does the MARCH get <u>more relaxed</u> or <u>more tense</u> for you as it moves along? How can you tell?	8. More relaxed More tense? <u>IDEAS:</u>_____ _____
9. Does the MARCH seem to end <u>up in the air</u>, or do you have a feeling of a <u>final ending</u>? What influenced your choice?	9. In the air? Final ending? <u>IDEAS:</u>_____ _____
10. If this were movie music, which kind of MARCH do you think this was? What are your reasons?	10. a. wedding b. protest c. funeral d. 4th of July parade IDEAS ⟶

Example 6.1

Teaching Guidelines

1. Read directions aloud using an overhead of the handout.

- Explain the questions or other response options.
- Make sure everyone has a pencil.
- Be sure you can locate the music on a CD. Otherwise, prerecord the selection alone for quick accessibility.

2. Play the recording three times, as described earlier, allowing no talking.

- If need be, announce the question number to help guide students' attention. This should be the only talking by anyone.

3. Discuss responses in considerable detail. Some special considerations include:

- A show of hands—"How many people chose answer (a) for number 1?"
  - ➪ Whenever students should raise their hand to respond, *raise your own while asking the question* in order to remind them to raise theirs!
  - ➪ For high order questions choose several students by name and ask what features they heard that supports their answer.

Get students to reveal, in their own words, how discerning their listening has been. The cognitive bases for high order responses often depend on recognition and identification of instruments, terminology, and "facts" students have learned in composition and other lessons. Through such transfer, listening "tests" and applies earlier learning to "just listening."

- Repeat this discussion process for each choice.
  - ➪ Keep in mind that discussions of an item get boring when they become too long. Later items on the form also depend increasingly on memory, which rapidly fades.

Discussion seeks to cognitively strengthen the likelihood that students will notice (in focal attention) the attensive quality or musical feature in question in the future— including, first of all, the very next listening during the same lesson.

- Students of this age perceive much more than they can readily refer to. Therefore, they need **prompts** and **cues** of various kinds.

Many attensive qualities are, in fact, secondary "refinements" that students are not used to paying attention to, but can easily attend to if given direction or help. Thus, the teacher tries to bring focal attention on *precocious perceptions* that are at first only "background" or subattentional influences that previously have been tacit, and thereby to bring these "refinements" into conscious awareness and greater use.

- Instead of just saying "Good" or "OK" ritualistically, use plenty of varied "comebacks" and feel free to qualify remarks or to probe further: for example, "That's interesting, but what about . . . ?"

- Do not make the discussion sound as though the answers to a test are being checked. Rather, truly engage students; get them to discuss each other's answers.

- Avoid or discourage responses that express dislike. Whether they *like* the particular piece is less important than getting them to find the newly-highlighted attensive qualities *interesting*. Stress the attensive quality and its potential in other contexts they may find more pleasing.

How to Develop Question and Answer Lessons

1. Listen several times without a score

- Make a list of the attensive qualities *you* hear in the order of their appearance. You will not use them all, but the result will be an overall "aural map."

- Eliminate those that are unsuitable; for example, too subtle or spaced too close together.

- Write directions and questions for the remainder.

2. Visual layout

- The box-like "frames" in Example 6.1 make visual reference easier.

- Type your handouts; students take more seriously what the teacher has taken seriously enough to prepare neatly.

- As cues, *italicize or underline key terms* (for example, questions 5 and 6 in Example 6.1) or places where *answer choices* are previewed in the question (for example, questions 7, 8, and 9 in Example 6.1)

3. Writing final directions

- Keep questions short and simple and choose vocabulary carefully. Complicated directions are ill suited.

- Where helpful, use graphic designs (e.g., answers 1, and 2 in 6.1) and one or two word choices (e.g., answers 3, 5, 6, 7, 8, 9, and 10).

- Avoid suggesting that "music makes . . . " or "music expresses . . . " feelings, ideas, and so forth. Instead of asking "How does the music *make* you feel?" or "What does the music *make* you think of now?" stress *constructivism*; thus: "What feeling can *you* associate with the music?" or "What color (image, etc.) do *you* think goes with the music now?"

- Do not end questions with a fill-in-the-blank. This reads like a test.

- For low-order directions, begin with "what": for example, "What instrument plays the theme now?" Where a choice of answers is given, begin with "which" (e.g., question 6 in Example 6.1)

- Avoid the word "best." With low-order questions, an answer is either correct or it is not. In subjective, high-order directions, use expressions such as "do *you* think" or "do *you* feel" (e.g., questions 1, 2, and 3 in Example 6.1).

- For high-order questions and directions provide a "follow-up" probe that allows students to consider the (low-order) reasons, perceptions, and the like, behind their response (e.g., questions 1, 2, 3, 7, 8, 9, and 10).
- Provide space for the student to write short reminders of these follow-ups (e.g., 7, 8, and 9). For longer responses, tell students to write their thoughts on the back of the handout (e.g., for 1, 2, 3, and 10).

4. Organization

- Directions that should be in the students' mind throughout the entire piece should go first: for example, "How many times does the *theme* appear?"
- Directions that ask students to reflect on the overall piece generally are placed last (e.g., 10 in Example 6.1).
- Otherwise, directions should be spaced to proceed *sequentially* throughout the piece.
- Ideally, none should be so close in time as to rush their responses nor so far apart as to lead to mental dawdling.

5. Balance

- Directions should typically favor high over low order by at least 60/40 percent. This inspires *constructivist* thinking and allows them to feel positive about the lesson.
- Insure that high-order directions depend on lower-order cognition; focus on such low-order cognitions during the discussion of their high-order responses.
- Always try to end with one or two questions that cause students to reflect holistically on the piece (e.g., question 10 in 6.1)

6. Production and revision

- Word processing allows easy storage and retrieval and facilitates revision.
- Revisions are likely before the format, pacing, and wording of questions work well. Even then, over the years some revisions are often needed to accommodate a new generation of students.

2. GRAPHIC SCORES—"LISTENING MAPS"

Graphic scores (charts, or listening maps) provide visual references that guide students' attention throughout the piece. They serve the same purpose as a real musical score. In fact, for short easily reproduced pieces, students can benefit greatly by learning to follow a traditional score.

For some pieces, a simplified score can be made to follow. See Example 6.3 on pages 154–155.

Similarly, graphic listening scores can and should often incorporate notation of themes or motifs, rhythmic patterns, and the like. See Examples 6.4 (pages 155–156) and 6.5 (page 156).

Graphic scores, listening maps and notated themes can also be used in conjunction with *numbered directions*. For the first listening students follow the "score." Then, for the second listening, they use the "score" to help answer each of the questions.

- Note that themes can be notated on a staff (A in 6.6 on pages 157–158) or sometimes by indicating directional changes without a staff (B, and Coda).

Sometimes questions can be keyed to a score by placing the question numbers at the desired locations in the score (Example 6.6a, 6.6b). Sometimes the choices for a response can be included right in the "score," particularly by having students choose among two options. For example, in a piece with an easily recognized theme, students can write in the instrument(s) that play the theme in different sections (see "Soprano + ?" in 6.7). Or, when sections repeat at different dynamic levels, students can write in (or choose) the appropriate dynamic marking. Places where the music gets gradually louder or softer, faster or slower can also be identified.

- Of course, lessons involving vocal music will have words that are central to how the graphic is organized.

- Do not overlook the possibility of having students perform with certain portions of the piece. For example, they can conduct along, changing their pattern to "follow" the music. (Performing with a piece usually allows the piece to be somewhat longer than for "just listening.")

- They can also clap or tap a rhythmic motive each time it appears: for example, refer to 6.4.

Some teachers create scores where students perform throughout the entire listening. This is suitable for the concrete learning of primary grade students. But where "just listening" is necessary for older students, performing along with the entire recording is counterproductive.

- After students have physically responded to an attensive feature, end the lesson with "just listening." The physical response will help them to hear it now in the holistic context.

Teaching Guidelines:

1. Using a transparency, familiarize students with *how to follow the "score"*—that is, what the symbols and letters, represent; how sections and themes, are shown; and how their eyes should move up and down or across the page.
   - If questions are keyed to the "score" (e.g., see 6.6b), those references in the "score" (e.g., 6.6a) should be pointed out.

2. If there are particular themes and rhythms notated in the score, preview these *aurally* so students can easily recognize them (e.g. 6.3, 6.4, 6.5).
   - If there are several themes first make a little recognition game of aurally distinguishing between them (e.g., first 2 measures of A and B in 6.3).

3. Play the recording and have the students follow the "score" projected on the screen, not their own handouts!
   - "Steer" them through the "score" by pointing on the transparency as the piece unfolds.

4. For the second hearing, students follow their own "scores."
   - If the piece is challenging, have students "just listen" by following their *own* "scores" for the second listening, *then*, on a third listening, they respond to the questions. A fourth listening puts the attensive qualities back into holistic context.

The Wild Horseman

Robert Schumann

Example 6.2

The Swan - from "Carnival of the animals"

Example 6.3

Continued

Example 6.3

The Nutcracker Suite
"March"

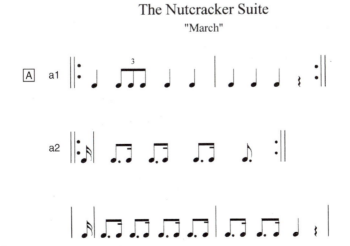

Example 6.4

Continued

Example 6.4

First movement from
Eine Kleine Nachtmusik
by
Wolfgang Amadeus Mozart

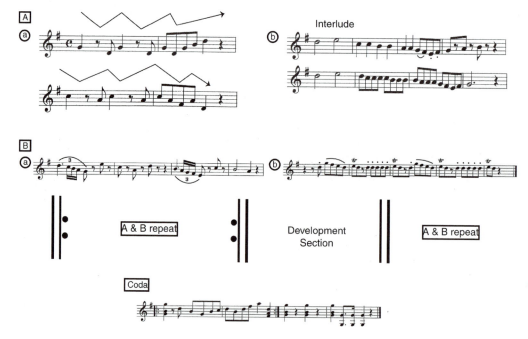

Example 6.5

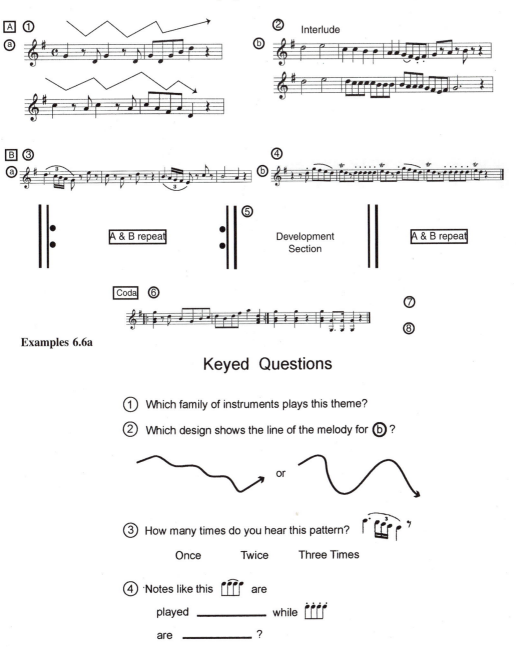

Examples 6.6a

Keyed Questions

① Which family of instruments plays this theme?

② Which design shows the line of the melody for ⓑ ?

or

③ How many times do you hear this pattern?

Once   Twice   Three Times

④ Notes like this   are

played ——————— while

are ——————— ?

⑤ In the development, the composer "plays" with the theme
from A and B. Circle the 2 themes you think he used the most.

Examples 6.6b

Continued   ⑥ The CODA sounds most like?

        Aa   Ab   Ba   Bb

⑦ Did any instruments besides the strings play?

⑧ Circle any adjectives you think describe the musical
feeling of this piece. What are the musical reasons for each?

cheerful	majestic	serious	dramatic
heavy	calm	sad	restless
broad	active	light	gloomy
refined	happy	careful	tender

Soprano: + Organ	There were shepherds abiding in the field, keeping watch over their flock by night.
Soprano + ?	and, lo, the angel of the Lord came upon them, and the glory of the Lord shone round about them; and they were sore afraid.

Soprano
+ ?
	and the angel said unto them:
	  "Fear not; for behold, I bring you good tidings of great joy,
	  which shall be to all people.
	  For unto you is born this day in the city of David, a Savior,
	  which is Christ the Lord."

Soprano + ?	And suddenly there was with the angel a multitude of the heavenly Host, Praising God and saying:
Woman + Men Men	Glory to God, glory to God in the Highest and peace on earth.
Woman + Men Men	Glory to God, glory to God in the Highest and peace on earth.

Soprano
Alto
Tenor
Bass
	goodwill
	                    goodwill
	        goodwill
	goodwill

Example 6.7

Continued

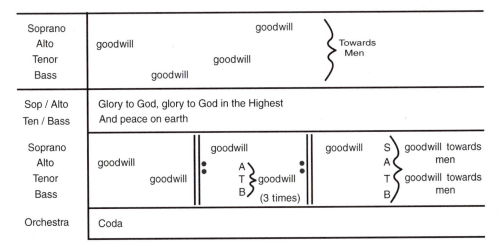

Soprano Alto Tenor Bass	goodwill goodwill goodwill goodwill (with "Towards Men")
Sop / Alto Ten / Bass	Glory to God, glory to God in the Highest And peace on earth
Soprano Alto Tenor Bass	goodwill ... (3 times) ... goodwill towards men
Orchestra	Coda

Example 6.7

Later*

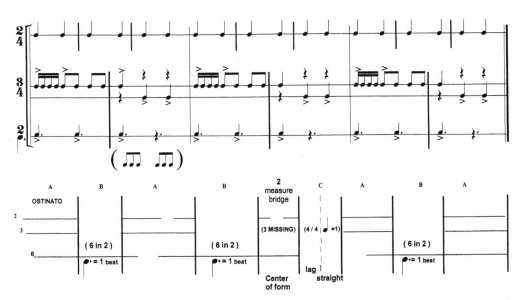

* Cat Stevens -- "Foreigner Suite" Album

Example 6.8

How to Develop Graphic Scores

1. These lessons require considerable preparation time and often some graphic creativity.
2. *The first version the teacher produces is rarely successful* and some revision is usually needed.

   In the case of graphic scores, the graphics themselves—for example, size, layout, clarity, and so on—often need improvement.
3. Unlike standardized listening lessons, pacing and spacing directions amount to *aurally guiding students sequentially through highlights from beginning to end.* Therefore, graphic scores require the teacher to account in some way for virtually the entire piece.
4. Teachers should not "impose" their idiosyncratic way of hearing a piece by how they visually represent the organization of a piece. They should also avoid highly personal programmatic interpretations.

5. After the second listening, lead a discussion focusing on the various attensive qualities to which the "score" points.
   - If questions have been used, these should also be discussed in some detail.
6. Play the recording a final time.
   - Over time, encourage students to listen this final time without using their "score."
   - A brief final discussion stresses the potential of the attensive qualities for other music and lessons—especially composition lessons (Chapters 4, 5).

"Program music" usually involves a certain picture or idea that inspired the composer. However, a listener's response need not reflect the "program" (i.e., story, picture, literal idea) the composer had in mind. The musical qualities, not the "story" or "picture," are what is musically interesting. Even where the "program" (usually the title) is known, it need not dictate the response. For example, whether the piece is "about" the *Flight of the Bumblebee*, a mosquito, a housefly or a hummingbird, the focus should be on attensive and other relevant musical qualities. In fact, a clever hype can pose the question of what else the music could (or could not) be "expressive of."

II. REUSABLE FORMATS

Unlike the first two types of listening lesson, these lessons involve "forms" that can be used with more than one piece. The teacher simply provides the specifics that adapt a given format to the piece at stake. When these forms are used over several years with different literature, the resulting familiarity with the form benefits transfer of learning and listening habits generally. Adapt the basic forms suggested in Examples 6.9 through 6.19 (on pages 161–176) to suit the students' age level and other variables; for example, vocabulary.

3. INSTRUMENT CHECKLIST FORM

	Sections →					
STRINGS	VIOLIN					
	VIOLA					
	CELLO					
	BASS					
WINDS	FLUTE					
	CLARINET					
	OBOE					
	BASSOON					
	SAXOPHONE					
BRASS	FRENCH HORN					
	TRUMPET					
	TROMBONE					
	TUBA					
PERCUSSION	TIMPANI					
	SNARE DRUM					
	BASS DRUM					
	CYMBAL					
	GONG					
	BONGO					
	TOM-TOM					
	TRIANGLE					
	CHIMES					
	XYLOPHONE					
	MARIMBA					
OTHER						
	PIANO					
	ORGAN					
	OTHER:					
VOICE	SOPRANO					
	ALTO					
	TENOR					
	BASS					
	SOLO					
	DUET					
	SMALL ENSEMBLE					
	LARGE ENSEMBLE					

When the recording is finished, turn this paper over and write your ideas on how the instruments used in this composition contribute to the unity and variety (organization) and feelings (expression).

Example 6.9

This form focuses on individual instruments, families of instruments and, especially, their role in the organization and expressiveness of music. Use it with music where instrumentation is varied but clearly central to the expressive and formal organization of the music.

- Blank boxes are for specific or unusual instruments used in particular pieces.

- Similar forms should be evolved for world music, rock and jazz groups, and so forth.

- The directions at the bottom should be used religiously as the basis for the discussion. Otherwise the lesson will become excessively low order. With it, high-order responses dealing with form and expression are elicited in terms of the low-order components related to tone quality.

Teaching Guidelines

1. On a transparency, show the information students need to copy onto their forms for the present piece. Minimally this will include filling in the verse or sections numbers at the top, and any additional instruments.

2. "Sections" typically represent formal organization (e.g., ABACA; Theme, Var. 1, Var. 2, etc.). However, where no clear formal divisions exist—notably with through composed music—they can be numbered and pointed to by the teacher as they aurally unfold.

   - Each such point should involve a clear change that students can easily recognize or should begin with some highly recognizable feature (e.g., a cymbal crash, a major change of dynamic level).

3. Verses can be simply be numbered (e.g., "verse 1 / chorus / verse 2 / chorus", etc.).

   - Choral pieces can use keywords as shorthand indicators of sections: for example, for Handel's *Hallelujah Chorus*, "hallelujah," "kingdom," "he shall," and so on.

4. Preview the use of the form in relation to your priming strategy.

5. Play the recording three times.

   - The first time, students listen while watching the transparency as you point out the changing sections or verses.

   - Discuss responses after the second listening.

   - Listen holistically the third time; that is, without pointing on the overhead.

6. Avoid any impression that this is merely a test of instrument identification.

   - In fact, students' responses will not be identical.

   - While some responses will be wrong (e.g., hearing a saxophone where there was none), others vary between listeners because even experienced listeners do not notice the same instruments, particularly when background instruments are part of the texture.

Distinctions are often influenced by recording and playback variables. For unfamiliar music, even sophisticated listeners cannot tell the difference between an oboe and an English horn or between a viola in its low register and a cello in its upper register. Such subtle differences between instruments are thus not suitable attensive qualities for lessons based on recorded music!

7. To focus on an instrument students are *unlikely* to recognize by name, call it the "mystery instrument" or "instrument X" for purposes of the checklist and preliminary discussion.

   • In the discussion, use its real name and discuss it in comparison to similar instruments.

The purpose of this checklist is to highlight the important relationship between orchestration and formal and expressive features of the music. Instrument identification is *used*, then, to focus on important aspects of composition that have to do with the composer's orchestration, not *taught* for its own sake! In fact, with the exception of using the "mystery instrument" to focus on an unfamiliar instrument, *students should already be able to recognize common instruments*. The discussion is predicated upon such readiness—informally learned outside of school or as developed formally in previous listening lessons—and the lesson will not succeed without it!

4. GENERAL CHARACTERISTICS SURVEY

This form helps students focus on from three to seven or more attensive variables at a time. A piece is selected because these variables are prominent at different points in the music.

Lessons using this form cannot succeed if students are not already familiar with the attensive variables from earlier lessons. Appropriate readiness needs to exist in order to predicate a lesson on, "melody," "mood," "text," or "harmony." For example, when students are at the readiness stage where for "melody" they can only draw the shape of a line or describe it as smooth or jagged, then *that is how they will listen.*

However, the selection can be chosen to *also* introduce a new refinement (e.g., the melodic use of scale steps or chord skips) that serves as readiness staging for subsequent melodic compositions. The lesson therefore summarizes and provides an opportunity for transfer of learning from *earlier* lessons while at the same time serving as the basis for *subsequent* lessons.

QUALITIES ⟶

Sections

Example 6.10

This form is used in essentially the same way as the instrument checklist, except that the format is horizontal. Sections (or verses) are listed along the left and right margins, and reference to attensive qualities is positioned across the top.

- A teacher might focus on attensive qualities that are drawn from the list of generative themes; for example, melody, harmony, rhythm, mood, meter, line, texture, tone color, text, tempo, and mode.

> The word provided by the teacher is a *keyword*. Thus "texture" might be expected to elicit responses concerning "thickness" or "thinness." "Melody" or "line" would elicit comments involving melodic shape and direction or other features learned by composing melodies (e.g., uses mainly "steps"). "Meter" would focus on recognizing meter changes, and so on.

- Other possibilities might be more specific, such as specific melodic or rhythmic motifs, key uses of a particular instrument, and so forth.

Other factors to keep in mind when designing such a format:

- The boxes are only used to jot short "reminders" for later discussion.

- Younger students will be able to keep track of only three or four keywords (i.e., attensive qualities); middle school students can keep track of more—*if* some require only single word responses. Therefore the number of boxes from left to right should be between four and six. This allows the same form to provide continuity from fourth through eighth grade.

- As with the instrument checklist form, sections can be defined in terms of the actual musical organization, or along arbitrary lines (see points 2. and 3. under Teaching Guidelines for the Instrument Checklist mentioned earlier.)

Teaching Guidelines

1. Make a transparency of the *specifics* students need to copy onto their forms *for this lesson.*

2. Preview and clarify what is meant by, or expected in relation to, the *keywords* provided.

If keywords are not clarified, students will put "yes" under 'melody' instead of describing it as "jagged," drawing the shape of its "line," or writing "AB" to represent its two-part organization. Similarly, if *any* mood adjectives are acceptable, then point this out. But if the keyword "mood" is to elicit only a *choice* between happy and sad (perhaps to parallel the alternation of major and minor "modes") or between tense and relaxed (perhaps to parallel the variable dealing with consonant and dissonant "harmony"), then make sure students know this.

---

3. Play the recording and have the class listen but not respond.
   - Point to the verses or sections on the transparency so that students become familiar with the *length* of each section and any patterns of repeated sections, refrains, and so on.

4. Clarify questions or confusions concerning the sections and general directions.
   - Before listening the second time, review the keywords and the types of responses expected.

5. Listen again, this time with students writing their responses in the boxes.
   - As they listen, still use the transparency to guide students who are unsure "where we are" in the music.

6. Discuss students' responses in depth according to the Basic Lesson Format (pages 145–146) provided earlier.

7. Listen a final time—without pointing on the overhead!—and discuss or summarize responses in terms of the attensive variables focused on in the lesson, and their potential relevance for other kinds of music.

5. FEELINGS/INSTRUMENTS RESPONSE

This form can be used to keep track of two different sets of variables: Changes of *feeling tone* over the course of a piece; or the presence and absence of *families of instruments* and their relation to the overall organization of the piece. *One or the other is used*, not both for the same piece on the same occasion.

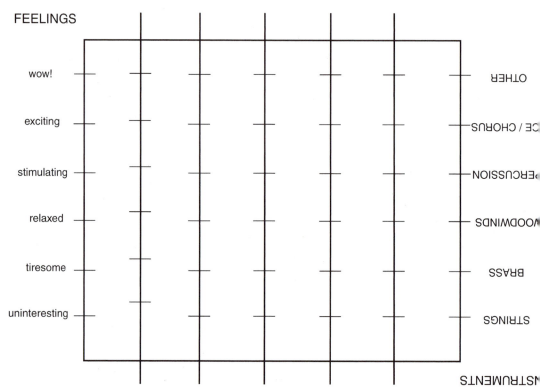

Example 6.11

Feeling Tone:

- Relevant adjectives are listed vertically along the left side in advance.

It could trace the continuum of the six degrees of feelings such as is shown in Example 6.11. Or it could describe a continuum of another type, such as "tension" or "love" *that the class agrees to in advance.*

Come prepared with a basic proposal (that can be altered after discussion) rather than wasting time having the class construct the continuum: for example, for music that is expressive of "love," such a proposal for a continuum might be "none," "interested," "attracted," "steady," "serious," or "intense."

• Students draw a continuous line to represent their changing responses

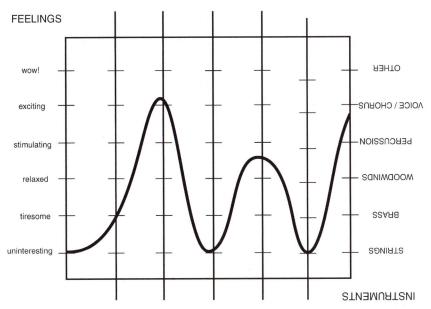

Example 6.12

Instrumental Families:

• Turn the form upside down and the categories are already in place.

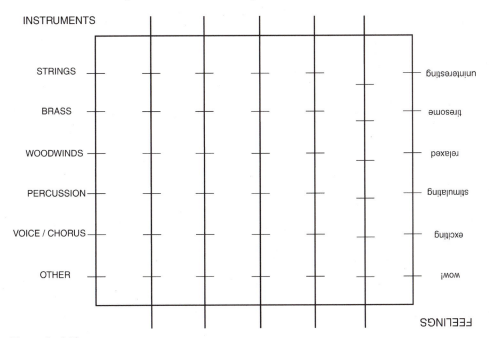

Example 6.13

- "Other" is used for solo or nonstandard instruments.

- Students draw a straight, but often discontinuous, line to show the *presence* of a particular family:

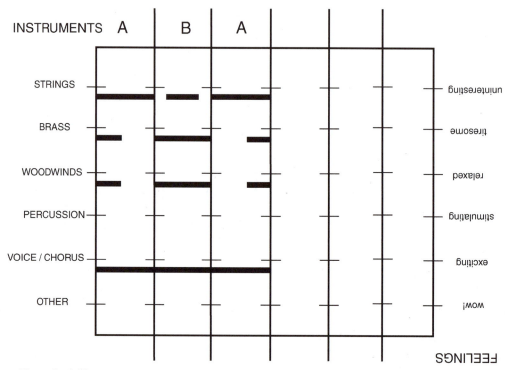

Example 6.14

- Students need to be attentive to the simultaneous use of families and to the prospect that once a family has entered the texture, it may not continue throughout the whole section or verse. This often requires an additional listening, for a total of four times.

Teaching Guidelines

1. Preview the form in terms of the priming strategy: For example, "If this music was being used in a love story, let's determine what kinds of ups and downs of love are felt by the couple involved."

2. As before, students listen the first time without responding while you signal the beginnings of sections.

3. "Charting" is done during the second listening; discussion follows.

4. Listen a final time to summarize *their* conclusions.

6. CONTINUUM CHART

This form is used to record changes in the relative presence (or degree) of *one attensive variable*. Therefore it is best used in compositions that feature one clear attensive quality that changes in significant ways (e.g., "dynamics" in 6.15).

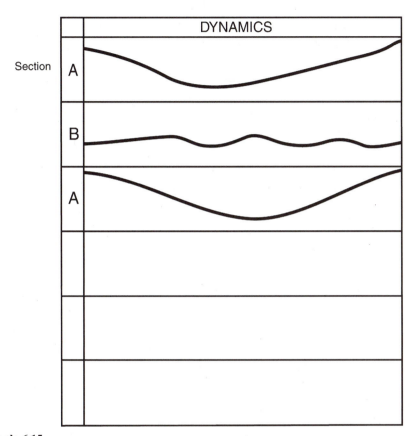

Example 6.15

Some examples chosen from among the generative themes explained in Chapter 3 are:

- Tension versus relaxation
- Dissonance versus consonance
- Thinness versus thickness of texture
- Mood changes (happy/sad, excitement/calm)
- Dynamic changes (loud/soft)
- Tempo changes
- Activity (movement) versus static levels
- Interest or feeling levels

The variable is charted by drawing a continuous line in the section (or verse) box. The higher or lower the line, the greater or lesser the presence or intensity of the variable. The form works best for shorter pieces where each section of verse is approximately 15–25 seconds in length. A horizontal page format increases the length of the box. This is often most suitable for students in grades 4 and 5.

Teaching Guidelines

1. The same general pattern should be followed as for the previous reusable forms.

2. *An important difference*: During the first listening, students need to get a "feel" for how long the verses or sections are and, therefore, how quickly to draw their lines. If they do not pace their lines, they quickly run out of space.

   • During the first listening, students watch as you draw a *straight* line on the transparency at the required pace.

   • Younger students can also follow in the second listening as you move a *capped* pen at the proper pace on the transparency.

3. Due to this pacing requirement, sections or verses should be very *similar in length*.

   • If the form is to be used when the A section is much longer than B, have students shorten the B box *in advance* by putting an "X" through the unused portion.

4. The form is best used where (for example, in an ABACA piece), the line that results for each A section will look very similar and will also be contrasted clearly with B and C.

   • This form is well suited to comparing different jazz solos in the same composition, different verses of a song or choral work, and so on.

5. Because this form is so straightforward, the discussion is especially important. Therefore preplan discussion questions and strategies.

   • The discussion after the final listening should serve as readiness in regard to the relevance of the attensive variable for subsequent uses; for example, "What are some ways we could use this in a sound composition?"

7. "WHAT I HEAR/MY FEELING" FORM

This format allows the teacher to determine which attensive qualities students *already* hear most readily. Unlike the previous forms, here there is no "given" focus. Instead, students simply indicate what "sticks out" to them—what they find most notable or interesting—at different points in the section or verse. Sections that inspire varying responses for the beginning, middle, and end of a section are best.

Teaching Guidelines

1. This form also depends on students gauging the timing of their three responses. Therefore, follow points 2 and 3 from the previous form here, as well.

2. Some students may not know what to write in the "What I Hear" column but can nonetheless usually write something about their feelings.

	What I Hear	My Feelings	
			Early
			Middle
			Late

(Left vertical axis label: **Verses or Sections of a Composition**)

Example 6.16

- Then, give **prompts** and **cues** that help them work backwards from their feelings to the features heard that they think were responsible for those feelings. This process must be used if students are to become more conscious of attensive qualities.

3. The simplicity of the form once again disguises the subtlety and practice required in conducting an effective discussion. In particular:

- The range of responses will be considerable since students are freely attending to what they most naturally notice. Therefore, the teacher must work to *relate different responses along similar lines.*

  For example, "John heard many brass instruments at this point but you were noticing the percussion; yet you both agree with most of the others that the loudness and tempo of the music in the middle of this section is really important to your feelings of excitement."

- Without discussion, the teacher is left knowing only *that* students perceived vastly different attensive qualities.

- The overall point is for students to realize that while we often hear different "things," these often result in comparable *kinds* of responses.

4. In the final discussion, make a class list of the kinds of "things" students wrote in the "What I hear" column.

- Note which attensive qualities are *not* indicated in students' responses? *These need cognitive strengthening in subsequent lessons of all kinds.* "Missing" qualities that *have* been the focus of past lessons of various kinds are also of concern. They need more emphasis.

- Note which attensive qualities are most common? What "refinements" can be added? For example, they are hearing "tension," but only in relation to dynamics, not melodic direction, dissonance, instrumentation, and so on.

5. Teachers should regularly collect this particular form to learn how well *individual* students listen.

- Transparencies can be given in the future to those whose listening is most discerning, therefore promoting discussions that help those whose discrimination is underdeveloped.

8. COMPARISON RATINGS GRAPH

Using this form, students show their discrimination of the relative strength or presence of the featured attensive variable. Unlike the Continuum Chart (6.15), it does not attempt to trace changes *during* a section or verse but differences *between* sections; for example, where "tension levels" between sections are contrasted.

Comparison Ratings

To be ? rated:

Turn the page over and write the reasons for each of your rating decisions. Can you explain or describe how some people might have a different rating?

Example 6.17

Focus can be on feeling states, such as:

- Tension
- Interest
- Intensity (of mood)

Or it can be on cognitive variables, such as:

- Dissonance
- Density (of texture)
- "Fit" between music and word meaning

Each vertical column represents sections or verses. Students place an X or check mark at the place that represents their individual judgments. Make sure they also follow the directions at the bottom of the page.

This form can also be used to make comparisons between different recordings of the same piece—usually a popular song, a show tune in its original versus pop setting, two jazz versions, and so on.

Teaching Guidelines

1. Discuss each selected focus to review and refresh students' thinking about the musical variables in question.

2. Since students will basically make only one rating for each section, they need to be directed not to make their rating prematurely—until they have heard most of the section. Make sure sections are not so long that attention wanders.

3. The total number of sections should be noted in advance and the same numbers written on the back of the sheet so that comments concerning each section are separated.

4. Sometimes this form can be used by two or three students who confer on their ratings and, most important, their reasons.

This form can easily be used to direct student's selective attention during the listening stage of student compositions and class performances.

- After a sound composition performance by one group the other groups can confer (as in point 4) to evaluate how well the composition handled the stated criteria. In such uses, the vertical lines will represent each different composition heard.
- When listening to performances of groups of, say, student instrumentalists who have been practicing a certain piece (technique, chord, etc.), the form can be used by the other groups to rate, say, the consistency of the tempo, accuracy of pitches, and chord changes. In this case, the *keywords* "tempo," "pitches," and "chords" would be written on the top lines of each of the first three vertical columns, and the word "overall" over the fourth, where the "overall impression" can be rated. This process "motivates" the work of each composing or performing group and makes the audience members more aware of these variables in their own performances and general listening.

9. COLOR RESPONSE FORM

This form elicits mood (**affective**) and subjective responses of various kinds through color metaphors. It is particularly useful in discussions with fourth and fifth graders who do not know how to describe music yet.

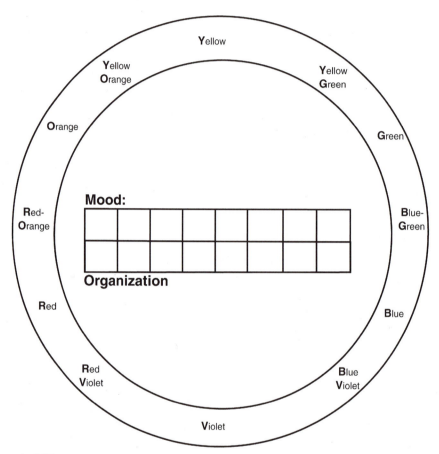

Example 6.18

- The form is set up as a color circle. In a color circle, not only do colors blend gradually into adjacent colors but, more importantly, *contrasting colors are directly opposite each other.*
- If possible, make a poster of a real color circle arranged just like the form.
- The sections (ABACA) or verses (1, 2, 3, 4) of the music are indicated in the lower row of boxes labeled "organization."

Teaching Guidelines

1. A preliminary discussion about color references for moods is useful.
   - For example, "What does it mean when we say someone is in a 'blue' mood?" "What colors do you associate with feelings of happiness?" "What colors are used in life at serious events? Happy events? Why?"

2. Based on their mood response, students select a color for each verse or section by writing its name (or first letter: Y, YG, etc.) in the "mood" box that corresponds with the section.

- The selection should therefore have clearly contrasting moods for each section! Thus, an ABACA piece would typically elicit the same or close (adjacent) choices for each A section and contrasting colors for B and C.

3. As with any kind of adjective, it is important always to ask students for the "What did you hear?" behind their choices of colors; that is, for the low order perception that supports their high order response.

4. People with **synesthesia** actually do "hear colors." But that is not the point of this process.

- Instead, use the students' color associations with moods to help them focus on the features that were the basis for their intuitive musical mood responses.
- Avoid suggesting that students are *supposed* to be listening for or actually hearing colors.
- Discussion can also refer to bright versus dark, or light versus deep shades.

> Color responses are useful mainly with younger students or those who at first have difficulty discussing music. Such students often relate simple color references to musical responses and feel safe in volunteering their answers. As in any discussion, however, they may need *prompts* and *cues*: for example, [prompt] "What did you hear in the music that sounded 'blue' to you? [cue] Was it the slow tempo, or maybe the melody or harmony?"

10. ADJECTIVE CIRCLE

This form is based on one used by the psychologist Kate Hevner to study mood responses. Her form utilized adult vocabulary. Consult with a language arts specialists to determine the best words to use for students at different grade levels.

- This adjective circle is constructed very much like a color circle: Adjacent groups of words are very closely related in terms of *affective* qualities. Therefore, group A and B are similar and group B and C are close, but A and C are more distinct. And, as with a color circle, directly across from a group is its opposite feeling. Thus A and E, B and F, C and G, and D and H all represent the greatest degree of mood contrast.

- The blank lines allow students or the teacher to add vocabulary. For example, a student might add "floating" in group C (while another student might add that same word to group D).

- The columns of lines at the bottom represent sections of the piece. Have students write the verse number or section label on the short line above each column. As they listen, they select adjectives from groupings A–H and write the *words* on the lines for the section in question.

- This form is most effective with music where sections have distinct moods. Corresopndingly, only one or two adjectives will be used and the class will tend to select them from the same or adjacent groups.

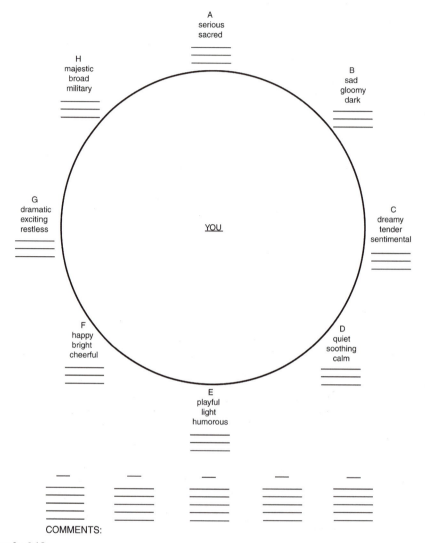

A
serious
sacred

H
majestic
broad
military

B
sad
gloomy
dark

G
dramatic
exciting
restless

YOU

C
dreamy
tender
sentimental

F
happy
bright
cheerful

D
quiet
soothing
calm

E
playful
light
humorous

COMMENTS:

Example 6.19

Teaching Guidelines

1. Since this lesson depends heavily on language, students must understand the meanings of the words.

2. Preview the form the first time it is used to discuss the close relationship of mood between adjacent groups (e.g., H and A, or A and B), between increasingly distant groups (e.g., H and B) and opposite groups (e.g., H and D). It is important that students are aware of these factors.

3. After students have made their responses:
   • For each section have a *show of hands* for each of the eight groups of words.

"How many people chose a word from group A for the first verse? How many from B? How many from C?" Continue questioning through letter H.

- Keep a tally on the chalkboard for later discussion:

A	10
B	8
C	3
D	2
E	0
F	0
G	0
H	6

- From each display of hands (for example, from among those who raise their hands for A), choose several students to give musical reasons for their choices. Continue this pattern for the words in the other groups.

- Once that process is (quickly) completed, discuss the overall *pattern of responses* for the particular section or verse.

↪ In the tally model, responses were grouped at the top right of the circle (H, A, B, and C) rather than the bottom left (D, E, F, G). *This kind of pattern is very typical* and needs to be noted because, once again, it shows that responses can be similar, yet different.

↪ Some responses will be predictably atypical of any such pattern. For example, in the tally model, the two students that selected group D are idiosyncratic but their perceptions and reasons *should* be pursued. A brief discussion may in fact reveal perfectly adequate perception coupled with a bizarre reasoning: For example, "I chose happy from group F because even though this was slow and low pitched and sounded like a funeral, I was thinking of the murderer who is happy he killed the guy; so, for him, the music is happy!"

↪ Some students who choose idiosyncratic words or groups often (a) are not really trying (i.e., just answering to comply); or (b) are trying to attract attention by "being different" or "weird." However, because the teacher is not concerned as much with the words or groups chosen as with the underlying perception, these students are not "off the hook."

- Continue in the same manner for each section of the piece, stressing the important similarities between students' responses and the (usually) subtle differences.

4. Always stress the compositional variables that are the bases for the adjectives students choose.
   - As always, subjective responses need to be linked to an awareness of particular musical features or compositional techniques.
   - Most of these should have been featured in past lessons of various kinds and are present evidence of transfer of learning.

The adjective circle is particularly well suited to emphasize how similar perceptions can evoke varied responses. Therefore, it is particularly useful in establishing that listening is an active process of "reaching out" aurally and that this selective attention can be different in terms of the types of features that "stick out" for different people. Similarly, they learn that a response is constructed or created by them in terms of their thoughts, their lives, and their individual experiences.

Reusable Formats—Common Considerations

1. Using a transparency, preview each format in terms of the priming strategy with specific attention to the focus of the lesson. Have some students work on transparencies!

2. Students do not respond during the first listening; instead, they familiarize themselves with the music by following the form. Pencils should be used and need to be on hand in order to to distribute.

3. After the first listening, clarify any questions or confusions. As the format itself becomes familiar, the musical features to be focused on must increasingly challenge them.

4. *The discussion after the second listening is the most important part of the lesson.* With the timed saved by the form's flexible use, comprehensively plan discussion questions and strategies. Include all students, not just those who volunteer!

5. The discussion after the final listening should be *holistic* and should focus the lesson on past and future transfer of learning.

6. Collect these forms from time to time to assess individual progress. As a rule, do not grade responses.

7. Many of these forms can be used as **homework**—for example, for "listening notebooks"—where students listen and respond to their own recordings or music on the radio and TV.

8. Many forms are useful for other kinds of listening projects, particularly in connection with **learning stations**.

9. All these forms are useful for the listening stages of composition lessons, particularly sound composition lessons.

10. All students should keep completed forms in their folders or portfolios.

III. INFORMAL DIRECTED LISTENING

Informal listening lessons are "informal" only because, with one exception, they do not use a stock handout. If a handout is prepared, it is generally very simple to prepare and for a one-time use. While addressing the same kinds of musical features and generative themes as in lesson formats 1–10 mentioned earlier, the listening directions are few and the responses relatively straightforward. Hence, there is little need for complex planning or production.

For the same reasons, however, these lessons are best used for (a) uncomplicated selections where attensive variables are striking; and for (b) "everyday" kinds of listening.

The latter focuses on improving discrimination and the now richer quality of what is otherwise only "casual" listening that too often misses interesting or important musical details. Most of the following suggestions profit from a mixture of "formal" lessons (using the previous ten lesson formats) and "informal" formats.

11. FAMILIAR SONGS (E.G., FROM FILMS, MUSICAL SHOWS, FOLK SONGS, AND POP MUSIC)

- Songs where students already know the words or can easily read along as they listen (e.g., a ballad) are suitable. The words can be shown on a transparency to guide and organize their listening.
- When listening to (or watching videos of) musicals, each piece should be handled as an informal listening lesson, with its own focus and discussion. Stress the "fit" of the words and music, and the different arrangement of voices and instrumental forces. This is a good way for students to learn the different roles of arias, recitatives, small ensembles, large choruses, and dance.

12. SHORT INSTRUMENTAL COMPOSITIONS OF A SINGULAR CHARACTER, SUCH AS "CHARACTER PIECES" FOR PIANO—(E.G., SCHUMAN "THE HAPPY FARMER" OR EXAMPLE 6.2)

- If the score can be shown on a transparency, students can follow as the teacher points to each new measure (e.g., Example 6.2). Because the music is simple to follow and straightforward in mood (often programmatic), these pieces can be successfully listened to without a score, too. But since following a score while listening to a recording is a listening praxis some find enjoyable or beneficial (e.g., in studying music), some experience following a score is recommended as a option for later life.
- Typically the overall "character" of such a piece is the focus: for example, "Why do you think the composer called this piece the 'Happy Farmer'? What sounds happy? Why a farmer, not a coal miner? What are other titles that might fit just as well? What kind of film or commercial might this music be good for? What moments in your life feel like how this music sounds?"

13. PERFORMANCES IN CLASS

- *Treat important class performances* (see Chapters 7, 8) *as directed listening for the 'audience.'* Focus specifically on the targeted criteria or goals; for example, whether the tempo is steady, the pitches or chords accurate, whether the "ensemble" is 'tight,' and so forth.

- The music itself can also be a point of focus; for example, when pieces that students are performing have features that can serve as a basis for students' own compositions (see no. 16 that follows).

- Have half the class sing or play a tune and the other half accompany (e.g., on guitars, electronic keyboards, etc.). Record it and complete an informal listening evaluation of the performance.

- Singing in unison, rounds, and parts should periodically be recorded; then complete an informal evaluation of the performance. This evaluation should develop *criteria for improvement* and should be followed immediately by some additional practice and a "final" recording—possibly for "our class album."

14. SHORT VIDEOS (OR SELECTED SEGMENTS OF LONGER VIDEOS)

- Excerpts from film or TV dramas, commercials, documentaries, and the like can be studied in terms of the music used—its qualities, effect, successful contribution, and so forth.

- Folk, modern dance, and ballet videos are useful, as are videos of jazz performances and world musics.

- Cases where music composed for one praxis (e.g., a "classic" of any kind) is used in other interesting ways (e.g., as film music or as a commercial) are beneficial, as are comparisons of the relative effectiveness of music used in two similar situations (e.g., music for two different dramatic scenes).

- Music videos can be acquired (or rented) as well. Particularly recommended are:

> Paul Winters' "Canyon Consort," chronicles a raft trip down the Grand Canyon during which music was composed from and performed in nature (PBS Home Video)
>
> "Kodo," physically athletic Japanese folk drumming (SONY Video)
>
> "Riverdance," the Irish dance spectacular (Columbia Tristar Home Video)
>
> "Stomp," the percussion/dance ensemble (mentioned in Chapters 4 and 5) that uses everyday objects as percussion instruments (HBO Home Video)
>
> "Amazing Grace with Bill Moyers," an account of various versions of this famous song (PBS Home Video).

15. WORLD AND MULTICULTURAL MUSIC

- Much of this music is not originally intended for "just listening," yet it surely holds potential interest for audiences so inclined (e.g., the "Kodo" group mentioned just above also has CD recordings available).

> ⇨ Lessons should stress stylistic features in relation to the culture and focus on improving students' general aural acuity.
>
> ⇨ Comparisons between cultures (e.g., African versus Japanese drumming; music for different religious or ceremonial uses) should focus on stylistic differences and highlight the praxial value of music as made in its natural setting.

- For dance projects to such music, *first listen to the music in some depth* before teaching, devising or improvising steps and other movements. This way, students learn to focus on attensive qualities and musical features that can transfer to their own compositions and other listening.

16. SHORT PROGRAMMATIC PIECES IN RELATION TO SELECTED PICTURES OR STORIES

- Use several magazine pictures or art reproductions, at least one of which reasonably relates to the programmatic idea that inspired the composer, but where at least one other picture ought to be a *realistic alternative* (e.g., for the "Aquarium" section of Saint-Saëns' *Carnival of the Animals*, have a suitable underwater picture of fish, but also perhaps a picture of a very foggy or misty scene).

> ⇨ The piece is played and students are asked to select the picture that "looks like the music sounds or feels" *to them*.
>
> ⇨ Discussion focuses on the musical qualities in relation to students' choices, and particularly on how more than one picture might be suitable even though the composer started with another in mind.

- A similar procedure is used with brief story lines.

17. PIECES TO BE USED QUICKLY AS READINESS STAGING FOR SOUND AND MELODIC COMPOSITIONS

- Such readiness staging is a prime occasion for using informal listening. For example, existing melodies can be listened to once or twice as the first stage of a composition lesson where students will attempt to compose their own melody in the same form, using similar melodic movement, and so forth.

- Such listening to models works just as well as *follow-up* to a composition lesson when students' compositions are compared to how a "real" composer handled the same compositional problems.

Common Considerations for Informal Listening Lesson Formats 11–17

1. These listening lessons feature only a few simple directions or questions that point to the salient attensive qualities the teacher wishes to emphasize. See, for example, the questions modeled under lesson format no. 12.

   - As the teacher gives the *complete directions,* they are written on the chalkboard, whiteboard, or teacher's transparency in a "shorthand" form. In the case of the questions modeled for lesson format 12, this "shorthand" might be: (1) "happy" and "farmer?" (2) "other titles?" (3) "film or commercial?" (4) "your life?" These serve as brief reminders of the complete directions.

   - The complete directions must be *clear.* The short reminders must be easy to read since students will in fact refer to them.

2. Students should be expected to make any *written* observations, thoughts, and ideas *as* they think of them.

3. Be clear about expectations for *overt* responses (e.g., conducting with the meter, tapping the rhythm of a theme each time it occurs).

4. The "preview" hearing associated with lesson formats 1–10 is not *usually* needed with 11–17 since these informal lessons have no complex form or format to become familiar with.

   - In some cases, students benefit from listening to the entire selection one time without writing or responding. For example, in the case of format 16, they should listen to the whole piece before starting to write their answer, so what they hear inclines them to relate to one particular picture rather than another.

   - In most cases, students can begin to write or respond right away.

   - With really simple use (e.g., format 17) it may be necessary to listen only twice—although most other listening lessons usually benefit from three hearings.

   - In the specific case of no. 13 (and no. 18 that follows), one hearing of the recording is usually all the time the teacher can afford.

5. The *discussion* stage of informal lessons is especially important. Since little time is spent preparing *materials,* planning should be devoted to preparing a strategy for thorough and beneficial discussion.

TWO SPECIAL TYPES

18. THE LISTENING STAGE OF A COMPOSITION LESSON (SEE CHAPTERS 4 AND 5 FOR APPLICATION DETAILS)

All composition lessons that end with performances for the rest of the class (in particular, all sound compositions) should be treated as informal directed listening lessons. Therefore they need their own separate planning!

- Some of the forms described previously may be suitable, but are used only on the basis of one listening.
- Whatever compositional elements are being focused on should also be the focus for listening.
- Encourage a written response of students' responses, however informal (i.e., scribbled).
    - ⮞ For example, have students make a list of their ideas concerning how, and how well, the elements were handled, or have them draw the shape of the melodic line they hear, or determine how many passing tones went up rather than down.
- Discussion of *each* sound composition performance should be extensive. It is by means of the discussion that students engage in *reflective abstraction* and thus in *cognitive strengthening* of the musical features under consideration.
    - ⮞ Features addressed in sound compositions should become more attensive for other listening!
- When students listen to melodies composed in class (their own included), they should be directed to listen for the compositional criteria that are at stake, not just whether the music is "nice" or whether they "like it."
- All discussion should always clarify the criteria or musical variables in ways that can transfer to subsequent lessons and especially to out-of-school listening.

19. "EAR TRAINING"

These lessons do not focus on "just listening" for purposes of holistic musical responses. Rather, they develop aural skills that transfer to holistic tasks—particularly in connection with the various formats of melodic composition presented in Chapter 4. Therefore, they should never be used for their own sake or as tests! They should be taught with their specific transfer value clearly in the mind and results should be "tested" in action—that is, applied in the actual holistic context to which they are relevant—not in isolation.

> These lessons should be approached more as "games" that **practice-in-action** the skills to be acquired, and not as a skill-drill. In fact, it is best to use them regularly in connection with the related composition formats from Chapter 4.

Melodic Contour—"Dot-to-Dot Notation"

These lessons improve students' aural discrimination of melodic line. The primary focus is on changes of melodic direction, but without requiring specific interval identification. It uses a handout like this.

1	2	3	4	5	7	8	9	0	1	2	3	4	5
•	•	•	•	•	•	•	•	•	•	•	•	•	•
•	•	•	•	•	•	•	•	•	•	•	•	•	•
•	•	•	•	•	•	•	•	•	•	•	•	•	•

Example 6.20a

The teacher works from a transparency of the same handout.

1. The "dots" represent individual pitches and the numbers above represent the sequence played.

2. Point to the lowest of the three dots under no. 1 and play middle C; then to the middle dot under no. 2 and play the next D and connect the two dots with a line:

Example 6.20b

3. Then you can play either middle C again or the next E and ask the class which dot, the lowest or the highest, should be connected.

4. This can be followed by an example that features a repeated tone.

5. With this preliminary modeling of the process, have students actually indicate their own responses. At first, use only variations of C, D, and E. Before each pitch is played, announce the number about to be played.

This pattern of pitches

Example 6.20c

should result in this pattern of connected dots.

Example 6.20d

6. Play the pitch pattern a second time asking students to check their lines for accuracy.

7. Then repeat the entire process, one pitch at a time, this time drawing the correct line for each example on the transparency.

8. Locate any places where students had problems and clarify their aural confusion by playing the two pitches again while singing the "skipped" pitch.

9. Repeat steps 5 and 6 with a different example.

10. Results can be checked by having individuals or the class call out each interval. For example, ask, "The interval between pitch 1 and pitch 2 is . . . ?" and the class answers whether it is a:

"step"—up or down (for scale steps),

"skip"—up or down (for "thirds" of any kind); or

"repeated tone."

Once students can accurately handle three pitches, add a fourth by using a handout that has four lines of dots. Then you can move to at least five lines so that leaps of 1–4–1 and 1–5–1 and 1–3–5 can be practiced. Encourage students to sing the "skipped" pitches. Always reserve the lowest dot for the "tonic."

The dots are a *simplified notational system* that allows students who cannot yet use *standard* notation to nonetheless practice hearing basic intervals and melodic direction. The dots do *not* show step and half-step differences and therefore any attempt to apply dot-to-dot notation to standard notation will be confusing. Students who start with the dot-to-dot procedure in fourth grade can typically use standard notation by middle school because, among other learning, they have been using standard notation in their compositions and performing.

Rhythmic Patterns

This type of practice focuses on identifying rhythmic patterns by ear and eye and is typically used to aurally reinforce the *rhythmic emphasis format* of melodic composition suggested in Chapter 4. Approached as a "game," students can be encouraged to practice this discrimination with considerable benefit.

1. Begin with four measures of different rhythms that use the same basic note values; label the measures A, B, C, and D:

Example 6.21

- Practice each *individually* by tapping the rhythm (or speaking it using solfege syllables).
- Then perform (at least two times) various 4-measure *arrangements* of A, B, C, and D for the class. For example:

Example 6.22

- Students should determine by ear the order in which these measures appeared—which, for Example 6.22 would be A, B, C, and D.

2. A more difficult variation on this lesson is to perform a 4-measure arrangement that uses only three of the original four measures.

   - Students are challenged to determine which choice is *not* used, then to determine the rhythm of the "odd" measure on their own.

3. Students can, individually or in teams, notate 4-measure arrangements of their own (as in 6.21 and 22) *that they think they can perform accurately* but that will be challenging for the rest of the class to perform.

   - As students gain skill performing rhythms in performance classes (Chapter 7 and 8) they can be expected to perform the examples themselves, as individuals or at least as a class.

4. Extract rhythms of melodies students are likely to recognize (e.g., standard sing-along songs, folk tunes, current pop tunes, etc.). Play "name that tune" just by *looking* at the rhythms (i.e., trying to "hear" them with the "inner ear").

   - Give students time to study each example.

   - Perform the rhythm for the class, (a) as a last resort and, (b) to confirm the correct answer.

5. If guitar (or autoharp, Omnichord, Qchord, lap dulcimers, etc.—see Chapter 8) is part of instruction, the rhythm of strum patterns should be made a focus of aural practice. At the very least, some effort should be made to help students learn strum patterns by ear—that is, just by listening, not at all by watching.

Chord Changes

These lessons practice identifying specific *chord changes* and *points where chords change* (i.e., **harmonic rhythm**). They should be used in connection with the *harmonic emphasis format* of composing tonal melodies (Chapter 4) and for performance lessons involving chording instruments (see Chapter 8).

1. Create "games" that involve chord recognition and have students circle the chords they think the teacher has played:

1	2	3	4	5	6	7	8	9	10
G	G	G	Ⓖ	G	G	Ⓖ	G	G	G
F	Ⓕ	F	F	Ⓕ	F	F	F	Ⓕ	F
Ⓒ	C	Ⓒ	C	C	Ⓒ	C	Ⓒ	C	Ⓒ

Example 6.23

2. Continue in the same manner with a melody students know *but have not used chords in connection with before.*

- Provide the words or just the tune on a handout, and have students indicate the chords that are used at certain points. Either tell them the key and use, say, C, F, and G symbols; or use Roman numerals. Use both systems over time so they practice listening in both ways.

Amazing Grace

Example 6.24 *Using a Tune*

3. A different version uses a simple handout that shows the choices at the particular point in the words or melody. Students circle their choices as they listen.

Amazing Grace

A-mazing grace! How sweet the sound. That saved a wretch like me!

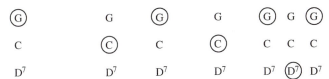

I once was lost but now I'm found: Was blind, but now I see.

Example 6.25 *Using Words [bold = circled]*

SUMMARY AND CONCLUSION

"Just listening" is very unnatural for most students, even many adults! The concert audience is a relatively recent invention in Western music history. Most other listening in the world, instead, involves habits and practices that depart in varying degree from the full attention expected at Western concerts of the standard repertory—or even at jazz and other kinds of "concert music."

Nonetheless, students benefit greatly from learning to "just listen." In particular, such lessons are the prime means by which the teacher is able to improve and expand the detail and depth of students' aural capacities. Therefore, whether the situation is "formal" (as at a concert) or "informal" (as at a wedding or jazz club), when students can hear more "from" or "in" music of any kind, their response and musical benefits are richer.

No musical praxis is more accessible to people than listening! The responsibility of the general music teacher, then, is twofold:

1. To enhance student's aural acuity. What type of music students listen to and under whatever conditions, they will simply "hear more" and be able to respond more richly.

2. To promote other listening options or "tastes" students can find rewarding beyond their current singular focus on "pop" and teen music. This is done by modeling what listening is "good for" in life in relation to different styles, genres, and types of musical praxis.

With action learning, perception is enhanced by using a wide range of musics. None is advanced at the expense of another. Just the opposite is the case: Students' *musical choices are expanded* through listening to music in class that they would not otherwise have encountered outside of school.

However, this diversity also presents the problem of "depth versus breadth." If students encounter only one example of jazz music, one choral piece, one African drumming recording and so on, *breadth* exists but not with the *depth* needed to be musically independent, to aurally discriminate appropriately, or otherwise empowered to make real and informed musical choices.

The solution is to ensure that musicianship skills featured in listening lessons are *general* enough to transfer to a *range* of musics! Beyond that, teachers need to select a well-balanced diet of musics. Students' backgrounds—including regional and ethnic tastes—and the resources that are available should be taken into consideration and opportunities should be sought to bring adult amateur musicians and performers into classes.

The Listening Program
Familiarity enhances the likelihood of students' interest in, liking of, and discriminative capacities for a particular music. In addition to repertory selected specifically to relate to composition and performing lessons:

- Feature lessons that use a particular kind of music that can be a likely source for students' future listening pleasure; for example, jazz.

- The total listening "program" should feature a range of musics; for example, jazz, contemporary idioms, traditional music of selected ethnic groups (depending on local conditions), and so on.

- Music selected from the European canon should also include multiple examples from different historical periods, but with the heaviest emphasis on "modern" music.
- Use the kind of **rubrics** described in Appendix B as **summative evaluation** to assure that aural acuity is improving in concrete ways.

CHAPTER SEVEN

SINGING

GENERAL INTRODUCTION TO RECREATIONAL PERFORMANCE

> This introduction provides an analysis of amateur performance praxis *in general*—that is, recreational performing as its own musical value and as its own curricular focus in general music classes. It introduces concerns common to both to the *singing* emphasis of this chapter and the *instrumental* performance addressed in the next chapter.

Aside from listening, dancing, and other uses of music, performance itself is a primary source of personal pleasure, interest, and meaning. Such pleasures, however, are not intended only for professionals and experts. Performance by **amateurs** as **recreation** is, without doubt, a far more common praxis than highly trained performance. Historically, however, this has not been the case.

The "Music Appreciation" Tradition

Traditional aesthetic theory* has been concerned mainly with listening to "art music" with discernment based on *connoisseurship*. Such theories of so-called "music appreciation" generally concede only minor importance to the performer. Instead, "the work," said to be autonomous of time, place, performer, and listener, is the primary source of appreciation.

Traditional aesthetic theory has also dealt almost exclusively with notated music of the European standard repertoire. It has typically ignored, excluded, downplayed, marginalized, or actively denigrated aural traditions and improvised musics because the score *is* regarded as the "work" and without a score there can be no autonomous meanings. This eliminates as "good music" most of the music performed in the world and accounts for the historical lack of world musics in music education at all levels.

The rise of aesthetic theory in the eighteenth century also promoted the professionalizing of performance. With the rise of public concerts, the new middle class that was vying for cultural primacy with the old aristocracy began to attend concerts in part to be *seen* as "classy." Therefore they made less and less music for themselves in the home and elsewhere. Prior to the invention of aesthetics in the mid-1800s, of course, social and cultural refinement meant being able to join in amateur musical performances of various kinds (such as madrigal singing as after-dinner entertainment). But with middle class acceptance of the idea that only professionals have the technique and other knowledge to properly render the profound aesthetic meanings claimed for a work, informal and personal uses of music increasingly gave way to "just listening" to professional performances. Amateur and other forms of personal music making

---

*The reader is reminded that "traditional aesthetic theory" refers to neo-Kantian aestheticians, not the use of the term "aesthetic" by pragmatist and phenomenologist philosophers (see **aesthetic theory**).

took on a decidedly second class status and amateurism was often derided by professionals and other experts (e.g., "Amateurs teach amateurs to be amateurs!"). Today, then, a "musician" refers only to a trained professional not to someone who regularly performs music.

School Ensembles

The consequences of these developments for music education have, as a result, become confused. On one hand, performance ensembles have dominated music education. Even though, by their nature, most school-based ensembles cannot begin to approximate the exacting requirements for artistry placed on performance by orthodox aesthetic criteria, the assumption still prevails that performance of "good music" at any level *automatically* amounts to an aesthetic *education*. Furthermore, the assumption is widespread that the pleasures of performance are aesthetic, even though traditional aesthetic theory describes aesthetic responding as a cerebral, intellectualized, abstracted, disembodied kind of experience and denounces the whole idea of "aesthetic pleasure" as improper because, then, music is no longer "for its own sake" but for pleasure!

Nonetheless, ensembles continue to dominate music education on the assumption that performing in ensembles for eight years develops "music appreciation" and makes students into connoisseurs who will continue to listen to the kind of music they performed in school, even if they do not perform it anymore. The evidence that performance ensembles routinely develop future listening devotees, however, is nonexistent or to the contrary!

One reason listening appreciation is not sufficiently influenced by school ensemble performance is that *audience listening* and *performance listening* are not the same praxis. Performance-based listening certainly *can* contribute to audience listening, and vice versa. However, the typical ensemble program does not regularly or directly apply performance listening to audience listening (e.g., via listening lessons). Thus few, if any, skills, habits, inclinations, or preferences are developed specifically for audience listening and, not surprisingly, graduates show no increased inclination to attend band, chorus or orchestra, concerts as adults.

Worse, most school musicians no longer perform after graduation. The benefits and pleasures of ensemble participation have been largely social and have addressed adolescents' social needs—while they are still in school! But given the assumptions that (a) ensemble performance automatically elicits and develops aesthetic appreciation, and that (b) being in an ensemble automatically promotes future audience listening, instruction typically overlooks promoting amateur performance for lifelong recreation. In fact, perhaps because of the bias for listening appreciation, rarely is performance as a lifelong recreation typically stressed in the overall curriculum. If it were, instruction for chamber and solo performance of all kinds of literature and performance genres would be featured for *all* students—and not just the minority in ensembles.

Performance in General Music Classes

General music instruction has also focused on the kind of knowledge teachers believe will, someday and somehow, be applied by students as future audiences of "good music." The tradition has been for general music teachers to "teach concepts" assumed to be necessary for having or improving aesthetic experience. Most performing "activities" and "experiences" in class are intended, then, to promote "music appreciation" as listeners, not to serve the explicit curricular purpose of promoting lifelong recreation as *amateur musicians*. While physical education classes promote amateurism in sports, far too few general music "grads" can read music, match pitch, sing comfortably, or perform on real instruments at a beginning level, despite six to eight years of music classes in which there has been considerable singing and performing on "classroom instruments"—instruments not typically used by adults.

Furthermore, because folk and indigenous instruments are not used in European concert literature and do not serve as pre-band instruction, the most popular instruments in the world are typically not even included in the curriculum! With the occasional exception of guitars and recorders—the first as a gesture to "youth culture" and the second as "pre-band" instruction in reading music—many general music classes feature *only* classroom instruments. These are used mainly to "teach concepts," the eventual application of which is assumed generally to involve *listening*. Since "music appreciation" is generally associated with listening, then, general music teachers have not traditionally seen themselves as teaching performance as source of lifelong musical enjoyment. Not surprisingly, then, general music classes traditionally fail to promote interest in, or skill on, *real* **social instruments**.

With the **praxial theory** of music (upon which this text is based), all kinds, types, and traditions of performing—from beginning competence, to expert amateur, to virtuosic artistry—are valued for their contribution to the performer's "good life." Amateur performance is therefore valued and stressed for its own sake as a curricular action ideal of ensembles and classroom music. Recreational and avocational performing on folk, indigenous, and ubiquitous instruments of various kinds (and according to local traditions, availability and interest) is then a mainstay of an action-based general music program.

People who make music for themselves and for family, friends, and "audiences" such as church congregations or retirement communities contribute to the musical life—or musical "liveliness"—of the local community and to society in general. Praxially speaking, they are rightfully entitled to be called "musicians" for the same reason that amateurs who play golf are called "golfers."

Any musical praxis affords a range of skill and rewards from neophyte all the way to expert. A basic criterion of a curriculum based on praxis, then, is to help students to develop to a basic level where, at the minimum, they begin to enjoy and derive **"good time"** from performing music, yet where they are also aware of other models of skill or specialization toward which they can aspire. This is the state of "breaking 100 in music" mentioned in Chapter 1.

CONDITIONS FOR "BREAKING 100" IN PERFORMANCE

1. *Functional music reading* sufficient to serving lifelong involvement
   - The goal of music reading is the ability to translate notation into real time performances that can then be played at the desired tempo through practice.
     - ⇨ In relation to *instruments* this means development of facility in fingering pitches and chords and performing rhythms correctly.
     - ⇨ In relation to *singing* this entails "vocal reading"—the functional ability to sing from a score "at sight" and developing an "ear" to hear and correct mistakes.

Music reading serves both singing and instrumental performance. Learning to read music via an instrument enables the individual to pursue that instrument as a performance outlet. But it also directly improves vocal music reading—as is demonstrated in any school, church, or community choir where the best music readers are those who also play an instrument! Therefore, minimally, *an action-based program for performance praxis will insure that students read music functionally on an instrument.* The voice, in any case, should be approached as a separate instrument.

2. *Musicianship relevant to at least that performance medium* where the student is able to function *independently* of a teacher or other direct help (e.g., parents)

- Useful musicianship is the focus, not theory for its own sake. In *general* music class, this amounts to *general musicianship*—that is, knowledge and skill broadly applicable enough to serve as an entrance to *many* beginning-level performance practices.

    ⇨ Once a particular praxis attracts a student, then more specific musicianship skills will be practiced through engaging in that praxis.

- Basic musicianship for any particular praxis is an interaction of psychomotor and cognitive *skills.* Cognitive "knowledge" or "understanding" must be learned and applied "in action" through a kind of apprenticeship of "learning by doing," not as inert facts, disjointed information, abstract concepts, or as isolated skill-drill.

    ⇨ Such skills are evaluated holistically in terms of **authentic assessment**.

- Furthermore, students must be able to apply such skills independently. If they do not exhibit independent musicianship *now*, there is little reason to believe that they will be able to do so as adults.

3. *Proficiency suitable to personal "good time"* yet informed by expert models

- Despite falling short of the highest exemplars of a particular praxis, amateur performance is *rewarding* in its own way and provides it its own "good time." (*Amat*eur, of course, comes from the Latin *amat*, meaning lover.) Amateur musical performance then shares something with, for instance, amateur golfing. Millions of people "play" golf and find it rewarding despite knowing better than nongolfers how limited their skills are compared to professionals.

- On the other hand, familiarity with expert models—particularly as "spectators" (see point 5. that follows)—promotes a background in the traditions of any praxis. And, in relation to various personal variables (such as time constraints and innate ability), amateur musicians (and golfers) typically benefit from knowing how much better they can become with more practice. However, not everyone has time to be an expert.

There is a sense in which "competence" can be defined as the technical ability that serves "good time." Dissatisfaction with poor putting sends some golfers to the putting green to develop more expertise. "Breaking 100" always depends on personal values—key among which, importantly, are balancing the time demands of a busy life with recreation! Such personal considerations end up governing the criteria of proficiency judged "good time" for each amateur's situated conditions.

4. *Practicing strategies* for learning new music and advancing technique

- Technique comes from practice, but practice is *not* a matter of *mere repetition.* Rather, practice results only under conditions of **intentionality**—that is, where students (a) have a *clear idea* of what is to be achieved, and (b) are consciously *trying to* achieve that improved musical result.

  ⇨ In effect, this means that general music classes devoted to teaching skills must be somewhat like *rehearsals,* but where individuals practice to improve their *personal* skills, not just the collective result.

  ⇨ It also means that considerable monitoring of progress must be directed toward *individual students*—including teaching *self*-monitoring.

Always singing as a full class provides no feedback to the teacher or to any given student concerning *individual* ability to match pitch, read music, or the like. Aside from providing little impetus for improvement, then, such teaching also fails to meet the student's need to achieve.

- Effective practicing also requires strategies for *how to practice*. These should be demonstrated to an entire class, at first as step-by-step procedures that students are expected to demonstrate (step-by-step) individually.

  ⇨ As a repertory of such strategies is taught, students must be encouraged (and given the opportunity in class) to practice on their own and must be made as *accountable* for the results as they are with their math lessons.

- The difference between *drill* and **practice-in-action** is crucial.

  ⇨ Out of context drill (such as golfers practicing at the driving range) is "work" and in itself not usually "playful." It is willingly undertaken only when the individual clearly sees the effort as improving the "good time" of actually "playing" (golf or music) and is rewarded (and motivated for the future) only when "playing" is more likely to have "good time" as the result.

  ⇨ Accordingly, practice in the classroom setting is best approached as *practice-though-playing* in a holistic musical context, for musical purposes and rewards!

5. *Familiarity with a basic listening repertory and models of performances* relative to the performance medium in question

- Performance cannot be taught properly in the absence of listening models! A curriculum devoted to enhancing performance skills for lifelong pleasures must provide a rich background of listening involving the performance medium to be studied.

> ⇨ Aside from inspiring students *to* practice, such listening gives them models *of* excellence.

> ⇨ Exemplars also promote an informal, intuitive kind of musicianship that simply cannot be taught in any other way.

Amateur performers attend more concerts and they collect recordings involving "their" performing medium and literature interests. Listening skills developed in relation to *individual* recreational performance therefore promote audiences and appreciation better than large ensemble or whole class performance. For example, whether the medium is singing or playing guitar, models from a variety of styles should be featured, not only to benefit performance but also with a view to the pleasures of listening, as well.

---

6. *Resourcefulness for locating music, recordings, information, and help* for continuing musical involvement or progress

- If students are going to continue to actively perform outside of class and after graduation, they need to know how and where to locate music, recordings, and information relative to their performing interests.

> ⇨ Teachers provide music for in-class performance; but students are otherwise clueless concerning where to find music on their own. Therefore they need to learn to use resources found in libraries, music and record stores and, of course, the Internet.

Summary
"Breaking 100" in music depends on:

- Learning to *read music* functionally in one or more performance mediums;
- Developing a level of *musicianship* that functions independently of a teacher;
- Achieving *technical proficiency* suitable to the praxis and to a beginning level that *presently* is "good time."

A praxial program for "Breaking 100" will stress:

- How to *practice* for the purposes of learning new music and advancing skills;
- Developing a basic *listening repertory* relative to the performance *medium*;
- *Locating information and other resources* that promote a lifelong hobby of playing and listening.

With these conditions in mind, we now turn to a specific consideration of singing. For economy and focus, however, the reader is reminded that issues common to *both* singing and to performing on instruments are explained in connection with singing. Details concerning instrumental performance are found in Chapter 8 but the common issues addressed next will not be repeated there.

SINGING

MATCHING PITCH

Singing depends, of course, on facility in matching pitch. By the intermediate grades, an effective general music program should have assisted most students in matching pitch. However, some students may still have difficulty. And, of course, new students who cannot match pitch will move to schools where students have already learned to sing in tune.

Matching pitch depends on three closely related variables: (a) Processing the *external* pitch to be matched in the "inner ear" as short-term tonal memory; (b) "hearing" that pitch *inwardly* as the "target" for the vocally produced pitch; and (c) comparing and adjusting the vocally produced pitch to (a). Step (c) takes place not just as "hearing" the external pitch, but also "sensing" it inwardly through bone conductance and body resonance.

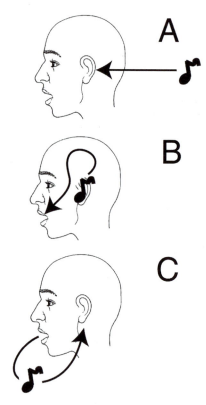

Example 7.1

Students with normal hearing usually have no difficulty with (a) at this age. They can tell whether a sung or played pitch is the same or different from a previous example. If they cannot, they need just such practice. The instructional problem, then, is helping them with (b) and (c).

Basic Strategy

1. Have the student vocalize an upward glissando by imitating a *slow* siren. A comparable hand movement in vertical space should accompany this "slide" from low to high.

- Develop a **kinesthetic** *association* between voice and hand, for example, using the hand to represent the pitched sound of a buzzing bee, tracing a course of flight up and down.
- Draw various lines on the chalkboard (or whiteboard) for the student to execute (with both hand and voice) in various patterns (up and down).
- Students at first can actually trace their fingers along the drawn lines and then step back away from the chalkboard and "perform" the same pattern (still using hand movement).

2. Using the same process, have the student sing scale degrees. Start on any pitch they sing.

   - Glissando through, and hold scale steps to "hear" and "feel" the relationship between vocal pitch and hand movement.

3. Then *you* should produce and *sustain* a pitch in the middle of the student's vocal range.

   - The student attempts to match your pitch by humming. This enhances the bone conductance phase of hearing.
   - Move the *student's* hand slowly up or down as the student follows with a slow vocal *glissando* in the required pitch direction until the pitch is matched.
   - *Sustain the now tuned pitch* for several seconds and ask the student to focus on how matching your sustained pitch "feels."
   - Students also need to "feel" what unison is *not*.
   - After holding a pitch, move a little above or below the matched pitch; hold it, then "resolve" it back to matching!
   - Practice the preceding exercise with several different pitches.
   - Beginning with a given pitch, sing *scale steps* without the glissando. Still use the hand movement.

4. Now trace out basic melodic motifs of familiar tunes—for example "Hot Cross Buns"—using only scale steps 1, 2, and 3.

   - *Tune-up the first note* using the first three steps explained in point 3. Then move deliberately from step to step, correcting errors by using the second step in point 3.
   - Wean students of dependence on the need for your corrective help.
   - With your fingers almost touching theirs (and facing each other), have the student move his or her own hand in sync with yours.

5. On the chalkboard, draw three lines, about a foot long, one over the other. Use roughly the same degree of spatial separation you have been using in vertical space to represent separate scale steps.

   - Tune-up (as in 3.) the bottom pitch with yours, which is treated as the tonic. Point to the next line up (step 2 of the scale) and have the student follow by actually touching the opposite end of the same line while vocally matching your pitch. And so on for the third scale degree.
   - Explore a variety of patterns using the first three scale degrees, including the interval of a major third.

- Once facility is accomplished, the lines can be spread out in a pattern that carefully traces a simple melodic pattern—for example, first 2 measures of "Do-Re-Mi"—*but without rhythm.*
- Then, use the actual pitch notation for the same tune (on quarter notes).

6. At some stage of points 4. and 5., stop singing along with the student—except for tuning-up the first pitch.

- Many students catch on quickly in one short session. However, future work is often necessary.

Nuts 'n' Bolts 'n' Cautions

1. The basic remedial process requires individual attention before or after school.

- Every general music student needs to match pitch to sing in church and socially (e.g., caroling, sing-alongs, etc.)

2. Some coaching of pitch matching can take place in small groups.

- *Children can match the pitch of children's voices most easily* and the basic strategy works best by having students match a pitch produced by other students.

3. It does no good and considerable harm if some students are regularly allowed to sing "off pitch" when the rest of the class sings in tune.

- You need to consider how to tactfully and efficiently monitor and assist individual students in order to do them the favor of providing the skills for a rich musical life.
- Some steps of the basic strategy can be adapted for large group help.
    - ⮩ For example, tune-up the entire class on the first pitch (having them move arms and voices according to your model), and similarly tune-up tricky or otherwise weak passages pitch by pitch.

4. Students need the opportunity to hear their own performance.

- Frequent but brief opportunities for solos should be included. This eliminates reliance on the group and helps in learning to monitor one's own singing (pitch, tone, etc.). Solo singing is best begun in the primary grades where self-consciousness is rarely a factor. Then, in the later grades, singing alone is not a "big deal."
- Do not sing as a whole class exclusively! The *averaging effect of large numbers* makes whole-class singing sound better than an individual or smaller group and therefore misleads teacher and students alike. Use a variety of strategies for having segments of the class sing.
- For example, boys then girls; by rows (or, if seated in the preferred circle, x-number of students from the circle; for example, count off by five and have the "ones" sing, then the "twos," etc.), according to hair color, the color of the seats they are sitting in, all students with red socks, and so forth.
- While singing in groups, *listen carefully to individual voices.* Where possible, an individual may be briefly isolated for on-the-spot help. However, most problems can be addressed as though for the whole class (group or "part")—if they don't need the help, they don't mind.

- Do not sing along with the class! This hinders your monitoring of individuals and, worse, makes the performance sound better than it really is.

5. Male teachers have a disadvantage when it comes to teaching pitch matching to *un*-changed voices in the elementary school (and girl's voices thereafter). Matching pitch is even more difficult when the target pitch is an octave lower than what they can sing. Options:

   - Sing falsetto (i.e., in head voice) or use an alto or tenor recorder.
   - Sustain the target pitch on an electronic keyboard by using the built-in "voice" or "chorus" setting. Standard pianos cannot sustain the pitch and the timbre can confuse the process, but sometimes helps.
   - Have students produce the pitch to be matched (e.g., to tune-up a first note).

6. Women teachers have comparable problems working with the chan*ging* and chan*ged* male voices in middle school. Similar options should be used.

7. Exploring the difference between the speaking and singing voice can assist some students who do not immediately progress using the basic strategy.

   - Try calling out a name, as though calling a person who is a long way away, by sustaining (singing, not shouting) each vowel on a pitch: John - - - nie - - - (3 seconds on each syllable, using a falling minor third).
   - Have the student *speak*, then *sing* a sentence on a given pitch (any pitch).
   - Mark or point out certain syllables on which to *raise* the pitch (inflection): "My name is <u>Tom</u>my and <u>I'm</u> in <u>fifth</u> grade."
   - Choose different syllables for *lower* inflection: "My <u>name</u> is Tom<u>my</u> and I'm <u>in</u> fifth <u>grade</u>."
   - Sing (chant) slowly on a single pitch.
   - Stop on the highlighted syllables and sustain the raised or lowered pitch.
   - Change the starting pitch several times.
   - Sing all highlighted syllables on the same pitch: use whole steps and thirds, both up and down.
   - Mix pitches to be used on highlighted syllables. Sing by rote, not eye:

My name is Tom - my and I'm in fifth grade.

Example 7.2

VOCAL DEVELOPMENT

1. Fifth and sixth grade singers can produce a lovely and satisfying vocal tone.
   - A good tone should always be stressed.
   - Developing the head voice is important.
   - Attention to posture, breathing, and phrasing are important in all singing lessons.

- Expressive singing will produce results that these singers can hear and appreciate.

- Provide opportunities to 'critique' singing tone, phrasing, and expressiveness.

2. In general[†] in fifth and sixth grade girls can sing in a range from around $b^\flat$ or middle c to f^2 or g^2 while boy sopranos have a range of roughly a to e^2. However, except when working specifically to extend the ranges, sing mostly in a middle range.

   - By sixth grade, many boys' voices will drop a step or so lower than their fifth grade voices, while retaining their soprano quality.

   - This is the first step in the boy's *changing* voice.

   - If unison songs are sung in this somewhat lower range, girls are denied becoming comfortable with their higher ranges. This can explain why many girls progressively resist singing in their upper ranges.

   - Part singing that places boys on the lower part might seem to solve this problem, except that both boys and girls should be expected to sing *each* part.

   - Unison singing is therefore progressively a problem. As a result, some singing by boys and girls alone is advised, with the nonsinging group functioning as 'critical' listeners.

3. Different authorities have reached different conclusions concerning the **stages of development** of the *changing* boys' voice.

   - However, after an evolution that begins generally in sixth grade, the boys' voice typically settles for a while in middle school into what might be called a "teen baritone" which (again, authorities differ somewhat) can produce pitches from the vicinity of an octave below middle c to around d^1 or e^1.

     - ⇨ These singers are rarely comfortable at either extreme: lower pitches are often all but inaudible and the higher pitches often sound painfully strained. For them a middle *tessitura* should be used.

   - This is only a transitional stage!

     - ⇨ Some "teen baritones" will become "teen basses" (singing down to a G)— some as early as seventh grade. Some "teen basses" will become adult basses and others adult baritones.

     - ⇨ Other "teen baritones" will (if encouraged) develop the top of their ranges and become adult tenors.

     - ⇨ *Do not refer to "teen baritones" as "basses"* (e.g., in SAB music) since this misleads those who would otherwise develop into real *tenors* to *not* develop their upper ranges—thus creating a shortage of tenors!

   - In middle school, at least three different ranges need to be accommodated: women's voices (see the next point), boys with chan*ging* voices, and those with chan*ged* voices.

[†]Different researchers find slightly different results, or label similar results differently. See 3 following, as well.

- A traditional strategy assumes that all girls can sing in a range of about middle c to e^1. Boys are asked to sing a tune that has a range of an octave in the key of G or A.

  ➪ Boys who can mostly sing in the middle octave of the piano will be those with chan*ging* voices.

  ➪ Those who can sing mostly down the octave will be those with chan*ged* voices.

  ➪ Those singing in the upper octave will still be boy sopranos. Note: They decidedly prefer *not* to be called sopranos and do not like it to be obvious when they are singing "girls' parts"!

- Unison singing requires a careful negotiation of a key to accommodate all three ranges without straining. Failure in this criterion jeopardizes their willingness to sing.

  ➪ Pitch matching and other vocal problems are also worsened outside of a comfortable range.

4. The female voice, at this age, also undergoes subtle changes. Before puberty the voice is light and in the range suggested previously in no. 2.

- With the arrival of puberty, a "break" between the head and the chest voice becomes apparent, somewhere around a^1. Singing above the break is often breathy, while below the break, the chest voice—also used for shouting and cheering—is stronger and clearer.

- Some breathiness will disappear naturally as their bodies mature, but focus should be on proper breathing for building a strong, clear head tone. Girls also need to become comfortable negotiating the break between the chest and head voice.

- Many girls do not like singing above the break: It takes more "work" and sounds 'operatic' while, in contrast, singing in chest voice is "cool," like the "belt-singing" of pop singers. This attitude needs to be discouraged! It denies girls from developing their full ranges and hinders many kinds of recreational singing when being "cool" is no longer relevant.

READING PITCHES

The *ability to read music at a functional level for personal use* is the most important skill that could be taught in a general music class, since it opens wide-ranging possibilities for performing. Yet singers who read music most typically learn this skill by playing instruments or singing in chorus. The remaining majority of graduates served by general music classes typically do not learn to read music functionally.

Basic Issues

1. Many teachers do not advance beyond having their classes sing rote songs because they have no specific curricular goal for teaching students to read music vocally. Instead, they use "rote songs" to "teach concepts" for eventual application for listening.

- In an action-based program for praxis, music reading is a central goal.

2. Rote singing (imitating the teacher or a recording), of course, is the opposite of music reading. When rote singing is still the rule (not the exception) in grades 4–6, the "fun" of singing is gained at the loss of teaching vocal music reading.

3. A good deal of the weakness in teaching music reading arises from the problematic interaction of *two clusters of skills* that are best addressed *separately* at first:

> (a) pitch *matching* and other issues related to gaining control over the *singing voice*; and
>
> (b) *reading notation*—both pitch and rhythm.

Students who cannot *match pitch* with assurance cannot learn to *read notation* through *singing!*

- The voice is an instrument, and students need reasonable control of the vocal instrument before it can be used to read music.
- Attempts to teach pitch matching and music reading *simultaneously* consistently results in failure of both, with negative consequence for students' attitudes toward both skills.

Basic Strategy

1. *Music reading*—the ability to translate pitch and metric notation accurately and functionally into sound—*is most efficiently and effectively taught systematically using instruments.*

   - Pitch matching does not interfere with learning to read music, then, since the instrument provides the notated pitch.
   - Therefore, at least to begin with, performing from notation (i.e., reading music) and vocal pitch matching are best addressed separately.

2. The choice of an instrument for homogenous instruction will vary according to locale, student interests (and age), school resources and, of course, the teacher's ability. Following are some common choices.

   - Recorders are sometimes used.‡ They are inexpensive, easy to care for and can be taken home for practice. They also have positive transfer value to instruments such as flute and clarinet. Recorders are also "real" instruments.

The main instructional issue with the use of recorders is that some practice is required to produce a pitch in the appropriate register. *This should be mastered first.* A model where the mouthpiece can be separated from the body of the instrument is recommended so children can practice holding and fingering the instrument with-

---

‡In modern Japan, most students learn to match pitch in playground singing games before they even enter school. Even so, music reading in the national curriculum is taught in the primary grades using recorder. "Official" student bookbags even have a slot for the recorder so it can be carried conveniently from school for home practice.

out the temptations of blowing into the mouthpiece. Some schools ask families to buy the recorder and then buy back those recorders that students do not wish to keep. These are loaned to students who cannot afford instruments.

- "Flutophones" and pennywhistles are an option. These wind instruments easily allow students to produce a pitch. The former, however, has a very poor tone, looks like a plastic toy or classroom instrument (which it is—and such perceptions become more important beginning in fifth grade) and has little use outside the classroom. The pennywhistle, however, is a "real" folk instrument and it is available in different keys.
- Electronic keyboards are ideal in many respects:

    Producing a pitch is no problem.

    Multiple key signatures can be used.

    Visual familiarity with the keyboard itself is an asset for understanding steps and half steps, other intervals, and chord construction (see Chapter 4).

    Chording functions makes these instruments self-sufficiently satisfying to play. (They can also be used along with guitars, autoharps, and so on, just as a "chording instrument" for accompanying melodies in class).

    Even inexpensive electronic keyboards provide all kinds of interesting auto-effects—various timbres and rhythmic accompaniments.

    They are a frequent source of recreational performance. That is why they are widely sold in electronics and department stores—and so a collection can be purchased over time for school use when found on sale.

    Advanced electronic keyboards are used in connection with MIDI-based computer software. Familiarity with them opens a world of musical possibilities.

    Larger electronic keyboard allow students to learn to read the bass clef.

    Finally, electronic keyboards are an inviting introduction to a standard piano (acoustic or electronic) with its recreational possibilities.
- Keyboard-like instruments are often utilized. Tone bells, step bells and, of course, Orff instruments share the first three advantages of electronic keyboards. These are, however, only classroom instruments and do not model lifelong use.

    They are, however, ubiquitous in primary classrooms and in the absence of other resources can certainly be put to good use.

    However, beginning as early as fifth grade, students often start to view such instruments as "childish" and their intentionality for using them can therefore suffer.
- Folk and traditional instruments can be employed. A wide range of folk and traditional instruments have been used by successful teachers, for example, lap and hammered dulcimers, Celtic harps, ocarinas, and harmonica, just to name a few. Regionally popular folk and ethnic instruments should also be considered.

3. The readiness staging of instruction with instruments is discussed in Chapter 8, page 229.

4. Once students are able to accurately perform instruments from notation, they have the readiness for transfer of learning of music reading from playing to singing.

(a) Students must *predictably match pitch,*
(b) across at least the *vocal range demanded by typical songs,*
(c) *before* reading skills learned via instruments can *transfer* to singing!

Some Suggestions:

- Play a song using notation, first on instruments and then vocally. This helps the association between sight and sound.
- It is at this stage that a suitable *solfège system* for *pitch* reading can be employed.

    Some teachers favor a syllable system of "variable do" solfège. The Kodaly system (and variants) is perhaps most well known. Solfège also accommodates (at much higher levels of practice) accidentals.

    Other teachers prefer using numbers that correspond to scale degrees. This builds on transfer of learning from melody writing (Chapter 4).

    Still others use the names of pitches (which, in effect, is "fixed do" solfège).

- Critics of using scale degree numbers or pitch names point out the rhythmic implications of saying "sev-en" or "B flat" on a single note value.
- However, as discussed next, because "beginners (of any age) can focus on only one feature at a time," *pitch* reading and *rhythmic* reading *are best separated* at beginning stages.

While advocates will claim that *their* system is absolutely better than all of the others, more often the teacher's comfort, familiarity, and consistent use of a system—any system—are the determining factors. *Different teachers get equally good results using different instructional "tools"!*

- Rhythmic reading can be separately addressed by using a *rhythmic* solfège system consistently from kindergarten through grade 8. Teachers who are jointly responsible for a program—general music and instrumental teachers—need to agree on using a consistent system; or on a progression from one system to another between levels.
- Eventually (but sooner than later), teachers should approach a new song first by vocally sight reading it, *then* playing it on instruments, in order to confirm accuracy or help with tricky passages.

In elementary band lessons this is the preferred sequence since a valve can produce any number of pitches. In order for students to know when they have produced the wrong note, they need to already have the correct pitch or rhythm in their "inner ear." However, *at first* the process is reversed in general music class by relying on the predictability of instrument pitch production for teaching music reading, while vocal pitch matching is learned separately and then pitches are confirmed using instruments.

- After students can match pitch vocally and can perform from scores on instruments, *vocal music reading* can proceed as its own **primary focus**. Then, seeing the note should progressively result in "inwardly hearing" the correct pitch and rhythm and producing it *vocally.*

  Then the primary focus of instrumental lessons should be on improving instrumental tone and technique and expanding the repertory (of keys, styles, etc.), rather than as a readiness stage for music reading.

  However, instrumental and vocal reading will always be mutually advantageous in the general music or instrumental classroom.

All music reading, instrumental and vocal, should be constantly related to and derived from melody writing lessons (Chapter 4) to encourage transfer of learning!

- *Understanding how melodies are constructed* is central in *learning to perform melodies from notation.* Such cognitive and analytic skills naturally assist music reading: for example, awareness of skips of chord tones, repetition of rhythmic and melodic motifs, and so on.
- A recommended first step to a reading attempt (instrumental or vocal), then, is to *analyze a melody according to criteria learned in melodic composition lessons.*

All melody-writing lessons are also opportunities to stress music reading.

- *Students' melodies should often serve as first lessons in music reading.* This enhances transfer of cognitive musicianship to performing and, in any case, students have the intentionality to perform their own tunes because they want to hear them.

RHYTHMIC-METRIC READING

The benefits of *addressing pitch* and *rhythm/meter separately* were already mentioned. Each is a separate skill involving different cognitive knowledge.

- In general, *beginners (of any age) concentrate best on one new challenge or focus at a time.*
- Therefore, students need to be able to accomplish each skill separately before they can put the two together.
- Then a separate stage of practicing combines two previously separate skills into one (more complex) new skill.

Basic Strategy

1. Use a *consistent system* for rhythmic reading—either traditional counting or, more usually some kind of rhythmic solfège where syllables are assigned to note values.

    • Whatever system is adopted for rhythmic performance reading should also be used in all phases of melody *composition* that deal with rhythm!

Systems for reading pitches or rhythms are to performance as training wheels are to riding a bicycle. The system will help when they learn new music on their own (e.g., in choirs) but eventually they need to be weaned from the system to function in real-life situations. Classes need to practice translating notation into sound in real time without directly using the system—except for corrective purposes.

---

2. Underlying any system of counting must be a functional understanding of meter. And at the heart of meter, is the need to understand *simple* and *compound* meters.

In their zeal to simplify rhythmic reading, some teachers mistakenly teach that " the top number of a meter signature tells us how many beats there are in a measure, and the bottom number tells us what kind of note gets one beat." That is true only for simple meters. The *top* number of a *compound* meter signature does *not* represent the number of "beats" but, rather, the number of subdivided "counts." (See 7.3.)

    • Therefore, for example, compound-duple (e.g., 6/8) has *two beats* per measure (each a dotted quarter note), subdivided into *six counts* (each an eighth note).

---

3. The following (repeated here from Chapter 4) accurately represents meter and thus simplifies teaching meter and rhythmic reading.

METER

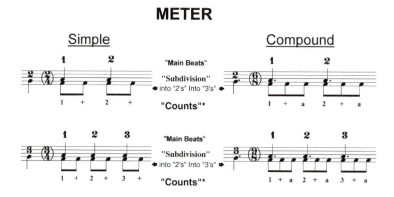

*The teacher's preferred rhythmic syllables should be used

Example 7.3

4. Make and post a huge chart that shows 7.3 for students to use as needed. Over time, wean students from using the chart.

5. Whatever rhythmic reading system is adopted, it should be used for the part of the chart pertaining to "counting": for example, "1 & 2 &" or "1 tah 2 tah" for simple; "1 & ah 2 & ah" or "1 tah tey 2 tah tey" for compound.

6. All the lessons in Chapter 4 that focus on rhythm should always be occasions for practicing rhythmic reading!

Nuts 'n' Bolts 'n' Cautions

1. The exact terminology adopted for 7.3 is not important. Some teachers might prefer to refer to "beats" and "subdivided beats" rather than "main beats" and "sub-beats."
   - However, *absolute consistency should be observed in terminology*—not only between different general music teachers in a district but between general music and instrumental teachers throughout the system!

2. "Counts" *is* a useful term for either writing in or otherwise ac*count*ing for beats and sub-beats.
   - At the beginning stages of rhythmic reading, have students actually write in all the counts. Do this lightly, then erase for subsequent classes. Otherwise, at least do this *as a class* on a transparency of the score.

3. Be clear when asking if the music "moves in twos or threes?" whether reference is to "main beats per measure" (i.e., simple duple or triple meters) or "subdivisions per main beat" (i.e., simple versus compound meter).

4. In addition to the note values shown on the chart, all versions of duple, triple, and quadruple meter should be the focus of lessons: where, for example, eighth and half notes are the "main beats."
   - For example renotate a 4/4 piece as 4/8, or 4/2 and perform it.
   - Renotate familiar tunes in a different meter (e.g., "Jingle Bells" in 4/4 rather than 6/8) for the class to perform.
   - Or, as part the rhythmic composition format (Chapter 4, pp. 96–99), have one group rearrange and another group performs the arrangement.
   - Early attempts at reading should feature both styles of meter signature side-by-side, as in 7.3. Eventually use only the traditional meter signature.

5. Finally, dancing, other movement (e.g., drill-team marching), and drumming usually improve students' rhythmic-metric reading.
   - Moving to different meters and in different rhythms (e.g., drumming, clogging, square dancing) gets rhythm and meter "into the body."
   - Dancing is useful in relation to ethnic musics, as well as for its social potential.

PART AND HARMONY SINGING

Singing in some type of harmony is one of the most satisfying of musical experiences. Therefore functional music reading is not complete until students can read and carry their own part in various kinds of part music. So, as reading progresses, part-singing should become a new focus.

Basic Strategy

1. Begin by learning to read a simple and short canon or round as a *unison song*.

2. Solidify the tune in their "inner ears" by using "silent singing":

   • Sing a few measures from notation, then (while mouthing the words silently), "hear" the next few measures, then reenter singing—hopefully in tune. Repeat, alternating the measures sung silently.

   • The experience of silent singing can be previewed by asking students individually to "sing mentally" (while mouthing words) a favorite song.

3. After students can both sing and *play* a tune:

   • Have half sing and half play it, and then reverse the groups. This helps students deal aurally with the distraction of a different part. It also insures that they read the music, not simply perform it by ear.

4. Finally, sing the song as a two-part round or canon.

   • First, have half sing one part and the others play the other part.

   • When first singing both parts, *do not use words.* Have one "part" sing the tune on the syllable "lah" and the other half on "loh." Thus each group hears itself better as a "section" and is less confused by the other part.

> This strategy of singing on contrasting vowels
> is useful for early stages of *all* part-singing, and in choir.

   • Once students can do this well, then sing both parts on words.

5. Expand the process to three and four-part rounds.

OTHER PART-SINGING LESSONS

1. *Partner songs* These are two different songs that have the same chords and so fit together when sung at the same time, for example, "Three Blind Mice" and "Row, Row, Row Your Boat." Many partner songs are featured in commercial song series and arrangements.

   • First sing and play each separately.

   • Then, sing one and play the other, then switch.

   • Finally, sing both.

2. *Countermelodies and descants* These arrangements feature a melody in counterpoint of some kind that accompanies the original melody. Usually the second melody is rhythmically and melodically distinct. The most useful are those that are musically interesting in their own right.

   • Again, teach the original tune and the second one separately, then one vocally and one instrumentally, then combine them vocally.

3. *Part-song arrangements* Start simple, for example, expanding to two parts at cadence points. Make sure everyone gets to perform both the tune and the harmony.

- With harmony parts (including partner songs and countermelodies) each part can first be performed with half the students singing and half playing (then reverse). Once students' ears become accustomed to where and how to move melodically, then all parts can be sung.

Nuts 'n' Bolts 'n' Cautions

1. All the previously described lessons depend in early stages on (a) first performing the parts on instruments, (b) then combining singing and playing parts, and (c) finally singing all parts together. Therefore:

- Competence with playing instruments from notation is a readiness "prerequisite."
- In classes where this is not possible (or curriculum does not address instrumental performance), some benefit is gained from the teacher performing new parts on an instrument while the students all sing the part they already know. This at least introduces the "complication" of singing along with a new part.

2. Unless the *eye guides the ear*, parts are learned only by rote. Whatever the pleasures of just singing a song, no progress will be made in developing music *reading* skills.

- This is one advantage for using instruments in the readiness staging of part-singing lessons. Because students can rarely play a part by ear, they have to use the score. Students who *can play*, but *cannot* match pitch well yet (or refuse to sing) can still be productively engaged.

3. Some *singing harmony by ear* should also be attempted. This models the process and pleasures of many "sing along" kinds of occasions.

- Sing a harmony part while the class sings the unison song (or have half the class just listen).
- Do this several times, on several occasions, always singing the same harmony part.
- Encourage students to "sing along" with that harmony part. Those who *can* "hear" it will sing it while the rest will remain on the melody.
- Use "sing along" or "barbershop" kinds of harmonization such as "You are my Sunshine," and the like.

4. Students struggling to match pitch will struggle all the more with harmony or second parts. They should sing "the tune" until they have the vocal and ear training readiness for part-singing.

Musical independence is encouraged when the whole class does not function as a "chorus" all the time. Instead, for example, once two-part songs are learned as a "chorus," subdivide the class into "duet groups" of perhaps, 4–6 singers per part. Thus the "duet" is performed by a total of 8–12 singers, with the rest of the class acting as a discriminating and appreciative audience.

LEARNING AS PRACTICING

Singing, performing with instruments, and learning to read music all require practice. Lessons must provide plenty of practice. However, practice is not simply repetition. **Practice** is repetition undertaken *mindfully* by students in light of specific performance goals and assessment criteria. To practice effectively, students need to identify 'right' from 'wrong' notes and how to correct the latter. Independent musicianship requires that they eventually be able to do this on their own!

However, many teachers avoid practicing skills in class lessons because they worry students will become bored. In actuality, however, students are intrinsically motivated when mastering skills they find interesting and satisfying. And it meets their *need for achievement!* The key, then, is to focus on short-term rewards and pleasures.

1. Skill-based practice should set goals that can be achieved *within the lesson itself.*
   - Students should be able to *do* something new or better than before the practicing.
   - At the very least, use the **rubrics** described in Appendix B to *guide practice* and as **summative evaluation**.

2. Such improvements should be easily noticeable by the students, and *they* ought to be the primary judges of whether or not the goals in question have been reached.
   - *Listening to and critiquing their own performances* according to certain criteria (e.g., rubrics) is a minimal requirement of all practicing and a major means for developing musical independence.
     - ⇨ For example, a singing lesson that focuses on pitch accuracy can be recorded as a basis for improvement by the class.
     - ⇨ Or, one half the class can critique a performance by the other half, until the whole class performance improves.
     - ⇨ Use "auditors": for example, four students are chosen to audit and critique a class performance according to set criteria. Their comments serve as the basis for improvement. Then four different auditors listen, and so on. Regularly rotate the auditors so that all students get experience.

3. Concert-like performances (for a given "rehearsal") are motivating.
   - Prime practicing by performing when the classroom teacher returns to pick up the class. Students will practice with more intentionality, and they enjoy performing for their teacher.
   - Prime a rehearsal to result in a recorded performance. In a subsequent class, listen to and critique the recording as a basis for additional improvement.
   - Prime a rehearsal to produce a recording that students know will be heard by other classes at their level. This introduces **comparitition** as a motivation for practice. Be sure that each class gets to hear the performance of at least one other class.
   - Rehearse to contribute to a "class album"—that is, a collection of performances (singing, playing of standard, and class-composed melodies and sound compositions) that have reached a "polished level," as decided on by the class. Students can "dub" their own copies if they want to take them home. Some teachers may arrange for inexpensive CDs to be made.

- Teachers who maintain a Web site devoted to student compositions and in-class performances can rehearse with the possibility of selected performances being heard on the Web site for a set period of time. Students can be part of the selection process (thus listening to the "best" of other classes) or, in any case, should understand the teacher's selection criteria.

Nuts 'n' Bolts 'n' Cautions

1. Notice that rehearsing, by its very nature, depends on and incorporates a great deal of listening according to pre-stated criteria, on the basis of which students then **act adaptively** by trying to improve the performance.

2. While the teacher must certainly diagnose shortcomings, it is counterproductive when the teacher makes *all* corrections!
   - Ultimately, students need to be able to self-evaluate *that* an error (or weakness) exists, *what* the error is (or *why* it is weak), *how* to fix it, and *whether* it is fixed.

3. Such self-diagnostic skills are the essence of **independent musicianship** and a condition of lifelong use.
   - Independent self-monitoring enhances the present and future effectiveness of students' *performances*.
   - It also develops criteria for *listening* to performances, for example in concerts. Even students who do not continue to perform become more discriminating listeners in regard to performance values and variables themselves (e.g., tone, steady tempo, etc.).

4. *Listening to expert models* should be a significant part of any performance-based curriculum!
   - Performances by student musicians—high school and collegiate—are very useful in this regard.
   - Invite visiting artists and, especially, local amateurs. The latter are often central in helping students to understand "breaking 100 in music" as a possibility for their own lives.
   - Have fifth grade students listen to the performances of sixth grade students, and so on up the grades. This motivates students toward the next highest level of progress to which an age group can aspire.
   - Commercial videos and CDs should be used, and performances by adult visitors and student musicians should be videorecorded for future use.

General Considerations

1. Repertory for singing should be personally rewarding now while serving as a basis for further interest and development after and outside of school.
   - In general, "less is more"! That is, a limited repertory carefully selected and practiced to the level of producing functional skills and musical independence (at least to a beginning level) is more effective than a wide-ranging repertory 'surveyed' only superficially.

2. Singing in the middle school, often beginning in seventh grade, is resisted by some students. Some of this attitude is a natural (but mistaken) development

that comes with early adolescence—the impression that classroom singing is "childish" and not "cool." With boys, it is often related to voice change and to an impression they have—despite all the male rock stars—that singing is uncool for boys (or is intimidating in front of girls).

- This mind-set often arises when, rather than developing notable skill improvement, past classroom singing has involved mainly musical "fun and games" that pre- and early adolescents associate with the primary grades. Aside from not rewarding their need for achievement, such singing is not seen as relevant to soon-to-be "young adults."

- Therefore, a program for systematically teaching singing (pitch matching, tone production, range enhancement) and music reading should begin *no later than fourth and fifth grade*. Then middle school students are more respectful of and interested in increasing vocal skills along lines suggested in this chapter.

3. Repertory for middle school singing and music reading lessons must be chosen carefully in line with their interests.

- At the very least, they need to feel that "real music" is involved, not "children's songs."

- Lyrics suited to their cognitive and intellectual development (see Chapter 2) are crucial criteria of songs they prefer to sing—especially in middle school!

- Students will also take more interest in "real" songs that are serving as models for their own melody compositions. They are often eager to sing their own songs.

4. Above all, and despite any reluctance, *middle school students must be encouraged to keep singing* and *to improve basic music reading*. Gains made in the intermediate years must not be allowed to wither from disuse.

- Attitudes and values at the end of middle school usually continue into high school and adulthood.

- Middle school is, then, the last chance to inspire some lifelong interest in music and, simultaneously, is a springboard for high school and adult interests and activities.

- General music classes taught along lines suggested here will increase participation in high school general music electives and choir.

CHAPTER EIGHT

RECREATIONAL INSTRUMENTS

INTRODUCTION

Amateur performance on instruments is a bona fide source of **"good time"** and deserves its own curricular focus beyond its role in teaching music reading. However, learning to play "real" folk, **social** or recreational instruments as a basis for lifelong amateur performance is too infrequently an explicit curricular goal of general music curriculums.

> An action-based general music curriculum seeks to "turn on" students to the pleasures of personal performance on social and recreational instruments—including those who already study piano and orchestral instruments privately or who play in the band or orchestra. And the instrumental instruction described in this chapter also develops the type of musicianship that influences listening skills and habits, even for those who do not continue playing past their school years.

Many considerations for selecting instruments and ideas for their use in teaching *music reading* were explained in Chapter 7 (pages 201–212). Choice of instruments for class use is also influenced by:

- budgets controlling which and how many instruments can be afforded.
- the teacher's ability to play and teach several instruments.
- the size and layout of the instructional and storage spaces.
- important differences concerning each of the instruments chosen for inclusion.

> Specialized sources should be consulted for details concerning teaching individual instruments.

BASIC ISSUES

1. TEACHING BASIC *MUSIC READING* AND *INSTRUMENTAL TECHNIQUE* ARE BEST FOCUSED ON *SEPARATELY*

Pitch and rhythm must be produced on an instrument with technical assurance *before* efficient and (from the student's point of view) satisfying progress can be made with music reading. Some students struggle with one or both skills and focusing on these two separate skills simultaneously invites confusion and consternation.

Once *basic music reading*—for example, in C, G, and F major—is mastered, then new literature with its new technical challenges becomes the **primary focus**. New literature should be chosen with this technical progress in mind. The closer the literature progresses to adult or "real-life" models the more naturally it will advance technique (e.g., new fingerings, alternative fingerings, new strums, etc.)

When *reading* lessons are the focus of the moment, students should not need to struggle with the basics of technique—with the exception of learning a new fingering, chord, and so on. However, any students who take private lessons or are in ensembles usually already read well enough to focus from the first on fingerings and instrumental technique.

Technical progress on the instrument sufficient to initiating lifelong recreational interest is the central focus of this chapter! Therefore, technique lessons should:

- Assume *readiness* with the basics of music reading and,

- Always begin by *reviewing* and *previewing* any relevant music reading aspects of a lesson: for example, meters, key, tricky rhythms, and pitch patterns such as chord skips, and so forth.

2. THE SELECTION OF INSTRUMENTS IS VERY IMPORTANT

When resources permit, simply allowing some *choice* increases students' interest and intentionality and, as a result, the likelihood of practicing—particularly when instruction starts in middle school. Choices can be "guided" if there is reason to suspect that a given student is more likely to succeed with one instrument rather than others.

- Teaching all students the same instrument is simpler in terms of pedagogy and resources, but carryover to playing outside of school is greater when students choose instruments that interest them (for whatever reason).

- An assortment of different instruments also allows greater variety in the kinds of combinations and literature performed in class.

- Combining melody and chording instruments is especially recommended since it allows tunes to be accompanied by harmony and enhances transfer between tonal composition lessons (Chapter 4) and performing lessons (Chapters 7, 8).

- Electronic keyboards are ideal for the reasons listed in Chapter 7. Playing melodies and chords are both easy to accomplish and transfer value to life is high.

- Guitar is a popular choice, though for teaching music reading for purposes of singing it involves the separate step of learning tablature! The baritone ukulele is self-sufficiently satisfying, works well with smaller hands, and can eventually lead to guitar.

- Depending on the region, banjos, lap and hammered dulcimers and other folk instruments are attractive for lifelong personal enjoyment.

Band and orchestral instruments students already own can introduce the complications of transposition if students are to play and practice together in the same key. This can occasionally be worthwhile if students who quit studying an instrument can be gotten to play it again under classroom circumstances. However, the slower **learning curve** of such instruments—not to mention the loudness level contributed by wind instruments—can be a burden. Students who already study band and orchestral instruments are usually interested in studying folk and traditional instruments in general music class,* and learn quickly.

---

*Violinist's, however, can learn "country fiddlin' " in general music class—something not usually allowed in their regular lessons. Their advanced status, however, will require more independent planning.

3. SPECIFIC CONSIDERATIONS FOR CHOOSING INSTRUMENTS

a. *Expense* Not only must the acquisition of instruments be considered; the upkeep of instruments, and how easily they can be moved and stored (and possibly damaged) is also important.

- High quality instruments are usually a better investment in terms of wear and tear, playability, tone, and ease or frequency of repair.
- Repair and replenishment of strings, and so forth, must be considered in terms of budget, but also in terms of local availability. Using instruments for which parts or repair expertise are not locally available makes you dependent on mail-order merchants.

b. *Storage and access*

- Instruments that are set up permanently in the classroom (e.g., electronic keyboards, hammered dulcimers, etc.) save time but need to be protected from unsupervised use and abuse.
- Otherwise, storage space must be available, accessible, and easily secured or monitored.
  - ➪ Storage rooms can be conducive to "traffic jams" when getting or returning instruments! Sending students in "waves" avoids chaos, though this wastes class time.
- Some instruments are sensitive to temperature and humidity change and typically require more expensive and more frequent repair. String replacement is a constant problem for guitars, mandolins, ukuleles, and the like.

c. *Tuning* Stringed instruments need to be tuned frequently even under ideal storage conditions. This consumes more class time than those requiring no tuning or minor touch-ups.

d. *Personal use* The likelihood that students can and might want to acquire their own instruments—while they are students, and later in life—should be an important criterion!

- Personal ownership of the instruments (even inexpensive instruments, such as recorders or pennywhistles) enhances the likelihood of home practicing!

- Cooperative arrangements with local music merchants can be mutually advantageous. In return for reduced prices for instrument purchase and maintenance, the curriculum promotes the number of students who purchase their own instruments.

- Electronic keyboards are often "on sale" at local stores, especially after Christmas. Over time enough of the smaller ones can be acquired to outfit an *entire* classroom.

Electronic keyboards are perhaps the most ideal choice for many classrooms

- They instantly produce a pitch (unlike, e.g., playing a recorder) and require no tuning or maintenance (just periodic replacement).

- Because melody and harmony can be performed together (with built-in rhythmic accompaniments, which is a major "plus" in students' minds!) performances are holistic and musically satisfying—which is, no doubt, why their recreational use has led to an entire industry. Therefore, their ubiquity in the "real world" makes them a natural candidate for use outside of school and throughout life!

- Units that have earphones are a distinct advantage for silent practicing!

- Having a few larger, more "high tech" keyboards increases the possibility students will want to purchase their own. They are also an "incentive": Once students have practiced a piece on a more basic keyboard, they can play (or record) it with the richer enhancements available on the more sophisticated instrument.

- Instruments not readily available in typical music or department stores are less likely to be acquired for home use in the future.

    However, Internet searches can locate sources for mail order of any instrument.

    Students playing these instruments should *in any case* be assigned to search Web sites for their instruments. In addition to purchase information, they will find clubs, events, recordings, sources of literature, and so on.

Teachers should do Internet searches on their own. This is the best way to locate information on prices to compare to local merchants, teaching materials, recordings, videos, even interest groups of amateurs, and so on.

- Teaching handbells in class (and starting handbell choirs) makes sense where local churches have handbell choirs. In any case, schools that develop student interest and skill can enable local churches to start such ensembles. However, handbells are expensive and require considerable care. A variety of less expensive *hand chimes* are available from various manufacturers and are best for classroom use. Then only one set of handbells is required for public performances.

e. *"Standard" instruments"* Some, such as piano (acoustic, but especially electronic pi- anos) and electric guitars (including bass guitar), can be considered for middle school students due to their eventual relevance for "garage bands," church use, and so on.

- Rock (i.e., 'pop music' generally) is an important musical praxis and there is no reason it should be ignored or excluded as a performance medium in schools.

Popular melodic and chording instruments of various ethnic traditions can be con- sidered when such groups are represented in the community. This increases the like- lihood for out-of-school use in life—for example, in family traditions, seasonal festivals, and celebrations. Even if the teacher is not able to improve student per- formance on instruments learned at home, the opportunity for their inclusion in class will enrich the musical environment and improve cultural understanding. It also opens the door for having local groups serve as models by performing in class or concerts.

- For purposes of simultaneous use in class, however, only instruments can be chosen that use a basic chromatic scale and the presence of such in- struments increases the problems of heterogeneous instruction explained next.

- Various kinds of drumming lessons included as part of multicultural or world mu- sic study need *curricular* separation from instrumental instruction that teaches mu- sic reading and harmony (e.g., such as "hearing" when to change a chord)—al- though steel drums and various kinds of marimbas (e.g., African) are possibilities.

f. "Classroom instruments" These are instruments that require little or no skill to play and, thus technical progress is not required. As a result, such instruments rarely chal- lenge or reward many students' **need-for-achievement,** nor are they musically satis- fying as students get older. Furthermore, because they are not seen as "real" (or do not have their own available "literature") and are not even typically available in mu- sic stores, they are unlikely to transfer to lifelong recreational use. An exception is the *zither* trademarked as the Autoharp® and it's various electronic cousins.

- Nonetheless, where only classroom instruments are available, they should be used to their fullest to teach music reading, to model the importance of practice, and as a musical "outlet" for students who have no other performance possibilities.

- Some classroom instruments can be used to play (and introduce) music of other instrumental media that can initiate interest in that medium: for example, Orff instruments used to play steel band arrangements, or tone bells used to play hand- bell literature—especially where steel bands and handbell choirs are after-school options. Then, in-class lessons promote membership in ensembles that use "real" instruments.

If resources are limited, students in grades 4 and 5 should be taught basic reading skills using classroom instruments.

These reading skills are applied in grades 4 and 5 to singing (see Chapter 7) and then to recreational, social, and ethnic instruments used in middle school classes.

Under typical conditions, use of "real" instruments begins in grade 6.

Avoid, if possible, using instruments in the middle school classroom that students associate with "elementary school." Orff instruments are a major exception, though by middle school, all key bars should be in place when the instrument is used.

4. *ADVANTAGES* OF USING A SELECTION OF ASSORTED INSTRUMENTS IN CLASS

- Through the models provided by classmates (i.e., "That looks like fun!"), students will develop an interest in another instrument and pursue it instead (or in addition) to their own.

- Students can choose instruments that align with their abilities (see no. 5.). Some can excel on a simpler instrument but will struggle on others. Transfer students who are instantly "behind" should be encouraged to begin on simpler instruments.

- Combining melody and chording instruments in the same class promotes important transfer of learning to and from melodic composition lessons that focus on harmony. When only melody instruments *or* chording instruments (e.g., usually guitars) are used, such musical and educational richness is missing.

- For the same reasons, performance lessons involving heterogeneous instruments are more ensemble-like and therefore more musically satisfying. Class "albums"—recordings of class performances—can be produced, and classes can even perform at assemblies of younger students, at retirement homes, and the like.

- "Small ensembles" can be created within the class (e.g., one or two of each instrument in the class) that practice together to produce recordings that they can take home.

Such "small ensemble" performances are the most effective and efficient bases for student self-assessment and teacher evaluation of progress. Students produce written 'critiques' and such recordings are far more efficient than setting up individual "tests"—not to mention, students often perform better when not under the pressure of a solo auditing.

5. COMPLICATIONS OF HETEROGENEOUS GROUPING

- The teacher needs facility on each instrument.
- Very careful management staging and readiness staging need to be planned.
  - ⇨ Different steps and directions are required for each instrumental group.
  - ⇨ Some instruments that are simpler to play will be learned more quickly than other instruments, and students need to focus on refinements while others focus on basics.
  - ⇨ Readiness staging involves keeping track of the different sequences of skill development natural to each instrument. For example, melody players can play in

a new key just by learning one new fingering, while the new chord needed for that key usually entails more skill and practice by guitar players.

- Literature has to be arranged by the teacher so that students can play together often.
- Most importantly, the literature and arrangements must incorporate pedagogy for teaching *all* the instruments, *simultaneously*, from the *beginning*. This means that *students must be able to progress at their own rate within a group context.*

  ⇨ This involves a difference between *individual* and *multiple* sequences of technique development.

Individual Versus Multiple Sequencing of Technical Progress

Individual sequencing

In traditional instrumental teaching, students move at their individual pace through a *sequence of literature* that progressively elicits technical progress. The sequence of technical improvement for an individual, then, involves simply changing the literature! However, students inevitably progress at different rates. This pedagogy becomes progressively problematic for group instruction because students quickly get "out of sync" with each other's rate of learning. Group lessons for beginners given by instrumental teachers often proceed on the basis of individual sequencing (usually the next tune in the method book)—and quickly run afoul of it, as well! The only saving grace is that such groups are small and involve the same instrument. Even then, some of the large dropout rate of beginning group instrumental lessons can be attributed to this problem.

- With *individual sequencing,* students gain new technique *at their own rate* by moving to ever-*different* literature.
- But precisely because individuals learn at *different rates,* even small group instruction on the same instrument is progressively difficult to coordinate.

Multiple (or parallel) sequences

In teaching diverse instruments in large groups, traditional sequencing based on individual progress is especially doomed to failure. Not only do *students* have different **learning curves** but, as mentioned, different *instruments* are easier or harder to play! Therefore, in classes where students will play together—which is a primary feature and value of such instruction—technique needs to be improved using *common literature!* While that literature is varied, and often introduces new technical challenges (keys, fingerings, etc.), in a general music class setting, it cannot be the sole or even primary basis for technical progress.

Multiple sequencing involves all students playing the *same literature* but at multiple levels of technique.

This entails making arrangements that provide for *multiple levels of technical progress* per each piece and, thus, that accommodate *parallel sequences* of technical improvement on different instruments (see 8.3). Students perform together, but on a part that suits their present stage of progress.

In Example 8.1 a basic arrangement of "Skip to My Lou" features the traditional tune and a harmony part for "duet" playing.*

- Students playing *melody instruments* (e.g., recorders, pennywhistles, keyboards) would first practice the tune.

- Those who learn it quickly would then practice the duet part, which has the same rhythm but some different pitches.

Example 8.1

*Examples 8.1–8.2 are drawn from: Rick Bunting, *Teaching Traditional Music and Instruments: A Classroom Approach.* (Traditional Music Materials, 8 Kirby Street, Bainbridge, NY 13733).

- Variations 1, 2, and 3 of the tune progressively challenge quicker learners with increased technical demands.

- The piece is performed with all or preselected parts playing together. Students who just learn the basic tune are still able to make a positive contribution and achieve satisfaction. And, they will be motivated to progress beyond the next basic tune to its variations and harmony part.

- Those who cannot even play the basic tune yet can, in group performance, play the "simplified" version—which uses the pitches they have been practicing, but in a rhythmically and melodically simplified form.

Notice that Example 8.1 (page 220) also provides for chording instruments (see no. 6 following—"Chording instruments"). The chords are shown in boxes and the strums indicated as slashes showing the metric accents.

- At first, harmony players just perform basic strums (or, for keyboards, actual block chords—not the "one finger" auto-chord function!) in the indicated meter.

Simplified

Skip To My Lou

Variation 1

Skip To My Lou

Example 8.1

Continued

Variation 2

Skip To My Lou

Variation 3

Skip To My Lou

- As the students improve (and perhaps become bored), more interesting strums (or keyboard figurations) and techniques are taught (e.g., as shown in 8.3 on p. 224). This allows them to progress and makes the overall result more satisfying for everyone (especially for recorded performances).
- Students having trouble with a new chord—the fingering or hand shift—can, for now, play only the chords they know.

Example 8.2 demonstrates a melodic arrangement of the traditional tune "Rakes of Mallow" that features three different levels of expertise on the way to learning to play the basic tune.

- The basic tune is scored on the bottom staff. On the very top staff is the simplified version; it features all the pitches needed to play the basic tune, but in simpler arrangement so that slower learning students can perform successfully with the other parts. The middle staff is intermediate in technical difficulty; it includes all basic notes of the tune but the fast moving eighth notes of the original tune will require more technique.

- A two-part version of this tune can be arranged in the same format as 8.1 so that the entire process can result in duets.

Rakes of Mallow

Copyright 1986 by Rick Bunting

Example 8.2

A pedagogy based on multiple sequencing requires the teacher to develop a *parallel sequence* of technique *stages* (i.e., **readiness staging** of *technique*) for each instrument in class. Each technique stage for one instrument has a parallel stage for the other instruments.

Example 8.3 shows this parallel sequencing of technical stages for guitar, recorder and keyboard. The sequence of staging moves from most basic at the top to progressively more advanced skills as you move down the sequence.

Parallel Sequencing of Comparable Technique Stages**		
Guitar	**Recorder**	**Keyboard**
Strum open strings	Play one note	First chord (left hand)
One finger chords	Add new note(s)	Add new chord
Full chord(s)	Melodic exercises	Add new chord
Bass/strum	Melodic exercises	Broken Chord(s)
Simplified melody (tablature)	Simplified Melody	Simplified Melody
Melody	Melody	Melody
Duet	Duet	Duet
Variation(s)	Variation(s)	Variation(s)
Melody and chords	Variation(s)	Melody and Chords
Example 8.3		

6. CHORDING INSTRUMENTS: GUITAR, BARITONE UKULELE, MANDOLIN, LAP DULCIMER, KEYBOARDS, ETC.

Players of chording instruments can profit from learning to play melodies on their instruments (see, e.g., 8.3, guitar tablature), if for no other reason than it teaches music reading skills that can then transfer to singing. (The publication from which 8.1 and 8.2 were drawn also includes tablature for melody playing on guitar and mandolin, and tablature publications are widely available.)*

   a. In order to prime the intentionality of guitar players, for example, teachers must be prepared to prime—by personal example, or at least by video—the virtues and values of the possibilities such melodic skills provide for guitar players.

   b. At the very least, students should be encouraged to play "walking bass" kinds of patterns and "fills."

**Chart by Rick Bunting.

c. One advantage keyboards have is that students can learn to play both the tune and the chords.

7. PRACTICE FOR PROGRESS

It is a safe conclusion that if students do not practice and are not held accountable for progress, they will make little headway.

Do not just leave students to their own practicing ideas. Students need to be taught *how* to practice, and they need plenty of *opportunities* to practice *in class* and, if needed, after school.

Timed practice: A period of clock time within a lesson during which students are assigned to practice acquiring a certain skill, literature, and so on, that they will need to be accountable for at the end of that time period.

Supervised practice: Practicing under the supervision of the teacher, who monitors and helps correct students' mistakes

Guided practice (coaching): Diagnostic hints and suggestions for how to overcome certain technique problems such as a hand-shift. Advanced students can often provide this function.

Basic protocol:

1. Preview and model, step-by-step, a particular *practicing format* (see page 226) suited to the learning at hand.

2. Then, lead the class through the individual steps of the format.

3. Assign *timed practice*, during which the teacher must quickly monitor individuals' practicing and give specific coaching.

When several individuals have the same or similar problems, stop and reiterate (or revise) the *practice format* for the benefit of all rather than waste time making the same comments over and over again to individuals.

---

4. The class (or instrument group) performs together several times, therefore affording the teacher one final opportunity to assist those in need.

5. Finally some individual accountability must be provided by which each student's practicing is assessed (see "Accountability" page 227). Have, for example, groups of three or four (on the same instrument) perform the same music together and focus on and evaluate individual performers (while the remainder of the class is asked to listen and constructively critique); or use the "small ensembles" of mixed instruments mentioned earlier.

- <u>Practicing formats</u>—are "set" routines, strategies, and gimmicks for overcoming customary problems. These should be taught in class as models for a student's own practicing. Each format should be presented as a sequence of *readiness stages*. For example, the following model can be useful for beginners learning a new part on most melody instruments.

  a. Practice *saying* the names of the notes, in order, out of rhythm.

  b. Say and *silently finger* the notes, in order, out of rhythm (turn keyboards off).

  c. Play the pitches slowly, in order, *on equal note values*. Gradually speed up the tempo.

  d. Preview and practice *speaking* the rhythms; for example, on "tah" or rhythm syllables.

  e. *Play* the rhythms, slowly, *on one pitch*, observing rests, and so on. Gradually speed up the tempo.

  f. Combine pitches and rhythms at a slow tempo.

  g. Speed up the tempo.

  Additional steps may be added, as applicable to a particular instrument or skill: for example, practice formats are especially useful for hand-shifts on fretted instruments and piano. What is important, though, is that different practicing formats for common problems be used for *in-class practice*.

- <u>Out-of-class practice</u>—depends on student access to the instruments in question and, of course, parental interest and cooperation.

  a. In an action-based curriculum for praxis, it is important, however, to *eventually get students regularly practicing and playing outside of class*.

  b. Students who are not progressing in class (or transfer students) should practice after school, in school.

  c. Letting students take (certain) instruments home for use and practice needs to be carefully considered in terms of (a) possible damage to the instrument, and (b) what to do if the student is not in school (or "forgets" to bring the instrument—for example, your only mandolin—from home) the next time it is needed in class.

  d. Start after-school "clubs" which in effect will be "ensemble-classes" that, with minimal teacher coaching, *practice-in-action*. Such clubs function best when they have "gigs," or performance goals in mind (e.g., to make a recording).

- *Effective practicing*—takes places under the conditions of intentionality and accountability.

- *Intentionality*—comes into play when the students have interest in and derive musical pleasure from *progress*. Progress, then, becomes its own reward and motivates further practicing.

- *Student accountability*—is the responsibility on the part of individual students for showing progress via formal assessment.

8. ACCOUNTABILITY

An action-based program for praxis involves a substantial *commitment to the inclusion of instrumental instruction.*

Instruments are not simply used casually or sporadically, or merely to "teach concepts," or to "experience" various cultural differences. Rather, the curriculum is committed to advancing all students to predescribed *functional levels* on at least one instrument. *Students,* then, need to be accountable for their practicing and the *teacher* needs to be accountable for the effectiveness of instruction, as well. Accountability motivates intentionality and "application" in the same way that assignments do in all other subjects.

1. *Short-run accountability*: Frequent constructive "critiques" function as diagnoses and suggestions for on-going practicing,

   - Timed practicing is recommended. Shorter assigned times produce more intense practicing when assessment follows. The teacher should audit and critique results.

   - Regularly have students critique themselves (and each other), with the teacher then assessing their critiques.

2. *Middle-range accountability*: A progression of specific literature for which all students must attain basic competence (however defined, and whether or not "graded").

   - These take the form of "repertory lists" that students "pass-off" or "check-off" as they demonstrate competence.

   - "Passing" an item ought to be guided by **rubrics** that describe and rate at least: *tempo* (both consistency and acceptable metronome speed); *technique* (e.g., fingering, chord, shifts, etc.); *tone* quality and *intonation* (where applicable; i.e., neither is an issue for electronic keyboards); *accuracy* (with notation); and overall *musical effect.*

   - Individuals can indicate readiness to be "tested" for purposes of "passing" an item. But it is usually more efficient to hear "small ensembles" that allow you to hear and evaluate the adequacy of each player. At **summative evaluation** points, performances can be for the class as the audience. Otherwise the teacher listens to one "ensemble" while the rest are still practicing.

   - Repertory checklists (and recorded "albums" of "finished" pieces) should be a significant part of student evaluation and can be included in student portfolios.

   - Different repertory lists should be selected for each grade level. When such requirements are strictly maintained, students will expect to be held responsible for these skills, even if it means practicing after or outside of school.

A primary consideration in selecting repertory is the *parallel sequencing of technique stages* (see 8.3). In addition, repertory lists should be very carefully chosen to provide: (a) a reasonable selection of typical *technical skills* for the instrument(s) in question; (b) new *musicianship* skills (i.e., knowledge of keys, chords, etc.) typical for the literature; (c) *sequential progress* of the first two factors such that students

build on previous stages of expertise in developing ever *new expertise*, (d) that approaches or approximates levels needed for *musical independence* and "good time."
Note: Have students play at least one of their own composed melodies as part of their list of requirements!

3. *Long-run accountability*: **Authentic assessment** needs to be summative, thus taking place at key points during study—including in subsequent years.

- Summative evaluation is crucial when students move on to new teachers in middle school.

- Students' *reading* readiness should be tested at the beginning of middle school instruction: (a) *Pre*-tests identify curricular weaknesses at earlier levels and, (b) identify students—especially transfer students—who need *remedial* help.

- Students can be *post*-tested at the conclusion of each grade level or at the end of middle school by means of an independently prepared piece from a list of choices. (a) This indicates the degree to which the action ideal for recreational performance is being met; and, if not, what areas in general need to be improved by curriculum and instruction; (b) post-tests provide a certain amount of incentive for students to practice (as long as this "incentive" does not become "pressure" that is strictly extrinsically focused on the test); and (c) they provide tangible evidence of progress and accomplishment: "This is what I can do that I couldn't do before I received instruction."

4. *Variable student accountability*: (a) Some instruments simply require more practice; and (b) individual students exhibit a wide range of capability and thus accomplishment, even when they practice equally well.

- Provision (a) needs to be taken into consideration in constructing repertory lists, planning parallel sequencing, writing rubrics, and so on.

- While (b) is taken into consideration during instruction by the variable versions of literature mentioned, final results will still find some students making less progress than others.

The "bottom line" for Action Learning is not to arrive at a grade; it is whether and to what degree a student has made progress that at least approaches a beginning level of proficiency for lifelong interest. Therefore, criteria that take a student's initial or natural abilities into consideration are recommended over "absolute" standards applied equally across-the-board. This is the only reasonable policy where transfer and special students are taught.
The use of the type of **rubrics** explained in Appendix B is highly recommended.

5. *Teacher accountability*: The means and materials of instruction are judged to be successful in terms of the total number of students who (a) develop a recreational inter-

est in their instrument and (b) a beginning level of musical independence sufficient to making more progress on their own.

- To insure independence, over time students should be allowed to begin new music on their own. And, as mentioned, summative evaluations should be based on an "independently learned" piece.

BASIC STAGING OF INSTRUMENTAL LESSONS

The specifics of management and readiness staging vary greatly according to the instruments, the classroom, the curriculum, and the like. The following basics are recommended to guide both management and readiness staging.

1. Students should know when they walk in the classroom whether instruments are the focus of today's lessons. Then they should go directly to get instruments, tune them, or whatever the routine is that the teacher requires.

   a. Some teachers prefer the planning convenience of having set "instrument days." Then students automatically know that, "it's Tuesday and we'll use instruments today."

   b. Other teachers work performance classes into more natural "fit" with melodic composition lessons and listening lessons. Though planning is more complicated, this "fit" enhances transfer of learning.

   c. Some routine for retrieving and preparing instruments (i.e., getting then out of cases, set up, tuned, etc.) is needed to save time, and this is beneficial because this age group needs strict operational guidelines.

Avoid teaching a "unit" devoted entirely to playing since this leads to the many problems of **lockstep teaching**.

For similar reasons, avoid "units" devoted solely to melody writing, sound compositions, and so forth, as well.

---

2. Seating arrangements contribute to ease of instruction.

   a. The use of music stands and chairs that facilitate good playing posture are important necessities, not luxuries.

   b. Arrange for players of similar instruments to sit together. Then when helping for instance, with a particular chord, the teacher can move physically close to the "guitar section" of the class, and so on for other instruments. Such seating also facilitates timed practice by groups.

      - Care is needed in selecting a permanent location for larger instruments, such as keyboards and hammered dulcimers.

   c. An open arrangement of some kind that creates a center "stage" for the teacher avoids the teacher needing to climb over or through a row to help or monitor students in the next rows. The pattern can be square, round, "rounded square" (as shown) and, if needed, use two rows (only) of offset chairs.

```
        X   X   X   X   X   X   X
    X                               X
    X                               X
    X                               X
    X               stage           X
    X                               X
    X                               X
    X                               X
        X   X               X   X
```

This central "stage" is also the best location for a centrally placed microphone (suspended from the ceiling, if possible) that is used to record class and individual performances. An omni-directional microphone is best. The recording system should always be in place so you do not have to fuss with equipment instead of helping students.

3. Once students have their instruments and are in their assigned locations, it is time for tuning (or for checking their own tuning).

Students need to know how to tune their chosen instruments
if they are going to practice and enjoy them on their own!

   a. When teaching *basic tuning*—that is, of an instrument to itself—the first stage of any lesson has students tune their own instruments, with the teacher checking and assisting as necessary.
      • Teach the tuning of each instrument separately; assign groups timed practice until you can get to their group.
      • Once students can tune their own instrument to itself, they should be expected to do this as part of their ordinary routine *upon entering the room!*
      • Then, as a stage of the lesson, teach the class how to tune-up as an "ensemble."

   b. *Ensemble tuning*—tuning an instrument to itself *and* to other instruments (especially those with fixed pitch, such as keyboards, pennywhistles, etc.)—should be at least "rough." But take more time when making recordings.

Instruments too badly out of tune are poor models for cultivating listening, or are musically unsatisfying.

> Furthermore, when struggling beginners play a new chord in unison, on badly out-of-tune guitars, for example, can make it impossible for students or the teacher to judge whether the correct chord was played.

4. As a rule, begin each instrumental lesson with a performance of a piece *the class already knows and enjoys playing.* The first stage of a playing class should be a musical "turn on," so get the students' intentionality **primed** *for* playing *by* playing!

5. Next: (a) *Introduce some new "problem"* that will occupy everyone. This usually involves some new *musicianship* skill (e.g., new key) or some new *technical* stage (see 8.3). However, (b) sometimes students are assigned to *resume practicing* (i.e., improving or mastering) *a previous assignment.*

   a. When a new "problem" is presented, careful management staging is required: (1) Prime student interest (usually by your own performance that previews both the literature and the more satisfying results of the new skills); (2) demonstrate and explain the new skills introduced; (3) provide for students' first attempts; (4) give further demonstrations of and suggestions concerning the skills (if possible, use students who are enjoying some success already as models); (5) assign *timed practice* during which (6) you anticipate the guidance and *practice formats* most likely to be helpful; (7) supervise practicing; (8) finish (for today) with a class or "small ensemble" performance that demonstrates what "we accomplished today" and, more importantly, "what we still need to work on next time" (i.e., accountability).

   b. When "next time" comes around, the teacher needs to refocus the problem, reprime students, and restage the timed practice, practice formats, and so on.

      • Students who progress more quickly are assigned the more difficult variations or a new technique stage (see 8.3). They can also be shown routine maintenance for their instrument (e.g., changing strings) and more advanced techniques (e.g., alternate fingering, new strums, etc.).

      • Students who struggle simply need more individual help—typically, adherence to the present practicing format, or a new format.

6. The process described in no. 5 cannot go on forever. For one thing, many students will always use however much time they are allowed.

   a. You need to have clear limits concerning how much time to allow before students are evaluated and before the class moves on to its next lesson—a lesson, for example, that might be a melodic composition or listening lesson that grows from or follows-up the performance lesson.

   b. From the first, then, have in mind not only *when,* but also exactly *how* students will be evaluated. This cannot follow a single routine since it often varies according to the literature. Grading or otherwise reporting and recording their progress should also be factored into the evaluation process.

Performances (individually or as a class) should regularly be recorded.
Recording "final" performances by a class or an individual demonstrates the satisfying progress that results from practice. Other recording can be used for self-critique purposes, therefore teaching self-diagnosis.

---

7. The transition to the next lesson needs to be kept in mind.

   a. Performance lessons need not take up an entire class period!

   • Some performance lessons are most useful, for example, as the culmination of a class period that *begins* with a melody-writing lesson and *ends* with students practicing their own melodies. Similarly, the melody that serves a performance lesson can lead during the same class period to a composition lesson focusing on similar compositional features.

   b. When performance *lessons* use a full class *period*, the teacher needs to consider:

   • The *sequence* of repertory and skills relative to developing both music reading and technical competence on the instrument;

   • The *readiness staging* needed to tie-in the present performance lesson with composition and listening lessons in the most productive way for insuring transfer of learning in both directions.

Connections between lessons over time—between any and all composition, performance and listening lessons—should usually be evident to students.
Otherwise they will regard individual lessons as freestanding and, as having no connection from one day or week to another. Such lack of transfer leads to ineffective learning, lack of a sense of progress (and, consequently, failure to meet students' need for achievement) and, most seriously, a lack of follow-through to lifelong use.

Nuts 'n' Bolts 'n' Cautions

   1. "On-task" behavior is advanced whenever certain *routines* are required (e.g., for getting, tuning, returning instruments, etc). These routines should be outlined on large, easily viewed posters.

   2. Use large posters (or personal handouts kept for future use) to indicate fingerings, and so forth.

   • Make sure students know how to use fingering charts and chord charts on their own so they can learn new literature independently.

   3. Routinely maintain instruments so that the flow of a lesson is not regularly impeded by, for example, broken strings.

   4. Students should have "folders" (portfolios) in which they keep the music they are practicing, and other class "products" (compositions, listening lesson forms, etc).

- Consider having two folders (or sections) in a portfolio: one for instrumental music and one for compositions and listening lessons.
- *Have students keep a pencil in their folders*—and in any case, have extra pencils on hand.
- And, as per no. 1., have a set routine for getting and returning folders. A filing system that assists students in *finding* their folders is also an asset!

5. Most instruments cannot be properly played seated in desks that have fixed arms. Just "propping" up music wherever a place can be found also contributes to poor posture and other problems.

6. Models (and motivations) of good performance should stem from the teacher. Also, invite adult models from the community to perform and, especially, older students (i.e., from the next highest grade level).

7. Make sure students treat instruments with care and respect.

8. The same goes for their music, which should not end up wrinkled, ripped, and so forth. Having students buy simple three-ring binders for their music leaves them with a "book" of pieces for the future. It also helps the individual sheets stand up on a music stand.

   - Plan room for the "holes" so they do not intrude into the score, and pre-punch the handouts. Encourage students to use "hole reinforcement" rings, but always have plenty on hand for ripped out holes.
   - Also, assemble a library of music for students to play (at home, after school, etc.) that goes beyond the required repertoire lists.

9. Legibility of the score—especially the size and relative placement of notes and symbols—is crucial.

   - Beginners are often influenced by how much physical space follows a note. Therefore they often hold notes longer or shorter according to *spacing* and fail to notice the note head, stem, dots, and so on.
   - Where possible, use notation software for a clear, professional look!

10. Find varied ways for students to perform together. This greatly increases the intentionality of both melody and harmony players since, without the other part, the music is not as satisfying.

    - Make interesting arrangements for small, mixed ensembles that interested and advanced students can play—usually after school.
    - Encourage "gigs" for interested after-school groups: for example, local retirement homes, a "concert" in a local library, during summer craft fairs, and church events.

11. "Playing along" with the class from time to time enhances overall satisfaction through refinements of accompaniment, and so on, that you add.

    - However do not "cover up" students' problems or play along with students *all* the time. They can become dependent on you, or they think their skills are more advanced than is the case. Worse, you cannot listen, observe, and diagnose as well while you are concentrating on playing.

12. Have an instrument "fair" where local music merchants bring various models of instruments that students might talk their parents into buying. The point is to encourage the possibility of acquiring an instrument and to make it easier for them to get information.

13. Practice rooms are useful once students can be trusted to practice effectively on their own. However, any room—including storage rooms for instruments, and so on—can serve this function.

14. For very helpful insights concerning playing and practicing, alone and with others, see: Stephanie Judy, *Making Music for the Joy of It* (Los Angeles: Jeremy P. Tarcher, Inc., 1990), Chapters 7–13 (pages 89–243).

Summary

At early stages of instruction, teaching (a) *music reading competence* via an instrument should be separated from advancing (b) *technical expertise* on the instrument.

- Early instrumental lessons should have the primary focus of gaining control of the instrument sufficient to using it to learn to read notation.

- Then primary focus should shift to *basic music reading*—except, of course, where "reading" a new note involves teaching a new fingering. Basic music reading—mastery of the notes and primary chords in C, G, and F major—can be accomplished at quite minimal levels of technical ability.

- Once basic music reading is mastered, primary focus of teaching and practice turns to gaining *technique fluency and control* of the instrument.

- This, in turn, requires careful choice of progressive literature and arrangements.

CHAPTER NINE

PROFESSIONALISM: PUTTING ACTION LEARNING INTO ACTION

INTRODUCTION

In teaching, as in life, the whole is always much more than the simple addition of its parts. In teaching, that extra something is the **professionalism** of the teacher in adapting, adjusting, altering, and advocating change, all according to local circumstances.

This chapter focuses on all the many conditions and constraints that require approaching teaching as a professional **praxis** because no **technicist**, factory model of music education can possibly account for the complexity of modern teaching. Instead, teaching as praxis entails diagnosing important variables and conditions as a basis for curriculum and instruction.

THE CLASSROOM

1. Nature of the space—Ideally, a classroom should be spacious but not so large as to hinder the teacher's ability to monitor students.

   - *Flexible* use of space is best since each of the lesson protocols in Chapters 4–8 has its own requirements. However, certain equipment typically needs a more or less *permanent* location (e.g., piano, recording equipment, computers, keyboards) and this requires careful thought.

   - *Multiuse* spaces (e.g., teaching general music in a choir room or auditorium) always create more problems than dedicated classrooms.

   - Use of adjacent rooms, such as practice rooms, should be considered. Classrooms that open to backstage allow use of the stage. Other dead spaces can be used when feasible: for example, space around choral risers and hall-like entryways.

2. Class size and nature—This interacts with classroom space but also has its own dynamics.

   - Very large classes are a challenge for management staging and class control.

   - Each class has its own "personality" and needs.

3. Seating

   - *Fixed seating* (e.g., in an auditorium) is always problematic. Use of the apron in front of the stage, the aisles, the back of the auditorium, or the stage itself should be carefully planned—either as the standard arrangement or according to the type of lesson plan. Chairs with stationary writing arms make it hard to play instruments. Chairs with no writing arms are a problem for writing and composing.

- Groups work best when they are physically separated by considerable space. All lessons profit when you can walk behind students, looking over their shoulders to see whether they understand directions, and previewing their work for discussion or improvement. Multiple-seating arrangements, therefore, are advantageous.

5. Organization

  - Careful planning is needed for instrumental storage and access, and for equipment and instruments that cannot easily be moved. The location of the sound system is crucial. Equipment for recording student projects should always be set up and ready to go.
  - Seating needs to consider sight lines to chalkboards, whiteboards, overhead projector screens, videomonitors, lighting, and so on. Multiple straight rows of chairs are the worst alternative! In general, any organization that creates a "stage" for the teacher and an "audience" of students is best avoided.

$$\boxed{\text{Teacher}}$$

$$\text{x x x x x x x x x x x}$$

$$\text{x x x x x x x x x x x}$$

$$\text{x x x x x x x x x x x}$$

Exceptions may be when viewing videos, and so on.

  - Many lesson formats proceed best when students are in a circular format where they can discuss face-to-face and see and hear performances better (see page 230).
  - Most lessons benefit from some specific rearrangement of the chairs (or, in auditoriums, for example, other alternatives). This changeover *within* and *between* class periods needs to be part of your planning!
  - Avoid placing the desk, piano, or any other equipment in a way that forms a physical barrier between you and the class; you need as much freedom of movement as possible to monitor students.

6. Physical conditions—Even if these are outside your control, any negative effects need to be considered.

  - Overly resonant rooms, for example, can lead to noise that is distracting to **field dependent** learners. Acoustically "dead" rooms, on the other hand, encourage some learners to be more tentative in their explorations since they sense that they can be too easily distinguished. This can contribute to class control, but it often discourages experimentation during sound compositions and the practicing needed for recreational instruments. Therefore it is important to adjust for such factors through management staging.
  - Ventilation, light control, sound seepage to and from adjacent rooms must similarly be considered in planning when the circumstances are unavoidable.

SCHEDULING

Given the incredible variety of scheduling differences in schools, a technicist, one-size-fits-all, factory model of teaching is impossible.

1. Total time

- In elementary schools where general music is offered only once a week for as little 30 minutes, teachers simply cannot attempt the same curriculum nor attain the same breadth and depth of results as can teachers whose classes meet more often or for longer periods.

For Action Learning, "less is best when done well."
Curriculum needs to consider the practicalities of class length and frequency. When time is greatly limited, curriculum must include fewer skills and less content but teach such to a functional level.

- Middle schools entail great differences of scheduling between individual schools and particular regions. Some schools offer general music class for grades 6–7, or 7–8, or at only one grade level.
- Middle school classes may meet everyday or on alternating days, but only for a "block" of weeks, not for the entire year. Each arrangement has its own conditions but the fragmentation of instruction has liabilities that need to be considered.
- The practical limitations of scheduling are a major determinant of curricular content. This means curriculum will vary greatly—even within the same district where scheduling varies between schools.

2. Length of class period

- *Short periods do not require much variety to sustain interest and intentionality.* Short periods should place primary focus on one or two instructional outcomes that can be adequately accomplished. With short classes, the "less is more" maxim is particularly apt because trying to accomplish too much usually fails to achieve anything in the way of functional learning. Readiness staging, scaffolding, transfer of learning, and a spiral curriculum are also more crucial since classes are often widely separated in time (see the next point). Longer *lessons* (e.g., sound composition, song writing, etc.) often need to be broken over two periods. The second segment, then, requires *re*-priming and *new* management staging.
- *Long class periods require changes of pace for variety.* Transitions from one type of lesson (e.g., song-writing lesson) to another (e.g., recreational playing lesson where students play what they just composed) within the same period need to be carefully planned. However, longer periods are less likely to require segmenting lessons over several class periods.
- Skills need time for guided practice. Skills develop more slowly with very short class periods. In fact, it may be best to avoid even attempting some skills under such conditions; instead, include skills that thrive on the singular focus of a shorter period.
- Finally, variability between sections of the same class levels means that not every fifth grade class, for example, can be taught using the same lesson plan.

3. Time between classes

- Classes that meet once a week for 40 minutes require different planning than those meeting twice a week for 20 minutes. Middle schools often sequester general music class into a "block" of, say, 10 or 13 weeks of everyday classes before students "rotate" to a new subject for the next "block."

- Fragmented scheduling is particularly difficult for skill development: for example, the boys' changing voice changes according to its own timing, not according to whether the boy is in music class this "block"; when learning to play an instrument a student may have last had instruction during the first "block" of the seventh grade and not again until the last "block" of the eighth grade—almost a year and a half! Worse, since students don't tend to stay in the same class "sections" each year, sections will contain students at widely different readiness stages.

- Under such conditions, general music teachers can only *diagnose the variables* and make whatever adjustments are possible. For example, teachers can have students with the freshest memory of fingering or chords help others who have not attempted such skills for eighteen months.

- Thus there is no simple solution, no technicist fix, no single "how-to" series of scripted lessons, no set "method" that can accommodate the importance of such unavoidable variables. Success requires diagnosis, judgment, and constant adjustment.

RESOURCES

1. Resources differ greatly *between* schools—sometimes even within the same district.

> Advocacy for general music resources (including, by the way, scheduling) often depends in part on the "publicity" general music teachers can attract to their programs. Suggestions for increasing the public "visibility" of the general music program have been made throughout this text.

2. Limited resources require sensible planning, especially concerning curriculum, and on developing an acquisition program that systematically unfolds over the years. One enterprising teacher wrote a new curriculum where all students would learn to play electronic keyboards. When the school board "rubber-stamped" the curriculum, it was obliged to provide the keyboards!

   - Plan an acquisition program that systematically unfolds over the years.

3. Teachers must also deal with the breadth versus depth decisions that arise at every point.

   - Thus, rather than accumulating a CD collection that includes a little of everything, recordings should be acquired according to a plan for depth across reasonable breadth.

   - Similarly, spending money on computers and software just to be on the technology bandwagon may waste money if such acquisitions can have only minor impact on instruction.

4. Resources need to be carefully planned in connection with curriculum (e.g., which instruments to teach), and according to scheduling, room space, and other conditions.

> • Inadequate budgets provide "reasons" for *limiting* what can be accomplished, but for teachers who are professionals, budget constraints are no "excuse" for accomplishing *nothing*!

CURRICULUM

The term is often misused and abused. For some it means, "whatever I teach." For others it entails adopting a technicist method or set of materials such as a song-series (and thus falling into "**methodolatry**"). However, curriculum properly involves three distinct considerations that need to be coordinated.

- *Written or formal curriculum.* This is a document by which the teacher (or faculty group) answers the question, "What of all that could be taught *under local conditions* is most important to teach?" For Action Learning, such a document is absolutely necessary in order to take into consideration all the variables described in this chapter, plus some yet to be discussed. However, the formal curriculum is only a comprehensive *hypothesis* concerning what is practicable and valuable. It (or any part) is tested "in action" and, like any hypothesis, must be adjusted, updated, reconceived according to the results it produces and to accommodate changes in conditions over time.

- *The instructed curriculum.* This is the instruction a teacher actually provides—whether or not following a formal curriculum. It amounts to what the teacher actually covers or attempts to teach. When teachers complain, "Well, I *taught it* to them but they didn't learn *it*," the "it" in question is the instructed curriculum. To call this the instructed curriculum points out that "instruction" and "teaching" are not synonymous! Rather, "teaching" should properly mean that students have *learned* from instruction!

- *The learned or praxial curriculum.* This is what the students are (a) able to do, know and use, (b) better or at all, (c) as a result of instruction. It could be called the "value-added" curriculum since it amounts to the value instruction adds to students' education and lives.

The Hidden Curriculum

Unfortunately, the learned curriculum can sometimes be *negative*. For example, too many English teachers, though trying to teach students to appreciate poetry, manage to unwittingly "teach" them to hate and avoid it. In music classes, similarly, force-feeding only Eurocentric classics often has the same effect (for the same reasons) and, worse, it "teaches" that other musics are not important enough to study. Including only "pop" or "children's" music in class similarly "teaches" a limiting message about the value of music in life.

Thus sociologists have identified a "hidden curriculum." This learning is not made explicit in the formal curriculum. It is the result of certain biases, assumptions and attitudes—of the teacher, of schools generally, or of dominant socioeconomic groups (which, in some communities can be, considered nationally, "minority" groups)—that are taught and learned tacitly.

Furthermore, as in the case of the English or music teacher who force-feeds a diet of classics on the **perennialist** assumption that curriculum ought to focus exclusively on developing an appreciation of "great works" and the consequent development of "good taste," the resulting hidden curriculum often backfires—that is, it turns students off to the very attitudes and biases being advanced; or, in failing to advance positive learning, leaves students with the attitudes and values they had prior to beginning instruction.

- Other background concerning curriculum was presented in Chapter 1 (pages 14–28) and Chapter 3 (pages 52–53, 64–71). Appendix A (page 250) features guidelines for developing an Action Learning curriculum. A sample of a formal curriculum for grade 6 is also included as a model.
- Specific instructional variables for implementing an Action Learning curriculum have been considered for each of the different lesson protocols in Chapters 4–8.

CLASSROOM CONTROL

The basic management staging process outlined in Chapter 3 and then particularized for each of the lesson protocols in Chapters 4–8 is a major instructional variable in minimizing "discipline problems." Additional variables also contribute to the classroom control or "discipline" that is so vital with this age group.

Classroom "discipline"

"Discipline" is not just a matter of adopting a certain "discipline method."

Book after book has been written extolling this or that *technicist model* of discipline and entire schools have adopted a single factory-model approach. The variables are once again too complex, too multilayered, and too dynamic to be easily remedied by any technical formula.

Instead, each teacher needs to develop a personal approach that takes into consideration everything already mentioned in this chapter. To these must be added any local norms and expectations for handling student behavior problems, including single-method adoptions by a school.

1. Discipline

Today the term implies "law and order" enforced by the teacher. However, the root of the word discipline is "disciple" and originally implied the *self-directed* following of a leader, idea, or cause—as in the "disciples" of religious figures or in academic "disciplines." While there can be no doubt that teachers regularly have occasion to "enforce" short-term control, nurturing *self-discipline* by helping students focus their intentionality on positive, musical actions and growth is the best long-term strategy.

- Because it focuses on tangible musical praxis that students can relate to and "see" as potentially valuable in and for life, Action Learning eliminates or minimizes much problem behavior that otherwise results from students who are bored or who intuitively resist the hidden curriculum at stake. As some coaches say, "the best defense is a good offense."

- On the other hand, the active learning style of Action Learning can inspire occasions of growth-typical "acting out," or overly enthusiastic participation—both of which need to be handled as they occur.

2. Problem behavior

This needs to be distinguished from **growth-typical** behavior. Of course, growth-typical behavior (e.g., the physicality between early adolescent boys) can be problematic. But growth-typical behavior is expected because it is "normal." It is not, therefore, necessarily a sign of some character fault, or of personal or social problems.

- Teachers need to *anticipate* growth-typical behavior and to *avoid or minimize* problem behavior by means of *management staging*. So, for example, transitions between lessons within a class period that involve students getting out of their seats and moving to new locations need specific directions for orderly behavior. The small steps of management staging generally help keep students "on-task" and make their participation more orderly and controlled.

3. Group dynamics

Social interactions, often subtle, are usually central to problem or growth-typical behavior. Even a "solo offender" may have been showing off for or prodded by "innocent" others. Avoiding and handling problems typically requires considering group dynamics.

- Some students are "leaders." Dealing effectively with them and their interactions with "followers" is beneficial.

- Negative peer attention is better than no peer attention for some students. Overcoming the social isolation of such students (e.g., by group work) is more successful than draconian means that often worsen the situation.

- Some students' need for achievement is fulfilled by being "bad": The only thing they feel "good at" is goading the teacher, bothering classmates, and the like. The various means detailed in this text for *musically* meeting students' need for achievement are the best solution.

- Teachers, too, are members of the group. Their "role" in the group is central in the classroom dynamic. There are two ways in which a teacher's "authority" role is achieved:

  Authoritarian, dictatorial, drill sergeant, demagogic "boss" or "push" teachers typically feature expression such as "*I* want . . . ," "*I* need . . . ," or "you don't do that in *my* class," and the like. They have to always "push" students because their curriculum is taught for its own sake in a teacher-dominated instructional style. This kind of authority is only formally *granted* by the institutional role of "teacher" and therefore is automatically demanded or assumed by the teacher.

  Authoritative, facilitating, "lead" teachers, in contrast, use expressions such as "Let's . . . " (i.e., "let *us*"), "*we* need to . . . ," and "*your* class is . . . ," and so forth. They "pull," "draw," and "lead" students towards student-centered curricular interests where the students are actively reaching goals they value. The lead teacher's authority is *earned*: it amounts to a respect that comes from successfully helping achieve results in which students feel they have a personal stake.

4. Roles

In all groups and institutions certain "social roles" are defined and follow almost "scripted" patterns.

- Students typically "cast" themselves in certain roles: bully, leader, beauty queen, macho man, nerd, teacher's pet, tough guy (or girl), sports idol, just to name a few. It is useful for teachers to try to diagnose such "scripts" when they cause problems in class and then rescript the alternatives. Often you only need to identify for the student the role being played; it is often not conscious or malicious. But your awareness often reduces or eliminates the behavior because students of this age do not like being seen as predictable.

- Entire classes (on a given day) may also engage in a "game" or "script" they do not even realize they are "playing." "Torture the substitute" and "defy the beginning teacher" are common games. Simply announcing the name of the game and prescribing the alternative best defeats such games: for example, "Ah ha, I see this is Knock-our-Books-on-the-Floor-Day; so *let's* all put our books under our desks so *we* will not be disturbed any further." Another game involves variations on the "Out-of-seat Game": going to the bathroom, pencil sharpener, frequent trips to the wastebasket, and the like.

- The role of "teacher" has a choice of many scripts. Already mentioned has been a boss or leader. Some typical negative roles teachers consciously or unwittingly "play" are: enemy, drill-sergeant, jailor, police officer, killjoy, and slave driver. But they can also be seen as friend, facilitator, even hero or model. The role of *friend* is recommended; however, it needs to be distinguished from being *one-of-the-guys*. A friend is someone whom you trust, confide in, respect, like, share interests with and, even, sometimes be angry or frustrated with, but quickly get over it. Being "buddy-buddy," however, leads to a kind of over-informality that obliterates "the line" that needs to be drawn if students are to respect the teacher's *formal* role in school and society.[*] Another desirable role can be that of substitute "parent" whose friendship also involves mutual respect, "tough love," and adherence to certain expectations.

CLASSROOM MANAGEMENT OPTIONS

Teachers typically think of classroom management as tricks and gimmicks for *reacting* to misbehavior. But, in fact, *proactive*, *constructive*, and *corrective* measures are more important in the long run.

1. Reactive options

Teacher reactions often involve punishment, reprimanding, and scolding; or more extreme measures such as making a point of moving students to new or isolated locations, sending them to "the office," assigning them to stay after school, or public ridicule or censure.

---

[*]The *informal* role of teacher falls to any person from whom one learns. Parents are primary in this role. However, formal roles also exist outside of school, for example with coaches in youth sports leagues.

- Such reactions sometimes handle the *immediate* problem but they rarely have any positive long-term effect.

- Moreover, these reactions often *worsen* the immediate situation! For example, they lead to *student reactivity* where the culprit "stands up to" or "talks back to" the teacher, acts disrespectful, makes a "scene," and so on. Furthermore, depending on the circumstances, punishment of a classmate can inflame peers and create hostility toward the teacher. This is almost always the case when the class sees the teacher's reaction as unfair, unwarranted, or excessive.

Some suggestions:

- Seek to employ *constructive* options first, whenever possible (see the next section).

- Never criticize the "personhood" of the student ("You *are* . . . "); rather, identify the offending behavior ("You *were* . . . and shouldn't"). Then direct it be stopped, and quickly resume the lesson.

- Remain calm! In fact, except in the case of emergency (such as breaking up fights), a "dramatic pause" coupled with the "evil eye" and frown of disapproval at least gives the teacher time to avoid an *emotional reaction* and to carefully consider alternatives. With rational and stable students, this is often enough. With unstable and irrational individuals, however, further action is usually required—if not at the moment, then when the episode is repeated or becomes more flagrant.

Warning!
A common game is "Getting-the-teacher's-goat." So, when a class or individual succeeds in "getting your goat," they have won, are positively reinforced by your show of emotion, and the problem will recur!

- Try humor! This minimizes hostility and gets your point across in a low-key way. Teachers whose humor is natural, quick, and sincere—a trait especially recommended for this age group—should use it in reacting to minor episodes.

- Use a *three-part assertion message*, said matter-of-factly:

    (a) "When you . . . (identify behavior)"

    (b) I/we/you . . . (describe negative consequences of the behavior)"

    (c) "because . . . (give reasons, usually referring to classroom rules or lesson)."

    For example, "(a) When you socialize with another group, (b) your group and that group both fall behind, (c) because it wastes time and we need to have these sound compositions ready to perform in 5 more minutes."

- Requests to "cease and desist," should neither be perceived as "begging," (e.g., "*please* stop . . . ") and thus as a sign of lack of resolve or confidence; nor as shouted commands, which create the image of the "boss" teacher or "enemy." Rather, they should be phrased as "reminders" of class rules, or past misbehavior (e.g., "Remember, we don't practice our sound compositions at full volume!"); or as "diagnostic" information that brings to an offender's attention whatever needs to be consciously avoided (e.g., "You're not raising your hand!").

2. Constructive options

These support good behavior or redirect poor behavior.

- *Physical proximity.* Move near (or behind) problem students. Be more or less "dramatically obvious" according to the situation. Lightly touching a misbehaving student's shoulder while continuing to teach can be effective, too.

- Use *signals, gestures,* and *cues.* These involve facial expressions of disapproval, surprise, alarm, feigned "puzzlement," looking the student directly in the eye, and the like.[†] Hand gestures, coupled with nonverbal cues can help: A "traffic cop" gesture of "stop where you are" may be all that is needed. *Tone of voice,* and *dramatic timing* of comments are also cues. Tone of voice conveys dissatisfaction as much as do the words; and dramatic pauses, or speaking very slowly (often in a kind of arrhythmic monotone), can convey the appropriate constructive message.

- Get students *back on task.* "Off-task" behavior often comes from confusion or indecision.

  Diagnose problems with the task itself—usually weaknesses of management staging. Consider whether it should be restaged on the spot so that students are not confused and thus frustrated.

  Deal with any common problems at one time rather than repeating clarifications to each individual or group

- Provide *proactive directions* more often than reactive complaints: for example, "You've got only 5 more minutes before we record these compositions" rather than "you're wasting time."

- Show interest in *student's* needs. Instead of "Get back to work!" try "What's the problem?" These should not be perceived as scolding, but as an inquiry into the reasons for off-task behavior.

- Remove *temptation* and distracting circumstances or objects. Take them away, move them out of reach, or move the students away from temptation.

- *Compliment good behavior* in subtle ways, preferably to individuals at the appropriate time.

Some experts disapprove of techniques such as "I like it when you . . . " or "Billy is getting to go first because he was sitting quietly" for being manipulative and other-directed and more like the behavior management rewards used in training dogs. Some problem students may occasionally benefit from a carefully administered dose

---

[†]However, direct eye contact has different meaning for certain ethnic groups, so do not assume that a student who "lowers his eyes" is guilty. In many cultures it indicates respect!

of such "behavior mod." However, "Keep up the good work," and "you're getting it just fine now," coupled with approving facial expressions are less manipulative forms of positive reinforcement.

- Use "we" messages, encouragement, helpful reminders and suggestions to stress the class as a group. "*We* are getting too noisy for any group to hear what it is doing, so *let's* work at half-volume until the final performance."

3. Corrective measures

- Do not ignore gross misbehavior or even repeated minor annoyances. This conveys weakness and indecision. Gross incidents do not usually go away by themselves and repeated annoyances often evolve into disruptions that are flagrant.

- On the other hand, mildly annoying or attention-grabbing behavior can sometimes be quelled by *nonreinforcement*—by ignoring it and thus not rewarding the student by drawing attention to it. In particular, students who regularly yell out answers without raising their hands can simply be ignored until they understand they will not be acknowledged until they follow the rules.

- Apply school and class rules "by the book," *fairly* and *consistently*. Play no favorites.

- Give choices, not threats. "You can either . . . (correct behavior), or you can . . . (negative consequence), it's your choice!" is much more effective than the threat, "If you don't . . . , you'll have to. . . . " However the negative consequence must be easily enforced. In the event of further noncompliance, do not repeat the choice; it has been made and the consequence needs to be applied.

- Negative consequences should be clearly negative. Such consequences as, "Well, since we can't work quietly we'll sit and do nothing" are not only *not negative enough* (especially if the class wins the "game" called "We don't want to do this anymore!"), but can lead to *further problems*. For example, this age is unlikely to "sit and do nothing" *quietly*; thus this consequence just presents a new round of difficulties. Consequences should also be reasonable or have a logical relation to the offense.

4. Proactive measures

As mentioned earlier, when it comes to classroom management, a "good offense" is often the best "defense."

Plan interesting and relevant lessons. Nothing is more proactive than making lessons that are interesting, challenging, and worthwhile. The tangibility and relevance of Action Learning, then, is especially geared for promoting this condition.

- Plan management staging carefully in terms of priming, pacing, variety, physical arrangement of room, transitions within a class period, and other such variables. Anticipating and then avoiding everything that might lead to disruption and off-task behavior is better than beginning class with threats and admonitions.

- Jointly decide with students on the "rules" of the classroom and the "consequences" for violations. Lead this discussion so that reasonable consistency exists between classes, yet where each class has a sense of "ownership" because the rules are *their* rules, not the teacher's.

- The teacher should be seen as enforcing rules for the benefit of the *class*, not because of the teacher's personal whims and hang-ups. Soft practicing, then, is for the benefit of the class, not because loud practicing annoys the teacher.

- Become self-aware of *your* tolerance levels and whether they are necessarily in the best interests of *students*. Some teachers can tolerate more or less hubbub in a class than others, but tolerating too much may not be in the best interest of easily distracted learners. Tolerating too little commotion may stifle and regiment a lesson that is instead supposed to be creative and exploratory.

Be especially aware of the behaviors that usually "trigger" certain reactions in you—personal hang-ups that may be unreasonable or counter-productive! Become self-analytical and self-critical about personal insecurities and traits that make you vulnerable to annoyance, or that are not relevant to the learning at hand.

- Analyze your "style" and "habits" of control and management by videorecording and audiorecording lessons regularly. Analyze the recording only after several days have elapsed.

- Be sure to establish a support system. Beginning teachers often assume that asking for advice is a sign of weakness. It is not! It is a sign of professional commitment to improve. Discuss issues with a colleague (or formal "mentor teacher" if the school has such a role) and ask for a 'critique' of your recorded lessons. Support can also involve a teacher in another school system or a teacher-educator from a nearby university. "Tricks that click" kinds of advice, however, predictably fail to "transfer" between teachers and situations for an infinite number of reasons.

- Always *prime* a lesson (and reprime segmented lessons). Nothing is more important than establishing productive *musical intentionality*.

A leading cause of behavior problems is a mismatch between the teacher's goals and the students' intentionality. When students are unclear about your goal for a lesson or have not had their intentionality primed so that such goals are more tempting and interesting, then misbehavior and off-task "acting out" will reign. Therefore, continually work to improve how lessons are primed; and do not forget to provide for a "crescendo" of mounting interest throughout the lesson (see Chapter 3).

- Be in charge, but without dominating. *Class* begins the minute the first student walks in the door, so do not allow disorder to develop that requires major efforts at restoring order when *instruction* actually begins.

- Model and demand good manners and the principles of democratic cooperation. Do not allow students to be rude and insulting and avoid similar conduct on your own part. Insist on "civilized" behavior of the kind that is expected if people are going to be productive and positive members of society.

Defensive Teaching

Teachers who teach *defensively* usually begin class with warnings and threats, and throughout class frequently use punishment, censure, and embarrassment. These may maintain order. However, (a) *the students are still in control* because these negative tactics occupy so much of the teacher's attention and time that productive learning is greatly reduced; (b) a defensive approach engages the *self-fulfilling prophecy* where students typically live up to negative expectations; and (c) when order is maintained through fear and intimidation, students typically *behave* in order to stay out of trouble rather than *to learn*!

Nuts 'n' Bolts 'n' Cautions

1. As has been stressed earlier, nothing is more important with this age than establishing routines, procedures, and clear expectations. However, do not just require them; teach and practice them until they are effective habits!

    a. *Teacher expectations*: Students need to be taught from the first such expectations as raising their hand to contribute, bringing a pencil to class, and so forth.

    b. *Procedures*: Establish step-by-step rules for accomplishing common tasks and needs; for exmple, tuning instruments, and so forth.

    c. *Routines*: Promote certain practices, such as *automatically* picking up folders upon entering the room, and *instantly* becoming silent at the teacher's signal.

2. On the other hand, while teachers need to be *consistent*, students will often take advantage when a teacher's reactions and habits become *predictable.*

3. The use of sarcasm, ridicule, and humiliation are rarely effective and often dangerous. Such tactics risk turning the entire class against the teacher who is perceived as "picking" on a peer. Such tactics can psychologically damage students who are sensitive, have a weak self-concept, or are insecure.

4. *Rational* and *stable* students who misbehave can most usually be dealt with by reasoning with them. They rarely require punishment! *Irrational* or *unstable* children react poorly to punishment—it often inflames their behavior—but they also do not respond as readily (or at all) to reasoning. Therefore they require much more individual attention in the way of proactive and corrective measures.

    - ADD students are not irrational, but they do require more proactive and corrective measures.

5. Rarely is an entire class responsible for a problem. Therefore, rarely should the class as a whole be blamed, punished, or censured. This only increases group hostility to-

ward the teacher (or toward the offenders) and has a negative impact on students who were behaving and cooperating.

6. Taking student misbehavior personally reflects teacher insecurity, vulnerabilities, and personal hang-ups. These need to be identified and overcome.

7. Some off-task behavior can be the result of vision or hearing problems. Move the student closer and bring the problem to the attention of school health officials.

8. "Catch" the problem student doing something *good*, rather than commenting only on poor conduct!

9. Deal correctively with misbehavior in a way that least disturbs the flow of the class. Do not let disorder, confusion, or anarchy develop.

10. Sometimes "change for its own sake" can be effective. A new physical arrangement of the classroom, a new routine or procedure (or variations on old ones) can produce short-term gains (or, if not introduced carefully, massive confusion).

11. Videorecord often.

    a. Sometimes focus the camera on *you*, diagnosing your nonverbal cues, tone of voice, speech clarity, and pacing. Then "practice" certain improvements.

    b. At other times, focus the camera on the *class* and look for conduct you should have been noticing or have mistakenly ignored. Among other things, simply the presence of the camera on the class on regular occasions assures students that the teacher now has an extra "eye" and that they cannot "get away with" sneaky misconduct because you see it on the video.

12. Remember that some students think they can only be good at being bad. Substitute positive, musical achievement for the need to attract attention by misbehavior.

13. Distinguish between distractions, disruptions, and gross misbehavior.

    a. *Distractions* are behaviors that momentarily distract the teacher or particular students. These vary from teacher to teacher and depending on the students involved.

    b. *Disruptions* interrupt the flow of the class. They should be addressed constructively, correctively, and quickly. When certain disruptions are frequent, planning should be proactive.

    c. *Gross misbehavior* usually brings the lesson to a complete halt. These are serious episodes and must be handled dynamically. How quickly and how professionally the teacher can resume the lesson is important: for example, a smile, tone of voice, calming, or reassuring words may ease the transition "back to work."

14. While teachers need to be psychologically insightful with students, *teachers are not trained psychologists*. Recurring behavior problems that appear to have fundamental psychological or social causes or complications should therefore be referred to school health officials. School counselors, social workers, and psychologists, for example, often devise a plan that requires the cooperation of all teachers who have that student and may also enlist the support of parents.

Warning!
Much student misbehavior is encouraged by boredom, confusion, lack of positive intentionality, defensive teaching, and so on. Thus when episodes are frequent or severe, the teacher needs to do some professional soul-searching concerning curriculum choices, planning, and instructional practices. Otherwise, teachers often "stick" with methods and content that, while comfortably familiar and convenient for planning and delivery, create recurring and uncomfortable disciplinary episodes because (a) the instruction is ill-suited to the developmental needs of the age or (b) fails to engage students with learning that is relevant to lifelong musicking. Such teaching quickly leads to a negative mind-set that blames students for a situation that is the teacher's responsibility to improve.

CONCLUSION

Imagine the irony of a doctor complaining to the nurse that all the people in the waiting room are sick! Students in schools are not exactly "sick," but teachers exist to meet students' educational deficiencies just as doctors exist to meet patients' health problems. Teachers have no more right to expect perfect students than doctors do to expect healthy patients.

Coping with less than perfect teaching spaces, schedules, and the other variables discussed in this chapter, are also predictable parts of the challenge of teaching. Just as it is unreasonable for pilots to expect only perfect flying conditions, it is just as illogical for teachers to expect ideal teaching circumstances. The satisfaction of successfully negotiating certain difficulties on behalf of "clients"—teachers' students and pilots' passengers—is, in fact, one of the rewards of professional praxis in both cases. This is an unavoidable part of the ethic that helps professionalized teachers rise above being mere "teaching technicians" who expect the smooth running predictability of an assembly line type of class regardless of differences between students or whether or not students are benefiting musically in lasting ways.

Teaching music as *praxis*, instead, involves a professional ethic focused on promoting the musical welfare of all students. Successful and contented teachers are those, then, who are motivated by the challenges facing them and who take pleasure from successfully negotiating what they anticipate will be uneven terrain. Action Learning teachers have the added benefit of "turning on" students to the lifelong pleasures of musicking.

CURRICULUM

AN ACTION LEARNING PARADIGM
FOR CURRICULUM DEVELOPMENT

Action ideals guide Action Learning. Such ideals, however, are not utopian or idealistic; they are realistic aspirations that simply have no single kind of perfection. For example, striving for love, peace, and happiness are all action ideals.

Such "ideal objectives," first of all, guide human action in certain directions, and *results are judged in part by the conditions and criteria indicated by the ideals*. The ideal of "good health," then, is not attained at any one time in any one form; yet it serves to guide the direction and decisions of a physician's praxis, *and* it provides general criterion for judging the pragmatism of results from the point of view of the client.

Secondly, such ideals are "ideal" because they are relative to the variable needs and criteria of the individuals served by praxis. Thus action ideals for love, peace, or happiness are all relative to an incredible variety of situations and conditions, yet guide our actions.

An action ideal (a) determines the direction and course of human action (i.e., praxis or "doing"), (b) *and* serves as the basis for evaluating the degree of success of the praxis. What is ideally "good" depends on a variety of conditions that differ between one praxis and another, and even on different occasions for the same individual.

Music is governed by all kinds of action ideals. For example, *a score is an action ideal.* Its performance is relative to a multiplicity of conditions and therefore no performance can ever attain "perfection." This keeps the interest of audiences over time and guides the continuing practice and study of performers.

Professions, too, are characterized by action ideals. Already mentioned is the physician's commitment to "good health." From this comes the ethical injunction to "do no harm."

In order to be **professionalized**, teaching needs to be guided by action ideals. The action ideals that follow distinguish curriculum development for Action Learning from other approaches.

GENERAL ACTION IDEALS OF ACTION LEARNING IN MUSIC

Three *General Action Ideals* guide the process of writing an Action Learning curriculum and indicate general standards or criteria for evaluating the *learned* curriculum.[*]

---

[*]See Chapter 9 (pages 239–240), for important distinctions between the *written* (or formal), the *instructed*, and the *learned* (or praxial) curriculum.

General Praxial Ideal

This standard points to the action ideal of "breaking 100 in music"—that is, of developing a more positive realization of the *personal relevance of active musical involvement*, outside of and after graduation from school, on the part of each student.

- Students should be more aware of a greater range of *musical choices* they can put into "action" now and throughout life.

- *Real-life models* of such likely outlets for musicking are the major focus of instruction and serve as the holistic means by which such ends are fostered and evaluated.

- The underlying ideal is to help each student make musicking "basic" to life because it is "good for" the many functions it makes more special and for the ways it creates **"good time."**

General Musicianship Ideal

This standard involves the ideal musicianship skills and knowledge minimally needed to *be able to* "break 100" in one or more of the real-life forms of musicking identified by the Praxial Ideal.

- *Functional knowledge and skill* are taught and are directly put "into action" by means of one or more of the likely models of musicking that the curriculum indicates for the Praxial Ideal.

- *Musicianship* that can serve several kinds of musicking is most ideal, but at least should be pragmatic for one kind.

- *Competency* sufficient to functional *musical independence* is the underlying ideal.

Attitude Ideal

The ideal here is that students will *want to* continue to apply musical learning and skills "in life" outside of school. This could also be called the "value-added" ideal.

- Attitudes, values, and rewards of instruction and learning need to be immediate so that students are more likely to want to continue to be involved in learning and using music in their lives *now* as a basis for the future.

- Such values provide the conditions for "breaking 100" in music, and the ideal is to inspire at least a significant degree of *personal satisfaction and achievement* through classroom music.

- Competent *amateurism* is the underlying ideal for the "general student," but the special needs of the talented few also must be identified and nurtured.

  These three action ideals determine the *general* conditions of Action Learning. They govern the formulation of the more specific *Functional Ideals* that are the *formal curriculum*. This planning by teachers proceeds by considering a series of guiding questions for each General Ideal.

GUIDING QUESTIONS FOR DEVELOPING FUNCTIONAL IDEALS

1. *For determining the Praxial Dimension.*
   a. What types of musical involvement are already most typical in the lives of people who are committed to the ongoing personal benefits of music in their lives?

    b. What forms of musicking are many musically interested adults *not* utilizing as much as they would if music teachers oriented instruction in such directions?

These questions identify the most conceivable ways in which ordinary, generally well educated people can continue to be musically involved in "real life." General music teachers must address two more specific questions and clarify what is functionally ideal for their curriculums.

- Of all the ways in which ordinary people can continue to be involved with music (a. and b.), which are *most likely* to reach the largest number of people? Which, therefore, are most **utilitarian**?

- Of those ways of musicking, which collection of several is *most teachable* in the local situation[†] and has the greatest possibility for **pragmatic** results?

> This sifting process creates a *Praxial Dimension List* that constitutes the "real-life" musicking the particular curriculum will model and promote.

  2. *For determining the Musicianship Dimension.* The following guiding questions are asked for *each* item on the Praxial Dimension List:

    a. What do adults who are involved musically in such ways have to *know* or *be able to do* in order to participate at a satisfying and comfortable level?

    b. What *general musicianship knowledge* and *skills* do these forms of musicking share at some level?

    c. Of these provisions, which are *minimally necessary* to "breaking 100" as an amateur?

> A premium is placed on the "less is more" criterion; more musicianship skills can be added if (or once) instruction predictably meets those judged to be minimally necessary to an "independent beginner" status.

  3. *For determining the Attitude Dimension.* These questions are also answered for *each* type of musicking on the Praxial Dimension List:

    a. What *attitudes, values, and rewards* need to be encouraged by instruction to promote the intentionality and personal values favorable to the Praxial Dimension?

    b. What kinds of *intrinsic* values from present instruction will promote the kind of *self-direction* that motivates an individual to take part as an amateur without needing *extrinsic* motivation?

[†]The potential for transfer of learning from one praxis to another in such a collection is a major consideration. When a praxis that is highly unique is included in such a collection (e.g., teaching didgeridoos as opposed to, say, recorders or keyboards) it promotes little or no transfer value to any other praxis (e.g., melody composition, most listening lessons) and is consequently uneconomical in use of time and resources.

c. What kinds of *satisfactions* lead to self-motivation?

d. Which are most predictably nurtured if promoted as self-sufficient goals of instruction?

These provisions insure that instruction is not only successful in developing musicianship, but that the process of acquiring and using such musicianship rewards students and accordingly promotes continuing interest in the praxis at stake. These conditions are the criteria for "breaking 100 in music."

Curricular thinking and planning of this kind reveals that some range of particular praxes of singing, performing on instruments, listening, composing, arranging, and rearranging will typically be given focus in an Action Learning curriculum.

A FORMAL ACTION LEARNING CURRICULUM: FUNCTIONAL IDEALS

I. The General Action Ideals just considered pointed to three ideal and guiding standards—one each devoted to praxis, musicianship, and attitudes (values). Each *Functional Ideal* in an Action Learning curriculum therefore also consists of three *dimensions*:

- *Praxial Dimension.* This indicates the particular real-life or holistic musical actions from the Praxial Dimension List (see pages 251–252) on which the particular ideal will focus. For example, the action ideal for "Recreational Singing" in the model following (page 260) focuses on promoting singing in community groups, solos of various kinds, and singing as a recreational activity.

The praxial dimension insures that instruction will promote holistic results based on "real-life" musical praxis. The recreational singing of the model, for example, will importantly dictate the choice of literature: rather than the typical children's songs from a song-book series, the ideal in the model points to the kinds of music that students are most likely to sing in real life.

- *Musicianship Dimension.* This standard outlines the *musicianship knowledge and skills* minimally needed *to be able to* take part in the kind of musical praxis identified by the Praxial Dimension. The functional ideal in the model includes pitch matching, singing in tune, healthy vocal production, independently carrying a part, and music reading.

This list will vary for each functional ideal according to the Praxial Dimension. It will also differ between teachers and schools according to schedule and resources. Whatever is addressed, however, should result in *functional musicianship* appropriate to the grade level.

- *Attitude Dimension.* This "value added" standard focuses on promoting the *attitudes, values, and rewards* needed if students are going *to want to* take part in the musicking identified in the Praxial Dimension. The model seeks to promote enjoyment, vocal self-confidence, and the attitude that learning to read music will increase satisfaction.

Without positive "participation values" pegged to the musicking specified in the Praxial Dimension of a Functional Ideal, students are unlikely to want to learn to, or to continue to, be involved. Instruction must promote these values as *ends-in-themselves*, rather than force musicianship skills on unwilling or passive students who would not want to transfer such skills to real life. Rather than musically sterile, atomistic skill-drills that "turn off" students, the curriculum should models the pleasures of the "real-thing."

II. The total number of Functional Ideals indicates the scope or *breadth* of the curriculum. The model curriculum addresses six (see pages 259–262):

   1. Listening

   2. Recreational singing

   3. Sound composition and song writing

   4. Performance on classroom instruments

   5. Performance on soprano Baroque recorder

   6. Performance on baritone ukulele

The musicianship and attitude standards for each in the model hypothesize the *depth* to be addressed at the sixth grade level.

III. The beginning of the model shows the philosophical thinking that should introduce a formal curriculum document.

- The "Philosophy of Music" statement deals with two issues: What is music? and, What is music "good for" in life? This helps insure that instruction focuses on "music" and its values rather than on fragmented concepts and information *about* music or fragmented skills.

- The "Philosophy of Education" states a personal philosophy of "schooling." It answers the question, "What is schooling good for?" and clarifies the "value added" approach to schooling. Such a statement, however, must consider the school's explicit or tacit philosophy and community expectations.

- The "Philosophy of Music Education" answers the question, "What value should formal music education add to students' informal musical learning?"

These philosophical considerations should actually be the first step in writing a curriculum. They should clarify the teacher's thinking for the pragmatic purpose of deciding on the content of instruction and the kinds of tangible outcomes the curriculum should promote. They also serve as a rationale that explains the Functional Ideals of the curriculum itself to administrators and parents.

Such philosophical clarification is all the more important when a group of teachers writes curriculum. Reaching some sense of philosophical consensus promotes reaching agreement concerning curricular choices on which collective efforts can be focused—horizontally, at the same levels, or vertically, at subsequent levels. What cannot be agreed upon can still be included in "personalizing" the praxis of individual teachers.

Nowhere are any particular "methods" or "materials" dictated. Instead, teachers are free to approach the Functional Ideals of the curriculum in their unique ways, as long as they succeed with reasonable efficiency. However, the action theory supporting an Action Learning curriculum will naturally feature the kinds of musical praxis and teaching protocols described in Chapters 4–8. Furthermore, the shared framework of the Action Learning paradigm (see Chapters 1 and 3) creates a sense of *community* that helps teachers communicate in the same terms despite their somewhat different instructional approaches.

IV. There must be some systematic attempt to evaluate students and make them accountable for the formal criteria stipulated in each action ideal. But teachers also need to engage in self-evaluation and be accountable to each other, to students and to the community for the tangible results they have hypothesized.

   1. The *formal curriculum* hypothesizes that certain tangible outcomes are most ideal.

   2. The methods and materials used by each teacher in the *instructed curriculum* hypothesize the best ways to produce those values.

With Action Learning, monitoring the *learned curriculum* evidences both sets of hypotheses and **authentic assessment** is therefore always involved, whether at the curricular level or concerning the primary focus of a particular lesson!

Certain curricular outcomes may not be judged as ideal as previously hypothesized (e.g., students *en masse* show little interest), or are just not practicable given local conditions. On the other hand, the Functional Ideals may be reasonable but the methods and materials, and how expertly they are used, may require new choices or more expertise.

V. Grading and other alternatives for evaluating, reporting, and recording progress are dictated at state and local levels in endlessly variable forms. The following points deserve consideration, however.

   • First, curriculum and instruction exist not to generate *grades* but learning! Grades, as a form of extrinsic feedback, *can* motivate learning but, without care, often at the expense of the intrinsic rewards of musicking.

   • Second, *feedback* in the form of *evaluation*, *reporting*, and *recording* of progress, and the *diagnosis* of needed improvements is more important to learning than grades. Grades (or other forms of progress reports, whether anecdotal, portfolio, rubric based, etc.) should not become the focus of student intentionality so that the value of learning becomes extrinsic rather than a matter of intrinsic satisfactions.

VI. Planning grid. Notice that the model includes a "grid" (pages 262–264) in which all musicianship components are given a shorthand reference for each Functional Ideal (in the left hand column) and in relation to the *generative themes* (across the top) that the teacher has selected for emphasis in his class. The grid typically takes two pages fastened together side by side.

- A blank version (i.e., with nothing specified in each "box") is used for each class section to record lessons devoted to a particular ideal in relation to a particular theme. A check mark or date can be entered for each such lesson.
- This prevents the teacher from overlooking or overdoing certain types of lessons.

VII. Aligning a curriculum with published standards.

- Direct Alignment: With direct alignment, national or state standards end up *being* the curriculum rather than promoting accountability or "quality control" *for* curriculum. For example, *directly* "teaching a standard" tends to assume that some value has been advanced once the standard has been "covered" by one or several lessons. However, because standards are presented in lists of disconnected and separately measured criteria students can demonstrate individual standards adequately and still not be able to apply them in *holistic synergy* in *real time* in a *real musical praxis* that is *meaningful* enough to interest them for future use—all of the foregoing italicized criteria being the "standards," instead, of an Action Learning curriculum.

"Standards of Care" versus Standardized Results
The "helping professions" involve "standards of care" because *standardized results* are impossible when people are involved. Professional praxis appropriately always takes situatedness into consideration. This means that the "quality control" and "accountability" that published standards attempt to promote in teaching must actually take a form that is unique to the situation or individual. Chapter 9 considered only the most obvious of such situated variables.

- Indirect Alignment: Standards can be addressed by curriculum *indirectly*, rather than taught to *directly* with a one-to-one relationship between an individual lesson and an isolated standard. An Action Learning curriculum will produce comprehensive results that indirectly "cover" individual criteria provided in most lists of standards. However, results are holistic and authentic, not atomistic, and are unique according to the local curriculum.

Published standards can be used, then, to ensure the inclusion of certain content and skills. In this way, they can guide the writing of a formal curriculum that, however, addresses such learning holistically.

The local curriculum, if successfully instructed, will meet—in *holistic, action-based, and personally relevant ways*—most of the standards published by national and state organizations. If necessary or helpful, a chart can be added to the written curriculum that matches the musicianship dimensions of the holistic Functional Ideals to separately published standards, showing exactly which standards are addressed in that course.

CURRICULUM MODEL

"Curriculum for Grade 6"
T. J. Smith, Long Island NY
PHILOSOPHY OF MUSIC

Throughout history human beings have invested significant time and energy to music. In all cultures, music accompanies and enriches life's experiences. Whether for personal leisure, entertainment, and emotional expression or simply to provide a meaningful alternative to silence, music clearly fulfills important practical human needs.

As is demonstrated by every society all human life is involved with music. Regardless of lifestyle or personality, everyone encounters music throughout daily endeavors. In our society, music serves its purposes in various ways. Motion picture films are incomplete without the enhancing element of a musical score. Humans travel miles in automobiles occupying themselves for hours with music on the radio. Technology has provided more compact and portable electronic units to satisfy the human need for constant access to music. Communities flock to theaters and concert halls to see musical theater productions, operas, films, and live concerts of all musical genres. A major part of society devotes hours to practice, performance, or composition of music for reasons they find to be central to their lives. All cultures traditionally incorporate music in many areas of life and thus the world is flooded with musical opportunities, uses, and experiences. In short, music is always *good for something*; it possesses unlimited purposes, fulfills significant human needs, and provides seemingly essential elements to the quality of life.

As an art form and a discipline, music involves the subjective experience of individuals; that is, humans perceive music in a personal and very distinctive manner. Thus, music possesses a uniqueness that suits the individuality of human beings. Whether performing for an audience, composing for an ensemble or listening among others, music, like all art forms, distinctly touches humans.

Humans are clearly endowed with a natural interest in music. This is apparent at a very early age. Children sing songs on the playground and adore television series filled with music. Humans seek involvement and often absorb themselves with musical experiences. Music is a natural response to and enhancement of life's experiences: happiness, sadness, anger, longing. Music is good for human beings in many ways, but most of all, music is good for *being* human.

PHILOSOPHY OF EDUCATION

Society is fraught with challenges today. Personal subsistence requires basic skills and a wealth of knowledge needed to prosper and to function as productive members of society. Beyond personal survival, individuals must learn to coexist with other members of society. They need to attain the social skills and behaviors necessary to live among other beings; they need to learn to conform to the existing conditions of society or be prepared to make changes in the expectations prescribed by society. Humans strive for distinction in a crowded world, but each must learn to share his or her uniqueness and at the same time respect the individuality of others.

The school is thus an essential institution. It can empower students with the skills necessary for obtaining a productive place in society, and it helps to nurture student individuality. The classroom also offers opportunities to practice vital social skills. Thus, students work together and learn to cooperate. They learn to communicate, offering opinions and contributing their own personal ideas and talents. Along with providing social opportunities, schools also guide students intellectually. Students develop language skills, analytical thinking, problem solving, and cultivate a desire for knowledge. Students encounter experiences in schools that prepare them for life's decisions.

Personal exploration and nurturing of self-identity are major aspects of education. Students actively participate in a wide variety of experiences and learn how to work cooperatively with others. The maturation process is a rocky road where each student develops personal values and cultivates a positive sense of self. Schools should offer students meaningful experiences that identify, nurture, and develop talents, interests, and skills that are of likely value to the students. Students engage in situations that provide personal satisfaction and, ultimately, should obtain a greater self-worth.

Individuals who experience meaningful educational situations will actively set intrinsic goals, make value judgments, and develop new ideas. Schools are designed to nurture individuality through social, creative, and intellectual involvement in order to steer young members of society toward success.

PHILOSOPHY OF MUSIC EDUCATION

Music education leads students through positive and meaningful experiences with "the doing of music." With these experiences, students develop an intrinsic desire to actively participate in musical "doings" outside of the school and farther along in life.

The primary objective of the music program is to foster these intrinsic values. Effective music education leads to student involvement in music outside the classroom. Students engage in "real-life" activities that lead to successful musical results. The curriculum outlines "Action Ideals" which are predicated on the existence of such "real-life" uses. The "ideal" objectives such as listening, song writing, performance on classroom instruments, recreational singing, or performance on soprano Baroque recorder are general areas from which activities will be drawn. These action ideals intend to prepare and motivate students for participation in "real-life" situations such as community ensembles, community theaters, and other recreations. The action ideals thus prepare students for a rich musical life in the future.

The music classroom provides students with opportunities to practice essential musical and social skills. Students work with one another to reach specific goals. All contribute their own creative ideas and talents to the group. Students learn to share their opinions and cooperate with others to reach successful musical results. These activities involve students in the hope that they might pursue such a positive musical cooperation later in life.

Meaningful, "real-life" musical experiences in the classroom teach students musical skills. Active participation in listening, performing, and composing will expose students to musical skills such as music reading, aural discrimination, and the exploration and use of creative thoughts. Thus, students will gain the social skills needed to work efficiently with others and will practice the musical skills needed to independently engage in musical activities.

Music education is not merely the study of music history and abstract musical concepts. The music classroom is a place where students develop intrinsic values and intentionality concerning music, as well as applying learned skills to the "doing" of music. Thus, the music classroom offers students meaningful musical experiences that lead to a positive attitude toward music, successful social involvement and a desire to pursue music as one of life's many rewards. The "doing" of music is a major part of "being" human. To musically educate students is to prepare them for a lifelong involvement with music.

FUNCTIONAL ACTION IDEALS

Functional Action Ideals are the "ideal" objectives of the curriculum. They serve as the focus of musical growth. Lessons are drawn from each Action Ideal in order to provide meaningful experiences that facilitate musical skills and foster a positive attitude toward music involvement.

I. Listening

Praxial Dimension

- Listening to public performances (chorus or band concerts, rock concerts, etc.)
- Listening to recordings of various musical styles according to personal preference
- Listening while actively participating (dance, party, cabaret dinner)

Musicianship Dimension

- Recognizes and identifies the expressive and formal role of various timbres
- Identifies musical contrasts (dynamic levels, tempi, pitch frequency)
- Describes organization of the musical work (identifies different/similar sections)
- Has appropriate listening criteria for various Western music styles (classical, folk, jazz, rock)
- Can distinguish between compound and duple meters (beat groups of three or two)
- Responds intuitively to "mood" or "feeling" of the piece
- Makes informed choices concerning personal preference
- Demonstrates proper listening behavior appropriate to individual performance situations

Attitude Dimension

- Enjoys listening to recordings or performances of various musical styles according to personal preference
- Seeks new listening experiences
- Respects other's choices regarding musical preference or opinion

- Values the need for proper listening behavior inherent to individual performance situations

II. Recreational Singing

Praxial Dimension

- Singing in community choirs
- Singing in musical theater productions
- Solo performance (community choirs, weddings, musical theater roles)
- Singing as a social or personal recreational activity

Musicianship Dimension

- Matches pitch and sings in tune
- Utilizes healthy vocal production (breath support, proper phonation)
- Demonstrates vocal independence in ensemble singing
- Maintains an established steady beat
- Reads standard vocal notation using the solfège system
- Follows basic music symbols (dynamic levels, rhythmic values, pitches)

Attitude Dimension

- Enjoys singing for personal use
- Demonstrates self-confidence in regard to singing voice
- Sings comfortably among others
- Enjoys singing in ensembles
- Interested in improving singing by practicing healthy vocal technique
- Values the importance of music reading

III. Sound Composition and Song Writing

Praxial Dimension

- Writing original songs to be performed by community or church groups
- Writing original songs to be performed by small bands/groups (rock, folk)
- Writing arrangements of original or well-known tunes to be performed on social instruments
- Composing sound pieces for personal use (e.g., slide shows) and recreation

Musicianship Dimension

- Creates sound compositions using nonconventional instruments that meet effective criteria of form and expression
- Uses nonconventional notation effectively
- Writes simple melodies derived from a given harmonic structure using conventional notation
- Uses conventional notation correctly and transcribes music legibly
- Can read melodies written by themselves or other students
- Arranges original melodies for performance on classroom instruments (including melodic and rhythmic instruments)

Attitude Dimension

- Enjoys composing original melodies and writing arrangements
- Enjoys working cooperatively in small groups creating expressive sound compositions
- Demonstrates confidence and pride in personal or group work
- Respects the compositions and performances of others
- Values the needs for a legible notational system

IV. Performance on Classroom Instruments

Praxial Dimension

- Playing percussion instruments (hand drum, tambourine, claves, bongos, conga, etc.) to accompany singing in community performance ensembles
- Performance on melodic instruments (xylophones, tone bells, etc.) to accompany community performance ensembles
- Preparation for study of band or orchestral instruments
- Playing classroom instruments as part of a recreational ensemble

Musicianship Dimension

- Can technically play each instrument correctly
- Matches established tempos and keeps a steady beat while performing
- Can read and perform rhythmic patterns on percussion instruments
- Can read and perform simple bourdon accompaniments on melodic instruments
- Can read and perform simple melodies on melodic instruments
- Accompanies classroom singing and/or movement successfully
- Selects appropriate instruments according to the mood or style of music
- Values the need for care and maintenance of classroom instruments

Attitude Dimension

- Volunteers to play instruments as solo or accompaniment
- Enjoys playing instrument well enough to participate in ensembles
- Enjoys improvising with others and alone
- Respects the instruments and cares for them properly
- Respects the performances of others

V. Performance on Soprano Baroque Recorder

Praxial Dimension

- Playing solo recorder in community ensembles
- Preparation for study of band or orchestral instruments
- Performance in small recorder ensembles
- Functional music reading for lifelong use

Musicianship Dimension

- Can finger and play notes D4, E4, F4, F♯4, G4, A4, B4, C5, D5

- Can read and perform simple melodies
- Accompanies classroom singing or movement
- Can perform independently in two- and three-part recorder ensembles
- Cares for and maintains the instrument properly
- Can independently learn songs for performance in class

Attitude Dimension

- Volunteers to play instrument on solo melodies or accompaniment
- Enjoys playing instrument well enough to participate in ensembles
- Values the need for music literacy
- Respects the instruments and cares for them properly
- Respects the performances of others

VI. Performance on Baritone Ukulele

Praxial Dimension

- Accompanying community ensembles
- Accompanying recreational singing
- Preparation for study of guitar in middle school
- Performance in ensembles such as rock groups, pit bands, or folk groups

Musicianship Dimension

- Can refer to parts of the ukulele
- Can read chord symbols and finger G, G^7, D, D^7, e, A, A^7
- Accompanies classroom singing and movement activities
- Uses proper fingering techniques and various strum styles
- Can sing and play simultaneously
- Cares for instrument appropriately

Attitude Dimension

- Volunteers to play instrument as solo or accompaniment
- Enjoys playing instrument well enough to participate in ensembles
- Respects the instruments and cares for them properly
- Respects the performances of others

CURRICULUM PLANNING GRID

The Curriculum Planning Grid presents the detailed content of the curriculum. It aids in planning daily lessons by providing a complete overview of curricular goals.

A smaller, blank version will be used to record lessons on a regular basis. The record will insure that the lessons are focusing on all the elements of the curriculum. The table will also provide a broader picture for use in revising aspects of the course and evaluation of the curriculum.

Page One	Duration/Meter	Intensity	Notation	Social/Other
Singing	Sings in meters of 2, 3, 4, and 6. Maintains an established steady beat. Responds to conductor.	Can define and follow dynamic markings.	Reads notation using solfège. Defines and uses notation for rhythm and pitch.	Uses healthy vocal production. Sings and blends well with others. Respects other singers.
Recorder	Performs rhythms of simple melodies accurately.	Follows dynamic markings.	Reads simple melodies. Fingers D4, E4, F♯4, G4, A4, B4, C5, and D5	Cares for and maintains instrument properly.
Ukulele	Strums correctly for meters of 2, 3, 4, and 6.	Follows dynamic markings.	Reads chord symbols on lead sheets and scores.	Identifies parts. Cares for instruments.
Classroom instruments	Matches tempos and maintains a steady beat.	Follows dynamic markings. Chooses appropriate dynamic level to accompany.	Performs from rhythmic and pitch notation accurately.	Identifies instruments by name and demonstrates proper use. Cares for instruments.
Listening	Distinguishes compound and simple meters (as groupings of 2 or 3). Recognizes tempo changes. Identifies meter changes.	Recognizes contrasts resulting from changes of dynamic levels.	Uses score/sound map to follow musical features. Notates rhythmic patterns. Diagrams melodic contour.	Makes informed choices for preferences. Demonstrates proper audience etiquette.
Composition	Uses rhythmic variety. Notates rhythmic values and meters correctly.	Creates sound compositions that use varied dynamic levels according to criteria for form and expression.	Notates sound compositions using clear graphic notation. Uses conventional notation as needed.	Works cooperatively. Listens respectfully to others' compositions. Provides constructive feedback.

Page Two	Linear/Melody	Harmony	Timbre/Style	Organization/
Singing	Matches pitch. Sings in tune. Uses Curwin signs.	Holds own part in ensemble singing.	Differentiates between vocal styles.	Reflects formal organization in performance.
Recorder	Correctly fingers simple melodies.	Plays harmony lines with confidence and independence.	Distinguishes between also, tenor, and soprano recorders.	Reflects formal organization in performance.
Ukulele	Sings and accompanies self and others simultaneously.	Follows chord changes. Hears when to change chords.	Appropriately strums for accompanying singing and movement activities.	Reflects formal organization in performance.
Clasroom instruments	Performs simple melodies on melodic instruments.	Performs simple bourdon accompaniments on melodic or chording instruments.	Selects appropriate instruments according to mood or style of music.	Reflects formal organization in performance.
Listening	Identifies melodic direct, phrasing, mode (major/minor), repetition of themes.	Responds to harmonic changes. Distinguishes between melody and harmony. Identifies mode.	Recognizes expressive and formal role of timbre. Identifies timbres. Describes texture and mood.	Describes form by distinguishing between similarity, contrast, and repetition.
Composition	Composes to given criteria. Plays own melodies. instruments.	Arranges melodies for classroom rhythmic and melodic timbral variety.	Creates song composition to effective criteria of expression. Uses criteria.	Creates sound compositions and song according to formal

ACTION EVALUATION

Action Evaluation is a system that endeavors to assess evidence of musical growth. Students are evaluated according to their performance, participation, and attitude in each area of the course. The Action Evaluation is customized to suit each student based on individual weaknesses and strengths. Evaluations are kept on record for reference during recommendations, conferences, and evaluation of the effectiveness of course curriculum.

An essential part of the Action Evaluation also involves continuing evaluation of the course curriculum itself. Evidence of meaningful learning is the primary goal of the curriculum. Constant revision and remodeling of the curriculum to improve results is imperative.

EVALUATION

- Objectives: Objectives are the Functional Action Ideals that specify musical growth, proficiency, and performance, as well as student attitude and effort. Ideals for recreational singing, performance on classroom instruments, performance on baritone ukulele, performance on soprano Baroque recorder, critical listening, sound composition, and song writing serve as the vehicle for developing proficiency in each area of study. Evaluation of the student's performance within each objective will seek evidence of learning.

- Weight for Importance (WFI): Individual objectives will be weighted differently according to each student's strengths and weaknesses. To insure that each student receives an equal opportunity for success, total possible weighing will be identical. A four point system will be used.

- Level of Performance (LOP): Each student's performance will be rated based on a prestated four point quality ranking system for each objective in which 0 = no progress or achievement and 4 = desirable progress or achievement.

- Score: The score is determined by multiplying the Weight for Importance (WFI) and the Level of Performance (LOP) for each objective.

- Total Score: The total score will represent the sum of the individual scores for each objective.

- Comments: Comments will provide explanations for LOP ratings as well as feedback regarding performance for each objective. Comments might include specific goals for students or areas of focus and need-for-improvement for next term.

- Grade Average: The following formula will be used:
  - The total WFI will be multiplied by four, which is the highest level of performance.
  - This number is divided into the total score.
  - That total is multiplied by four to create a Grade Point Average.
  - The scale below will be used to convert the GPA into a grade.

4.0	3.7	3.3	3.0	2.7	2.3	2.0	1.7	1.3	1.0	0.7
A	A−	B+	B	B−	C+	C	C−	D+	D	D−
96	93	90	87	84	80	78	75	72	69	66

EVALUATION OF THE COURSE

Evaluation of the course involves tangible evidence of pragmatic learning. The primary objective of the "learned curriculum" is to develop an interest and competence in music and music involvement. Students exiting the course should demonstrate the competence and interest for an active involvement with music later in school and in life.

Further evidence of course effectiveness will be manifest in later years of schooling. Observation of students in the middle school and high school will serve as a model for improvement in the formal and instructed curriculum. Student's involvement in musical opportunities at the higher level, a positive attitude toward music, and active interest in music performing, composing and/or listening will provide significant feedback. Most importantly, the level to which the student engages in musical activities outside of the school and for his own enjoyment will indicate the success and/or failure of elements that make up the course.

Criticism and improvement in the methods of teaching, lessons, and teacher performance will be obtained through videotaping in the classroom.

APPENDIX B

DESIGNING AND USING RUBRICS

A rubric is a comprehensive analysis of a task, project, or assignment that describes important *criteria* according to various *levels of quality* in a way that provides feedback, diagnosis, and evaluation. When students undertake such tasks, they understand in advance the teacher's criteria and expectations because rubrics are clear and concise. Used regularly and from year to year, rubrics support future learning

For example, one teacher developed this rubric as part of several other criteria for song writing. It can be used for a given project, or as a comprehensive report of achievement.

Song Writing	Basic	Developing	Competent	Proficient
Constructs melody from given chords.	Creates basic whole/half note melody based on chord roots.	Uses roots, thirds, and fifths with basic rhythms.	Uses roots, thirds, fifths, and travels between them with varied rhythm.	Uses 'color' notes in addition to basic chord tones and creates interesting rhythms.

Here is another, by that same teacher, as part of several criteria for singing. This is more likely to be useful as a comprehensive report.

Singing	Basic	Developing	Competent	Proficient
Matches pitches on the piano	3-note span within the student's vocal range	3–5 notes	5–8 notes	Over an octave

Notice that such a rubric can also simply function as a checklist that describes, rather than labels achievement. Rather than individual labels, the following could be used (with or without descriptors) by having the teacher check the box that best describes the student's achievement.

Singing:	Beginning ⟶	Developing ⟶		Proficient
Matches pitches on the piano	3 note span within the students vocal range	3–5 notes	5–8 notes	Over an octave

Numbered "levels" can replace labels to represent gradations of achievement (compare the following to the earlier version of the same rubrics).

Song Writing	1	2	3	4
Constructs melody from given chords.	Creates basic whole/half note melody based on chord roots.	Uses roots, thirds, and fifths with basic rhythms.	Uses roots, thirds, fifths, and travels between them with varied rhythm.	Uses 'color' notes in addition to basic chord tones and creates interesting rhythms.

Where grades need to be calculated, the numbers circled can be translated into Grade Point Averages, where, for example 4 = A, and so on. Thus, for song writing, if there are, perhaps seven overall criteria, the total points will be divided by seven, with 4.0–3.76 as A, 3.75 to 3.5 as A−, 3.49–3.26 as B+, and 3.25–3.0 as B; and so on.

That such arithmetic *appears* "objective" should not conceal the arbitrariness of the assigned values. One teacher might have A+ = 4.0–3.75, with the remaining values redistributed so a B+ = 3.0–2.75, and so forth. Other teachers might prefer to use letter grades with the rubric, and then calculate overall grades by translating the letters into numbers, then back into letters grades according to some formula. And rubrics need not adopt a pattern of four levels. Sometimes three or five may be most appropriate in a given protocol. In any case, much subjective judgment based on the teacher's own musicianship and knowledge of students is always involved.

Finally, rubrics can be designed for individual courses (or levels) or as a comprehensive way of evaluating overall standards and the success of teaching. Therefore, the rubric for pitch matching means one thing if intended to rate students in grade 3, as opposed to students in grade 6 or 8!

It should be evident that rubrics provide more feedback than "naked" grades, such as a report card that includes the following:

Melody writing   B−

Pitch matching   D+

Rubrics can also be used as an adjunct to anecdotal and portfolio forms of reporting progress. In a portfolio, for example, the section containing samples of a student's melodic compositions can include a comprehensive rubric evaluation. The included sample compositions provide the "data" to discuss with students and parents. Similarly, in anecdotal reports, rubrics can be included, for example, as bar graphs, so parents can compare progress to fixed descriptions of achievement.

APPENDIX C

RESOURCES

The best source for the most up-to-date teaching materials and other resources is the Internet. Web searches using popular search engines will reveal an incredible variety of sources and links for further searching, specific information and titles, sources for purchasing materials, and the like. These are much more current and detailed than what can be published here. Many of the catalogues and organizations listed below have Web sites with links.

ARTICLES, INSTRUCTIONAL VIDEOS, AND SO ON

Andrade, H. G. "Using Rubrics to Promote Thinking and Learning." *Educational Leadership* (February 2000), 57/5: 13–19.

Arnett, P. L. "Managing the Music Classroom With Technology." *Learning and Leading with Technology,* 23 (1996); 14–17.

ASCD staff. "Problem-based Learning" [2 Videos]. ASCD, 1250 N. Pitt St., Alexandria VA 22314-1453; www.ascd.org.

Austin, J. "Technocentrism and Technophobia: Finding a Middle Ground for Music Educators in the Next Millenium." In *Technological Directions in Music Education,* edited by D. Sebald. San Antonio: IMR Press, 1993.

Beery, L. "Appropriate Voicings for Middle School Choruses." *Choral Journal* (March 1996): 15–20.

Bowyer, D. W. "A New Approach to Computer-Assisted Instruction in Music Theory for Elementary and Middle School Children." *Dissertation Abstracts International,* 53/01 (2000); 100–110.

Daniels, R. D. "How to Select a Notation Program." *Teaching Music* (December 1993): 36–37.

Forman, G. and C. Twomey-Fosnot. "The Uses of Piaget's Constructivism in Early Childhood Education Programs." In *Handbook of Research in Early Childhood,* edited by B. Spodek. New York: MacMillan, 1982.

Gilstrap, R. L. "The Electrified Classroom: Using Technology in the Middle Grades." *Childhood Education,* 73/5 (1997): 297–300.

Gousouasis, P. "An Organismic Model of Music Learning for Young Children." *Journal of Computing in Childhood Education,* 5/3&4 (1994); 273–284.

Hall, M. "Dance in the Music Classroom." [w/selected recordings and videos]. *Teaching Music,* 6/1 (August 1998): 30.

Hermanson, C. K. and J. Kerfoot. "Technology Assisted Teaching." *American Music Teacher,* 43/6 (1994); 20–23.

———. "Using Situated Learning and Multimedia to Investigate Higher-Order Thinking," *Journal of Interactive Learning Research,* 10/1; 3–24.

Hesser, L. A. "Effectiveness of Computer-Assisted Instruction in Developing Music Reading Skills at the Elementary Level." *Bulletin of Research in Music Education,* No. 104 (1990): 59–61.

Hickey, M. "Assessment Rubrics for Music Composition." *Music Educators Journal,* 85/4 (January 1999): 26–33.

Higgens, W. "Technology." In *Handbook of Research on Music Teaching and Learning,* edited by Richard Colwell. New York: Schirmer Books, 1992.

Keyes, C. "Teaching Improvisation and Twentieth-Century Idioms." *Music Educators Journal,* 86/6: 17–22.

Lehman, P. "Grading Practices in Music: A Report of MENC." *Music Educators Journal*, 85/5 (March 1998): 37–40.

McCarthy, M. "Dance in the Music Curriculum." *Music Educators Journal*, 82/6 (May 1996): 17–21.

MENC/GAMA Guitar Task Force. "Guide to Guitar in the Classroom." *Music Educators Journal*, 85/5 (March 1998): Special Insert Booklet.

Ohler, J. "The Promise of Midi Technology: A Reflection on Musical Intelligence." *Learning and Leading with Technology*, 25/6 (1998): 6–15.

Reese, S. and A. Davis. "The Systems Approach to Music Technology." *Music Educators Journal*, 85/1 (1998): 24–28.

Rasmussen, K. "Dance Education: The Ultimate Sport." *Education Update* (ASCD), 41/5.

Robinson, R. L. "Starting a Guitar Class." *Teaching Music* (December 1993): 34–35.

Ruggiero, V. R. "Bad Attitude." *American Educator*, (Summer 2000): 10.

Rutkowski, J. "Conducting Research in the Music Classroom." *Music Educators Journal* (March 1996): 42–44, 62.

Sewall, G. "Lost in Action." *American Educator*, (Summer 2000): 4.

Snell, K. "On Music Cognition and Music Education." *Canadian Music Educator*, 40/2 (1999): 29–33.

Stitt, R. "A Study to Determine Effects of Computer-Assisted Instruction on the Middle School General Music Curriculum." *Bulletin of Research in Music Education*, No. 18 (1993): 47–57.

Swaine, M. "Interface the Music." *MacUser* (September 1993): 13–14.

Sylwester, R. "In Search of the Roots of Adolescent Aggression." *Educational Leadership*, 57/1 (September 1999): 65–69.

Sylwester, R. "The Neurobiology of Self-Esteem." *Educational Leadership*, 54/6 (February 1997): 75–79.

Traver, R. "What is a Good Guiding Question?" *Educational Leadership* (March 1998): 70–73.

Waters, B. "Ideas for Effective Web-Based Instruction." *Music Educators Journal*, 85/4 (1999): 13–17.

Webster, P. "Computer-Based Technology and Music Teaching and Learning." In *The New Handbook of Research for Music Teaching and Learning*, Richard Colwell, ed. New York: Oxford University Press, 2002.

Weintraub, D. "Improving Retention in Music Fundamentals through the Use of Computer-Based Instruction." ERIC document #336072.

Williams, D. B. "Pioneering New Trails Through the Wilderness of Music, Computer, and Communications Technologies." *Association for Technology in Music Instruction Newsletter* (October 2002). www.music.org/sqk_blat/October.

Woody, R. H. and J. M. Fredrickson. "A Partnership Project: Integrating Computer Technology and Orff-Schulwerk." *General Music Today*, 13/2 (2000): 8–11.

CATALOGUES, SOURCES

Backyard Music [source of inexpensive yet long-lasting and functional cardboard lap dulcimers], P.O. Box 9047, New Haven CT.

Educational Video Network [Music video], 1219 Nineteenth Street, Huntsville TX 77340.

Facets Multimedia: Music on Video Catalogue [Video], 1517 W. Fullerton Ave., Chicago IL 60614.

Films for the Humanities and Sciences [Videos, CDs and CD-ROM], PO Box 2053, Princeton NJ 08543-2053; www.films.com.

Friendship House [Teaching aids], PO Box 450978, Cleveland OH 44145-0623.

General Music Store Catalog [classroom instruments, books, teaching aids], 19880 State Line Rd., South Bend IN 46637.

Insight Media: Music and Dance on Video & CD-ROM, 2162 Broadway, PO Box 621, New York NY 10024-0621.

MENC Professional Resources Guide, issued yearly.

McCormick's Software Avenue [Music and music education software], PO Box 577, Arlington Heights IL 60006; www.mccormicksnet.com.

Music in Motion [books, recordings, teaching aids]. PO Box 833814, Richardson TX 75083-3814.

Music Treasures Co. [Books, recordings and videos], PO Box 9138, Richmond VA 23227-0138.

Music Technology Guide: Technology Solutions for Music Educator [MIDI, recording equipment, computer hardware and software, recordings, books and videos]. Lentinine's Music Inc., 844 North Main Street, Akron OH 44310.

Oak Publications [A publisher of materials and music for traditional musical instruments, such as those cited in Chapter 8; for example, folk guitar, banjo, mandolin, Autoharp, pennywhistle, 'fiddle', dulcimers]. 33 West Sixtieth Street, New York NY 10023.

Suzuki Musical Instruments [Classroom instruments], PO Box 261030, San Diego CA 92196-1030.

The Resource Guide: Products and Solutions for Music Educators. SoundTree, 316 South Service Road, Melville NY 11747-3201 www.soundtree.com.

Teacher's Video Company Music Catalogue, Global Video Inc., PO Box MUP-4455, Scottsdale AZ 85261.

Traditional Music Materials [cited in Chapter 8 as a source for teaching heterogeneous traditional instruments in group instruction], 8 Kirby Street, Bainbridge NY 13733.

West Music [classroom instruments, recordings, music], PO Box 5521, 1212 Fifth Street, Coralville IA 52241.

Wireless Audio Collection [recordings, cassettes], Minnesota Public Radio, PO Box 64454, St. Paul MN 55164-04554.

BOOKS, COLLECTIONS, PAMPHLETS, MAGAZINES

Airasian, P. W. and A. R. Gullickson, *Teacher Self-Evaluation Took Kit.* Thousand Oaks CA: Corwin Press, Inc., 1997; 2d printing.

Armstrong, T. *Multiple Intelligences in the Classroom.* Baltimore MD: ASCD, 1997.

"Assessment in Music Education," Special Issue of the *Music Educators Journal*, 86/2 (September 1999).

Attention!: The Magazine for Families and Adults with Attention-Deficity/Hyperactivity Disorder. CHADD, 8181 Professional Place, Suite 201, Landover MD 20785; www.chadd.org. Published bimonthly.

Berz, W. L. and J. Bowman. *Applications of Research in Music Technology.* Reston, Virginia: MENC, 1994.

Blazer, B. *A Child's Guide for Concentrating: For Kids with ADHD.* Shire Richwood Inc. 1-800-536-7878; contents also available at http://www.health-center.com/adhd/, 1999.

Blum, R. E. and J. A. Arter. *A Handbook for Student Performance Assessment in an Era of Restructuring.* Baltimore MD: ASCD, 1997.

Blythe, T., et al. *The Teaching for Understanding Guide.* San Francisco CA: Jossey-Bass, 1997.

Brandt, R. S. *Education in a New Era: ASCD 2000 Yearbook.* Baltimore MD: ASCD, 2000.

Brooks, J. G. and G. Martin, *In Search of Understanding: The Case for Constructivist Classrooms.* Baltimore MD: ASCD, 1993.

Caine, R. N. and G. Caine. *Education on the Edge of Possibility.* Baltimore MD: ASCD, 1997.

———. *Teaching and the Human Brain.* Baltimore MD: ASCD, 1991.

Carr, J. F. and D. E. Harris. *Succeeding with Standards: Aligning Curriculum, Assessment, and Action Planning.* Baltimore MD: ASCD, 2001.

Charles, C. M. *Building Classroom Discipline*, 6th ed. (New York: Longman, 1998).

Curwin, R. L. and A. N. Mendler. *Discipline with Dignity*. Baltimore MD: ASCD, 1988.

Danielson, C. *Enhancing Professional Practice: A Framework for Teaching*. Baltimore MD: ASCD, 1996.

Danielson, C. and Arbrutyn. *An Introduction to Using Portfolios in the Classroom*. Baltimore MD: ASCD, 1997.

Denyer, R. *The Guitar Handbook*. New York: Alfred A. Knopf, 1982.

Delpit, L. *Other People's Children: Cultural Conflict in the Classroom*. New York: The New Press, 1995.

DiGiuolio, R. *Positive Classroom Management: A Step-by-step Guide to Successfully Running the Show Without Destroying Student Dignity*. Thousand Oaks CA: Corwin Press, Inc., 1995; 3d printing.

Dunn, R. and K. Dunn. *Practical Approaches to Individualizing Instruction*. West Nyack NY: Parker Publishing, 1972.

EMI Classics/IDG Books. *The Teacher's Guide to Classical Music for Dummies*. IDG Books Worldwide, Inc., 919 E. Hillsdale Blvd., Suite 400, Foster City, CA 94404; www.dummies.com; www.idgbooks.com.

Fosnot, C. T., ed. *Constructivism: Theory, Perspectives, and Practice*. New York: Teachers College Press, 1996.

Music Memory Bulletin [collections of "listening maps"], issued yearly by: University Interscholastic League, Box 8028, University Station, Austin TX 78713.

Harmin, M. *Inspiring Active Learning*. Baltimore MD: ASCD, 1994.

Havinghurst, R. J. *Developmental Tasks and Education*. New York: Longman, 1979.

Heinich, R., M. Moldenda, J. Russel, and S. Smaldino. *Instructional Media and Technologies for Learning*. Englewood Cliffs, NJ: Prentice-Hall, 1996.

Hollowell, E. M. and J. J. Ratey, *Driven to Distraction* [ADD]. New York: Simon and Schuster, 1994.

Hood, M. V. *Teaching Rhythm and Using Classroom Instruments*. Englewood Cliffs NJ: Prentice-Hall, 1970.

"Integrating Technology into the Classroom," Special Focus Issue of *Educational Leadership*, 56/5 (February 1999).

Jacobs, H. H. *Mapping the Big Picture: Integrating Curriculum and Assessment K–12*. Baltimore MD: ASCD, 1997.

Jenson, E. *Teaching with the Brain in Mind*. Baltimore MD: ASCD, 1998.

Judy, S. *Making Music for the Joy of It*. Los Angeles: Jeremy P. Tarcher, Inc, 1990.

Kaplan, P., and S. Stauffer. *Cooperative Learning in Music*. Reston, VA: MENC, 1994.

Kessler, R. *The Soul of Education: Helping Students Find Connection, Compassion, and Character at School*. Baltimore MD: ASCD, 2000.

Kohn, A. *Beyond Discipline: From Compliance to Community*. Baltimore MD: ASCD, 1996.

————. *No Contest: The Case Against Competition*. Boston: Houghton Mifflin, 1986.

Lambert, L., et al. *The Constructivist Teacher*. New York: Teachers College Press, 1995.

Lave, J. and E. Wenger. *Situated Learning: Legitimate Peripheral Participation*. New York: Cambridge University Press, 1991.

Marlowe, B. A. and M. L. Page. *Creating and Sustaining the Constructivist Classroom*. Thousand Oaks, CA: Corwin Press, Inc., 1997.

Miller, R. *What are Schools For? Holistic Education in American Culture*. Brandon, VT: Holistic Education Press, 1990.

Paynter, J. *Sound and Structure*. Cambridge: Cambridge University Press, 1992.

Perrone, V., ed. *Expanding Student Assessment*. Baltimore MD: ASCD, 1991.

Pomperaug (Connecticut) Regional School District 15. *A Teacher's Guide to Performance-Based Learning and Assessment*. Baltimore MD: ASCD, 1996.

Schafer, R. M. *Creative Music Education.* New York: Schirmer Books, 1976.

Seifert, K. L. *Constructing a Psychology of Teaching and Learning.* New York: Houghton Mifflin Company, 1999.

Slattery, P. *Curriculum Development in the Postmodern Era.* New York: Garland Publishing, Inc., 1995.

Sprenger, M. *Learning & Memory: The Brain in Action.* Baltimore MD: ASCD, 1999.

Swears, L. *Teaching the Elementary School Chorus.* West Nyack NY: Parker Publishing, 1985.

Sylwester, R. *A Celebration of Neurons: An Educator's Guide to the Human Brain.* Baltimore MD: ASCD.

Tanner, T. B., and J. Hanmer. *ADHD: A Guide for Families* (Clinical Tools, Inc, 5001 Baum Blvd. Suite 720, Pittsburgh PA 15213; contents also available at http://www.health-center.com): 1998.

Tomlinson, C. A. *How to Differentiate Instruction in Mixed-Ability Classrooms.* Baltimore MD: ASCD, 1995.

Wiggens, G., and J. McTighe. *Understanding by Design.* Baltimore MD: ASCD, 1998.

Williams, D. and P. Webster. *Experiencing Music Technology.* 2d ed. New York: Wadsworth, 1999.

Wiske, M. S., ed. *Teaching for Understanding: Linking Research with Practice.* San Francisco CA: Jossey-Bass, 1997.

Wong, H. K. and R. Tripi. *The First Days of School: How to Be an Effective Teacher.* 2d ed. Baltimore MD: ASCD, 1991.

Zeigler D., C. A. *Teaching Teens with ADD and ADHD: A Quick Reference Guide for Teachers and Parents.* Bethesda, MD: Woodbine House, 2000.

INTERNET AND COMPUTER SOFTWARE AND CDS

Guitar on-line: www.activeguitar.com, www.guitarnotes.com, www.harmony-central.com.

www.childrens'music.org. Twenty-two links to a variety of sources.

www.creatingmusic.com. Online music composition-based software provided by composer Morton Subotnik.

M.U.S.I.C Musicians United for Songs in the Classroom, Inc. www.wpe.com/~musici/ A group dedicated to the use of popular music in the classroom; site features an absolutely huge list of links to music education sites!

"Morton Subotnik's Making Music." An interactive composition CD for ages 5 and up. Available through Kagi.com.

"Morton Subotnik's Making More Music." For ages 8 and up. Available through Kagi.com.

Wholenote—The Online Guitar Community: www.wholenote.com.

SOURCES OF MUSIC SOFTWARE FOR THE ELEMENTARY SCHOOL:

Electronic Courseware Systems. 220 Boylston St., Chestnut Hill, MA 02167.

Ibis Software, 140 Second Street, Suite 603, San Francisco, CA 94105.

Maestro Music, Inc., 2403 San Mateo, N.E. Suite P1, Albuquerque NM 87110.

Temporal Acuity Products, Bldg. #1, 300 120th Avenue, Bellevue, WA 98005.

APPENDIX D

MIDI WORKSTATIONS

COMPUTER MUSIC WORKSTATION

Simple Student Workstation...

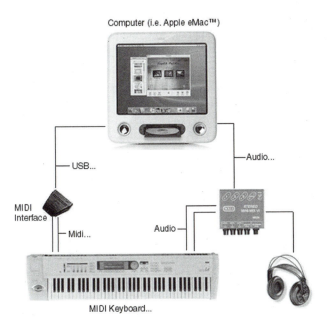

Computer (i.e. Apple eMac™)

USB...

Audio...

MIDI Interface

Midi...

Audio

MIDI Keyboard...

Adding a CD burner allows the making of CDs, for example, of students' compositions. Multi-user "labs" or areas of the classroom allow multiple students to compose and record their compositions.

MIDI SEQUENCER PROGRAMS

Sequencer software allows the recording of sound on sound. Students can edit and print their compositions in standard or graphic notation.

Freestyle: www.motu.com

Micrologic: www.emagic.de

Cakewalk: www.cakewalk.com

INTERACTIVE COMPOSITION

With this software students compose or improvise via the computer.

Band in a Box: www.pgmusic.com

Rock, Rap, and Roll: www.silverburdet.com

Jammer: www.soundtrek.com

Fruityloops: www.fruityloops.com

Acid Pro: www.sonicfoundry.com

Making Music and Making More Music: www.creatingmusic.com

NOTATION PROGRAMS

Students can use this software to compose, edit, and print their music using standard notation, or to give compositions done by hand in class a "professional" look.

Finale: www.codamusic.com. On this website is a free notation program called "Finale Notepad" that students can use at home to notate, print, and playback their compositions with or without a MIDI keyboard.

Sibelius: www.sibelius.com

COMPUTER-ASSISTED INSTRUCTION

This interactive software is used for ear training and fundamentals of traditional theory. Lessons are offered at various levels and typically proceed to advanced levels, according to a student's progress.

Practica Musica: www.ars-nova.com

Auralia: www.risingsoftware.com

Music Lessons: www.mibac

Music Ace: www.harmonicvision.com

MPEG AUDIO

These so-called MP3 files are compressed music files that can be stored on a computer, or copied to a CD. This is a popular way of sharing and playing music using a computer and teachers can use this technology to display and hear student compositions on a Web site. Many are free and can be downloaded from the Internet, or come included with typical home computer programs by Apple and Microsoft.

Apple iTunes: www.apple.com

MacAmp/WinAmp: www.winamp.com

SoundJam: www.soundjam.com

Windows Media Player: www.microsoft.com

A CRITICAL GLOSSARY OF
KEY IDEAS AND TERMS

accommodation, assimilation In Piaget's theory, cognitive development results when existing cognitive structures (**concepts**, action-schema) adapt to new experience in one of two ways. Where an established action-schema can be used successfully to process a new experience, the new experience is *assimilated* to that schema. *The schema is reinforced* and enriched and the future effectiveness of the schema and its likelihood of use are increased. When assimilation is futile (because the experience is too novel), the *schema itself is changed* to *accommodate* such novelty. "Learning" amounts to *restructuring the schema* so it will be more broadly effective for the future.

accountability Responsibility for producing certain results or reaching certain standards. *Teachers* need to be accountable for producing the benefits they claim for curriculum and instruction. *Student* accountability involves making students responsible for assignments and practicing.

action An action is purposive and mindful; as opposed to what "happens to" an **agent**, it involves "trying to" accomplish a certain result (see **intentionality**). It is the "doing" that results from **agency**. Contrast to **behavior**.

act (acting) adaptively See **adaptive action**.

action ideals These are broad *regulative* or *guiding goals* for human situations that can have a "good" but never "perfect" attainment (e.g., good marriage, good health, a "good performance"). Given differences between people and **situated** conditions, action ideals are realized in different ways or degrees. All professions that deal with people are guided by action ideals, not the standardized results that characterize making things. Action ideals modeled on **real-life** musical praxis serve as the basis of an Action Learning **curriculum**. For example, recreational performance can be set as a curricular ideal for all students, yet realized differently by each.

Action Learning A **model** of planning and teaching that adopts a **praxial** theory of music and that thus focuses on schooling for **real-life** uses of music. See Chapter 2.

action theory Accounts for human **action** in terms of relations between **intentionality** and certain physical and cognitive acts. Actions are explained in terms of goals, purposes, reasons, and intentions an **agent** is "trying to" bring about. Action theory is of interest to philosophy, sociology, and cognitive psychology; and is assumed by philosophies of law—for example, the idea of a "motive" for murder, that is, of "intentional" homicide.

action research Studies undertaken to improve teaching praxis. Action research is **situated** in the conditions to which it will apply and is carried out by the teacher or faculty who will use the results.

aesthetic theories of music and music education In this text, mention of "aesthetic theories" refers to neo-Kantian aesthetic traditions, not pragmatic and phenomenological philosophy where the word "aesthetic" is used in a different sense. Neo-Kantian aesthetic theories—there are many, all different—argue that the value of music is the contemplation of pure "Beauty" for its own sake. Most contend that aesthetic "Beauty" is (somehow) "in" autonomous musical "works" and that aesthetic experience realizes these embedded and *intrinsic values* by means of a required "aesthetic attitude." This "disinterested perception" means the listener is to put aside personal interests and adopt a "detached" attitude. Aesthetic contemplation is therefore set off from or above everyday life. Thus, when music is *used* in any way it is said to be no longer fully (or, for some theorists, at all) aesthetic because it is is not for pure contemplation but, rather, serves *extrinsic values*. Aesthetic theory developed in connection with European "classical music"—though the *connoisseurship* it sometimes involves is not the only way music lovers value that repertory. Therefore, aesthetic theory does *not* account for most "world music," which *is* pragmatic to one degree or another and thus **praxial**. The term "aesthetic" is sometimes casually (but confusingly) used to refer to any "expression" or "feelings" occasioned by music. However, the psychological term **affective** describes these "mood" responses more adequately. Another confusing use of the term is to refer to the "sensuous" aspect of musical perception. However, in order for aesthetic "Beauty" to transcend time, place and person, as is required by orthodox aesthetic theories, "aesthetic meaning" must be mental (i.e., abstract, cerebral, intellectual and cognitive) not "embodied" (i.e., experienced bodily). These and other contradictions and discrepancies are argued over by aestheticians to no final solution and are countered by **praxial theories of music** in favor of a **pragmatic** position that music is never autonomous and "for itself" and that, instead, its value is a matter of what it is "good for," only one such possible use being **"just listening."** Traditional aesthetic theories of *music education* tend to take the form of teaching so-called "music appreciation" as a cognitive matter of learning "concepts" concerning the structure of the *discipline* of music. This development of connoisseurship is focused on contemplation rather than many other everyday uses of music that enhance life, including other kinds of listening than "just listening."

adaptive action, acting adaptively Adaptive action results when an individual reflects on the consequences of an **action**. When the anticipated results are unsuitable, a new action is hypothesized and "tested." Teachers should provide for adaptive action by providing opportunities for students to judge the adequacy of results against criteria or expectations and then, if needed, improve their actions. **Transfer of learning** adapts a previous learning to a novel situation.

adolescence The **stage** of physical, emotional, social and mental development arising with **pubescence**. No such stage is distinguished in many "traditional" societies; instead, pubescence leads directly to adult **roles** and responsibilities. Modern society, however, has reserved adolescence as a transition between childhood and adulthood when certain important developmental **growth tasks** (e.g., self-identity, self-esteem) need to be fulfilled. Since there is no accepted definition of adulthood, the upper limits of adolescent are not fixed.

affect, affective response, affective qualities The term is broad and is often used interchangeably with psychological and physical experiences of "feeling," "mood," or "emotion." According to Piaget, affects interact with cognition.

affordances of music Physical things "afford" (allow, make possible, or facilitate) a wide range of uses, many of which go well beyond their intended purposes. Thus a rock can "be" a hammer, a hammer a nutcracker, and a tennis ball a dog toy. Music provides similar affordances according to how people use music. A given 'piece' thus affords a wide range of uses (i.e., meanings) for example, controlling moods, creating a sense of identity, making events special, therapy, celebration, worship, the "good time" of recreational performance, and so forth—all according to personally unique circumstances, variables and intentions (see **intentionality**). The idea of musical affordances accounts *sociologically* for the value of music in everyday life; it is distinguished from *musicological* analyses that presume inherent, fixed aesthetic qualities that scholars then attempt to analyze.

agent, agency An agent is an individual who acts in order to bring about a result (i.e., acts with **intentionality**). A *change agent*, then, is someone seeking change of a certain kind. Teachers are change agents for learning, but can also change society according to what and how they teach.

aleatory Music composed or performed according to random criteria. Thus two performances are considerably different.

amateur The word comes from the Latin for "lover" and refers to a person who engages in **musicking** for nonprofessional, avocational, and **recreational** benefits. Skill is therefore developed to a level of *personal* reward and satisfaction and, as a result, amateurs can range in skill from very basic to quite expert.

apprenticeship An apprentice is a beginner who learns by working with a master "on the job" by first doing basic, then increasingly realistic tasks, until capable of functioning independently. **Action Learning** is an apprenticeship in **musicking**.

assimilation See **accommodation**.

atomism See **holism**, **synergy**.

atonal Music that has no tonic pitch or key center.

attensive, attensive qualities and variables Attensive *qualities* are those features in*tensive* enough to attract *atten*tion. Such qualities, however, are not "objective"; they vary considerably from person to person. Thus people who play an instrument naturally find the sound of that instrument attensive and they are more likely to "attend" to it in **focal awareness;** and teens often find a "good beat" to be naturally attensive. The purpose of **directed listening** is to help students acquire a deeper and broader range of attensive qualities so their responses can go "deeper" into musical details. Listening *for* such certain attensive qualities **cognitively strengthens** those features in **subception**.

attitudes Attitudes are mental dispositions that incline an individual to respond in one way versus others. Attitudes have **cognitive** components involving belief and opinions, and **affective** components involving feeling tone, emotional associations, and subjective judgments.

authentic assessment, authentic learning Authentic assessment takes the form of classroom approximations or simulations of the holistic, **real-life** use(s) for which the learning is intended. Authentic learning (a major concern of Action Learning) involves knowledge and skill predicated on out-of-class and lifelong use, adjusted according to the developmental level of students.

authoritarian versus authoritative To be *authoritative* is to possess the knowledge and ability to help others improve and reach their own goals of excellence. It is *earned* authority. To be *authoritarian* is to have been *granted* arbitrary power to enforce one's authority over others, regardless of whether results are helpful or even desired. As one aphorism puts it, "authority that has to wield authority has lost its authority."

behavior, behavioral activity "Behavior" is technically distinct from **action**; the latter is under the control or direction of **intentionality**, but the former is reactive or spontaneous. Thus a wide range of unintended observable responses, movements, processes and operations, are considered behavior. Some *behaviorists* go so far as to deny the existence of ideas, intentions, and feelings. However, not all "unconscious" mental activity is simply behavior. Certain repeated actions originally guided by intentionality can become progressively *routinized* (or *normalized*) via **subception** so that **focal attention** can be directed to other matters. However, when such routines bring unsatisfactory results (e.g., playing a wrong note), attention can once again be restored in order to **act adaptively**. Practicing musical skills operates this way.

brainstorming The focused but unrestrained generating of ideas, solutions, plans, alternatives, suggestions.

brainstorming groups A form of **cooperative learning** where a group freely generates alternatives before a final plan is narrowed down and chosen. Sound compositions often begin this way.

canon The standard repertory of Western "classical" music.

cognition, cognitive Thinking, reasoning, remembering, understanding, conceiving, conceptualizing all understood as internal *mental* **actions** (processes) and **concepts** (or *action-schema* as Piaget called them).

cognitive strengthening Listening involves a **synergy** that is greater than the sum of its contributing parts. However, the more a listener is capable of cognitively focusing aural attention on a constituent part of a whole, the greater the influence of that part in future **holistic** responses. Thus, for example, by focusing on certain metric processes and details over time (via various listening and composition lessons) the potential role of metric change or organization becomes cognitively strengthened in future perception. Any **attensive quality** can be cognitively strengthened; first, by the teacher directing attention to it, then by having students practice perceiving and responding to it in a variety of relevant contexts. The result will be that students simply hear more or more "deeply." Cognitive strengthened features are sometimes in **focal awareness** while others operate through **subception** in **subsidiary awareness**. What is "in" focal and subsidiary awareness (i.e. "foreground" and "background") frequently shifts in normal listening.

"comparitive," "comparitition" Students have keen interest in comparing themselves and their accomplishments with their peers. Unlike **competition**, where by definition for every winner there are losers, such "comparitition" contributes to self-definition by comparing Self with "others." Some psychologists stress that much valuable learning is acquired through observing the models of others.

competition In education, a circumstance where one student achieves personal goals (i.e., "wins") at the expense of other students who fail to achieve their goals (i.e., "lose"). An educational strategy that is predicated on one or more students "failing" to reach personal goals is risky, especially for the fragile psychosocial development of pre- and early adolescents.

concepts This word is widely misunderstood in teaching and has no stable meaning outside of a particular theory. Generally considered, concepts are abstract "categories" formed on the basis of common properties. (Piaget, on the other hand, referred to cognitive structures as *action-schema*, thus emphasizing their action potential over simple categorizing.) Over time, properties that all "cats" or "drums" seem to have in common (despite their many differences) are mentally abstracted (by **reflective abstraction**) away from the "things" themselves, as purely *mental categories*. Being mental, these structures are, by definition, *abstract*. However *open concepts* are open to change with new experience (e.g., experience with lions, not kitties, and with timpani not hand drums)! Thus they progressively grow to be evermore powerful *hypotheses for action* (see **accommodation** and **assimilation**). *Closed concepts* are generally *formal* or *fixed* by definitions. Fixed concepts, such as an "octave" or "key signature" have commonplace definitions that are usually learned in such terms; formal definitions literally "create" a concept that previously did not exist, such as Einstein's concept of "relativity." Much "concept teaching" mistakenly treats open concepts as closed by treating the concept as a *fixed verbal statement, label* or *definition* (i.e., an abstraction) that needs to be exemplified by musical experience: for example, "Pitches in a melody can move up or down, or stay the same." After having students "experience the concept," the unsuspecting teacher at best has taught a label that, as a closed concept, remains abstract and **atomistic** rather than **holistic** and functional. Action Learning, in contrast, provides experiences with holistic praxis and, according to the tenets of **constructivism**, students thus formulate their *own* concepts through "experiences" that are *experiments* where concepts are treated as *hypotheses* for action and **reflective abstraction**. Those that "work" in bringing about desired results (**intentionality; accountability**) are *functional*, not abstract! To be functional, then, concepts should be taught as *cognitive skills* for "doing something," not as labels or inert abstractions "known" for their own sake. The "openness" of concepts allows for differences of developmental stages and for varied musical **affordances** between individuals.

concepts-in-action These are *functional* concepts; concepts at *work* (and thus very close to what Piaget called action-schema: see **concepts**) To be able at all to "do" or "understand" or even "have" certain experiences, involves concepts-in-action. In their unrefined form (unelaborated by **assimilation, accommodation, cognitive strengthening, reflective abstraction**, etc.), Piaget saw them as "precocious" because children can "do" or "experience" many things long before they have *formal* conceptual understanding or labels; that is, before "formal operational thinking" (see **Piaget**). Thus, pre- and early-adolescents already "have" many concepts-in-action and thus already "know" (cognitively experience) much that they cannot express, define, or label in formal operational terms: for example, "tonality," "melody," "12-bar blues" and so on. *Reflection* on what they already know or can do (e.g., "not falling off my bicycle is what adults are calling 'balance' ") is a process of *abstraction* that builds on precocious concepts-in-action and promotes strictly abstract thinking. Labels are mainly useful for guiding selective attention or discussing music. In general, however, most concepts-in-action are **tacit**: Like concepts of "love" or "in tune," they cannot be adequately put into words and can only be seen in action.

constructivism This theory stresses that learners create their own concepts. Conceptual knowledge is "formed" by a learner's *active processing*. It is not "*pre*-formed," then transmitted by a teacher and received by a passive student. Rather, it is "*in*-formed"—*inwardly* (mentally) formed—by **reflective abstraction** of experience and other data. The *in-formation of* concepts and the inevitability and relevance of their sub-, un- or pre-conscious aspects is a tenet of much recent cognitive psychology, *not* a theory of teaching. However, to meet the conditions of cognitive constructivism, teachers use their own "in-formations" to set active learning tasks and experiments where students "make sense" of—that is, *in-form* or construct—their own understanding from the experience provided by those lessons. Piaget's "genetic constructivism" stresses the predictable unfolding of the stages of development he theorizes for each learner (see **Piaget**). Lev Vygotsky's "social constructivism," however, stresses a learning community—teacher, peers, even models outside of school—that produces a collective influence without which individual learning is less effective (or fails to develop at all: e.g., "ensemble" playing or "accompanying"). Such learning via social interaction unfolds not in stages but in terms of situated conditions. It stresses the value of **cooperative learning**. The two models can, however, interact.

context, context effects, situatedness Context theory stresses that action, and thus teaching and learning, is influenced by the context in which it occurs *and* in which it will be used. Where learning, for instance, is supposed to apply outside the classroom, then the *classroom context effect must approximate or model the situations to which the learning is supposed to apply*. Thus learning acquired only to pass a test, earn a grade, or to avoid punishment is, in this theory, overly and narrowly situated for school, not to eventual use outside of and after graduation from school. "School music," then, has little impact on real-life musicking. *Situatedness* thus adds to *context* the **intentionality** for which the praxis (musical or educational) exists. **Praxis** is always situated. It varies according to the (a) particulars of a specific context or situation, and according to (b) natural differences between practitioners—including, especially, their intentions. Music, in the praxial view, is therefore always situated: The same score performed for different intentions (e.g., worship versus a secular concert) takes on different meanings and values. And musical composition, performance, and listening obviously are always situated with respect to the particular composer, performer, or listener. See also **transfer of learning, authentic assessment, affordances of music**.

contract learning activity projects/performances Such **independent** or **individualized** study is similar to a **learning contract**. Instead of focusing on general knowledge (e.g., how scales are constructed), contract learning activity projects or performances emphasize specific, tangible projects, performances or products, such as composing or performing a melody. See **goal cards**.

cooperative learning Learning resulting from cooperation in groups rather than through **competition** or **independent learning**. Various *small group formats*, such as **learning groups, jigsaw groups, simulations, study teams, peer tutoring, brainstorming**, and **role-playing** are employed to benefit each group member. Cooperative learning can, however, be **individualized** for a particular group when a certain mutuality of interest or ability exists; for example, small instrumental ensembles in class.

critical theory This terms identifies the social theory of thinkers associated with the "Frankfurt School" of social research early in the twentieth century. *Critical* theory is critical of the *traditional* theory associated with the models of knowledge based on the natural sciences, especially when the sciences—however useful in their own realms—are taken to be the only valid knowledge, or when applied as "social engineering." Traditional theory claimed to be "value free" and thus to reach "truth" that was disinterested and uncontaminated by human subjectivity. Critical theory, instead, sees values and the subjectivity of any human **life-world** as central to human knowledge claims. It is concerned, then, with the kind of social changes that empower people to improve their choices for action. Applied to education, critical theory seeks a *critical pedagogy* that empowers learners to choose and act in their own best interests. In relation to music education, it is "critical" of any **ideology** because ideology limits rather than expands musical choices.

cue See **prompts and cues**.

curriculum The term is used to refer to: (1) a formal written document, that is, the *formal curriculum*; (2) the instruction a teacher actually provides (whether or not a formal written document is at stake), that is, the *instructed curriculum*; and (3) what students can do or know (at all or better) as a result of instruction, that is, the *learned or praxial curriculum*. **Action Learning** is concerned with all three. Thus teachers need a written document (1) to clarify their goals, (2) to guide their planning and teaching, and (3) to use to judge the success of teaching and learning evidenced by students.

directed listening The directing of **focal awareness** to certain musical features, processes, or details. This process of *heightening selective attention* is designed to make the kinds of music qualities student do not naturally attend to more **attensive** for them in the future.

dyads This refers to **cooperative learning** teams of two. Often the simplest way of using such group learning is to quickly pair off students who are sitting next to each other. Almost any lesson can use dyads without much extra planning.

embodiment In traditional **aesthetic theory**, aesthetic experience is strictly mental and abstract. Thus bodily manifestations (visceral and affective states) are denigrated, downplayed, or intentionally ignored! However, recent cognitive psychology and newer trends in philosophy stress beyond question that (a) most abstract concepts (e.g., the concept of "in") have an embodied, that is, physically experiential basis (e.g., having bodily been "in" various enclosures) that is extended by metaphor (e.g., being "in trouble"); and that (b) the perception of musical sound itself involves certain embodied processes, feelings and other consequences beyond simply the biological bases of hearing. Therefore, **praxial theory** recognizes important aspects of musical experience as implicating bodily learning and responding; for example, how jazz syncopation is physically "felt."

enculturation, enculturating See **socialization**.

Erikson, Eric The **stage theory** of this psychologist involves psychosocial development. There are seven stages, of which two encompass the school years. *Industry versus inferiority* is a stage that arises in middle childhood, ages 6–12 years. During this "latency" period, children must learn to develop confidence in their intellectual and social skills. Failure to achieve such productive relations and results can lead to a sense of inferiority, to alienation, or to thoughtless conformity—all of which can result when students fail to develop musical competence and confidence. During adolescence, ages 12–19, the **growth task** is to develop a coherent *identity and self-concept*. *Identify diffusion* or *role confusion* amount to an unstable sense of Self and a resulting difficulty with relationships.

ends and means In this text "ends" refer to tangible products or other observable results of an **action**, and "means" refer to the processes and materials by which action transpires. However, with **praxis** and **action theory**, "process" and "product" are not separated and both the "doing" and the "done" are equally sources of concern, knowledge, and value. This applies to teaching as well as learning.

empowering, empowerment This refers to the freedom to be the author of one's own history. Its opposite is being controlled by political, economic, social, or cultural **ideology**, or by unconscious influences and **paradigms** resulting from **socialization** and enculturation. "Empowering teachers" means returning to them much of the decision making that has come into the hands of administrators and government officials. Empowered teachers "empower" students to have and make more musical choices than would otherwise have been the case.

essentialism *In philosophy*, this is the view that the "essence" of what something *is* can distinguish it from other things having different essences. It is the view that every thing has a "true nature" and to know that thing is to know this essence. *In music*, this view seeks some ultimate *aesthetic essence*, that is, what "music" *is* or in terms of which "music" is defined. The idea is subject to wide criticism in philosophy and is rejected by holistic approaches (see **musics**). *In educational theory*, essentialism is a reaction against **progressivism**. In contrast, it stresses academic "basics" over practical knowledge and teacher-dominated instruction as "essential" to being generally well educated.

existentialism The idea that "existence precedes essence" is central to existential *philosophy*; it means that the nature of one's Being is not predetermined. It results from the freedom or necessity to choose our Self and values through our actions. Thus human Being—who we are— is always in the process of Becoming, not given or fixed forever. Similarly, meanings, values, and guidelines for action come from reflection upon the circumstances and results of our choices, and are not absolute or eternal. While this philosophy is perhaps most notorious in its atheistic forms, its origins are traced to Christian sources, in particular the Danish theologian Søren Kierkegaard who took exception to traditional accounts of religious dogmatism in favor of stressing that religion is a "leap of faith" in the absence of rational "proof." Kierkegaard thus inspired later existential theologians (e.g., Paul Tillich, Gabriel Marcel, Martin Buber) who all stress choice-making over rule-following as the basis of moral life. Existential *psychology* stresses self-actualization; that is, helping the individual functionally create (or reorganize) Self. A main tenet of all existential views is the emphasis on the *personal creation of meaning, value, and Self* through one's personal **actions.** It is this theme that supports the **action theory** of Action Learning.

"expressive of" By this expression philosophers distinguish that music does not *directly express*, say, sadness; it can only be *expressive of* sadness. Saying that, for example, "music expresses sadness" assumes that "sad music" somehow actually "contains" and "communicates" *actual* sadness. This assumption is rejected by philosophers of music who argue instead that music only *sounds* sad to us in the same way the face of a Saint Bernard (to use the classic example of philosopher Peter Kivy*) only *looks* sad, even though the dog is not *actually* sad. So just as the face of a Saint Bernard can be expressive of sadness despite the fact the dog is not actually sad, music is similarly expressive of (i.e., affords, resembles) a variety of psychological states; for example, "sadness." "Sad music" does not literally "contain," communicate, or create sadness any more than an "angry sky" actually contains, communicates, or creates anger. Rather, the observer projects or attributes such a state onto the object or situation. The distinction is important for considering whether meaning is fixed "in" the music or variably in the "in the response" of a given listener to **affordances** of the music. Teaching or inferring that "music expresses sadness" or anything else presents a philosophically discredited view of musical expression! Emphasizing, instead, that music can be "expressive of" a range of states allows the student to *actively create* his or her own **affective response**, not to *passively receive* or *interpret* a preformed meaning presumed to be somehow hidden in the music like a coded message. All mention of musical "expression" herein refers to music being "expressive of" (being a projection of) affective states, not as "expressing" aesthetic messages in some absolute, impersonal, timeless way.

---

*Peter Kivy, *Sound Sentiment* (Philadelphia: Temple University Press), 1–12.

extrinsic versus intrinsic *Extrinsic* rewards, motivations, or intentions are external to an action itself. The value is separated from the act of doing. Thus grades, prizes, competition, praise and the like are all extrinsic rewards. *Intrinsic* rewards, and the like, cannot be separated from the doing. The action may have extrinsic consequences but is done mainly for its own rewards. Thus exercise can result in a strong heart and weight control but can also be done foremost as recreation. When extrinsic intentions are the inducement for musicking, intrinsic rewards are rarely discovered. In fact, intrinsic rewards are often corrupted by extrinsic motivations. Grades and competition in music often corrupt students' initial intrinsic interest. Extrinsic and intrinsic are also used by **aesthetic theory** to distinguish pragmatic use of music from what it claims to be the inherent and absolute value of purely contemplating music for its own sake. Praxial theory rejects the distinction and argues instead that the two are different sides of the same coin: music *is* inherently valuable, but only as this or that **affordance** determines its praxial value of the moment.

field-dependence, -independence Field *dependent* students are influenced more by perceptual information that is extraneous to the task at hand. They also naturally see things in large, connected but general patterns and need to be helped to see details. Field *independent* students can ignore presently irrelevant perceptual information and more easily perceive relevant detail. Field independence improves with age and education. Thus, older students are not as easily distracted by perceptual stimuli in the classroom. Field influences are also related to **learning styles.**

fine motor control Motor skills are **kinesthetic** acts central to skilled performance. *Fine motor control* involves small muscles and quick reflex motions while *gross motor control* involves large muscles and larger movements and slower motions. Most musical skills involve both, but expertise involves fine motor control.

focal awareness/attention Any perception involves a wide array of stimuli. Yet, we can generally focus our attention on only one "part" at a time. (This is particularly the case with beginners of any age.) When a listener focuses attention on one **attensive quality** it is said to be in focal awareness or focal attention. Other musical qualities, for the moment at least, are in secondary or **subsidiary awareness.** They provide the "background" against which the "foreground" of focal attention operates. Often, for example, novice listeners hear only the "tune" in focal awareness and "harmony" remains as background. However, with instruction, the chords themselves can come into focal awareness—be more interesting—while the tune momentarily has subsidiary interest (see **directed listening**). In psychology, discussions of *figure/ground* relations are generally given with visual references, but similar foreground/background effects are involved in aural perception.

futurism This view is critical of schools stressing the past to the detriment of preparing students for the ever-changing and unknown conditions of the future. In particular it is critical of the traditional "factory" model of education that stems from nineteenth century industrial models where schooling amounted to an "assembly line" for producing industrial workers. Such schooling, it is argued, fails to prepare students for a postindustrial society. Today, emphasis on technology sustains support from the futurist view.

generative themes These themes or broad topics "generate" learning at increasingly higher levels of refinement or application. They aid, therefore, in **transfer** of learning and help develop the process of a **spiral curriculum.** They are contrasted with **units** of instruction that focus on topics or themes as self-sufficient or self-contained emphases. They are further distinguished from **lock-step** curriculums that proceed by means of following one self-contained unit with another.

goal cards These are mini **learning contracts** or **contract learning activity projects** that can be accomplished quickly, often within a one or no more than two class periods, or as **homework.** They are very useful as **readiness staging** for contracts, projects, and as remedial or catch-up study (e.g., for new students). They are put on sturdy cards for ease of use and filed for future access. They can be *combined sequentially as packages* that lead from the beginning to more advanced levels of a learning.

"good time" As used herein, "good time" is not to be confused with "fun." "Good time" is time well spent, not wasted or just "passed" to have it behind you. The English word "worthwhile" literally means "good time." "Good time" is a major intention of *amateurs* and of much unusual *praxis*.

growth tasks These developmental tasks involve challenges, crises, or needs that occur at certain **stages** of development that should to be dealt with successfully *at those stages* if the problem is to be brought functionally under the individual's control. Around adolescence, a major growth task is the increasing differentiation of "Self" from parents and family, and the need for self-esteem and a positive self-concept (see **Erikson**, Eric). In humanistic psychology, Abraham Maslow proposed a hierarchy of *growth needs*, each level of which needs to be fulfilled before the next level can be attained. The bottom levels involve so-called "deficiency" or "D-needs" for food and protection, feelings of safety and love, and self-esteem. "Being" or "B-needs" arise as self-actualization (i.e., bringing a Self into being) on the foundation of successfully fulfilled D-needs. B-needs also facilitate "peak experiences" in the spiritual and artistic realms.

growth typical In **stage** theories of development, such behavior is typical or predictable at a particular stage. Being 'typical' does not, however, infer that growth-typical behavior that is *negative*—for example, the shoving and pushing of early adolescent boys—is acceptable! Because stages theories presume that subsequent stages improve on and consolidate the gains of earlier ones, the continuation of such problem behavior into the next stage is neither typical nor often good and implies that the need in question is still "unfinished business."

harmonic rhythm The timing of chord changes in connection with the melody, meter, and rhythm of a piece.

high order questions/responses These are highly complex, unique, and thus musically meaningful in terms of an individual's subjectivity. They are not, however, purely relativistic since the basis of any high order response will be **low order** perceptions and responses of one kind or another. High order *questions* promote high order *responses*.

holistic, holism versus atomistic, atomism Holism stresses that the "whole is always more than the sum of its parts." Thus no whole can be taught effectively by addressing its parts as individual "atoms" or bits and pieces. For example, teaching "melody" (as a **unit**) in isolation from "harmony" or "rhythm" (etc.) is *atomistic* and results in knowledge that misrepresents the musical "whole." On the other hand, it *is* possible to focus on a "part" in a holistic context. Thus composing a melody to given chords and rhythms focuses on melody construction, but in a holistic context. Atomistic teaching lacks holistic musical interest and rewards. Action Learning seeks to be as holistic as it can be by focusing on parts in relationship to the musical wholes to which they contribute.

homework Action Learning encourages learning to continue or develop outside of class. However, homework best takes the form of projects that will be monitored and evaluated in class: composing songs, rhythm pieces, listening lessons (for example, that are predicated on TV music), and so forth, are ideal. Homework can be organized along the lines of **independent, individualized instruction, goal cards,** and **cooperative learning**.

humanism, humanistic In general, a view that stresses human welfare, dignity, and the creation of meaning in human terms or for human benefits. In philosophy and psychology the view has led to an emphasis on *self-actualization*, the "bringing into being of one's Self" and one's values. The focus is on the choices that an individual makes to create personal meaning.

ideology, ideological In the *neutral* sense, an ideology is any system of ideas and values that comes to characterize or serve a particular group. Thus it is accurate to speak of the ideology of teacher's unions and state and national music education organizations. However, there is a *critical* sense where ideology becomes so self-serving and self-focused that it acts in ways that advance its "goods"—its vested interests, so to speak—as being in the best interests of *everyone*, even when they do not understand or accept such supposed values as being "good" for *them*. Music teachers become *ideologues* when they impose their own musical ideologies on students to the exclusion of other reasonable possibilities. Music education based on traditional aesthetic theory constitutes an ideology because it excludes or devalues multicultural, world, folk, recreational, and everyday musical praxis in favor of performing and contemplating Western Art music.

independent study, learning Group or individual instruction undertaken independently of the teacher, such as **learning contracts, contract-learning activity projects,** and **goal cards.** Independent study may or may not be **individualized.**

individualized learning Instruction prescribed for the particular **learning styles,** needs or interests of a particular student, or for a group of students sharing mutual needs. Individualized learning can also be **independent study,** and **cooperative learning** can be individualized for a group.

inner directed See **other-directed.**

intentionality As used here, this important philosophical term from **action theory** refers to the personal attitudes, values, goals, and needs behind anyone *"trying to"* achieve a certain result. Having such intentions is not the same as "motivation" because one can have a "motive" (e.g., good reasons to lose weight) without developing the intentionality to act (e.g., actually "trying to" diet). Intentionality is *musical* when the student is "trying to" bring about a *musical* result. Otherwise (and unfortunately), it can be **extrinsic.**

intrinsic See **extrinsic.**

jigsaw groups Such **cooperative learning** is planned when each student already has or must acquire a particular contribution to make to a group problem or project, for example small ensembles in class with each student on a different part. But other kinds of cooperative effort also work well, such as when each student carries out a different task that contributes to a group result—for example, sound compositions. With planning, this approach can profitably include mainstreamed students, students with language problems, and transfer students whose musical skills are different from the rest of the class.

"just listening" This refers herein to "audience listening"—usually in concerts but also to recordings—where **focal attention** is strictly on the sounds, not the setting or social praxis. It is distinguished, then, from the attentive listening done in connection with *non-concert* kinds of musical praxis, such as worship, ceremony, mood setting, **melodrama,** and so on. As used here, then, "just listening" is not the *contemplation* of pure "Beauty" assumed by aesthetic theories of music. "Just listening" produces its own praxial rewards depending on the variable **affordances** and **intentionality** at stake, which can range from intellectual interest to mood manipulation.

kinesthetic The "body sense" or awareness of the position of muscles, tendons, and joints in carrying out skilled acts.

learning contracts These projects are done as **independent learning.** The teacher must provide structure, guidelines and criteria according to: (1) a detailed description of the learning; (2) recommended methods, materials, and step-by-step procedures; (3) a timeline; (4) assessment procedures; (5) evaluation or grading criteria. They deal with general or broad skills and learning, whereas **contract learning activity projects/performances** similarly organize tangible performances, compositions, reports, and so forth. See **goal cards.**

learning curve A learning curve is a particular pattern of progress that varies according to the individual or the task (e.g., in learning to play an instrument). It has several "phases": (1) introduction and slow progress; (2) rapid gains; (3) diminishing gains; (4) leveling off; (5) plateau. Without a new level of challenge (e.g., a new stage of technique), students can either *stall* or *regress* at the point marked "?".

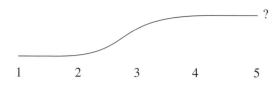

learning groups **Cooperative learning** where students with similar interests, needs, or projects work together. Study can be organized around a series of **goals cards** or as **contract learning activity packages**.

learning stations These entail **independent study** projects that students undertake as **independent study** or **cooperative learning**. The teacher assembles and organizes all materials and equipment in a specific location (the "station"). Work proceeds while others are involved at other stations or projects. Learning stations are best organized as **learning contracts, contract learning activity projects,** or **goal cards**. Stations take considerable time and effort to organize and thus are designed for repeated use.

learning style *Personal learning styles* involve the interaction of certain variables that influence learning: (a) *time*—people learn better at certain times of the day or when they are in the mood; (b) *attention*—learners have varying attention spans; (c) *field-dependence or independence*—the ability deal with peripheral distraction and to focus on details varies, and some students work better in quiet rather than a bustling atmosphere; (d) *perceptual preference*—some learn better by listening, others prefer to see or manipulate things, and some are flexible; (e) *working style*—some work well in groups, others alone; (f) *task direction*—some are self-directed, self-controlled, and self-starting and tend to stay on task without as much teacher direction; (g) *motivation, intentionality,* **inner direction**—students need more or less "external control" by the teacher; (h) *environment*—the formality or informality of the classroom, and activity within it influences learners so that, for example, room arrangements can have a bearing; (i) *responsibility*—students vary in the degree in which they can be trusted.

lockstep curriculum, teaching Instruction is organized into **units** of *self-contained topics*. Information is more or less piled up on previous "steps" until all are "covered." Typically, much of what was taught earliest is forgotten. Traditional approaches to general music have often involved lockstep units on melody, harmony, rhythm, and form (or units on historical styles, genres, etc.), each unit having its own unit test. **Transfer of learning** is a victim of this kind of teaching. Compare to a **spiral curriculum, transfer of learning,** and **readiness staging**.

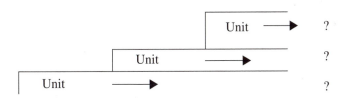

low order questions/responses These *responses* (or questions that elicit overt responses) have a "correct" answer. The *question,* "What instrument plays the theme?" calls for a low order response that is easily judged as correct. Similarly, "yes/no" and "true/false" issues are low order. Compare to **high order**.

lifelong learning Learning that has the generative capability of either serving a lifelong function, or that can continue to grow. Action Learning is predicated on the lifelong relevance of music learning. The opposite of lifelong learning is the "immunity" or "hurdle" theory of study. Thus once you have "had" (taken and passed) a general music class, for example, students are satisfied to have the hurdle behind them and feel immune from ever having to have anything more to do with that class content. Lifelong learning depends upon **transfer** of learning.

life-world In sociology and social philosophy this refers to the **situated** "everyday world" as experienced *uniquely* by a person. It is taken for granted as a fish does water but our life-world varies according the attitudes, values, beliefs, habits, perceptions and conceptions, stocks of knowledge, interpretative schemes, **paradigms**, and other subjective understanding that we have developed through enculturation and **socialization**. Despite being "personalized," much of our life-world is shared with others having similar cultural background and life situations. For **critical theory**, one's life-world can be a source of *un*-freedom if we are not critically aware of limiting influences, such as **ideologies**. **Empowerment** results in freedom from the undue control of the unconscious influences of the life-world, particularly those aspects that, unknown to us, are the sources of trouble and suffering. Differences between students' life-worlds are great and need to be considered in all curricular and instructional decision making. Teachers' life-worlds also vary with consequences for differences in their teaching.

mastery learning Teaching proceeds in terms of **readiness stages**. Each stage requires a particular level of mastery before students can move on to the next stage. *Instructional objectives* are thus organized according to graduated difficulty (e.g., repertory) and *mastery criteria* are defined for each level. Students continue to work at a level until they can "pass on" to the next or progress on their own. Since all students eventually "pass" all levels, mastery learning is an alternative to traditional tests and grades.

management staging Organizing a single lesson in separate steps or "stages." Each stage is timed, which contributes to efficiency by keeping students "on task" and serves as a short-term goal, thus rewarding "on-task" behavior. See Chapter 3.

"methodolatry" Uncritical devotion or faith in particular "methods" and "materials" used as recipes. This "how-to," or "cookbook" approach, sees teaching as a *technology of instruction* where teachers are workers on an assembly line (i.e., "the method"), rather than as a **professional praxis** requiring judgment and the development of ever-improved **praxial** knowledge. As a professional, each teacher's praxis will be as unique as, for example, a physician's or a lawyer's.

MIDI technology This combination of software and hardware allows computers to process and produce music signals. In the general music classroom the most typical use will be of electronic keyboards to enter or "input" for computer-aided operations.

model See **paradigm**.

modernism Most experts date the beginning of "modern" worldview with the Enlightenment in the late eighteenth century. Modern science began then and, along with a new belief in the power of reason, the era has been characterized by the belief that science, technology, and rational management can improve society. One form of Enlightenment rationalism was the eighteenth century "theory" of music that is still called "common practice." Another was the rise of **aesthetic theory**. Prior to this time, the arts were **praxial** and existed for pragmatic purposes. Aesthetic theory, in all the arts, however, has been under attack and revision since at least the early twentieth century with the advent of avant-garde and "anti-aesthetic" kinds of arts and music. Thus the nineteenth century ideals of aesthetic value and aesthetic greatness have given way to postmodern theories of art, such as the **praxial theory of music**. Thus *postmodernism* no longer accepts that human society can be rationally perfected, and suggests instead that "reality" is relative to cultural and other contexts.

multicultural As used in this text, this refers to musical subcultures existing *within* a pluralistic society; it is *not* a synonym for **world musics** since the latter often have their own multicultural subvarieties, at least at the level of the nation.

musical independence A *functional* level of *musical self-sufficiency* needed at least to attain a personal degree of satisfaction; musical competence in the absence of a teacher for lifelong use.

musicianship The knowledge and skills needed to be able to participate successfully (a) at all, (b) to a level of personal satisfaction, or (c) as an expert in a musical praxis. Where musical practices share important features, *general musicianship* serves several kinds of praxis—for example, **harmonic rhythm** is important to any praxis using chords. However, any praxis also has its own *unique* musicianship requirements.

musicking Rather than treating the word "music" as a noun, a static "thing" (such as a musical "work"), musicking stresses **action**, doing, process. It serves as a locution for "music making," but should not be limited to that. All "doings" connected with "music" are musicking; for example, composing, listening, music criticism and the like, and even audience behavior, choosing wedding music, and so on. Praxial theory stresses musicking as a "doing" in the present, while traditional aesthetic theory favors the idea of musical "works" statically rooted in the past.

musics Traditional views defined "music" according to **essentialist** traits and qualities that were supposedly said to characterize anything called "music." However, the increasing awareness of *musical pluralism* makes it clear that strikingly contrasting, even contrary traits distinguish different musical practices. Thus, "music" consists of separate "musics" in the same way that different "languages" constitute "language."

myelination Myelin is the fatty substance that forms a sheath around nerves and that 'insulates' them from 'short circuits' with other nerves. Myelination develops from the front to back of the brain and is typically 20 percent more advanced for girls from before birth until adolescence (after which there are no differences). Thus girls are better suited to many school tasks up until high school. This is particularly the case since the frontal portions of the cerebral cortex control future planning, selective attention, and self-control. Until parity is reached during mid-adolescence, then, boys are often somewhat "naturally" less adept at such matters.

need to achieve A theory by D. C. McClelland suggesting that successful achievement is sought for is own value. Such *achievement motivation* can be a prime reason for a student to practice a skill. However, without some *musical* rewards, learners are guided only by extrinsic rewards such as grades. When grades are no longer relevant (e.g., after exiting a course), effort to achieve will decline.

other-directed versus inner-directed These terms refer to the *locus of control* of **agency**. *Inner-direction* locates the source of self-control and **intentionality** as being with*in* the agent. *Other-directedness* locates the source of control as being in *other* people, such when students act only to impress parents, teachers, or peers. It might better have been called "outer-directed" since the controlling source is "outside" the Self. See also, **extrinsic** and **intrinsic**.

paradigm Broadly, a paradigm is a kind of "mental habit," set of taken for granted assumptions, or routine model for dealing with or understanding a common situation. Paradigms are the inevitable result of one's socialization and **life-world**. Once identified critically, however, they no longer "own us" and those we choose to observe can mindfully serve us. Paradigms are neither "good" nor "bad"; rather, they are "functional" or "dysfunctional." Most *teaching paradigms* are "soaked up" uncritically. Thus, teachers teach the way they were taught! Because such paradigms are taken for granted rather than fully understood, they frequently end up dysfunctional. **Action Learning** provides an empowering alternative that teachers can understand and choose as their accepted model for dealing with curriculum, instruction, and evaluation. The Action Learning paradigm is a general **protocol** for organizing thinking and monitoring the teaching and evaluation process. Specifics, however, must vary according to the teacher and situation. Such a paradigm, thus, establishes a common frame by which different teachers can communicate and cooperate while their teaching is nonetheless unique in its particulars.

peer tutoring, peer coaching Advanced students, or students with specific knowledge or skill (developed in or out of class), teach (tutor) other students in completing a project. Peer *coaching* supervises skill practice.

perennialism This education theory, like **essentialism**, is a reaction to **progressivism**. Rather than focusing on the child and the usefulness of knowledge, perennialists claim that time-tested "truths" and "great ideas" of (Western) history have perennial value and thus should be the basis of curriculum and teaching. The subject matter as a "discipline" is the focus and schooling is said to prepare for life best by developing a "disciplined mind." Perennialism in music is rooted in the idea of "great works" held to be perennially and universally valuable. Perennialism thus focuses on the *standard repertory* of "classics" and teaches music as a *discipline* of study instead, as is the case with progressivism, in terms life interest or relevance for students.

"performance strike" This is present when, "large numbers of students are refusing to perform at high levels, demoralizing the teachers who work with them. At times, performance strikes become organized resistance to authority . . . . But most often the students' refusal to perform appears as low motivation, low test scores and achievement, and a 'discipline problem' "† The conditions behind such mis- or dysfunctional behavior are the lack of relevance or "ownership" students are led to feel for the content or process of learning. It is the kind of "I don't care and you can't make me care" alienation that typically results for pre- and early adolescents from **essentialist** and **perennialist** teaching.

Piaget, Jean The cognitive theory of development of Piaget is a **stage theory** that analyzes cognitive development into four stages, each of which builds on the preceding one. The *sensorimotor stage*, from birth until 2 years, is based on coordination of sensory and motor activity. "Thinking," involves manipulating present "things" and during this period "things" become mental images that progressively take on "object permanence." The *preoperational stage* of thinking occurs from age 2 through 7. The action-oriented thinking of the previous period now expands to include words and other symbol systems of representation and during this time fully grammatical language precociously develops. The child can now begin to figure things out in predictable ways using words as well as by direct action (experimentation). The *concrete operational* stage lasts from ages 7–11. "Operations" now involve some abstract thinking, but are still mainly restricted to tangible or concrete objects, events, and processes. Learners can explore things and solve problems as long as these things are at hand. *Formal operational thinking*, the final stage, begins around age 11 and continues into adulthood. It progressively involves abstract thinking—logic and reasoning about relations, such as cause and effect—in the absence of concrete things. Former operational thinkers can use abstract symbols, can think about hypothetical possibilities, and can solve actual problems by *hypothesizing* (conceptualizing) before experimenting. Piaget's stages, however, focus on intellect and fail to account for social, emotional and artistic development, and they ignore intelligence of a nonverbal, nonsymbolic kind. See **constructivism, accommodation, assimilation.**

practicable, practical See under **pragmatic.**

practice Practicing is distinguished from *repetition* by the guiding and evaluating function of **intentionality.** Students who simply *repeat* passages or skills without a clear idea of the "right" notes or technique cannot correct their errors and thus do not learn, except accidentally. A lack of intentionality to improve also results in mindless repetition that falls short of practicing. However, even when technique remains unimproved, students (of any age) can have the intentionality to learn new repertoire at the present technical level and this effort does qualify as practice.

practice-in-action This refers to those times where by "playing" we also "practice" simply by "doing"—in other words, a **practicum.** Just "playing" golf with the intention of improving is such a practicum. The parallel of this idea for music teaching can be seen in good coaching; in addition to focused "skill drills," successful coaches also invent "game like" practice activities that are "playful" yet apply skills in practicums that approximate the eventual holistic act. "Scrimmages" are practicums. Musical "practice" benefits from similar "playful" resemblance to its eventual contexts of application. Isolated skill drill is beneficial only when applied to a practicum.

practicum See **practice-in-action.**

pragmatic, pragmatism This term is often used as a synonym for "practical" or "practicality." However, for teaching purposes a finer distinction applies: The philosophy of pragmatism holds that the meaning or value of a thing or proposition is seen in the consequences of its use. In other words, pragmatism is centrally concerned with *producing results that make a positive dif-*

---

†Ira Shor, *Empowering Education* (Chicago: University of Chicago Press, 1992), 21.

ference. In the case of education, teaching that makes no positive difference in terms of claimed or predicted benefits is not pragmatic—even though such teaching may be said to be "practicable" and "practical." "Practicable" literally means "capable of being put into practice" (i.e., capable of being put into *use;* "use*able*"). However, not everything that is practicable to teach or learn has pragmatic results. Teaching facts and information or concepts for their own sake is practicable (some teachers do it all the time); but such learning is quickly forgotten. The information taught may be "practical" in the sense that it is "intended for use," but if it is not taught in direct relation and application to the uses it supposedly serves, it will be forgotten and cannot usefully transfer to later use. "Practical" in a more general sense can refer to "use*ful*" learning in connection with praxis, such as "practical wisdom."

praxial theory of music and music education In comparison to the contemplation of hypothesized aesthetic absolutes said to be "in" musical "works" that are timeless (see **aesthetic theory, essentialism**), praxial theory values music as a **praxis**, a "doing" that serves an infinite variety of personal and social uses. The value of any music is seen in action, in the present, in terms of what it is "good for"; and that value is always **situated**, not fixed by the past (see **affordances**). All uses of music—from **"just listening"** at a concert or at home, to its role for worship, ceremony, dancing, advertising, or recreation—are acknowledged as valid! And "good music" is music that serves its intended purposes well. Music in everyday life is honored, not just concert music savored on infrequent occasions like a visit to a museum. Personal musical **agency** is especially valued; thus recreational performing, other amateur involvement, and personal meaning making by 'ordinary listeners' are respected as much as professional expertise and listening connoisseurship. *Praxial theory of music education* stresses such musical agency. Thus curriculum is predicated on promoting the use of music for enhancing everyday life and with developing skills and values that **transfer** from class to life because they are predicated on the kinds of **musicking** that are most likely in **real life**. Praxial theory is particularly suited for adolescents (including pre- and early adolescents) because it is directly in accord with their growth need for tangible learning and with how and why they already value and use music outside of school. It is also suited for school because, unlike the intangibilities of aesthetic contemplation, praxial competence is concrete and can be observed; thus teaching and learning can be evaluated and improved. See **modernism**.

praxis Praxis is any "doing" that serves a human purpose or good. Praxis, then, is concerned to bring about **pragmatic** results for an individual, group, or situation. Any praxis—for example, teaching, medicine, or musicking of any kind—is guided by **action ideals**, desired states of "right results" that regulate or control the **action** of the **agent(s)**. Thus **ends** of a desired kind are at stake in any praxis. This **intentionality** also involves diagnosing the **situated** conditions that will govern action and influence the intended results. Upon these basic considerations, the individual or group acts. However, such action is not simply a "means" of bringing about certain "right results"; it is also valued for its *process value*. Thus, playing music is rewarding and can be its own "right result," whether or not an audience is present. Praxis, thus, is synonymous in most regards with **action**. Knowledge learned from action ("doing") is called **praxial knowledge**.

praxial knowledge This refers to the knowledge that results over time from engaging in **praxis**— the "learning by doing" that, being so intimately bound to praxis, is usually only capable of being "seen" or "learned" in holistic action rather than from books. However, general and applied principles from **theory** also figure centrally in any praxial knowledge; theory "makes sense" of the data of experience, is useful for diagnosing problems, and hypothesizes new premises for future praxis. **Technique** involving practiced skills and routines is also important. However, theoretical and technical knowledge function in praxial knowledge in ways that cannot be separated from actual use. For these same reasons, the basis for learning any praxis is a **practicum** involving **authentic learning**.

preadolescence These are the years (ages 8–10) just prior to early **adolescence** when students begin to imitate and anticipate the behavior, attitudes, and values of adolescents. Generally these signs are seen no later than fifth grade, but are often observed beforehand. The onset of **pubescence** signals the end of preadolescence and the onset of early adolescence. See **transecence**.

primary and secondary focus Lessons should have a *primary* focus that the lesson is "about" or "for." Other learning will be of *secondary* focus. However, *connections* between primary and secondary focus are inevitable. Such overlap should be noted, but without losing track of the main emphasis. For example, a lesson having a primary focus on rhythmically organizing a tune will have secondary connections involving pitch selection. Thus, pitch selection ("tunefulness") should be of secondary focus so students are not distracted or confused by too many variables at once. As a rule of thumb, beginners (of any age) can concentrate or focus on one variable at a time!

priming The strategy by which **intentionality** is promoted in students for a particular lesson. Priming just does not announce the upcoming lesson, nor threaten or bribe students with **extrinsic** "motivations" about grades and tests. Rather it seeks to inspire, challenge, evoke, or elicit **intrinsic** interest by "tempting" students to engage in the lesson willingly. The "build up" or "selling" of advertising "hype" is implied, and thus some Action Learning teachers less technically refer to "hyping" a lesson. See **problem-based learning**.

problem-based learning This refers to projects that promote **authentic learning**. Students explore solutions to teacher-set problems based on their existing knowledge; but *new learning* is generated through *problem solving*—a major type of **constructivism**. Investigation and exploration, hypothesizing and testing of hypotheses in action are thus key ingredients. The teacher selects and poses ("**primes**" or "hypes") the problem, and is a resource guide, coach or tutor in its solution. Problem-based learning develops and practices problem-solving skills, particularly for the real-life praxes in question.

profession, professionalism In everyday parlance, any skilled work or occupation is often called a profession; for example, being a professional athlete or a professional truck driver. It is often in this "occupational" sense that teachers speak of themselves as professionals. However, in sociological terms, a true profession is a **praxis**. Such a professional "practice" (e.g., medical practice) is conducting according to applied **theory**, and especially **action ideals** that centrally elicit *ethical criterion* concerning "right results" for clients. Professional praxis—as with any praxis—is undertaken in part for the intrinsic pleasures of the process of praxis itself, although highly successful praxis may also bring financial or other rewards. Teaching comes closer to a true profession when conducted as praxis rather than as "**methodolatry**." This means basing teaching on (a) applied theory, rather than hand-me-down methods as teaching technologies; and (b) adopting an ethic of "right results" for students that focuses on improving praxis in order to "reach" evermore students, rather than continuing to teach using "set" methods and materials regardless of their results. Teacher accountability, then, is a prime condition of teaching as praxis.

progressivism This philosophy arose as a reaction against traditional teaching where the subject matter takes precedence over the relevance or interest for students. Such traditional "didactic" teaching (see **perennialism**; **essentialism**) relies on textbooks, memorization, and tests of factual data, assumes that learning is a matter of accumulating information transmitted by teachers to passive students, and that subjects are "academic disciplines" distinct from life. This agenda forces the teacher into an **authoritarian** role of enforcing standards and imposing "discipline." Progressivism, instead, puts the child and the child's interests at the center of teaching. Students are seen as active (see **constructivism**) not passive, and the school is seen as a microcosm of society. Thus, learning is related to personal life and to social issues outside of school, and schooling fosters a democratic model of society. In the progressive view, the teacher is **authoritative** and thus the teacher's knowledge, rather than being "forced" on students, is used to facilitate and guide students' active learning.

prompts and cues A *prompt* is used to help students respond to a question. For example, when a student struggles to answer, say, a question that asks for a mood response, the teacher can prompt with the choice, "Did it sound happy or sad, or light or scary to you?" A *cue*, on the other hand, is really a "clue" or even a "hint." Thus, when a student draws a blank on, say, a question about which family of instruments was playing, the teacher might offer, "Name one instrument you *did* hear. OK, the trumpet. And the trumpet is a member of which family?" Of course prompts and cues can be combined: if the teacher had said, "And the trumpet is a member of which, the brass section or the woodwind section" a prompt would have been combined with a cue. Prompts and cues facilitate discussions, especially with hesitant students.

protocol As used here, a protocol is a general practice or heuristic approach for a recurring situation; for example, "tuning up" is a protocol of an ensemble. The teaching protocols of Action Learning, then, are not set "methods" a teacher adopts; they are procedural guidelines, rules of thumb, problem-solving technique and general principles for teaching **praxis**. They are general models or patterns of praxis that help teachers understand how to plan and deliver their *own* lessons according to locally situated needs and conditions.

pubescence, puberty The word literally refers to pubic hair and thus to the onset of *secondary* sex characteristics. *Primary* sex characteristics determine whether an individual is biologically a boy or girl. Secondary sex characteristics include the appearance of pubic and underarm hair, breasts and menstruation for girls, and pubic and underarm hair, erections, and semen production for boys.

readiness Readiness is the preliminary learning needed if new learning is to succeed: for example, children need to learn how to match pitch before they can read music through singing. What is sometimes called *sequential learning* consists of a planned sequence of readiness stages for a particular learning domain; for example, a particular concept or skill. However, despite the fact that not all students learn in the same sequence, references to sequential learning often wrongly advance a *standardized learning sequence* that is the same for everyone. In this text, readiness relies heavily on **transfer of learning**—between all lessons, not just in one domain—rather than such standardized steps or stages.

readiness staging (also see scaffolding) The process of planning and building a "scaffold" of supports at early stages of learning that supports later stages. As used here, both terms refer to the **transfer of learning** by which one lesson is based upon an earlier lesson *and* promotes the **readiness** for subsequent lessons. Readiness staging is the process of progressive refinement that leads to increased competence with real-life musicking. Since there is no one correct sequence, different teachers will plan for readiness staging in somewhat different orders. However, a teacher's readiness staging for subsequent progress amounts to a hypothesis that needs to be tested in action and varied if need be; that is, for those students who are not benefiting.

real life, and real-life musical actions In this text, such references are to typical kinds of **musicking** that take place *outside of school* and the school years. Action Learning is concerned with modeling and developing, while students are still in school, the most typical outlets for adult musical involvement. Thus, for example, if students are expected "someday" to accompany recreational singing using the guitar, then this real-life musicking ought to be modeled to some level of **authentic assessment** of **musical independence** in school. This **holism** contrasts with teaching musical concepts and skills atomistically, for their own sake.

reconstructionism This theory of education sees schools as needing to "reconstruct" society by contributing to a new social order that would improve the human condition. In this manner it is related, in general, to **futurism** and to **critical theory**. Reconstructionism has promoted **multiculturalism**, gender equality, racial discrimination, and the like in schools today. Action Learning partakes of reconstructionism in its attempt to transform what has been called "a society of listeners" to one characterized by more varied, everyday, and active forms of amateur and recreational musical praxis.

recreation For some, this term implies any leisure or free-time pursuit or pastime. Used in this way, **aesthetic theories** often end up belittling amateur uses of music because most amateurs are seen as merely "fooling around" or "passing time" with music as opposed to being *serious* about music as an Art and, therefore, as not dedicated and skilled enough develop proper artistry. In **praxial theory**, however, recreation is thought of as *re*-creation. It involves "spending time" in ways judged to be "**good time**" because the Self is re-created (self-actualized) through musicking. Thus, the point of music education is to *self-actualize* in some way or degree through music; to "break 100 in music" by identifying one's "Self" with chosen musical "outlets." See also, **amateur, social instruments**.

reflective abstraction This is a process of (a) reflecting analytically on rudimentary actions ("precocious" actions, as Piaget called them), that is, on **tacit** and emergent **concepts-in-action**; then (b) abstracting a *conscious* mental representation or "idea" of such experiences (see **concepts, constructivism**). This process of "understanding" actions that were formerly intuitive or unconscious results in the progressive ability to *mindfully* use the newly constructed concept in the future as a *hypothesis* for action. For example, we learn our concept of love by reflective abstraction on "loving" actions, our own and those directed toward us. Similarly, we learn "form" by reflecting on "forming" or organizing actions of composing melody and sound pieces and by the **constructivist** "in-forming" of **directed listening**. Action Learning evokes precocious actions, and then gets students to progressively reflect (under the teacher's guidance) on the relevant features that will become the conscious concepts guiding future musical actions. Reflective abstraction is promoted by discussion, and by providing opportunities to **act adaptively**. The actual benefit of reflective abstraction depends on the cognitive development of the learner and the complexity of the learning.

rewards As used here, rewards are the personal benefits and satisfactions involved with musicking that stem directly from the praxis, not from grades, awards, popularity, and so forth.

role A social position or status that is characterized according to certain institutionalized expectations. Sociology sees roles somewhat as "scripts" people act out. Thus, to be a "student" entails "acting" the role "scripted" by the **paradigms** of schooling as a social institution. Ultimately, people are identified largely in terms of their roles. Thus "teacher" is seen as an interchangeable role and all "teachers" get grouped together. *Role conflict* arises when incompatible roles are at stake, such as when a "student" in fact knows more than a "teacher" or when a "teacher" who is also a "parent" must leave school to care for a sick child. Role *labeling* also masks the desirability that a "teacher" should always be a "student" of teaching and of music.

role-playing groups In these **simulations** students spontaneously "act out" their ideas. They have time to prepare, but not to compose their dialogue. Roles chosen should be seen as both "realistic" yet imaginative and should allow for full group participation. Example: "Your committee wants to hire (a certain popular recording group) for a dance and needs to convince your advisor that the music is good for dancing. Prepare then defend your *musical* reasons for wanting this group; I [or another group] will play the role of your advisor by challenging and asking questions."

rote, rote learning Mechanical learning or functioning that is gained by unthinking imitation. In school it often results from an injunction, such as "do it this way," or "it goes this way," that does not further elaborate on "why" or under what conditions and thus it fails to develop functional understanding, **musical independence, reflective abstraction**, and so forth.

rubrics Descriptors or criteria used to diagnose, rate, grade, assess, or guide student achievement. Descriptions identify a particular level of performance across a range of quality from "needs work" to "outstanding" (or similar labels). *Benchmarks* are in effect rubrics used at periodic intervals to guide or reflect overall progress. Rubrics are discussed in Appendix B.

sequencing See **readiness staging**.

scaffolding This term from educational psychology term refers to a building a framework or structure that serves as a temporary platform (thus "scaffold") upon which new learning can be constructed. See **readiness staging, constructivism**.

schooling "Schooling" is the educational process that occurs in schools. "Education" also occurs in the family, the church, and elsewhere.

signal A very obvious indicator that is quickly and clearly given to gain class attention, especially before beginning each **management stage**, but also in the event of general disruption. Many teachers clap a short rhythmic pattern that students immediately echo (and thus stop whatever they were previously doing).

simulations This form of **cooperative learning** has students consider alternatives for certain simulated problems. Example: "If you were a rock group and this (recording of an unidentified group) was your demo tape, what musical features would you point out in presenting it to a prospective producer." Similar to **role playing**.

situated, situatedness See **context, context effects**.

stochastic This is a particular kind of aleatory music that is predicated on random chance, such as throwing dice as a basis for certain musical choices.

social instruments As used here, these are instruments most typical for "social uses"—dancing, social singing, and so forth. Of course, just about any instrument can be used to accompany social uses, so here the reference is to those most commonly associated with amateur, recreational, and avocational musics, alone or with others, such as keyboards, folk guitars, and the like. Most **traditional instruments** (i.e., instruments in a particular folk tradition) are by their inherent function, social instruments—even when used soloistically as social entertainment.

socialization The process by which people learn to become members of a society. It is the sociological equivalent of what cultural anthropology calls "enculturation"—the acquisition of cultural norms, values, social roles and practices. In a more specialized sense, however, *primary socialization* is informal and takes place in the home, community, from the media, and so forth, while *secondary socialization* is formal and takes place in schools. Secondary socialization is part of "job training," even in professions such as music and teaching, where you learn certain **paradigms** and become accustomed to a particular **life-world** in order to "think" in terms of certain **roles**. Schools provide secondary socialization that fills in the gaps or even counteracts problematic primary socialization. Thus musical values, tastes, beliefs, and preferences socialized by the home and media can be at least augmented by formal schooling.

sorting function Educational sociologists and educational critics worry that schools "sort" or separate students on bases that reinforce and perpetuate existing social, economic, and racial inequalities. Music education, as traditionally conceived and practiced, can be seen as "sorting" students largely along lines dictated by the European "art music" tradition since school ensembles and curriculums tend to feature and favor this music exclusively over, say, garage bands or folk music ensembles. Thus an elite few who "have" talent for such music become the prime beneficiaries of music education while the "have-nots" remain largely un-benefited and left to their prior tastes and knowledge. General music classes are a prime opportunity to counter any such unfortunate process.

sound compositions, sound pieces Sound pieces are the "symphonies" of general music classes and allow students to develop musicianship skills and understanding relative to pieces that are longer and more complex than, for example, the tonal melodies they are composing. They are usually preplanned or improvised using limited or invented notation. Sound compositions have important transfer value for listening comprehension and skills. By means of **readiness staging**, a sound composition can lead into a listening lesson by preparing students to "hear" the same compositional variables in a recording. A listening lesson can similarly promote readiness for a subsequent sound composition.

special education, exceptional students, exceptional learners, classified students These and other variants are often used to refer to "students with special needs." However, general music teachers need to distinguish between *educable mentally retarded* (EMR) students, students with *learning disabilities,* such as handicaps of a physical, hearing, or visual nature (among the most common), and *gifted and talented* students who have a different range of special needs. All such special needs are beyond the scope of this text.

spiral curriculum This term has been associated with the psychologist Jerome Bruner who pointed out that early and necessarily precocious and rudimental involvement should be progressively elaborated to teach the "structure of the discipline"—that is, as formal, defined, and closed **concepts**. In the present text, however, instead of teaching *the discipline of music* for its own sake, references to spiral curriculum emphasize: a) the need to come progressively closer to **real-life** musical **praxis** by using evermore **authentic** models that, in turn, promote the relevant musicianship skills; b) the progressive elaboration of ever more complex and comprehensive open **concepts**.

stages of development Stage theories assume that development unfolds along an invariable sequence of steps or "stages." Each stage is seen to be unique in some way and successive stages are supposedly more complex because they integrate earlier stages. Weaknesses of stage theories include frequent exceptions to the developmental sequence, the exceedingly gradual and overlapping nature of developmental change, and the fact that development in certain areas of learning takes place according to its own logic or dynamic. Nonetheless, as guidelines for understanding human development, stages helpfully focus on broad and common traits.

staging Breaking a lesson into certain progressive "steps." See **readiness staging** and **management staging**.

study teams This term is similar to **learning** or **jigsaw** groups, but with special attention given to grouping students of *equal ability* and *similar interests.* Example: Learning to use computer software to notate a group composition or researching their common musical heritage.

subception The cognitive components of perception (and conception) that are "sub"-conscious or (momentarily) outside of **focal awareness**. The term *subattentional* is sometimes also used to refer to the parts of perception that are not in conscious attention. Such perceptions are "sub" or "below" the threshold of conscious awareness but nonetheless have an overall effect as part of the **synergy** and **holism** involved. In listening, musical features operating in subception at one moment may "surface" in focal awareness at another. Since we can be consciously aware of only one "thing" at a time, our attention often shifts between what (for us, not for everyone) is "in" the music background and foreground. Subception accounts for the richness of a musical perception—the presence and strength of the components collectively involved—and is a product of **cognitive strengthening**. The idea is closely related to **subsidiary awareness**.

subsidiary awareness Perception at any moment consists of many elaborately interconnected stimuli, only one of which can occupy **focal attention** at a given moment. Thus, when a novice listens "to" melody, it is "in" focal attention or awareness. Harmony, rhythmic organization, timbre, and so forth, all have a **holistic** effect through subsidiary awareness and **subception**; but the melody is the "foreground" of aural perception, so to speak, and other qualities (momentarily) provide the "background." With **cognitive strengthening**, listeners can respond to features in the perceptual foreground that formerly only served as background.

summative evaluations Herein, these are *lessons* where students integrate and transfer a wide range of prior learning by applying it to more comprehensive and thus "realistic" problems or projects. In order to insure that the prior learning of individual lessons can be applied **holistically** to a **real-life** musical praxis, **transfer of learning** is tested as students attempt to solve a *summative problem* independently. Summative evaluation "summarizes" what students have actually learned and what they still need to work on, and is the best way to evaluate teaching and learning. In Action Learning *formal tests* should take the form of summative problems that are graded!

synergy The experience of the sum being greater than the parts. Musical synergy is the result of all parts working together in a musical whole. Thus synergy is responsible for **holistic** musical experience. Synergy goes astray when teaching is **atomistic** and thus concerned only with parts in isolation. See **units**.

synesthesia A condition where a sensory experience associated with one sense modality (e.g., color) occurs when another modality is stimulated (e.g., hearing). Individuals with chromesthesia *literally* hear colors. For most listeners, however, color references to music function as metaphors for mood responses; for example," feeling blue" and "the Blues."

tacit knowledge/learning Conceptual or procedural knowledge that can not adequately be put into words; for example, the concept of "love" or the process of keeping one's "balance." It can be evaluated only "in action"; for example, singing or playing "in tune."

team-teaching Teachers are responsible in teams for teaching their respective subjects to a common subset of students whom they thus get to know better; or where teachers cooperatively plan and teach an interdisciplinary study.

technicist teaching Teaching conducted as a "technology" or one-size-fits-all "method." See "**methodolatry**."

technique, technical knowledge These concepts are distinguished from **theory** and **theoretical knowledge**, and **praxis** and **praxial knowledge**. Technique involves knowledge (a) used in a set way, (b) for a limited range of applications, (c) the value of which are taken for granted: for example, knowledge that allows an electrician to wire a house, or the flutist to play the correct notes. This knowledge is practiced in anticipation of the commonly accepted value of the predicted outcomes. Strictly **kinesthetic** aspects can sometimes be improved as out-of-context "skill-drill." "Mere" technique, however, is often of little good, especially in music.

theory, theoretical knowledge Greek philosophers distinguished between "theoria" (theory) and "techne" (**technical knowledge**), and "praxis" (**praxial knowledge**; "practical wisdom"). "Theory" involved "pure" knowledge developed and contemplated for its own sake rather than put to pragmatic use; for example, today's *aesthetic theories* of music. In modern use, *applied* theory (e.g., the knowledge of biochemistry possessed by a physician) is an important ingredient of any praxis. Thus certain *theoretical foundations* are essential to teaching as praxis (e.g., developmental and educational psychology) because, as the adage goes, "nothing is so practical as a good theory."

traditional instruments Broadly, these are instruments associated with the music of a particular cultural or national *tradition* (i.e., **praxis**): for example, the Koto in Japan, the Celtic Harp in Ireland. However, as used here, the term refers to the instruments used with "traditional folk musics" that continue to be played, sometimes at very high levels of skill, for their ongoing contribution to ethnic culture and **amateur** musicking.

transescence The transition from late childhood (8–10 years old; in the U.S., usually grades 4–5) to early adolescence (11–14, grades 6–8). **Preadolescence** is somewhat more specific in referring to the developmental stage just before **pubescence**.

transfer, transfer of learning This term is used in educational psychology to refer to the ability of a learner to *adapt* learning to new and somewhat novel situations (see **adaptive action**). Without transfer to real-life, learning is entirely **situated** in and for school. Generally, transfer is facilitated when learning is acquired by instruction based on models of the **musicking** to which it should or could apply. The more dissimilar the instruction is from the praxis (e.g., teaching facts for paper and pencil tests), or the more time between instruction and some kind of authentic application, the less likely it is that learning can or will be used in future situations. **Readiness staging** and **summative evaluation** promote transfer of learning.

units Self-contained topics or themes studied independently of other topics or themes. Students are typically tested at the completion of a unit. Then they move on to the next unit regardless of how well or poorly they did on the previous unit, because "covering the material" not **mastery learning** is the teaching premise. Learning is approached accumulatively rather than developmentally, as is the case instead with **generative themes**, **transfer of learning**, and **spiral curriculums**. See **lockstep teaching**.

utilitarianism This philosophy involves the *ethical* criterion of "the greatest good for the greatest number of people." The "utility" of an action or event is "good" when it promotes "happiness" or the "good life." A related view is called *act-consequentialism* where consequences of events or actions are judged in terms of benefits created. Critics of this view point equate it with hedonism and point to the difficulty of adequately defining "happiness." But for Action Learning, the benefits of musical enjoyment in the "good life" are unproblematic, and the idea of an "ethic" that stresses "good consequences" as the basis for "good teaching" is also reasonable.

values In the **aesthetic theory of music**, values are timeless and universal. "Good music" is absolutely "good." In the **praxial theory of music**, values are **situated** and "good music" is "good for" certain personal and social **affordances**. Even "just listening" to music is *worthwhile* in the praxial view—"worth while" literally means "good time."

vertical alignment of curriculum Insuring that learning and skill develop in an orderly and coordinated manner from one grade and level of school to the next. Horizontal alignment is between teachers of the same subject at the same grade level.

world musics This refers to **musics** of different nations or ethnicities.

Index